MOTHER OF BLISS

MOTHER OF BLISS
Ānandamayī Mā
(1896–1982)

Lisa Lassell Hallstrom

New York   Oxford

Oxford University Press

Oxford University Press

Oxford   New York

Athens   Auckland   Bangkok   Bogotá   Buenos Aires   Calcutta
Cape Town   Chennai   Dar es Salaam   Delhi   Florence   Hong Kong   Istanbul
Karachi   Kuala Lumpur   Madrid   Melbourne   Mexico City   Mumbai
Nairobi   Paris   São Paulo   Singapore   Taipei   Tokyo   Toronto   Warsaw

and associated companies in
Berlin   Ibadan

Copyright © 1999 by Lisa Lassell Hallstrom

Published by Oxford University Press, Inc.
198 Madison Avenue, New York, New York 10016

Oxford is a registered trademark of Oxford University Press

Library of Congress Cataloging-in-Publication Data
Hallstrom, Lisa Lassell.
Mother of bliss : Ānandamayī Mā (1896–1982)
Lisa Lassell Hallstrom.
p.   cm.
Includes bibliographical references and index.
ISBN 978-0-19-511648-9
1. Anandamayi, 1896– .   2. Hindu women saints—India—Biography.
3. Hindus—India—Biography.   I. title.
BL 1175. A49H35   1999
294.5'092—dc21   97–42456
[B]

Printed in the United States of America
on acid-free paper

To Devī,
in all her magnificent forms.

tasyai shrīdevyai namah

Prologue

O N AUGUST 28, 1982, IN THE foothills of the Himalayas, a funeral procession made its way between the Indian towns of Dehradun and Kankhal. It took longer than usual to make the twenty-seven-mile trip because the procession had to stop every few minutes to allow crowds of mourners to have their last *darshan*, or glimpse of the divine, of the Hindu saint whom they simply called Mā, or Mother.

By the time the body of eighty-six-year-old Ānandamayī Mā, or the Bliss-Filled Mother, reached its final destination at her ashram in Kankhal on the banks of the Ganges River, an unending stream of people had begun to gather to pay their respects. On September 4, *India Today* reported, "One could see them coming as far as the eye could see. They came in cars, rickshaws and on foot. Many were in a state of dazed shock." While some kept up a round-the-clock chanting of the divine name, other mourners continued, hour after hour, to *pranām*, or bow, in front of Mā's body, many weeping profusely. Among them was Indira Gandhi, who considered Mā her spiritual mother and had flown in by helicopter. Mrs. Gandhi left the following message of condolence at the ashram:

> Ānandamayī Mā was the living embodiment of devotion and love. Just with a glimpse of Her, countless problems are solved. She considered service to suffering humanity Her true religion. Her spiritually powerful personality was a source of great guidance for all human beings. I offer my homage to Her!

On Sunday, August 29, although Ānandamayī Mā was not officially a *sannyāsinī*, or ordained Hindu female monk, her burial was performed according to strict scriptural injunctions, presided over by some of India's most renowned brahman priests. She was buried as a realized being and her shrine was to become, from that day on, a place of worship and pilgrimage known for its spiritual power. Her twenty-eight ashrams, a charitable hospital, schools, and dispensaries would continue to be administered by the nonprofit society established in her name. Thousands of her devotees would continue to perform daily *pūjā*, or worship, to her in their household shrines, maintaining that, even though Mā had passed from this world, she still guided their every movement. Yet at the age of eighty-six, Ānandamayī Mā referred to herself as "an unlettered little girl" or, simply, "this body" and signed her name with a mere dot, maintaining that "in it is contained everything." She wrote no books, delivered no lectures. It is said that she never initiated people and encouraged people to follow their own guru's instructions and practice their own religion.

One crisp morning in October 1987, while studying in the Andover Library at Harvard Divinity School, I went to look for something in a small room used to catalogue rare books. On a table in the middle of the room I saw an enormous stack of books, photos, tapes, and films. On the front of one of the books I saw an extraordinary picture of a hauntingly beautiful woman. I was drawn to open the book, only to discover that this woman was the famous Hindu woman saint, Ānandamayī Mā, whom I had heard about on my trip to India in 1978. In fact, the entire stack seemed to have some connection with Ānandamayī Mā. I was told by the secretary that someone had donated the archive of this woman saint to the library and that it was in the process of being catalogued. Soon it would be relegated to the dark recesses of the archival bookshelves.

When I told my advisor, Diana Eck, about my discovery, she suggested that I write an article on the archive for the divinity school bulletin. The archive was a gold mine, and I was thrilled to immerse myself in it. The material seemed to provide a lens for exploring many of my interests in the study of the Hindu tradition and in the study of religion in general: gender and religion, women saints, the centrality of the guru in the Hindu tradition, and Hindu *bhakti*, or devotional practice. A little over two years later, on July 1, 1990, my family and I arrived by overnight train in Banaras, India, for a year of research on Ānandamayī Mā.

On September 20, 1990, I was traveling on a train from Banaras to Allahabad. I was on my way to meet and interview the most prominent biographer of Ānandamayī Mā, Bithika Mukerji. Professor Mukerji, Emeritus Professor of Philosophy at Banaras Hindu University and a long-time devotee of Mā, had completed two volumes of *From the Life of Anandamayi Ma* and was working on a third. I was thrilled to be meeting her at last, having corresponded with her for two years.

I was accompanied on the trip by three other devotees of Mā whom I had recently met at Mā's ashram in Banaras—Uma Chatterjee, a warm, lovely woman who was serving as secretary at the Banaras ashram; Annakutty Findeis, a diminutive, animated professor of German at Bombay University; and Annakutty's husband, Hans. Both women had been students of Bithika's, through whom they had met Ānandamayī Mā.

The train ride might have been interminably long (the train seemed to stop every few minutes for one reason or another) had it not been for the stories about Mā and the boisterous sharing of Bengali and American songs, punctuated with raucous laughter. At one point during the ride I asked my companions, "Why do you call Ānandamayī Mā *Mā*?" Uma responded, "It is the name we call our own mother. Your Mā is the closest person to you in the world."

When we arrived in Allahabad, we took a horse-drawn wagon to the grand Victorian house that was Bithika's family home. We were greeted very graciously by the strikingly handsome, brilliant, yet serene Bithikaji, or dearest Bithika, as they called her. Within minutes we were told that dinner was almost ready. Before dinner Bithika sat with her infant grandniece in her lap and allowed me to photograph her.

I was nervous and excited to be sitting down to a meal with the person I expected would be central to my research in India. Everything was beautifully prepared and strictly vegetarian. Among these highly educated people, whom I would come to know as typical of Mā's devotees, English was the language of choice. As the first course was being cleared, Bithika, wasting no time, asked me to tell her about my work. I said, "Well, I am very excited to be doing this study on Mā. You know, I have been interested in women saints for a long time." A look of alarm and even horror came over Bithika's face. "My dear Lisa," Bithika said emphatically, "Mā was neither a woman nor a saint!" She went on, "Once I was invited to give a talk on Mā at a conference on women saints but I refused. They obviously had no understanding of who Mā was!"

At first, all I knew was that I had said something terribly wrong. Slowly I realized what Bithika was saying: Mā could not be a woman or a saint because Mā was an incarnation of God. This encounter and the difficult questions that it raised were to reverberate within me in the months that followed. I was to discover that Bithika was in good company in thinking of Mā as God and God as Mā.

Acknowledgments

A S I CONTEMPLATE THE family members, friends, and colleagues to whom I am indebted for helping me carry this book from its inception through to its completion, I am overwhelmed with gratitude. Although the actual process of writing is something that one can do only alone, there is no doubt that without the support, inspiration, love, and good counsel offered so generously by so many people, it would have been impossible for me to have arrived at this destination. It is their confidence in me that fueled my journey and I hope that the final product is worthy of that confidence. In thanks . . .

To my friends and advisors,
  Diana Eck, for her vision of what it could be and her help in shaping it.
  John Carman, for his respectful and careful consideration of every word.

To my friends and teachers,
  Julia Leslie, for her initiating me into the study of women and *dharmashāstra*.
  Masatoshi Nagatomi, for his seeing me as a Sanskritist.
  Barbara Holdrege, for her example of passionate scholarship.
  Rachel Fell McDermott, for her integrity and boundless compassion.

To my friends and colleagues,
  Frederique Apffel Marglin, for her commitment to women's lived experience.
  Vasudha Narayanan, for her generosity and *saulabhya*.
  Kathleen Erndl, for her lifting up of Hindu *mātās*.
  Mary McGee, for her redressing of Manu.
  Charlie Hallisey, for his articulation of Marriott's transactional world.
  Bettina Baumer, for her perspective as a fellow insider-outsider.
  Elinor Gadon, for her dedication to the Once and Future Goddess.

To my fellow travelers,

Tara Doyle, for her devotion to friendship and her clarity of vision.

Paula Arai, for her insightful and encouraging words from a few steps ahead.

Heather White, for her inspiring company and her sense of what is important.

Suzin Green, for her humor and her vision of the longed-for paradigm shift.

Brenda Dobia, for her tantilizing proposal of a Shākta pilgrimage.

To Carole Bundy and Narges Moshiri, for being administrators with hearts.

To Olivia Hoblitzelle, Anne Yeomans, Rose Thorne, and Patricia Reis and all the women of the Interface Women's Spirituality Program, for sharing with me in the healing that can only come from the Goddess and for enabling me to truly graduate.

To Sonia Nevis, for accomplishing it when few even tried and for holding me to it, and to John Barbaro, for knowing that there was no way around it except through it.

To my friends who cheered me on, among them Hob, Beverly, Reenie, Peter, Steve, Margie, Kathleen, Urvashi, Durga, Dorothy, Deb, Glen, Gabby, Vern, Irene, Larry, Laurie, Jon, Joan, Phil, Suzanne, and Peter.

To David Caputo of Radical Solutions and Kitty Axelson Berry for much needed technical and editorial support.

To the institutions that generously supported this project, the Center for the Study of World Religions at Harvard University and the American Association of University Women.

To my editors at Oxford University Press, Cynthia Read and MaryBeth Branigan, for their expertise and support.

To the community of Ānandamayī Mā, for opening their hearts and homes to me and trusting that I would cherish their stories. Their faces and words will be with me forever, and I am ever indebted to them for helping me try to do the impossible, to understand Mā.

To my mother, Eleanor Comfort, and my sister, Julie Hunsdon, for their love and faith and to my mother-in-law, Elizabeth Petrie, for her support and inspiring example.

To my stepchildren, Christo and Anna, for their patience in getting to know me while I was immersed in this project.

To my children, Shama, Rama, Matt, and Nick, for their acceptance that they sometimes had to settle for less of me than they wanted or needed, for their willingness to spend a year in India full of unexpected adventures, and for their faith and love that has sustained me through the most difficult times.

To my husband, soul mate, and friend, Ted Hallstrom, for his faith from the beginning that I could do it, for his embracing of India with his whole being, for his unflagging financial and emotional support, and for his love throughout it all.

Amherst, MA
August 1997

L. L. H.

Contents

Transliteration Guide

ETERMINING WHEN AND HOW to transliterate the non-English words in this work has been daunting, because it draws on a combination of Bengali, Sanskrit, and English sources. Since this book is intended for a wide readership, I have chosen to take the following, less-than-purist, approach:

1. Sanskrit terms that can be found in English dictionaries generally occur without diacritical marks or italicization (e.g., guru, ashram, brahman). Other Sanskrit terms are written in italics, without diacritical marks, except for the long mark, or macron, that indicates a long vowel. Sanskrit vowels are pronounced as follows:

   a (as the "u" in "but": tantra)   ā (as in "baa": Mā)
   i (as in "it": Hindu)   ī (as in "magazine": *līlā*)
   u (as in "put": Upanishad)   ū (as in "rude": *pūjā*)

   The diphthongs are as follows: e (as in "prey": Devī); ai (as in "aisle": Vaishnava); o (as in "blow": moksha); and au (as in "now": Gaurī). The underdotted vowel, ṛ, is written here as "ri" as in "rich": Krishna.

2. Terms appear in the form most commonly used in interviews with Mā's devotees. Special note should be made of the term *kheyāla*. Although it is *kheyāl* in Bengali, it appears in almost all works on Ānandamayī Mā with an *a* at the end, as a Sanskrit word.

3. Place-names occur in their Anglicized form, without diacritical marks.

4. The names of contributors, Bengali authors, or Hindi authors who write in English (e.g., Bithika Mukerji) and familiar contemporary Hindu figures (e.g., Ramakrishna) appear in their Anglicized forms. The names of certain people around and including Ānandamayī Mā appear with diacriticals in their Hindi or Bengali forms (e.g., Bholanāth, Didimā).

5. The story of Mā's life in chapter 2 is written without diacritical marks, consistent with most popular literature on Mā.

MOTHER OF BLISS

Introduction

ONE OF THE MOST COMMON yet compelling questions posed by Western feminist theologians is, "How would our lives have been different if we had been raised to believe that God was our mother, all loving and all powerful?" This question has provoked a passionate interest in and nostalgia for ancient goddess cultures, such as those recently acknowledged to have flourished in the fertile valleys of Old Europe.[1] It has also led to an interest in reappropriating ancient goddesses of all traditions to help women and men create alternative models of Ultimate Reality that better reflect the female experience. The prevailing assumption of feminist theologians has been that a move away from patriarchal images of God as father or king and toward powerful yet compassionate female religious images would empower women and create a more balanced and humane society.[2] Feminist and liberation theologians have committed themselves to re-imagining a god or goddess who embraces and inspires all of his or her children.[3]

Yet, ancient goddess cultures are not the only resources for stimulating the reimagination of God as mother or for examining the impact on women and men of worshiping the divine feminine. India has one of the oldest continuous traditions of goddess worship in the world, and even today the Goddess is worshiped daily by many devout Hindus in both her multiplicity and her unity. The Great Goddess, or Mahādevī, is considered to have countless manifestations worthy of worship, from the fiercely independent goddesses, such as Kālī or Durgā, to the benign consort goddesses, such as Lakshmī or Pārvatī. The Goddess, no matter what her form, is considered by her devotees to be an embodiment of *shakti*, the dynamic creative power of the universe. In her forms as village goddesses, she is usually propitiated for specific requests such as healing the sick or granting blessings upon

3

important life passages, for example, childbearing. As the Great Goddess, she is envisioned as Ultimate Reality, both transcendent and imminent, and as such, she is responsible for the creation, preservation, and destruction of the universe. Those who envision Ultimate Reality as Devī or Mā and worship her both for the pleasures of this world, or *bhukti*, and for spiritual liberation, or *mukti*, are called Shāktas, or worshipers of the *shakti*, and comprise one of the three major sectarian divisions within the Hindu tradition.[4]

Perhaps even more relevant to the consideration of the relationship between goddess worship and women's experience is that in certain regions of India where the worship of the Goddess is most prevalent, such as Bengal, there is a belief that the Goddess can take birth as an apparently human being.[5] While the Christian conception of divine incarnation holds that Jesus Christ is the only incarnation of God on earth, the Hindu conception allows for multiple *avatāras*, or descensions of the divine into human form. Therefore, the god Vishnu is said to have been incarnated at least ten times; furthermore, Vishnu's incarnation, Krishna, is considered to have incarnated in contemporary religious figures. Likewise, Devī, the Goddess, has taken and will take many forms on earth. An examination of a phenomenon in which a living woman is determined to be an incarnation of the Goddess offers insight into the question under consideration.

In a related phenomenon, Hindu women throughout the centuries have been considered living saints and have been venerated as such. The women saints of the *bhakti*, or devotional tradition, such as Āntāl, Mīrābāi, Akkamahādevī, and Lalleshwarī, have been immortalized in poetry that is still sung as liturgy today. Scholars have begun to lift up their life stories, to compare and contrast them, to assess their impact on the women of their own time, and suggest their potential to empower contemporary Hindu women.[6] The number of contemporary Hindu women revered as saints is impressive, yet scholarly studies of their lives, their teachings, and their roles as exemplars for both women and men are, for the most part, yet to be pursued.[7]

Turning to the Hindu tradition of goddess worship and veneration of women saints to understand the potential of female religious images to empower women, however, raises a second question: "How can a culture that envisions God as Divine Mother relegate women to such an inferior and dependent economic, ritual, and social status?" It is understandable that one familiar with the Hindu tradition of goddess worship, on the one hand, and classical Sanskrit texts, such as the *Laws of Manu*, on the other, might ask such a question. The *Laws of Manu* is one of the best known of a genre of Hindu religious texts, called *dharmashāstra*, which articulate the righteous way of life, or *dharma*, and were composed by brahman men around the turn of the common era. It stipulates, among other things, that the *pativratā*, or the virtuous Hindu wife, should never do anything independent of her husband, that she should worship him as her only god, and that she should refrain from any other religious activity. Until recently, many Western scholars have assumed that the *dharmashāstra* paradigm of a Hindu wife's life of unquestioning obedience to her husband as her god has been normative or at least formative for most Hindu women. The impression that the brahmanical paradigm has held sway over all Hindu women has been reinforced by contemporary phenomena such as the recently publicized revival of the practice of suttee,[8] the ritual death of a Hindu woman on her husband's funeral pyre.

However, a recent upsurge of research has challenged this generalization. Western women scholars of the Hindu tradition have begun to respond to anthropologists from the developing world, such as Ifi Amadiume, Trinh Minh-ha, Vandana Shiva, and Leila Ahmed, who implore us to abandon an essentialist theory of gender inequality.[9] They also ask us to consider the multivalence of gender-related symbols, which, as Caroline Walker Bynum says, "may refer to gender in ways that affirm or reverse it, support or question it, or may, in their basic meaning have little or nothing to do with male and female roles."[10] And, finally, they ask us to "de-anthropologize" ourselves, to deconstruct our essentialist notion of "Hinduism" and of "woman," and look at the lives of particular Hindu women themselves. Many Western women historians of religion and anthropologists have begun to approach the study of women in the Hindu tradition with methodology based on attention to the particulars of women's lives, as related by the women themselves.[11]

Some scholars have challenged essentialist notions about "Hindu women" by focusing on particular Hindu women who are members of certain castes in certain regions who have rejected marriage and have chosen to live outside the realm of brahmanical dharma as renunciants, mendicants, and *yoginīs*. The work of Lynn Teskey Denton and Catherine Ojha on women ascetics in Banaras, India, has shed light on women who renounce the world and lead relatively independent lives, either within orders or on their own.[12] Furthermore, in predominantly Shākta communities, women recognized as *avatāras* and those considered to have particular spiritual power by virtue of their level of *shakti*, or power, have risen to prominence as gurus and often have large followings of men and women. There is a burgeoning field of research on Shākta women gurus, of which this study is a part.[13]

This study focuses on a particular Hindu woman whose life defies categorization yet provides access to some of the most profound and seemingly contradictory themes within the Hindu tradition, the contemporary Hindu religious figure, Ānandamayī Mā (1896–1982). Ānandamayī Mā was an illiterate Bengali woman who was widely revered as a saint, guru, and *avatāra*, or incarnation of God, for the last sixty years of her life. Hundreds of Mā's close devotees fully believe that God chose to incarnate as a baby girl, Nirmalā Sundarī, into a poor brahman family in Bengal in 1896. I choose the term "God" here, as does China Galland, "to draw on the resonance and power that such term can carry in Western culture."[14] Mā's devotees believe that this divine baby girl grew up to be their Mā, their personal Divine Mother, of whom they could ask every kind of question, with whom they could sing and dance, and for whom they would do anything she asked, because God the Mother always knows best. We will see that

Ānandamayī Mā's women devotees believe that they were able to enjoy a particular intimacy with God, as "Mā," because it was they who had the privilege of combing God's hair, massaging God's legs, and feeding and dressing God, as Mā took no interest in her own body and did not feed herself.

According to her spiritual biographies, Nirmalā Sundarī is said to have been exceptional from infancy. As a young child, she communed with animals and trees and often fell into states of trance. She was married at the age of twelve, but once she began living with her husband, Bholanāth, she was unwilling or unable to fulfill the role of a *pativratā*, or virtuous wife, as Hindu *dharmashāstra* would define it. Although in the beginning of their marriage, Nirmalā worked tirelessly to keep the house and care for Bholanāth, she never had sexual relations with her husband, and she began to withdraw more and more from everyday activities and spent a large part of her day in states of spiritual ecstasy. As news of her ecstatic states spread, she began to attract devotees who saw her as an extraordinary spiritual being. Bholanāth, while bewildered and frustrated at first, became convinced that his wife was a manifestation of the Goddess. After Nirmalā conferred spiritual initiation on herself, Bholanāth took initiation from her and began to relate to her as his guru. In a remarkable reversal from the perspective of *dharmashāstra*, he spent the rest of his life as his wife's disciple, caring for her physical well-being, as she seemed completely uninterested in her body, and mediating between her and her growing number of devotees.

By 1926, Nirmalā, by then called Ānandamayī Mā, the Bliss-Filled Mother, or simply Mā, had completely abandoned her *dharma*, or religious duty, as a Hindu wife and had begun her ceaseless travels around India, sometimes accompanied by her husband and attracting devotees wherever she went. From time to time, she sent her husband away to perform spiritual practices. After his death in 1938, she continued to grow in stature and influence, with such prominent figures as Kamala Nehru and her daughter, Indira Gandhi, numbered among her devotees. She was a focus of reverence, not only for her worldly devotees but also for many prominent male gurus and religious figures. In 1977, at the Kumbha Mela in Prayag, an enormous gathering of ascetics that takes place at four different sacred sites every six years, it is said that every day Mā gave *darshan* to thousands of ascetics, hour after hour, for eighteen days in a row. One of her devotees, Anil Ganguli, said, "Mā's motherly influence has inspired even the most contentious groups of ascetics to sink their differences and they have all joined in paying homage to Mā, the common object of adoration of all."[15] In the last decade of her life, Ānanadamayī Mā's devotees numbered in the hundreds of thousands, and ashrams, hospitals, and schools had been established in her name all over India. At the age of eighty-six, on August 28, 1982, Mā took *mahāsamādhi*,[16] or passed from the physical world, leaving behind no successor. Her ashrams continue to function in honor of her, headed by various male renouncers, or *sannyāsins*, and run largely by celibate women, or *brahmachārinīs*. Her thousands of householder devotees worship her daily in their homes and gather each week to participate in spiritual practices in her name.

Overview

In this book, Ānandamayī Mā serves as a lens through which to examine the following themes: the power and limitations of the *dharmashāstra* paradigm, the complex fabric of Hindu sainthood with its associated miraculous events, the alternative world of the Hindu female ascetic and guru and the accompanying mysteries of the guru–disciple relationship, and the imagining of God as Mother living in a human body. I have chosen to organize this study around four different aspects of Ānandamayī Mā: Ānandamayī Mā as woman, as saint, as guru, and as *avatāra* and Divine Mother.

This study begins in chapter 2, however, with my rendition of the life story of Ānandamayī Mā as told by her devotees. I hope this retelling, which is more concise and chronological than available biographies, will make Mā's life story more accessible, and offer a solid foundation for further analysis.

Chapter 3, "Ānandamayī Mā as a Woman," grapples with the fact that although Mā's life was highly unconventional from the perspective of the brahmanical paradigm, and although her devotees say that Mā was not a woman, they simultaneously insist that she was "the perfect wife." After describing the Hindu ideology of *strīdharma,* or the righteous way of life for the Hindu woman, it turns to an analysis of the development of the relationship between Mā and Bholanāth, comparing their relationship to the ideal relationship described in *dharmashāstra* texts. Finally, having established that Bholanāth and Mā were in most ways not husband and wife, but disciple and guru, it questions why Mā's devotees use the conventional paradigm to describe their relationship.

Chapter 4, "Ānandamayī Mā as Saint," begins by exploring the complex semantic field of Sanskrit and vernacular terms used to refer to a Hindu "saint" and enumerating the qualities often associated with Hindu saints. It goes on to consider Ānandamayī Mā within the context of "sainthood," particularly in relationship to the qualities of renunciation, egolessness, and unity awareness. After a discussion of caste within her community, it explores Mā as a *bhakta,* or devotee of God, enumerating stories of her *bhāvas,* or states of spiritual ecstasy. Finally, the chapter considers the stories of Mā's miraculous powers, or *siddhis,* indicators of the accomplishment of a yogi or *yoginī.*

Chapter 5, "Ānandamayī Mā as Guru," explores the paradigm of the guru–disciple relationship, beginning with a historical survey of the development of the cult of the guru within the Hindu tradition. Although Mā's devotees insist that Mā was not a guru, the majority of the chapter draws on interviews with Mā's close devotees that describe powerful direct and indirect initiation from Mā. It goes on to examine whether Mā functioned as a guru in assessing her disciples" states of consciousness and directing them in spiritual practices designed to lead them to spiritual liberation. Finally, it considers Mā's own words on the guru and on her role as a guru and whether she expected her devotees to model themselves on her and become like her.

Chapter 6, "Ānandamayī Mā as *Avatāra* and Divine Mother," examines the claim of Mā's devotees that she was not a human being but rather was divine in origin. It begins with a discussion of the historical development of the Hindu conception of divine incarnation and continues with a brief historical overview of the worship of the Divine Mother in South Asia. It goes on to enumerate devotees' answers to the question, "Who is Mā?" and examines Mā's own words on her identity. Finally, it considers how Mā wanted her devotees to relate to the Divine, focusing particularly on whether she expected them to exert self-effort to forge ahead on the path toward self-realization or to follow the *bhakti* path of surrender to God with its associated gift of grace.

Chapter 7 concludes by asking, "Did Ānandamayī Mā inspire her female devotees to model their lives on her life and to aspire to become like her?" It considers the ways in which Mā's female devotees benefited from her having been born a woman and also the ways in which Mā's message was "Do what I say, not what I do." Finally, it discusses the community's perspective on the relationship between gender and self-realization, on the relevance of the gender of God and of Mā, and on the relationship between grace and self-effort.

The methodological approach to this book has evolved, as much as possible, out of the material itself, as W. C. Smith and Mircea Eliade would have it.[17] It necessarily reflects the methodological pluralism of many contemporary scholars in anthropology and the history of religions.[18] Throughout, however, my primary commitment has been to the lived experiences of my contributors.

The prime method used for gathering the material for this study was in-depth phenomenological interviews, all but two conducted in India during 1990–1991. After interviewing two devotees of Ānandamayī Mā in the Boston area, I interviewed forty-two devotees in Bombay, Banaras, Haridwar, Dehradun, and Calcutta and seven other people who, although they did not call themselves devotees, had met Ānandamayī Mā and were deeply affected by their encounter. The interviews were relatively open-ended, but I asked nearly every contributor a set of seven questions. These questions frame the analytical sections of the study. The set of transcribed interviews with my contributors constitutes perhaps the most central of the three "texts" used in this study.

The second "text" is the set of transcriptions of informal sessions, called *satsangs*, in which Ānandamayī Mā engaged in questions and answers with groups of devotees. Recorded all over India between 1960 and 1981, these transcriptions, duplicates of which are part of the archive on Ānandamayī Mā at Harvard Divinity School's Andover Library, were given to me by an American devotee of Mā's. They were first transcribed and then translated into English by an Indian scholar in Los Angeles, hired by an American devotee.

The third "text" is the literature written in English on Ānandamayī Mā by her devotees, mostly during her lifetime—sacred biographies, published personal journals, collections of the testimonials of devotees, and collections of quotes from Mā.

The organization of this study evolved out of several methodological concerns, which have been addressed recently, primarily by anthropologists.[19] The first arises out of the challenge of encountering and trying to understand a culture with worldviews and ways of knowing radically different from one's own. The question arises: Is there a methodology for approaching a world which, from the Western perspective, seems beyond reason, in this case the Hindu world of living saints and human incarnations of the divine, replete with miracle stories, quests for self-realization, and spiritual experiences, all of which cannot be proved or measured?

Richard Shweder, in *Thinking through Cultures*, calls us to move beyond what he describes as conventional approaches to the encounter with the "other." One approach, dominated by positivists, maintains that there is only one dominant reality or way of knowing, that "seeing is believing." The other, dominated by radical relativists, gives permission to all realities but valorizes none. Shweder posits a third approach, the assumption of "multiple objective worlds."[20] The goal of post-Nietzschean methodology, says Shweder, is "to view the objective world from many points of view" and to be an "internal realist, seeing as best one can with the received dogma of the moment."[21] In the post-Nietzschean world, according to Shweder, "God is not dead; only positivism and monotheism are dead. Polytheism is alive and well. Its doctrine is the relativistic idea of multiple objective worlds, and its commandment is participation in the never-ending process of overcoming partial views."[22] In a similar vein, Diana Eck, in *Encountering God: A Spiritual Journey From Bozeman to Banaras*, articulates the difference between an inclusivist and a pluralist: "If we are an inclusivist, we include others into a worldview we already know and on the terms we have already set. If we are pluralists, we recognize the limits of the world we already know and we seek to understand others in their own terms, not just in ours."[23] From the perspective of multiple worlds, then, we hold the conviction that the world of the other offers a window through which to see reality, a *darshana*.[24] In addition, we hold that once one has looked through that window with an openness to the legitimacy of that world, one's own world is necessarily changed. Finally, we strive to present the world of the other in such a way as to honor these convictions. In this study, I have welcomed the opportunity to be changed by the *darshana* of the community of Ānandamayī Mā. To give the reader the opportunity to be changed as well, I have tried to evoke and not merely represent[25] their world.

A second set of challenges arises once we are within the world of the other. We must begin by acknowledging that within that world there are undoubtedly multiple voices and multiple perspectives. The context-sensitive methodology inspired by the Third World anthropologists acknowledges a need to first abandon essentialist notions of the universal subordination of women and then look at the lives of individual Hindu women.[26] This study looks for contexts in which Hindu women find empowerment, both within and outside the *dharmashāstra* paradigm. It does not generalize from a single woman's story. It also acknowledges and highlights different contexts that condition experience: caste, region, age, education. We do not assume we are talking about one world in this study, neither the "world" of the Hindu woman nor the "world" of Ānandamayī Mā's female devotees. More generally, this study strives to represent both female and male individual voices within the community. Furthermore, reflecting Carolyn Bynum's caution that gender-related symbols are multivalent and may not necessarily affirm gender and, thus, transform male and female roles,[27] this study raises the possibility that Ānandamayī Mā's female devotees may *not* have been empowered by her being a woman.

Once we are within the world of the other, a challenge particularly emphasized in the context-sensitive approach of the ethnosociologists of the Chicago school is to find indigenous concepts to describe what we are seeing.[28] The four aspects of Ānandamayī Mā—Mā as Hindu woman (*strī* or *pativratā*), as saint (*sant, bhakta*, or *sādhvī*), as guru, and as divine incarnation (*avatāra* or *Devī*)—seemed to me significant aspects of the cultural and religious landscape of which Ānandamayī Mā was a part. I also felt, despite the protestations of Mā's devotees to the contrary, that there was sufficient evidence to consider her as possessing each of these aspects. In this way I diverge from a strictly phenomenological approach in that I have not unilaterally accepted Mā's devotees' definition of what a study of Mā entails but have to a certain extent set my own agenda, based on the indigenous contexts in which I saw her reflected. By setting an agenda that I felt reflected the context within which Ānandamayī Mā lived, while letting her devotees speak for themselves within the established analytical categories, I hoped to achieve a balance between my scholarly voice and the voices of my contributors, between my analysis and the lived experience of Mā's devotees.

To ensure polyvocality as I invoke the world of the other and to preserve the integrity of narrative, I have included the verbatim stories of my contributors as much as possible. I have tried as well to include the voice of Ānandamayī Mā herself, confirming or challenging both her devotees' assumptions and the conclusions I have drawn from the devotees' stories.

Methodological Problems

There are two main methodological problems with this study. First is the challenge of remaining context-sensitive in terms of the specificity of vernacular language, region, and caste, considering that the community of Ānandamayī Mā, although primarily Bengali and brahman, is a pan-Indian, multilingual community. Bengali is the mother tongue of most members, Hindi is the mother tongue of some, and nearly everyone, especially the men, being highly educated, speaks English fluently. Because English has been spoken in Bengal for two hundred years, certain English terms, such as "saint" or "God," have been appropriated into the Bengali context and have their own meaning. Therefore, when it comes to the question, for example, of which word devotees used to describe who Mā was, while most said "God" and only secondarily used words such as "Bhagavān" or "Devī," it is difficult to assess what they would have answered if we had not been speaking English. Likewise, a devotee from Banaras in the Hindi-speaking heartland, might be Bengali and as such may have grown up within a Bengali Shākta context rather than a North Indian Vaishnava or Shaiva context.

Second, this study presents Ānandamayī Mā within a contemporary religious and social context. It does not attempt to present her in a historical or political context. Ānandamayī Mā as presented in all my "texts" was presented only within a timeless religious context. There were occasional allusions to a social context but absolutely no mention of the historical or political context. It is as if nothing else were going on in India at the time other than the spiritual activities of Mā and her devotees, although Mā's first decade saw the emerging Indian nationalist movement, and she matured with the Indian independence movement, lived through communal violence and partition, and died during the height of the rule of Indira Gandhi.

My decision to ignore the historical and political context leaves some interesting questions unanswered, for example, "What was going on in Bengal when Ānandamayī Mā left in 1932 never to return?" and the absence of interest in this kind of question on the part of the community is significant. It may reflect members' own lack of interest in worldly matters or a desire to honor Mā's complete indifference to politics and her insistence that sādhana, or spiritual practice, is all-important.[29] It is interesting to note, however, that the lives of many Hindu religious figures of Mā's time, such as Shri Aurobindo, expressed a marriage of politics and religion and a commitment to social reform.

Who Am I?

If a scholar, particularly one who engages in fieldwork, acknowledges that objectivity is impossible in an encounter between the self and other and that culture is always created in relationship, he or she must become, to some extent, self-reflexive and self-revelatory. As a co-creator of the culture that is the focus of this study, I feel obliged to reveal to the reader some of my own narrative, the story that conditioned my participation in the dialogue as well as my analysis of the data.[30] My particular background, which is somewhere between outsider and insider, clearly elicited the kind of responses that I received.

When I came to this study, I was no stranger to the Hindu tradition. Twenty-five years earlier, I had begun to read Indian philosophy. In 1975, I received initiation into a Hindu kundalinī yoga practice and began a daily practice of chanting and meditation. In 1978, I spent four months in India doing spiritual practice in the ashram of my guru. In 1984, I entered graduate school in religion, hoping to revitalize my transpersonal psychotherapy practice. I chose a program in which I could contextualize my spiritual practice within the Hindu tradition and the world's religions, in general. In the process, I discovered that I loved being a scholar and decided to go on to get a Ph.D. in Hinduism to engage in full-time teaching and research.

During my coursework, I found I could write about different aspects of the Hindu tradition with a certain insight that can come only from experience.

I came to my research on Ānandamayī Mā, then, with a certain kind of insider status, which I revealed to my contributors if asked. By the time I got to India in 1990, the word had spread within Mā's community that I had written a "beautiful article on Mā" in the *Harvard Divinity School Bulletin*. I arrived for each interview dressed in a sari, which drew appreciation from Mā's devotees. Almost invariably I would be asked before the interview began, "Are you a devotee of Mā's?" I usually replied, "No, but I am an admirer." I might then be asked, "Do you have a guru?" I would answer, "Yes, I have been initiated by a guru," If asked, I would tell them something about my practice. It is my conviction that the fact that I had studied with a guru, meditated, and chanted in Sanskrit every day inclined my contributors to reveal things to me that they might not have revealed to a "disinterested scholar."

I believe that my personal immersion in the philosophy and practices of the Hindu tradition has enhanced, rather than limited, my critical abilities as a scholar. Further, I hope that this study presents Ānandamayī Mā and her community in a way that both demonstrates my respect for them and fulfills my responsibility as a scholar to look with my own eyes and question what I see.

Who Are My Contributors?

Of the forty-nine people I interviewed for this study, forty-two considered themselves devotees of Ānandamayī Mā. The remaining seven, although they met Mā one or more times and were moved in some way by their contact, did not consider themselves devotees. Contributors were selected by a somewhat serendipitous process. The first devotees I met in the Boston area gave me the names of people who had been close to Mā whom they thought I should meet when I went to India. When I arrived in Banaras in July 1990, I went to Mā's ashram and met the secretary of the ashram, who introduced me to some of Mā's other devotees in Banaras, who in turn connected me with other devotees. Still, I was disappointed to find that Banaras was not the vibrant center of Mā's community that it had been in the 1970s, and the process was moving slowly.

In October, a young French scholar visiting in Banaras invited me to Kankhal, the site of Mā's *samādhi* shrine[31] and ashram. He was studying there with a well-known swami of Mā's and said he would introduce me to many *sannyāsins and brahmachāriṇīs*, or male and female renunciants, all of whom he said had been very close to Mā. In November and early December at Kankhal ashram and in neighboring Dehradun, I interviewed twelve of the forty-two devotees who were my contributors. In the same way, a devotee of Mā's whom I met in Bombay in early January told me that I would find many close devotees of Mā's in Calcutta and arranged for me to stay at the home of a prominent Calcutta businessman. My days there were full of interviews arranged by my host. In all, I interviewed seventeen devotees during my three-week stay in Calcutta, most of them householders. Ironically, the one person I thought I would work most closely with during my stay in India, Bithika Mukerji, I met only once and never interviewed, as she was involved all year in caring for her acutely ill mother.

Of the forty-two devotees I interviewed, there were twenty-five women and seventeen men. Twenty-eight were householders and fourteen were renunciants, and they ranged in age from thirty to eighty-two. Although I did not ask all devotees about their caste, it can be deduced from the surnames of householders that sixteen are brahmans, eight are *kayasthas* (a nonbrahman high caste), and three are *vaishyas* (merchant caste). I learned from the stories of the renunciants that of the six *sannyāsins*, or male monks, four are brahmans, one is a Parsee, and one a European. The one *sannyāsinī*, or female monk, is a brahman. Of the seven *brahmachārinīs*, or female celibates, four are brahman and three are *kayastha*. Thirty out of the forty-two devotees identified themselves as Bengali. If the forty-two devotees I interviewed are representive of close devotees of Ānandamayī Mā, which I believe they are, having read their names in the literature on Mā and having identified them in films and photographs of Mā, then an average devotee of Mā is a Bengali brahman, university educated, and English-speaking. The male householder devotees I interviewed tend to have government appointments or family businesses. The female householder devotees are not professionals; most are university educated and English-speaking and run the household. The renunciant devotees also are highly educated and decided to take vows of renunciation, either formally or informally, after their education was complete or even midcareer.

The remaining four men and three women interviewed in India were people who had met Ānandamayī Mā and been affected by that meeting but did not consider themselves devotees. Two of the men were brahman priests in Banaras, one was a Banaras businessman, and one was a European *sannyāsin* living in the ashram of another guru. Two of the women were living in that same ashram, and one was an Austrian scholar living in Banaras. I am grateful to have their perspective on the different aspects of Ānandamayī Mā to compare and contrast with the perspectives of her devotees.

Confidentiality

It will become apparent that, beyond the public level of discourse about Ānandamayī Mā that is accessible through the body of literature available on her, there is as well an esoteric level at which Mā's close devotees related to her and about which they only speak among themselves or possibly not at all. I believe that many of the conversations I participated in with my contributors tapped that level. Therefore, although my contributors understood that I intended to use their statements in this study, I have decided to give each of them a pseudonym. It is my hope that this step honors the trust and generosity they extended toward me.

What Were the Interviews Like?

The interviews with devotees and nondevotees alike ranged from somewhat formal to very impromptu. I had no research assistant. Only occasionally would a devotee accompany me to translate for the few people who spoke only Hindi or Bengali. In Banaras and Calcutta, I was usually invited to a devotee's house, served tea and sweets, and invited to talk about my project. I then showed them my tape recorder and asked permission to tape our conversation. After the formal part of the interview, I might be given a tour of the house, including the room used for worship and meditation, the *pūjā* room. In Mā's Kankhal ashram, the interviews usually took place outside, as we sat on a marble wall or on a bench, during the day or after the evening *ārati* or worship service. The formal part of most interviews lasted between one and two hours. I interviewed six contributors two or three times.

Although I usually asked particular questions, most interviews were conversational, informal, and covered a wide range of topics. The seven standard questions were: When did you first meet Mā and what was the meeting like? Can you tell me some experiences that you had with Mā that might help me better understand who Mā was? Who do you think Mā was? (Then, if they answered that Mā was God or the equivalent) Why do you think God came in the form of a woman? Is Mā your model for how to live your life? What is the goal of your *sādhana*, or spiritual practice? Has anything changed since Mā's *mahāsamādhi* [Mā's passing from the physical world]?

Several common themes or qualities were present in almost all interviews. The first, and perhaps the most important, was the almost unanimously held idea among Mā's devotees that "You cannot know Mā." I came to understand that what devotees meant was that Mā, being divine, was beyond knowing and certainly beyond describing in words. For example, when I interviewed Rupa Vishvanathan, an older woman devotee of Mā's in Kankhal, I explained, "So the task I have is to write about Mā for my doctoral dissertation." No sooner had I gotten these words out of my mouth than she said, "It is very difficult, because, to tell you the truth, it is very difficult to understand Mā. Because, you know, we have known her for nearly forty years. We met her nearly forty years ago. . . I think there are still things we do not understand."[32] A day later, Rupa was present as I interviewed Sita Gupta. I began by telling the two women that I wanted to hear about Sita's experiences with Mā so that I could better understand Mā. Rupa said immediately,

> OK, but one thing I can tell you now before we start—to understand Mā is impossible. Understanding must come from within you. It can't come through

a book, it can't come through me. It can only come through your own penance, your own way of life. Mā will reveal to you all the fruits from within you. I will say one thing, someone else will say another. You will only get more confused. . . . None of us are of that caliber to give you the complete understanding and the satisfaction, because it can only come from within you, from the pure Self which is Mā.[33]

This statement and the countless others like it mirror the conviction of the famous philosopher and devotee of Mā, Gopinath Kaviraj, stated in an article on Mā, that "no intellectual approach, however free from predispositions and prejudices, is capable of revealing the heart of truth."[34]

The unknowability of the divine is a powerful theme in the Hindu tradition. It holds that that no matter how many names we give God or how many perspectives, or *darshanas,* we pursue to understand the divine, God, as Diana Eck says, "exceeds the various ways of naming and imagining."[35] Eck goes on to say that Hindus are acutely aware that God language is "human language which constructs, approaches and apprehends, but never exhausts or fully comprehends the Divine."[36] Marilyn Waldman notes that the human struggle to know the unknowable has lead to two forms of piety: "the piety of determinacy in which one says that I am not on the right track unless I know everything for sure, and the piety of indeterminacy in which one says, I'm not on the right track if I do."[37] A Hindu statement of the piety of indeterminacy can be found in the *Guru Gītā,* a Sanskrit hymn of praise to the Guru: "He who thinks he knows not, knows; He who thinks he knows, knows not."[38] We will see that the devotees of Ānandamayī Mā reinforce her status as divine and maintain their own piety by continually speaking of her unknowability.

A second theme expressed by countless devotees was the feeling they were Mā's favorite child. People would say in kind of a whisper, "You know, Mā was *very* fond of me." One evening in Calcutta, I was speaking with Gita-Di Bose, a housewife who had grown up with Mā, about the fact that everyone had such a different relationship with Mā. She said, "And the funniest thing is that everybody felt, 'Mā loves me the most!' Everyone felt that Mā loved them especially."[39] At first, I wondered if this feeling was some form of arrogance on the part of certain devotees. But my husband reminded me that at his grandmother's funeral one of the grandchildren had said, "Grandma was the kind of grandmother who made each grandchild feel that they were her favorite." In the same way, Mā apparently made each devotee feel very special, despite the fact that each was one of hundreds of close devotees and one of thousands of people devoted to her.

The third theme present in almost all interviews was actually more of a quality, a certain deflection away from the personal. It was present in interviews with Mā's renunciant devotees. The most dramatic example was my interview with Swami Gitananda, the one *sannyāsinī,* or female monk, whom I interviewed. No matter how hard I tried to get Gitananda to speak about her personal experiences with Mā and her choice not to marry but to live with Mā as a renunciant, she was unswerving in bringing the topic back to *her* agenda, which was Mā. She had even brought a list of topics she wanted to cover, for example, the difference between the way Mā treated those who lived with her and those who came for occasional visits. She responded to all but one or two questions by saying, "I don't want to speak about myself. The story is too long."[40] Although this tendency was more pronounced with the renunciant devotees, perhaps reflecting the commitment they made during the process of *sannyāsa* initiation to die to their worldly lives, householder devotees also preferred to talk about Mā rather than about themselves.

This deflection of the personal was, to a great extent, modeled by Ānandamayī Mā herself. In chapter 6 we see that Mā constantly changed the subject when asked personal questions, especially if devotees were trying to get her to admit that she was God or the guru. She would nearly always turn the conversation around, asking devotees to focus on their own pursuit of God or the guru within. Furthermore, the language Mā used to refer to herself—"this body," "this little girl," or "this child"—deflected the listener away from her personality and toward the Absolute.

Thus, the interviews often reflected a tension between my agenda and that of the devotees. I was interested in finding out how contact with Ānandamayī Mā had impacted the lives of her devotees. I was looking for stories of transformation, of redirection, of before and after. While many contributors were willing to share these stories, especially the householders, they were more interested in documenting the greatness of Mā by recounting examples of her omniscience, her remarkable states of ecstasy, and her all-encompassing love. They seemed anxious to convince me that Mā was more than human. To some extent, they had difficulty relating to my "before" and "after" agenda. Why would I want to know about their limited lives or perspective? Most of them simply wanted me to know that *Mā* was their life.

The fourth common theme that emerged was the conviction that Mā had chosen me to present her to the West and that, therefore, the methodology I should use in this book was to "hold tightly to Mā's hand." I encountered this belief in my first interview, which took place in the Boston area with Elizabeth Walters and her visiting Indian friend and fellow devotee, Chandra Srinivasan, in 1988. Toward the end of the interview Elizabeth mused, "Who would have thought that this archive would come to Harvard, the most scholarly institution in this country and perhaps in the world, the archive of someone who did not reach out to Americans as some other teachers did? And it has come to you, Lisa."

Chandra added,

This universality makes me so happy. She has not chosen her own devotee, but she has chosen you. What is going to happen? You are going to have to start asking why, how? Be prepared. Because especially when you land in India, you will have to be very close to Mā and get the real essence as she wants it, not as you, Lisa, want it, or as the devotees want it, but as Mā wants it. You'll have to be very close. Just hold tightly to her hand.[41]

I was quite unprepared for this perception and this directive. However, it was not the last time I heard it. In Calcutta, Swami Samatananda, the head of Mā's Calcutta ashram, said,

> Sometimes Mā told us, "Why do you try to propagate my name? My name will be propagated in its own way, if God wants. Do your own *sādhana*. Try to know yourself. If God wants, my name will be all over the world. Don't worry." And now, it is through you, Lisa. In America perhaps so many people will be believing in Mā and seeing Mā's photograph.[42]

The consensus among Mā's devotees was that because nothing happens that is not Mā's will, or *kheyāla*, certainly my writing this book was her will, and therefore it was between me and Mā as to how it evolved. This belief is likely to have contributed to a phenomenon in which devotees, believing that there is no way to understand the divine, seemed somewhat mystified with my wanting to talk to them about Mā. They recommended, instead, that I forge an inner connection with Mā and receive the answers to my questions from within. Swami Brahmananda, the head of the Kankhal ashram said,

> If you are here for a week, don't examine her. Take the opportunity. Sit in the *samādhi* shrine, sit there as much as you can. Whatever time you have got, take it. Instead of coming this way and that, try to sit. I am certain that you will get some answers, some insight. Until you are rich, you cannot give money to others. You must know yourself. Ask, "What is my purpose in coming here?" Put these questions in your mind and sit and you will get some answer, definitely.[43]

When I returned from India, I attended a talk given by Iñes Talamantez, a Native American anthropologist, who spoke very movingly about the way to approach the other as a scholar. Approaching another culture with humility and respect, Talamantez said, entails allowing that culture to generate how one studies it. Instead of coming in with a set of questions, discover the indigenous methodology by asking one's contributors, "How should I go about this study?"[44] The community of Ānandamayī Mā told me from the beginning that all the answers to my questions would come from turning within to connect with my inner Self, which, according to the community, *is* Mā. If I had listened exclusively to Mā's community to determine how Mā should be studied, I would perhaps still be sitting in her *samādhi* shrine. Although I cannot say that I have fulfilled Talamantez's vision, I hope this study will be worthy of the community's confidence in me.

TWO

The Story of Ānandamayī Mā's Life

Though for a person like myself to write about Mā's life was like a dwarf's desire to touch the moon, still I wrote and felt it was good to do so. I knew that in learned circles this book would be considered worthless because I do not at all possess the necessary knowledge and intelligence needed to produce a book. But I thought that those who came in contact with Mā would read these anecdotes and experience bliss, and that the shortcomings in the language of the writer would not come in the way. . . . To those who have not seen Mā and who are coming to know her only through this book, I make an entreaty that if they misunderstand Mā's nature or character at any place, the failing is mine. There is no imperfection or shortcoming in Mā's conduct anywhere. Those who have met Mā will understand the truth of this statement.

> Gurupriya Devi, in the Dedication of
> *Sri Sri Mā Ānandamayī*, Volume 1

EACH OF THE SPIRITUAL BIOGRAPHIES OF Ānandamayī Mā begins, as does Gurupriya Devi's twenty-volume work,[1] with a note of apology in which the author-devotee tries to express the immensity, and even the impossibility, of writing about Mā's life. Mā, they tell us, is bigger than life and can never be "known." Yet, they feel it is their duty to share with those who have not had the good fortune to meet Mā the story of her life in the hope that the reader will obtain a taste of Mā's greatness and even an experience of her bliss.

There are an impressive number of spiritual biographies of Ānandamayī Mā and an even larger body of works in which devotees speak of their personal experiences with Mā. Seven major sacred biographies of Mā have been translated into or written in English, all but one written by life-long devotees of Mā and all but one written before her death. Mā's biographers witnessed overlapping portions of her eighty-six-year life. Because none of them was with her for her first twenty-eight years, they had to rely on the anecdotes told by Mā's mother, Didimā, who lived to be ninety-four, stories told by Mā's husband, Bholanāth, and Mā's own stories for information about her early life.

Two of the most important sources for Ānandamayī Mā's early life are the sacred biographies written by her two most respected early devotees. Gurupriya Devi (1899–1980), called Didi, or Elder Sister, provides the most detailed, primarily first–hand account of Mā's life in *Sri Sri Ma Anandamayi*. At present, seventeen of twenty volumes have been translated from Hindi into Bengali and five into English (the English version covers Mā's life from 1896 to 1938). Didi met Mā in 1925 and was nearly always at her side as her personal attendant until her own death in 1980. These volumes contain fascinating descriptions of Mā's activities annotated in daily or weekly diary entries, their only limitation that Didi primarily records only events she witnessed personally. The second book is *Matri Darshan*, written in Bengali and translated into English as *Mother as Revealed to Me*,[2] by the much loved and respected Jyotishchandra Ray, known as Bhaiji. Although only vaguely chronological, it contains detailed, firsthand stories. Bhaiji met Mā in 1924, became her devoted disciple, and ultimately left his wife and children for a life of renunciation until his death in 1937.

Many devotees suggested that I read Anil Ganguli's *Ānandamayī Mā: The Mother, Bliss-incarnate*,[3] published in English. Ganguli was also a renowned devotee of Mā's.[4] Chapters 3 through 6 recount Mā's life, and the rest of the book is a set of anecdotes organized by theme. Mā's early life is a retelling, since Ganguli met Mā in 1947. *Mā Ānandamayī Līlā*,[5] also in English, is the memoirs of Hari Ram Joshi, with some first-hand accounts of Mā's life between 1933, when he met her, and his death in 1965. The most inscrutable resource on Mā's life in English is *Svakriya Svarasamrita*, volumes 1 through 3, by Brahmacharini Chandan, a maternal cousin of Mā.[6] Chandan knew Mā all her life, took the vow of *brahmacharya*, or celibacy, in 1973 from Mā's mother, Didimā, and subsequently wrote these books to honor Didimā as her guru. Although very cumbersome and seemingly random, they include Didimā's accounts of Mā's early childhood and are the only source for many of them.

A more readable, Western-style account of Mā's life was written by Bithika Mukerji, a philosophy professor Emeritus at Banaras Hindu University. It is a lively, detailed account of Mā's life between 1896 and 1939. *From the Life of Anandamayi Ma*, volumes 1 and 2,[7] is largely based on interviews and the journals of Mā's early devotees. Mukerji is presently working on a third volume. She also published a condensed version of Mā's life and teaching, "Srī Ānandamayī Mā: Divine Play of the Spiritual Journey," in *Hindu Spirituality*.[8] The most accessible biography and the only one from an independent publisher is Alexander Lipski's *The Life and Teaching of Sri Anandamayi Ma*.[9] Although selective and without references, this work is as close to a scholarly account as can be found.[10] Lipski met Mā in 1965 while on a sabbatical leave from a professorship in Hindu religious thought and became quite devoted to her.[11]

The formats of Ānandamayī Mā's sacred biographies are similar. Most begin with her birth and chronicle her childhood and adolescence in some detail. They give particular emphasis to the years between 1918 and 1924, which they refer to as "The *Līlā* of *Sādhana*," or the play of spiritual practices, during which Mā engaged in yogic practices and initiated herself. The next ten years are also emphasized, as the number of devotees grew dramatically and Mā established her life-long pattern of renunciation and travel.

Most of the sacred biographies distill Mā's last forty years into a few pages or leave it out. There are several apparent reasons for this imbalance, some practical and some philosophical. Bhaiji's work takes us only up to 1938, when he died. Mukerji's work is apparently a work in progress, although we do not know whether she intends her volumes to cover Mā's entire life. However, the paucity of detail on Mā's later life may stem from the community's perception that Mā's "nature" was fully manifested by that time.[12] Furthermore, the contrasting plenitude of devotees' personal accounts during Mā's last forty years points to the community's emphasis on the timeless presence of grace in their lives. Dates and historical or social context are irrelevant to their testimonials. As Alexander Lipski says,

> From 1932 to the present Ānandamayī Mā's *līlā* [play] has been an uninterrupted outpouring of divine counsel, an incessant call to mankind to awaken from the sleep of delusion to the realization of the One who alone is real. . . . Instead of "significant" historical landmarks, Ānandamayī Mā's *līlā* (play) from 1932 to the present constitutes an unending procession of religious festivals, *kirtanas* and *satsangas* (meetings with her devotees).[13]

Mā's sacred biographies could be considered part of the traditional genre of Hindu hagiography, the written or sung account of an extraordinary person's life.[14] Since the sixth century B.C.E. there has been extensive documentation of the triumphs of the saints and sages of South Asia, possibly originating with stories about the lives of Gautama Buddha and of Mahāvīra, the founders of the Buddhist and Jain traditions. Although an occasional Hindu sacred biography emphasizes the struggles of a saint in the making, the "dark night of the soul" through which the saint must pass to know God, most establish the religious figure as more than human. Edward Dimock attributes this tendency to the cosmic significance of the *mahātma*, or great soul, who reflects a divinely established paradigm, the recurrent return to earth of God in human form at a time of the decline of righteousness.[15]

As early as the ninth century, in the sacred biographies of the philosopher Shankara, we find the tendency to present a religious figure as an incarnation of God who comes to earth.[16] Likewise, the ninth-century Tamil woman saint, Āntāl, is portrayed as an incarnation of the Goddess. The life stories of three later Hindu historical figures from Bengal—the sixteenth-century saint, Shrī Krishna Chaitanya; the nineteenth-century saint, Ramakrishna; and the twentieth-century saint, Ānandamayī Mā—are framed similarly. All these sacred biographies emphasize their subject's reflection of the universal, grace-bestowing power of the absolute.

Hagiography, or sacred biography, has been the subject of much recent interest and scholarship, in the field of Hindu studies as well as others.[17] In their introduction to *The Biographical Process: Studies in the History and Psychology of Religion*, Frank Reynolds and Donald Capps recognize spiritual biographies as "an extraordinary form of biography because they recount the process through which a new religious ideal is established and, at the same time, participate in the process."[18] This creative function goes hand in hand with their salvific function based on their teleology, described by scholars such as Charles Keyes, through which ordinary people gain access to the sacred as it is revealed through the life of an extraordinary person.[19]

Reynolds and Capps divide sacred biographies into two categories: those which "humanize" the biographical subject and those which "spiritualize" him or her. In the second category, "establishing the mythical ideal takes precedence over a simple chronicling of biographical facts."[20] Hindu sacred biography clearly chooses to "spiritualize" its subjects. The lives of Hindu saints are replete with miracle stories and descriptions of extraordinary states of consciousness and have been considered by most scholars to lack verifiable historical "facts." As a result, scholars have tended to emphasize the patterning of traditional Hindu sacred biographies upon a preestablished mythical paradigm.

In examining the life story of Ānandamayī Mā, however, we have the opportunity to consider the formation of the sacred biography of a living figure within a contemporary community. Unlike traditional sacred biographies—for example, those of Āntāl, which were written five to six hundred years after her death[21]—the sacred biographies of Ānandamayī Mā were written, in all but one case, while she was still alive; the anecdotes we are reading are being told and retold by people who were *present* during the incident.

The particular genre of hagiography of which Ānandamayī Mā's sacred biographies are a part is a contemporary genre in which devotees, believing the holy person to be divine in origin during his or her lifetime, recorded the person's life events and interactions with devotees. Anecdotes were collected and turned into publishable narrations by the biographers, who were also devotees. This genre seems to have originated with the sacred biographies of Ramakrishna Paramahamsa (1836–1886).[22] Like the Ramakrishna material and the material on successive charismatic figures, the sacred biographies of Ānandamayī Mā represent the perceptions, experiences, and beliefs of devotees of a living saint. As such, they present a unique opportunity to understand the contemporary Hindu phenomenon of an extraordinary person who evolves into a focus of worship. This study is representative of a new scholarly genre that takes up the challenge of examining contemporary sacred biography and its relationship to the phenomenon of contemporary Hindu sainthood.[23]

Because of the uniqueness of this opportunity, in the following section I provide a composite of the community's telling of the life story of

Ānandamayī Mā as represented in the seven biographies I have mentioned. In relating Mā's devotees' version of her life story, as much as possible as it is told, I hope to present it rather than to represent it.

Many of the spiritual biographies of Mā are overly detailed and achronological. I have condensed the traditional accounts by selecting anecdotes that appear in a majority of sources[24] to create a narrative that is not too cumbersome. I have tried to choose the closest firsthand account, and, in the rare case of disagreement about an incident, I acknowledge different versions in a footnote. In my desire to give the reader the flavor of a particular story as told by those closest to Mā, I use the devotee's actual or translated words.

Furthermore, I have directed my efforts toward a chronological presentation of the events of Mā's life to create a more accessible story line for future analysis. I emphasize the first phase of her life and condense her life after the death of Bholanāth, reflecting the choice of the most of her biographers. I also mirror her sacred biographies in occasionally narrating an event and following the narration with Mā's narration of the same event. Finally, I have tried to adopt a tone similar to that of the spiritual biographies, which is primarily devotional as opposed to analytical.

I hope that the fully referenced version of the story of Ānandamayī Mā's life related here will benefit scholars who wish to do further work on Mā. It will serve as a basis for the analysis in the following chapters of Ānandamayī Mā as a woman, as a saint and guru, and as an *avatāra*, or incarnation of God. It also takes its place in the series of tellings of Mā's life that shape the future of her community. Many may see it as having a potential salvific function for those who read it with devotion.

Ma's Life Story as Told by Her Devotees

Ma's Childhood

On April 30, 1896, in a humble cottage in the village of Kheora in the heart of primarily Muslim, rural Bengal, a devout Vaishnava brahman couple, Shri Bipin Bihari Bhattacarya and Srimati Mokshada Sundari Devi, gave birth to a girl, their second child. They named her Nirmala Sundari, or the One of Taintless Beauty. This baby girl was later to become known throughout India as Anandamayi Ma, the Bliss-Filled Mother, or simply Ma. Bipin Birhari Bhattacarya, known fondly as Dadamahashaya, belonged to the well-known Kashyapa lineage of nearby Vidyakut, claiming descent from the Vedic seer, Kashyapa. His family was proud to count two *satis* among their ancestors, as well as many pandits and gurus. Dadamahashaya's father was himself a guru, who, though he died early in his life, passed on to his son the proper form of worshiping the family deity, the Shalagrama Shila.[25] Mokshada Sundari Devi, known fondly as Didima, was also from a prominent Vaishnava brahman family of nearby Sultanpur, which claimed descent from a disciple of the Vedic *rishi*, Bharadwaj. Didima was also the offspring of a guru whose family had worshiped the family Shalagrama Shila from generation to generation and reverently remembered an ancestor who had performed suttee with great dignity.[26]

Both of Nirmala Sundari's parents possessed extraordinary spiritual sensibilities. Dadamahashaya was well respected in the villages of both his mother's and father's families for his "honest upright nature and his other worldliness."[27] He spent most of his time absorbed in the worship of the family deity and in singing devotional songs, accompanying himself on the *ektara*, a single-stringed instrument. He had a fine voice and was compared by the villagers to the famous Bengali poet, Ramprasad Sen, because of his *bhagavata-bhava-prema*, his quality of divine love. He rarely slept at night. One night he was so intoxicated from chanting the divine name that he did not even notice that a severe windstorm had blown the tin roof off the building in which he was chanting. When his wife entered, she found him still singing with great love in the pouring rain.[28]

Dadamahashaya's religious fervor was accompanied by lack of interest in worldly life. Before his marriage he had begun to wear the ochre robe of a *sannyasin*, or renunciant, but his parents called him home to marry the twelve-and-half-year-old, Mokshada Sundari Devi. For a year or so, the couple lived at the home of his father's family in Vidyakut, but after the birth of their first daughter, he again felt drawn to wander, singing God's name. He took his new wife and baby to live in Kheora with his mother. Thus, "although Shriyukt Bipin Bihari Bhattacarya Mahasaya was now leading the life of a householder, yet his inner feeling (*bhava*) seemed always to be in tune with divine union (*yoga*), the nature of which we do not know."[29]

Didima, however, being "full of wisdom, patience, dignity, and fortitude through difficulties,"[30] "remained in her innate bliss (*ananda*) and in her divine mood."[31] Although she lived in poverty, she "just kept taking care of her elders like her grandmother-in-law and her mother-in law day and night. Never was there in evidence even a shadow of any feeling of deficiency, complaint, worry or depressions in her."[32] She always displayed an "unchanged calmness of spirit, an abiding sense of contentment and sufficiency, and was never slovenly or bitter."[33] She remained the *Grihalakshmi*, the household embodiment of the goddess of fortune, of the family and even in his absence, "all her activities were rendered as seva to Shriyukt Bipin Bihari Bhattarcharya Mahasaya in his aspect as the Supreme Husband (Parampati)."[34]

During Dadamahashaya's absence, the couple's first daughter died in her second year.[35] After a time, some neighbors, feeling compassion for the young wife, sent for her husband to return from his ascetic wanderings. He returned to Kheora after three years' absence. Soon his mother, called Thakurma, or grandmother, having become concerned that her son's renunciant streak would jeopardize the family lineage, went on a pilgrimage to the Kali temple at Kasba to pray to the Goddess for a grandson. However, when she came into the presence of the image of Kali, she found herself saying, "If I am blessed with a granddaughter and she lives long, then on the occasion of her marriage, Shree Shree Kalimata will be worshiped with due ceremonial rites." After she had uttered this vow, she yelled, "Oh,

Hari, what is it that I have done! After coming here to pray for a boy, I have asked for a girl!"[36] As the Goddess would have it, Thakurma was to be Nirmala Sundari's playmate until she died just before her granddaughter's marriage.[37]

Soon thereafter, a second child was conceived to these kind, loving, and religious parents. Anandamayi Ma was to say later in her life, "Before this body[38] appeared, Father had abandoned his home. He had even donned the saffron robe for some time and spent his days and nights singing God's praises. This body appeared during his mood of renunciation."[39] Reflecting on the time prior to Ma's birth, Didima reports,

> Your Ma was to make her advent in this body, but even two or three months before that, such was the concurrence that I very often saw many Incarnations (avataras) in various forms, numerous deities and gods come near me in a vision—what a glorious manifestation! I could feel an indescribable environment. . . . I would, with an inexplicable inner experience, welcome and extend ceremonial reception (varan) to them with reverence.[40]

The birth itself was an unusual one. Didima did not suffer much pain in labor, and the baby was born after only ten minutes of labor. Those present at the birth were concerned when the baby was absolutely quiet after her birth. Later on, when Ma was asked about this, she replied, "Why should I have cried? I was watching the mango tree through the apertures in the cane matting at that time."[41] She had a fair and shining complexion and she "illumined Didima's cottage by the extraordinary lustre of [her] body."[42] Thus, Didima named her Nirmala Sundari, or One of Taintless Beauty.

Even as an infant, Nirmala was fully conscious. When she was four or five, she asked her mother, "Ma, didn't Mr. Nandan Chakravarty come to see me on the 13th day after my birth?" Didima had not remembered that previously.[43] When Nirmala was nine or ten months old, Didima relates that a radiant sadhu, or holy man, paid a visit to the house. He sat down close to the baby in the lotus posture and she crawled up to him. She gazed at him, "laughing, too, as if intimately familiar with him," and he looked intently at her, smiling all the while. Then he held little Nirmala overhead and "placed her feet reverently on his shoulder, head and other parts of his body in an extraordinary show of devotion and veneration and then sat her on his lap." Setting her down in front of him he began to perform puja, or worship, to her, bowing down before her. He said to Didima: "This whom you are seeing before you, this is Ma [the Divine Mother] and is so not [only of] men and women but also as permeating and transcending the universe. You will certainly not be able to keep Her bound to family ties. She will definitely not remain here."[44] The mahatma, or great soul, then vanished.

As a toddler, Nirmala was often seen in states of ecstasy, especially during kirtan, or devotional singing. Once when she was two and a half, she attended a nama kirtan, or chanting of the divine name, at a neighbor's house. She went into a trance like state, drooping over as she sat. Her mother shook her, bemoaning, "All the boys and girls remain seated. Only this one is in such a state!"[45] Another time when little Nirmala returned home from a *kirtan* in which a stanza was sung about Radha mad with love for Lord Krishna, she sat "deeply absorbed under a cluster of bananas. . . . [and] started singing the same stanza lispingly. As she continued Her singing, a flow of tears kept on drenching Her."[46] When asked about this later, Ma said, "I had experienced oneness with the prevailing *bhava* [emotion] of the *kirtana* singers."[47]

Mindful of the death of her firstborn, Didima, according to custom, used to place the infant Nirmala under the *tulsi* plant and roll her around it three times to invoke God's blessings. By the time she was a toddler, Nirmala would obediently go to the *tulsi* plant and perform the ritual herself. At around the same age, Nirmala would exasperate her mother with her "absentmindedness" while she was being fed. Didima would say, "You sit down for a meal and do not eat. Why do you always look up?" Later Ma explained, "I can tell you now that I used to watch images of the Gods and Goddesses coming and going [above me]."[48]

Even as a little child, Nirmala was irresistibly cheerful and adorable, and everyone in the village, Muslim and Hindu alike, wanted to carry her around and play with her. However, according to Hindu purity regulations, any child over six months old who was touched by a Muslim needed to receive a purificatory bath afterward. It is said that several times a day little Nirmala was picked up by her Muslim friends and returned, whereupon she was stripped of all her clothes and had water soaked with *tulsi* leaves poured over her by her mother.[49] In 1984, two years after Ma's *mahasamadhi*, when her devotees took a pilgrimage to Kheora, they were welcomed by Muslim devotees who said, "Although Ma was born into a Hindu family, She is also the Ma of the Muslims. She is our own Ma."[50]

Two more incidents reveal Nirmala's spiritual precocity. One day she was digging in the sand for several hours. Didima asked, "Why do you stay in the sun for so long?" Nirmala replied,

> There is a *Shalagrama Thakur* [divine image] in the *Thakurghar* [shrine of the image] and present in it are Krshna, Radha, and Rama Narayan and all such forms—so you were telling me, were you not Mother? Now in this heap of sand, too, are present all those forms and there are also still more forms, innumerable as they are.[51]

Again, when Nirmala was very tiny, it was *Vaisakhi Puja*, an auspicious time to offer a ripe mango to the deity. Didima, being extremely poor, was unable to buy a mango, and the tree outside the house only had green mangos, except for one ripe one at the very top of the tree. Little Nirmala, who had the habit of conversing with trees, went outside and came back with the ripe mango. Didima was angry at first, assuming that the child had taken it from someone else's tree. But Nirmala insisted that it fell from the top of the family tree, saying, "As you give me, so does the tree."[52]

Nirmala grew into a most unusual girl who displayed "unquestioning obedience, uncompromising truthfulness and unimpaired cheerfulness."[53] She had no sense of "I" or "mine" and often simply mirrored the emotions of those around her. She seemed to have no desires of her own "so the incentives to her behavior took shape out of the wishes of her companions."[54] She fetched and carried eagerly for everyone, and her sunny disposition earned her the nicknames Hasi Ma, Mother of Smiles, and Khushir Ma, Happy Mother. She was an invaluable help to her mother, who had six children in rapid succession after Nirmala, the much loved and relied Didi, or older sister.

Nirmala's obedience was a matter of her literal and "unquestioning acceptance of the bidding of others."[55] For example, one day Dadamahashaya told her to pause only at a comma when reading. After that, Nirmala would read in one breath. If she had to stop and take a breath, she would begin all over again. She "would read holding her breath with great difficulty, contorting her body in this effort until she came to a full stop and released her breath."[56] Once Nirmala was taken by an aunt to a fair in a nearby village. She was told to sit quietly outside a Shiva temple while the adults went into the village. Her aunt forgot about her, but when she returned several hours later she found her "sitting like a little statue, motionless, staring into space."[57] Sometimes Nirmala's literal obedience was disconcerting. Once when she was washing an agate cup, Didima saw her holding it a little negligently. She said, sarcastically, "You may as well drop it." Nirmala dropped it, and it shattered on the floor.[58]

On the rare occasion when Nirmala did something she was not supposed to do, there seemed to be a lack of consciousness or an intervening of divine will. For example, Ma reported later in her life an unconscious act of sacrilege:

> Mother used to caution me that the idol [in the family shrine] should not be touched. Most unexpectedly, however, the idol would often accidentally be touched by me, but invariably without leaving any impression on my mind as to what had been done. In fact, I would completely forget about it.[59]

Likewise, young Nirmala became moved to sneak out of the house to attend the Christian prayer meetings at the camp nearby. She would come back in a miraculously short time before dusk so as not to be noticed by Didima by means of a "strange sort of wavy movement in the air."[60] When asked about this later, Ma said, "The prayer they made at that time, the same prayer was also the form of this action." It seems that when the divine will became her will, her *kheyala*, the strict adherence to obedience did not hold. [61]

Nirmala seemed to have no emotion of her own. When she was eight or nine, her three younger brothers, ages six, four, and one and a half, died in quick succession over a period of six months. She "remained calm and showed no sign of mourning."[62] However, whenever her mother would begin to weep, Nirmala would "break out into such a torrent of heart-rending sobs that Mokshada Devi perforce had to forget her own sorrow in order to quiet the little girl."[63] When asked about this later in her life, Ma said that she had felt absolutely no pang of separation at the death of her brothers.

> She only cried out of a sense of duty to her lamenting mother. Whenever Didima wailed, Nirmala would play the role of a mourner. Her tears would

naturally touch Didima and induce her to pacify the grieved child. . . .
Absolutely unperturbed herself, this girl of inscrutable character thus played
to perfection [her] role.[64]

As she grew older, Nirmala continued to be fascinated with religious
subjects and to be drawn toward any religious event. She would accompany
her father when he did his *puja* and talked endlessly with her mother about
religious topics. Her greatest love was *kirtan*. Often she would wander off
and sing devotional songs by herself. In an uncommon show of emotion,
she would respond to the sentiment of the lyrics with tears streaming down
her cheeks.[65] In the village of Kheora, on special occasions there was often
nagar-kirtan, a chanting procession through the town. Nirmala would beg
her mother for permission to join the procession. Knowing full well the
strict purdah rules that were observed at that time in Bengal and shocked
that her daughter would consider joining a group of boys in the procession,
Didima would reply emphatically, "No." Nirmala would "remain grave and
calm for some time."[66]

Although Nirmala had received only informal religious instruction from
her parents, she displayed an uncanny knowledge of religious matters. Once
an older female relative of Nirmala's took *diksha*, or initiation, from a guru.
Soon she forgot the details of the required *mudras*, *nyasa*, and *asanas*,[67] but
she was afraid to ask Didima for help, so she mentioned it to young Nirmala.
Although the child had never seen anyone initiated, she gave her all the
details. Nirmala explained, "Hearing the words of [my Aunty], all that just
occurred spontaneously in this body."[68]

Nirmala continued to fall into trancelike states. In the middle of work
or play or at mealtime, she would become inert and stare into space with a
fixed gaze. Her mother would "shake and scold her or call her loudly by
name as if calling her from a distance. It was some time before she was
brought back to the consciousness of her surroundings."[69] Once during the
Durga Puja celebration at her maternal uncle's house, Nirmala fell into a
trance and began to recite some mantras. During the subsequent Kumari
Puja, the worship of virgin girls, her uncle, impressed by her supernatural
behavior, served the blessed food to her first.[70] Whenever Nirmala would
hear the sound of a drum, she would fall into an abnormal state. At one
such time she uttered, "There is one eternal sound only, from this point of
view. Know that the Supreme Sound abides in all sounds indeed!"[71] Some
of her relatives noticed that the child's states had an effect on them. Nirmala's
thakurma, or maternal grandmother, said that once Nirmala had said
something to her and that she had lost body consciousness for some time.[72]

Young Nirmala took complete joy in nature. She was always happiest
when she was outside. She would be seen "leaping and jumping in the air,
and dancing and singing, surging in exaltation and exhilaration. . . . The
void, air, light, water, etc., indeed all were [her] playmates."[73] Once the
thatched roof blew off the family cottage and everyone was very upset—
everyone except Nirmala, who laughed and danced, clapping her hands,
saying, "Now we can see the sky with its beautiful twinkling stars without

having to take the trouble to go out of the house. Now in and out are one in the same!"[74] In fact, Nirmala's gaze was so permanently fixed toward the sky that her mother often called her "camel-faced."[75]

Trees, flowers, and animals were Nirmala's intimate friends. When she talked to the trees, they seemed to shake a little. She would wrap her body in the parts of trees, caressing them with affection as she laughed and played in the breeze.[76] Flowers were the objects of endless hours of devotion. When "the *nandadulal* blossomed in the evening, Nirmala used to remain with that blooming flower until it was dark."[77] She also talked and played with birds and other animals, even snakes. Animals were irresistibly drawn to her. The following anecdote is told of Nirmala and her cousins going out to play.

> In a narrow village lane they came face to face with a herd of cows. . . . The children ran off. From a distance they looked back and saw Nirmala standing very still in the middle of the lane surrounded by the cows. Some of them had lowered their heads and were rubbing them against her body and licking her gently. When the herd moved away, Nirmala ran to join her friends.[78]

Didima worried about her daughter's future. She seemed so simple and acted so strangely at times. Yet Nirmala learned to do everything required of a young housewife, seemingly without any training: sewing, cooking, crafts. Although she only received two years of formal schooling, because of the distance to school and her mother's need for help at home, she had done very well. In spite of the fact that Didima called her by nicknames such as Ahalya,[79] which connote a lack of alertness, it seemed that Nirmala almost instantly learned whatever the schoolmaster assigned. When asked later about this, Ma said, "Reading and memorizing happened automatically."[80] Another time she said, "Somehow or other. . . . the meaning of unknown words would occur to me spontaneously."[81]

Ma's Marriage Is Arranged

When Nirmala was twelve years old, Dadamahashaya became concerned that his daughter's marriage had yet to be arranged. He asked Nirmala's youngest maternal uncle to read her horoscope, but the uncle took it and then refused to return it, although he was asked repeatedly to do so. As a result, Dadamahashaya worried that there was something inauspicious about it. In fact, Nirmala's uncle reported much later, the horoscope had predicted that Nirmala would "never be tied down to family life," a prediction which would not have been welcome at that time.[82]

Because Dadamahashaya was a member of one of Vidyakut's most-respected Bhattacarya families, he felt compelled to find a parallel match from the district of Vikrampur. The first proposal he received was turned down because Thakurma said she refused to marry her granddaughter to a widower. Next he traveled to the village of Dokaci to look for a suitable groom. While he was gone, Nirmala said, strangely, to her mother and grandmother, "I saw a police inspector." They were worried by this mysterious statement. Dadamahashaya returned with a man from Dokaci, who was seeking a bride for one Ramani Mohan Chakravarti, his brother-in-law, who worked for the police department in Atpara, district Vikrampur. Although Ramani Mohan was much older than Nirmala, his father, Jagatbandhu Chakravarti, then deceased, was from a distinguished brahman Bharadwaj family like Didima's. Ramani Mohan's brother-in-law questioned the young bride to be and her mother and seemed satisfied. The negotiations were completed quickly, and an auspicious date was set for the ceremonies.[83]

The marriage took place on February 7, 1909. The Maharaja of Tripura held Dadamahashaya in such high esteem as a devout, scholarly brahman that he offered the impoverished family his decorated elephants for the bridal ceremony.[84] The procession started from the Kasba Kali temple. After the *Vrddhi Kriya*, or prosperity ceremony, Ramani Mohan mounted an elephant and arrived in Kheora at a fixed time, the band playing ahead. All the guests from Vidyakut and Sultanpur had arrived. Nirmala, then twelve years and ten months old, had been made to sleep in a different house, facing east. During the wedding ceremony, Nirmala did everything exactly according to instructions. However, no one had told her how to perform *Shubha Drshti*, the first exchange of auspicious glances. When the time came for her to look upon her husband for the first time, she was "looking skyward at the spectators who had congregated in a group there."[85]

Toward the end of the marriage ceremonies, Sri Laksmicharan, a famous old village pandit, performed the *havan*, or fire oblation. He said to Ramani Mohan, "Grandson, you will not know what jewel you are taking home!" The pandit's son also remarked, as he looked at the young bride, "Her shining complexion is becoming visible through her clothing. She is not an ordinary person!" After the ceremony, Nirmala's youngest uncle feasted Ramani Mohan and showered the couple with many gifts, while keeping secret his findings upon reading Nirmala's horoscope.[86]

Nirmala continued to live with her parents for the next year in Kheora. Because Ramani Mohan had been told that his new bride had been a student at the lower primary school, he wrote her letters, although he, too, had had only a rudimentary education. Everyone in the village knew about the letters because very few letters ever came to the post office. When the first one arrived, Didima put it in a very prominent place for her daughter to take. It remained there for four days, since Nirmala had not been told to take it. Finally, Didima told her to take it. It was read amid much laughing and teasing, and Nirmala's friends sat down with her to compile an answer.[87]

Ma as a Daughter-in-Law

When Nirmala was fourteen, it seemed appropriate to send her to the house of her husband's family. However, because Ramani Mohan's parents were both dead, the responsibility of training the new housewife fell upon the wife of Ramani Mohan's eldest brother. Thus, Dadamahashaya escorted Nirmala to Shripur, to the house of Revati Mohan and his wife, Pramoda Devi. Revati Mohan was employed as a stationmaster. Ramani Mohan, himself, having lost his job at Atpara, was spending most of his time traveling all over East Bengal looking for work. Before leaving Kheora, Dadamahashaya drafted a few letters for Nirmala "in suitably respectful language, which she could copy, in answer to [Ramani Mohan's] letters."[88]

Before Nirmala's departure, Didima instructed her daughter to silently obey the orders of her husband and the elders of his family. When Nirmala and her father left Kheora, "[no one] could help crying with a mind heavily grief-stricken! It appeared from their mood and talks as if something very extraordinary had left the village."[89] After Nirmala's departure, Dadamahashaya and Didima left the maternal grandfather's village of Kheora and moved to Dadamahashaya's father's village of Vidyakut. Within the next four years, Didima gave birth to three more children, two daughters, Surabala and Hemangini, and a son, Makhan.

Upon arriving at Shripur, Ramani Mohan asked Nirmala to unquestioningly carry out the orders of the household elders in his absence. The household of Revati Mohan and Pramoda included their two sons, Kalipada and Ashu, and their daughter, Labanya, as well as Ramani Mohan's second eldest brother, Surendra Mohan, and his wife, Prafulla, who was even younger than Nirmala. Indeed, everyone agreed that during the four years in which Nirmala lived at Shripur, she was the model sister-in-law. She followed the instructions of her elder sister-in-law and her husband to the letter. She undertook all the household tasks "like a machine,"[90] with no trace of exhaustion. Moreover, "if any elder was about to do any work, she would take that work from her hands with a smiling face and do it Herself."[91] From earliest dawn until late in the evening, she fetched water, cooked, cleaned, looked after the children, and ran errands with cheerfulness, "quickness and neatness of movements."[92] She worked so continuously that she developed sores between her fingers and toes from having them in water so much. Some neighborhood women, for whom she sometimes scrubbed pots without being asked, questioned her, "What kind of person are you? Have you no feeling of pain in your body? Are you human?"[93]

Nirmala was much loved by Revati Mohan and Pramoda. Revati Mohan credited her with saving his life by nursing him through a serious illness. He once refused to let her visit her parents because he could not bear to be without her.[94] The younger children, Ashu and Labanya, also adored Nirmala. Once Labanya angered her mother by telling Nirmala that she wanted to address her as "Mother" instead of "Aunty." Many years later, during the 1960s, Ma had a reunion in Calcutta with her sister-in-law, Pramoda. Late one night the two women regaled everyone with a conversation about the old days. Ma said, "Look, all these housewives think that they are great experts in household work. Tell them whether I, too, did not look after your house satisfactorily?" Pramoda replied, "You cannot imagine how sweet and good she was. She not only did my entire work, but I will acknowledge that she never gave me any cause for dissatisfaction throughout the years that she was with me. Truly, such a spirit of *seva* is rare nowadays."[95]

There were times, however, when Revati Mohan and Pramoda wondered if Nirmala was a simpleton. Once, when the household was very anxious about a legal suit in which Nirmala's absent husband was involved, Pramoda commented, "What ill luck has befallen [Ramani Mohan]! And see, here is there the least worry or anxiety in her? What sort of person are you? Could you realize this situation? Look this is what has happened!" Nirmala listened and said, "Now may I go back to work?"[96] Nirmala always served food to everyone else and ate what was left over, sometimes going without adequate food. Pramoda finally insisted that Nirmala eat with her so she could ensure that the girl ate properly. When Pramoda was suffering from a skin disease, Nirmala would scratch her skin to relieve the itch and then refuse to wash her hands. She said, "Does one wash one's own hands every time after scratching one's own body?"[97] Nirmala followed *purdah* restrictions almost to a fault. She was so careful as not to let any man, even a relative, see her unveiled, that she often could not see what she was being told to carry.[98]

Thus, Revati Mohan's house was "the training center for [Ma's] 'outer manifestation' as a housewife. Her 'inner being' seems to have remained unrevealed during this period."[99] However, there were a few instances of trances, which were by and large interpreted as "spells of absentmindedness" or "sleepiness" by Ramani Mohan's family. Sometimes, while in the midst of work, Nirmala "would unaccountably become inert, as if sleeping." Once or twice, Pramoda

> was attracted to the kitchen by the smell of burning food. She found her youngest sister-in-law lying motionless on the floor amidst the litter of cooking utensils. When shaken and aroused, she would appear to be embarrassed at the damage caused and quickly set about repairing it. Pramoda thought she had been overcome by sleep and left it at that.[100]

In 1913, Revati Mohan passed away from complications of diabetes. Toward the end of his brother's illness, Ramani Mohan had returned to Shripur to help nurse him. Nirmala was in charge of the cooking for the *shraddha kriya*, or performance of the last rites, feeding many brahmans with great competence. For six months after Revati Mohan's death, Nirmala lived with Pramoda and the children at Atpara. When Dadamahashaya came to take Nirmala to Vidyakut for a visit, little Labanya said, "I shall not stay here at any cost without Aunty," and she rolled on the ground, weeping profusely.[101] But Nirmala left without her and stayed for six months with her parents in Vidyakut.

Meanwhile, Ramani Mohan continued looking for work, finding only temporary positions here and there. His communications with his bride consisted of a few letters and occasional gifts, which he would usually deliver during short visits to Shripur and later to Atpara. Soon after their marriage, he had bought two books for Nirmala, "but she found it difficult to read joined alphabets and to read according to lines and paragraphs. Therefore she did not read any books after this."[102]

Ma Joins Her Husband in Ashtagrama

In 1914, Ramani Mohan secured employment in the Land Settlement Department in Ashtagrama, also in East Bengal. Nirmala, by then eighteen years old, went to join her husband there. Bidding her a tearful good-bye, Didima gave her daughter the following instructions: "Now you must look upon your husband as your guardian and obey and respect him just as you did your own parents."103 Nirmala followed these instructions completely. "It can be said that throughout the lifetime of [Ramani Mohan] Mataji never did anything without his consent and permission."104

For sixteen months, Nirmala and Ramani Mohan lived together in Ashtagrama in the household of Shri Sarada Shankar Sen and his wife. In this household, as was true in Shripur, Nirmala was much loved and appreciated. Her personality so radiated joyfulness that Shrimati Sen decided that, since all mothers are addressed by their child's name plus "Ma" and Nirmala's childhood name was *khushi*, cheerfulness, she should be called Khushir Ma. Shrimati Sen said later, "When Khushir Ma came to the pond, the *ghats* [or banks] would be lit up by her radiant beauty."105 Nirmala's younger friends called her Ranga Didi, or Beautiful Sister. In addition, Nirmala's cooking was much appreciated and admired, and all the women of the household learned to cook like her.

It was here in Ashtagrama that Ramani Mohan's beautiful wife was first recognized as a "spiritually exalted woman."106 Srimati Sen's brother, Harkumar, was a highly educated though unstable man, prone to religious fervor, who had lost several jobs and was now living with his sister. Their mother had died just before Ramani Mohan and Nirmala's arrival, and they began living in her room. Soon thereafter, Harkumar entered Nirmala's room and said, "Now you are my mother, my mother who has come back to this room. On this *shashthi* day, you will have to give me a new *dhoti* [cloth wrapped and worn by men as pants]!"107 Thus, he became the first one to call her Ma. From that day on, Harkumar took every opportunity to serve Nirmala with great devotion. Nirmala, befitting a young wife, refused to talk to Harkumar or let him look at her. Yet, he faithfully performed *pranam*108 to her every morning and evening and asked for prasad, or blessed food, after she had finished eating.109 When she continued to refuse him, Harkumar appealed to Ramani Mohan. Ramani Mohan took pity on the devoted Harkumar and asked Nirmala to give him her *prasad*. Nirmala, having vowed to obey her husband, complied.

One day, unable to make his Ma speak, Harkumar said, "Daughter, are you made of stone! For a whole year, I have been asking you to speak to me but you do not say a word. If I were to call a stone 'Ma' the way I have called you, I would be able to put life into a stone!" Another day Harkumar prophesied, "Daughter, you will see, now I am calling you 'Ma.' One day the entire world will call you 'Ma.' Nobody has recognized you yet."110 His prophesy was not appreciated, however, because he lacked credibility. When Harkumar asked his Ma for a new name, she gave him the name Haribola, or the Song of God, and he proceeded to sing God's name very devotedly.

One night at the house in Ashtagrama, Nirmala said to her husband after dinner, "Let me sit for a while for *Harinam*.111 I shall retire later." Ramani Mohan did not object because he thought chanting might be good for his wife's delicate health. From that night on, Nirmala sat for *Harinam*, lighting incense and a lamp near a picture of Kali from a matchbox, which she had put on the wall. These evening sessions initiated a "restless stream of *bhava*," or religious ecstasy.[112] In time Nirmala began to sit for *Harinam* while her husband was at work, and the spiritual ecstasies continued.

It was Harkumar who become "instrumental in calling attention to the ecstatic states (*bhavavastha*) of Anandamayi Ma."[113] One day he pleaded with Ma to let him arrange a *kirtan* under her sacred *tulsi* plant. Nirmala asked her husband, and Ramani Mohan "was overjoyed." Harkumar cleaned the courtyard and had the walls plastered with cow dung in preparation for what was to be the first event at which Nirmala was publicly observed to be in a state of *bhava*. During the *kirtan*, Nirmala was seated inside the house on the bed of Madhu Baba's wife, who was ill.[114] After some time, she peeked at the *kirtan* through a crack in the door and saw the entire house fill with an amazing light. Her body fell down on the ground and rolled, breaking one of her conch bangles. The sick woman called her husband and the other men from the *kirtan*. They all thought Nirmala was suffering from a fit and tried to revive her with water. However, Nirmala's body continued to quiver.

> This pattern of thrilling was such that, under its impulse, Her body was lifted in the air with an upsurging movement, and nobody had the power to restrain it. There appeared in Her a combination of laughter and tears in a strange way. . . . [which] continued ceaselessly. What a unique phenomenon; the body in divine splendor with smile on the face! Externally and internally, a strange wave of joy, as in rhythm with the inhalation and exhalation of breath, was surging all through Her body. There was, at that time, freedom from any sense of shyness and hesitation which are normal under a veil. Even in those who were making an effort to lift Ma and seat Her, the touch of Her body seemed to transform their inner state in a strange way. . . . Those who performed this *kirtan* considered themselves fortunate and blessed. [115]

Later, in that same state, she remained seated, calm and motionless for a long time, "her face and eyes bathed in a radiant glow."[116] Ma described her state of bliss in the following way: "Just as perspiration trickles down a human body in an incessant stream, so blissful ecstasy (*ananda*) oozes out of every pore of this body."[117]

A second *kirtan* was arranged under the *tulsi* plant, and Nirmala again went into the same state of *bhava*. This time Nirmala ran toward the *kirtan*, arms up stretched and eyes upturned, and had to be restrained. Later Ramani Mohan said, "What is all this? I feel ashamed to face people," and decided not to hold *kirtan* for a while. After some time, however, Ramani Mohan was asked by his landlord to invite the famous *kirtan* singer, Gagan Sadhu, to sing in the drawing room of the house. Nirmala, in the back room, again fell off a cot, her body cold as if dead. She was carried to her room, and by dawn there was still no movement in her body. Everyone was very concerned, and it was decided to invite Gagan Sadhu back for a second *kirtan*, in hopes that it might revive Nirmala. This time, she was carried into the room where the *kirtan* was going on and laid on the other side of a curtain. By the end of the *kirtan*, she was still in a completely unresponsive state. She remained in a state of "drowsy exhilaration" for three to four days. It seemed that "since the day *kirtan* was initially performed under the *tulsi* plant, the moment [the singing of the name of God] reached Ma's ears, immediately, like the action of electricity, Her body would quickly turn abnormal."[118]

Rumors reached Nirmala's parents at Vidyakut that their daughter was suffering from hysteria. They wrote to Ramani Mohan asking if they should send medicine, but he reassured them that Nirmala was well. Her sessions of *Harinam* in the house continued and she began assuming different yogic *kriyas*, or spontaneous postures. When she attended spiritual readings, she would have to leave when she felt a *bhava* coming on and would stagger to her room. Other members of the household began to see her differently. Kshetra Babu, seeing her in a red sari one day, prostrated himself before her and addressed her as "Devi Durga." Writing to his wife he said, "I noticed Ramani Mohan's wife. She appeared like a burning lantern."[119]

During the time in which Nirmala lived with her husband at Ashtagrama, Ramani Mohan had reason to question whether he would ever have a normal, married relationship with his wife. As soon as they began to live together, Ramani Mohan "found a spiritual aura around his wife which precluded all worldly thoughts from his mind. He accepted her as he found her: gentle, obliging and hardworking, but without a trace of worldly feeling or desire."[120] It is said that

> when he first tried to approach Her physically, he supposedly received such a violent electric shock that he put for a time being all thought of a physical relationship out of his mind. He seems to have initially thought that this was only a temporary condition. That Nirmala was still such a child and that She would later become "normal." But the marriage was never physically consummated.[121]

Surely his wife was devoted to him. She ate his leftovers as *prasad*, did *pranam* to the water she used to wash his feet and drank it, and would even eat a bit of the earth touched by his feet before she took her meal. Ramani Mohan, seeing these acts of service, "remained charmed, feeling always as if a small girl was near him."[122] "However, he wondered, since there was nothing physically wrong with her, why was there no trace of worldly desire in her? Yet, simple-hearted and self-forgetful as he was, he remained under the influence of some invisible power, not knowing what it was and having within himself a feeling of reverence as well."[123] But sometimes, when talking to friends or relatives, he questioned the situation. Often they urged him to marry again.

In 1916, when Nirmala was nearly twenty, she became seriously ill and was moved to her parents' house at Vidyakut. When she left Ashtagrama, everyone bid her farewell with tearful eyes. At Vidyakut, in greater solitude and with fewer responsibilities, the *bhavas* and yogic *kriyas* that had come to her during her stay at Ashtagrama continued. Later Ma said of her time there, "In the dark, I sometimes perceived a strange effulgence enveloping my body, and that light seemed to move about with time."[124] Some report that at that time Nirmala used to cure the ailments of the sick people around whenever she felt moved to by the divine will.[125]

The Lila of Sadhana (1918–1924)

In the spring of 1918, Ramani Mohan was transferred from Ashtagrama to Bajitpur to work as a law clerk for the estate of the nawab of Bajitpur. After a brief visit to Atpara and her sister-in-law, Nirmala joined him in Bajitpur. She continued to fall into trance during *kirtan*. Once during *kirtan*, she was sitting next to the daughter of Ramani Mohan's supervisor. Feeling a *bhava* coming on, Nirmala called the girl's mother saying, "I do not know what my body is doing." The superintendent's wife fanned her and sprinkled water on her, but soon Ramani Mohan was sent for to take her home.[126] As a result, Ma later reported that her husband "used to take precautions to keep this secret from the neighbors. Whenever *kirtan* was sung I was not allowed to go outside. I used to roll along the floor of the room. However, in spite of all precautions, a rumor spread that Ramani [Mohan's] wife had been dancing during *kirtan* with a drum on her shoulder."[127]

In Bajitpur, Nirmala began to engage in intensive practice of *sadhana* as mantra repetition. While during the day she remained "the serene and pleasant-spoken young housewife," at night "she was a devout and dedicated seeker (*sadhaka*) fully occupied with the manifestations of the inner life."[128] After she had served her husband dinner around nine o'clock, she would prepare the corner of the room for her worship, clean it, and purify it with incense. While Ramani Mohan watched in awe,[129] she would then sit in a perfect yogic posture on the floor in the corner of the room and repeat the name of God. Sometimes her body would spontaneously assume intricate yogic postures and hand movements, coordinated with the speed of respiration, which could vary from very fast to so slow as to be almost nonexistent. It is said that "at that time a bright light emanated from her body and therefore she often covered herself with a cloth."[130]

Although Nirmala was performing these practices in the privacy of her own house, her activities did not remain secret for long.

> Through the apertures in the cane matting some people [saw] these marvellous movements and other actions performed by Ma, but no one understood the real importance of all this. Some believed that these actions were prompted by spirits or ghosts, others thought it was some kind of disease. On the basis of their individual beliefs people came and advised [Ramani Mohan] to show Ma to some exorcist or physician.[131]

When, even in the daytime, Sanskrit mantras and stanzas began to flow from Nirmala's lips in the presence of outsiders, Ramani Mohan decided to call in some spirit exorcists (*ojhas*) to try "to put an end to the improper behavior of his wife."[132] Two of them, upon seeing her, recognized her spiritual attainment. They simply exclaimed "Ma! Ma!", prostrated and went away. Once an exorcist came to see Ma at night and sat in one corner of her room. Ma was seated in another corner. The exorcist performed various kriyas and went outside for a while. Then he returned and filled a pipe with tobacco. Just as he was about to hand the pipe to Bholanath, he nearly collapsed. Bholanath supported him, yet the exorcist fell to the ground and started moaning. Then he began saying, "Ma! Ma!" Nervously Bholanath requested Ma, "Please do something to pacify this man." A strange condition became manifest in Ma—the man grew steady gradually. He recovered by degrees and then bowed before Ma and left. While leaving he said, "This is not our work. She is verily Bhagavati Herself."133

At the same time, Ramani Mohan consulted with Dr. Mahendra Nandi of Kalikach, a physician of great repute, who saw Ma and said, "These are all elevated states and not any illness. Please do not expose her to the gaze of all and sundry." After that Ramani Mohan stopped consulting people about Ma's state.134

In Bajitpur, many recognized Nirmala's state as extraordinary. A friend, Usha, visited her regularly, even though her mother-in-law did not approve. Once she secretly brought her son, who was very ill, to receive Nirmala's touch. He recovered, and Usha was convinced that it was because of that touch. She would say, "Do you know, although you are so much younger, I feel like calling you Mother!"135 In anxiety one day, Ramani Mohan sought out the advice of a venerated Vaishnava holy man. The holy man suggested that Nirmala might wear a *tulsi mala* around her neck to help her *sadhana*. When Ramani Mohan told Nirmala, she asked him to inquire of the holy man whether "*japa* performed on a *mala* is better than the *japa* of the mind." The holy man told Ramani Mohan that a *mala* was not necessary and that there was no reason to feel worried.136

Once a Shakta guru came to Bajitpur and, hearing of Nirmala's condition, asked to see her. The guru asked her to sit next to an image of Shiva. Ma reports, "This body automatically assumed yogic postures and spun around twice. The Gurudeva observed this. Thereupon he kept on sending me messages through others to the effect that he was a perfected soul and, if I so desired, he could be instrumental in communicating to me the direct vision of God. I merely listened to all those messages."137 The guru asked if he could perform *puja* at their house and they consented. At the end of the *puja* he decided to test Nirmala, asking her to sit on a certain *asana* and perform the purification with water. Ma reports, "I assumed the correct posture automatically. My hands started performing certain *kriyas*. The Gurudeva became frightened and at once asked me to get up from the *asana*." On another occasion, the guru started bragging that he had attained a certain yogic power called *Bagala Siddhi*. Nirmala yelled, "What, you have attained *Bagala Siddhi*! This is a complete lie!" Ramani Mohan was very upset at his wife's behavior, but the guru immediately broke down and confessed that he had, in fact, never attained any spiritual powers. Ma reports, "This body at once furnished him with the details of *mantras* and methods of worship required by him."138

From May 1922, there seemed to be a significant intensification of Nirmala's spiritual activities.[139] It was as if she had assumed the role of a *sadhika* (a woman who practices *sadhana*) in earnest. Ma reports, "One day in Bajitpur, I went to bathe in a pond near the house where I lived. While I was pouring water over my body, the *kheyala* [spiritual impulse] suddenly came to me, 'How would it be to play the role of a *sadhaka*?'" During her evening sessions, after her body assumed various yogic postures and hand movements, she would "sink into deep meditation for hours, her body still and motionless, sometimes like a rock and sometimes limp like a rag doll."[140] Thus, she "enacted the role of the *sadhaka* to perfection. It is to be called a role because even in this she remained self-sufficient, looking to nothing or nobody outside herself. It was in the nature of a manifestation, not an achievement."[141]

Each night during *namajapa*, Nirmala repeated the name of Hari, as her father had taught her to do. Ramani Mohan, a devout Shakta, apparently became perturbed by this. Ma says,

> One night Bholanath said to me, "We are Shaktas. Why do you always repeat 'Hari bol, Hari bol?' This is not fitting." I replied, "Then what should I chant? 'Jai Shiva Shankara, Vom Vom, Hara Hara'?' This body did not know any mantras, so whatever came I voiced. Bholanath was satisfied and said: "Yes, just recite this!" So from then onwards "Jai Shiva Shankara" was being recited .... With the repetition of "Jai Shiva Shankara" [the various spontaneous yogic postures performed by this body] became even more intricate. So many different *asanas* came about of themselves, one after the other—such as *siddhasana, padmasana, gomukhi asana*, etc. The strange thing was that while repeating the Name postures formed spontaneously and then, with an audible sound in the spinal column, this body would straighten out naturally into a completely upright pose. ... Thereafter the repetition of the Name would cease by itself and some kind of absorption (*tanmaya bhava*) ensued. [142]

Nirmala became "more and more centered on the inner life, until this process of interiorization culminated in an initiation, which in this case was as unique as the spiritual discipline which led up to it."[143] One day in July 1922, Ramani Mohan, under the advice of his sister-in-law, suggested to Nirmala that she get herself initiated by the family guru as soon as possible.[144] A month later, on August 3, on the full moon of *Jhulan Purnima*, a most extraordinary event occurred. Ma reports:

> Bholanath had had his evening meal. A hookah was got ready and given to him. He lay down smoking and watching what I was doing. The care with which I had wiped the floor of the room and then sat down in an *asana* seemed somewhat unusual to him. But after watching for a while he fell asleep. Here also, the curious thing is that the *yajna* and *puja* that have to be performed during the initiation were spontaneously carried out by this body. The *yajna stali* [vessel] was placed in front; all the various ingredients necessary for the *puja*, such as flowers, fruit, water, etc. were already there; although not everybody could see them, yet there was no doubt about their actual

existence. The *diksha mantra* emanated from the navel and was pronounced by the tongue. Then the mantra was written by the hand on the *yajna* vessel and *puja* and fire sacrifice were duly performed over the mantra, that is to say all the rituals prescribed by the *Shastras* for *diksha* were duly gone through. Later when my fingers were moving to count the *japa*, Bholanath woke up and saw me perform *japa*.[145]

On another occasion Ma said of her initiation, "As the master (*guru*) I revealed the mantra; as the disciple (*shishya*) I accepted it and started to recite it. The *mantra* now replaced the Names of God which I had been repeating earlier, as the realization dawned within me that the Master, the *mantra*, the Lord (*ishta*) and the disciple are One."[146]

Soon after Nirmala's self-initiation, her cousin, Nishikanta Bhattacarya, came to visit for a few days. He was shocked to witness the extraordinary evening behavior of his cousin and decided one night to challenge her. As Nirmala was meditating, Nishikanta asked Ramani Mohan what his wife was doing. Nirmala, fully veiled, lifted the veil and, with a stern expression, said, "Oh, what do you want to know?" Nishikanta, taken aback, took a few steps backward and asked respectfully, "Who are you?" Nirmala asked, "Were you frightened seeing that *bhava*?" She went on to say in an indistinct tone, "I am Mahadeva and Mahadevi [God and Goddess]." Then Ramani Mohan asked, "What are you doing?" Nirmala replied, "*Sandhya* and *nama japa*." Ramani Mohan said, "You are not allowed to do that without proper initiation from a guru." Nirmala responded, "I conferred it on myself the night of *Jhulan Purnima*."

Ramani Mohan then asked his wife when he should take initiation and from whom. Nirmala replied, "It will be Wednesday, the sixteenth *Agrahayan*. I will do it." She asked Ramani Mohan to go get Janaki Babu to confirm the date astrologically which he did. Jananki Babu was also was taken aback by Nirmala's appearance and asked her who she was. Nirmala replied with perfect composure, "*Purna Brahma Narayana* [The Absolute]." Janaki Babu told her that she was being naughty. Nirmala replied, "I am what I stated. You can stick to your views." They asked Nirmala for proof. At that moment

Mataji immediately started repeating many mantras and stotras and there was a great change in Her *Mahabhava* which frightened both of them. Janaki Babu and Nishikanta slipped away quietly while [Ramani Mohan] was directed to sit in front of Mataji. She then touched his *Brahma Talu* (center on top of the head). [He] immediately pronounced Om and went into a deep trance for hours.[147]

When Janaki Babu and Nishikanta returned, they were worried about Ramani Mohan and prayed to Nirmala to restore him. She did, and Ramani Mohan reported that he had had no body consciousness and had been filled with indescribable bliss.

In the months following her self-initiation, Nirmala

appeared a changed person even during the hours when she was not actually engaged in *sadhana*. She seemed withdrawn and there was a far-away look on her face. The erstwhile popular girl began to be shunned by her neighbors. Her companions and friends, puzzled and mystified, tended to avoid her. Nirmala, on the other hand, welcomed this solitude. Now that she was left severely alone, she had more time to devote to her sadhana.[148]

Nirmala's *sadhana* began to assume more concrete form. Although she had no previous knowledge of Sanskrit, Sanskrit hymns sprang spontaneously from her lips. When she was performing intricate yoga *asanas*, her long hair sometimes became entangled with her limbs and was torn out by the roots, yet she had no sense of bodily pain. Oftentimes she would go for long periods without food or drink.[149] "For long hours she would be on the floor, her face and body bathed in a light marvelous to behold."[150]

Ma later disclosed that in the months following her self-initiation she

"traversed the paths of all religions and faiths apart from the variety of forms of Hinduism. She had the *kheyala* to experience, as it were, the trials, hardships, and despairs of the pilgrim in search of God and also his state of blissful excitement. A vast range of spiritual experience was encapsulated within this short span of time for the benefit of all seekers of Truth.[151]

At night when the different stages of sadhana were being manifested through this body, what a variety of experiences I then had! Sometimes I used to hear distinctly "Repeat this mantra." When I got the mantra a query arose in me: "Whose mantra is this?" At once the reply came: "It is the mantra of Ganesh or Vishnu" or something like that. Again the query came from myself: "How does he look?" A form was revealed in no time. Every question was met by a prompt reply and there was immediate dissolution of all doubts and misgivings. One day I distinctly got the command: "From today you are not to bow down to anybody." I asked my invisible monitor: "Who are you?" The reply came: "Your Shakti (power)." I thought that there was a distinct Shakti residing in me and guiding me by issuing commands from time to time. Since all this happened at the stage of sadhana, jnana was being revealed in a piecemeal fashion. The integral knowledge which this body was possessed of from the very beginning was broken, as it were, into parts and there was something like the superimposition of ignorance. . . . After some time I again heard the voice within myself which told me: "Whom do you want to make obedience to? You are everything." At once I realized that the Universe was all my own manifestation. Partial knowledge then gave place to the integral and I found myself face to face with the One that appears as many. It was then that I understood why I had been forbidden to bow to anyone.[152]

It was also during this period that Nirmala began to display *siddhis*, or spiritual powers. A young friend of Ramani Mohan's had been unable to have children, but did not want to take another wife. According to Ma, he

told his father that after this body would get up from her asana after puja he would touch my feet and mentally pray for a son. . . . [When he did this] he at once fell down unconscious and therefore could not offer prayers. Hour after hour passed but he did not return to his senses. [Ramani Mohan] became frightened and requested me to see that he became alright. . . . When after a long interval he regained consciousness, he said it was impossible to describe the blissful ecstasy he had been plunged in all the while. Even though he had been unable to pray for a son as planned, yet, because it had been on his mind while touching me, he later did have children.[153]

Sometime later, there was a cholera epidemic, and Ramani Mohan became critically ill. Nirmala, "in her *kheyala*, declared, 'Let all the fingernails on my left hand be destroyed and may Pitaji recover!' There was an immediate improvement, which led to a complete recovery. A couple of days later, Mataji's nails decayed and eventually dropped off."[154]

As Nirmala had said, five months from the day of her self-initiation was the day designated for her initiation of Ramani Mohan, whom she had begun to call Bholanath, a name for Shiva. On that day

Bholanath decided to maneuver it so that he could not be initiated. . . . He always used to have breakfast before leaving for the office. But on that day, in his anxiety, he left without eating. At the appointed hour, Ma sent for him. He sent word that he would not come. Ma replied that if he did not come, she would be compelled to go to the office herself. Hearing this, Bholanath turned up without delay, for he knew Ma's nature very well. He was fully convinced that nothing was impossible for Ma. When he came home, he saw Ma pacing up and down. Incantations were emanating from her lips.

Ma gave him a dhoti to wear and told him to bathe and come back. When he came after a bath, Ma told him to sit steadily on a small carpet. Bholanath assumed the posture indicated and from Ma's holy mouth a "bija" mantra emanated. Ma told Bholanath to repeat that very name, forbade him to eat meat and instructed him to live a life of purity. Bholanath began to live accordingly.[155]

A short time later, in January 1923, Nirmala began a three-year period of silence, or *mauna*. She kept this silence very strictly, refraining even from gestures or facial expressions. Once during this period, Ramani Mohan's youngest brother, Jamini Kumar, came for a visit. He was very fond of Nirmala and was depressed by her silence. He followed her everywhere, imploring her to speak to him. One day Nirmala seated herself in a yogic posture and drew an imaginary circle around herself. She uttered some mantras and "then, with an indistinct voice, which gradually became stronger, she spoke to her young brother-in-law, while sitting inside *kundali*. After she wiped off the circle in the same manner, she got up and was silent again."[156] On a few other occasions, she followed the same procedure to temporarily break her silence. She also stopped visiting other people's houses during this period.

The Shahbagh Years: A Gathering of Devotees
(1924–1928)

In April 1924, Bholanath lost his post at Bajitpur and brought Nirmala to Dacca as he looked for new employment. Within a few days, he secured a post as manager of the estate of Nawabzadi Pyari Banu, known as Shahbagh

Gardens. Soon after they moved into the manager's three-room house, they were joined by Bholanath's nephew, Ashu. Although Nirmala was still cooking and performing household tasks, she continued to observe silence and was in states of trance and ecstasy much of the day. Her states of *bhava* began to interfere more and more with her work: "While serving food, her hand would stop midway; while cleaning utensils at the pond, she would fall into the water and lie half-immersed in it for a long time; she would get scorched by the fire of the kitchen oven or imperil herself in other ways."[157] Bholanath, fearing for her safety, asked his widowed sister, Matari, to stay with them, along with her son, Amulya. In August, Nirmala's youngest sister, Surabala, died at the age of sixteen. Bholanath, not understanding Nirmala's "absolute self-sufficiency,"[158] invited her parents to join them at Shahbagh to lessen her anticipated grief. Thus, within a few month the small house was full to overflowing.

During Nirmala and Bholanath's stay at Bajitpur, Nirmala had had a vision of a sacred tree somewhere near Dacca and sensed was that it was called a Siddheshvari tree. During their first few months at Shahbagh, Nirmala was taken by a childhood friend of Bholanath to visit an ancient, overgrown Kali temple nearby Shahbagh called Siddheshvari. In front of the temple, Nirmala recognized the tree of her vision, now fallen to the ground. The sacred site was reputed to be a *siddhapith*, or site where yogis had reached realization, and was associated with Shri Shankaracharya, the famous ninth-century philosopher.[159] In September 1924, Nirmala told Bholanath that it was her *kheyala* to stay at the Siddheshvari temple for a few days. Since Bholanath needed to work at Shahbagh during the day, it was decided that Dadamahashaya, Nirmala's father, would stay with her until Bholanath returned at night.

Nirmala spent her days at Siddheshvari in seclusion in the small back room of the temple. At night she would emerge to partake of fruit with Bholanath and his friend, Baul Chandra. On the eighth day, Nirmala asked Bholanath to follow her out of the temple and walk in a northern direction to a small clearing. She circumambulated a plot of ground, drew a circle, and sat down facing south. Mantras began to spring from her lips. She placed her right hand on the ground and leaned on it. What looked like solid ground yielded to her hand, and her arm plunged into the soil unimpeded. Bholanath pulled out her arm and suggested that they leave. Just then, warm, reddish water sprang forth from the hole. Nirmala asked Bholanath to put his hand in the hole, and when he did the reddish liquid gushed forth again. Later a brick platform was erected at this sacred site, and Ma used to sit on the platform surrounded by her devotees.[160]

The years at Shahbagh Gardens were characterized by the tremendous growth of the circle of those devoted to Nirmala and by her resulting transformation into Anandamayi Ma. From the beginning of their stay at Shahbagh, Bholanath invited more and more people to meet his extraordinary wife. Nirmala would first cook and serve the guests. After the guests had eaten, she "kept her head covered with a veil and came and sat near everybody only in obedience to Bholanath's orders. She would utter a couple of sentences if necessary only with Bholanath's permission."[161] Women, of course, had freer access to Nirmala, but eventually Bholanath asked her to speak more freely to the men who gathered for her *darshan*. It seemed as if "Bholanath intuitively knew that he must disregard conventions and set aside all feelings of possessiveness to make Ma accessible to the public."[162] As an increasing number of devotees gathered at Shahbagh, Nirmala warned her husband: "You must think twice before opening the doors to the world in this manner. Remember that you will not be able to stem the tide when it becomes overwhelming."[163]

But Bholanath continued to invite people. The people attracted to the young Anandamayi Ma were primarily *bhadraloks*, or respectable, educated people—professors, civil servants, doctors—many of whom were not previously religious. However, their contact with Nirmala transformed them from worldly people into devotees. One devotee, Usha Didi, is reported to have said to Nirmala during her first year at Shahbagh, "I have a desire to call you Ma. I do not feel sisterly towards you. I feel you are a mother to me." Ma replied, "Not you alone. One day many people of the world will call this body Ma."[164] And so it was, more and more people came to see Nirmala as their Ma. Two of her most famous devotees met Ma within a year or two of her coming to Shahbagh. Shri Jyotishchandra Rai, fondly called Bhaiji (brother) and considered by all devotees as coming "nearest to understanding Ma's personality,"[165] met her in Shahbagh at the end of 1924. Gurupriya Devi, Ma's lifelong attendant, came to Shahbagh to meet Ma with her father, Shashanka Mohan Mukhopadhyaya, a retired civil surgeon in December 1925.

During Ma's years at Shahbagh, people in Dacca held varying theories about who she was. Simple people believed that she was an incarnation of Kali and often called her Manusha Kali, or "Kali in human form." More sophisticated people believed that she was a self-realized being of extraordinary spiritual power.[166] Most people came to meet her out of a desire to be in her powerful spiritual presence. Some came for instructions, while others came for cures to ailments. Ordinarily Ma would say, "Pray to God. He will do what is best for his patient." Occasionally, when Bholanath implored Ma to cure someone's illness, Ma would take on that illness and Bholanath "became convinced not to ask her."[167]

Once the head trustee of the Nawabzadi's estate invited Bholanath and Ma to dinner and asked Ma to help the Nawabzadi win a legal case. Ma agreed but placed a hot coal in her hand, later explaining, "If yogic powers are used deliberately [for worldly gain], then the *sadhaka* has to perform penance (*prayashcitta*) for it."[168] Another time Bholanath asked Ma, "If it makes no difference to you what you eat, can you eat some of this chili powder?" Ma put a handful of the powder in her mouth and went about her housework, with no change of expression. Bholanath subsequently suffered from several days of bloody dysentery, which Ma dutifully nursed him through, remarking, "I have requested you so many times not to test me like this." Bholanath responded, "I shall not do it again."[169]

In 1925, some devotees requested that Ma perform the *Kali Puja*, the yearly worship of the Divine Mother in her manifestation as Kali. Ma reluctantly agreed, and the *puja* held at Siddheshvari came to be Ma's first public appearance. Bhaiji reports,

> An image of Kali was brought. Sri Ma sat on the ground in a meditative posture in absolute silence. Then like one overwhelmed with devotion, She started the *puja*, chanting mantras and placing flowers with sandal paste upon Her own head instead of on the image. All Her actions appeared to be like a doll's movements, as if some invisible hand were using Her body as a pliant tool for the expression of the Divine. Occasionally some flowers were strewn on the statue of Kali. In this manner the *puja* was performed.
>
> A goat was to be sacrificed. It was bathed in water. When it was brought to Mother, She took it on Her lap and wept as She stroked its body gently with Her hands. Then she recited some mantras, touching every part of the animal's body and whispered something into its ear. Thereafter She worshipped the scimitar with which the goat was to be sacrificed. She prostrated Herself on the ground, placing the knife upon Her own neck. Three sounds like the bleating of a goat came from Her lips. Afterwards when the animal was sacrificed, it neither moved nor uttered a cry, nor was there any trace of blood upon the severed head or body. Only with great difficulty one single drop of blood was at last drawn from the animal's carcass. All that time Sri Ma's face glowed with an intense uncommon beauty and throughout the ceremony there was a spell of great sanctity and deep absorption over all people present.[170]

Subsequently Ma would perform Kali Puja without the customary animal sacrifice, saying that "the true meaning of animal sacrifice . . . was sacrificing one's lower (animal) nature, living up to the fact that it was man's destiny to raise himself to his inherent divine status."[171]

Another incident took place at this first public *puja*. At a certain point in the ceremony, there arose a sudden violent storm. Ma "seemed to have become one with the very spirit of the storm" and "got up from her seat in the hollow swaying to the rhythm of the raging hurricane outside."[172] Ma's niece, Labanya, rushed forward and put both her arms around Ma and then fell away, unnoticed. People had begun to sing *kirtan* and followed the entranced Ma outside into the blowing rain. When the storm subsided, Labanya was found lying in a pool of mud and water, ecstatically singing, "*Haribol, Haribol.*" Even after a change of clothes, she seemed bewitched. Her mother, Pramoda, was angry with her and Ma and insisted that Ma bring Labanya back to normalcy. Ma took Labanya into another room and told Didi that the girl's state had resulted from her having touched Ma right before the *kirtan* had begun. Ma said, "Look, this state of bliss is coveted by *sadhakas*. She has come by it so naturally, but what can I do? Her mother is so determined not to allow any of this."[173] Ma then touched Labanya and tried to quiet her down. After three days she returned to normal.[174]

In January 1926, a *kirtan* party was held at Shahbagh to celebrate the solar eclipse, or *uttarayan sankranti*. It was at *kirtan* that Ma first displayed full *bhava* in public. The *kirtan* started at 10 A.M. while Ma was placing vermilion *bindis,* or dots, on the women's foreheads. Bhaiji reports,

> Suddenly the vermilion case dropped from Her hand. Her body sank down flat to the ground and began to roll on it. Then she slowly rose and stood on Her two big toes. Both hands were raised straight up, Her head slightly tilted to one side and a little backwards, and Her radiant eyes stared with a steady gaze towards the far end of the sky. A little later she began to move in that posture. Her body appeared to be filled with a heavenly presence. She paid no heed to Her clothes hanging loosely on her person. No one had the inclination to stop her. Her whole body danced on with measured beats in a most delicate way and reached the placed where *kirtan* was going on.[175]

Gurupriya Devi continues,

> Ma began to revolve in the midst of the *kirtan* singers. Her eyes were turned upward without a flicker of the eyelids, her face was shining with a supernatural glow, and her whole body was covered with a blood-red effulgence. Suddenly, as we were watching her, she fell onto the ground from the standing position. But it did not seem that she was hurt even slightly. As I have said, it was as if her body were moved by the wind. It seemed to have rolled to the ground along with the breeze. As it fell, the body started rotating fast just like a leaf or a paper blown about by a cyclone. We tried to hold down the body but it was impossible to control that speed. After awhile, Ma became still and sat up. Her eyes were closed and she was seated in a yogic posture, steady, grave, motionless. . . . A little later she started roaming around, singing, first softly and the loudly and clearly "*Hare Murare Madhu Kaitabhare, Gopala Govinda Mukunda Shaure.*". . . . What a beautiful voice it was! Even to this day, the hairs of my body stand on end at that remembrance. . . . Everything was new. Everyone was witnessing for the first time this *bhava* of Ma which had remained very secret all these days. . . Ma sat quietly for awhile, then her body fell to the ground. There was no pulsation at all, the breathing was very faint and slow. The eclipse was over.[176]

From this day on, Ma suggested that *kirtan* be performed every night at Shahbagh and, therefore, more and more people witnessed her "countless states of *bhava*."[177] Additionally, it was around this time that Ma began to speak more openly. At such times "her shyness as a daughter-in-law had totally disappeared, [and] she was speaking in a firm voice."[178]

By October 1926, Ma "had become widely known and Shahbagh was swarming with more and more people every day."[179] Her devotees asked Bholanath to persuade Ma to perform Kali Puja once again, as Ma was refusing their request. The day before the *puja,* Ma told Bholanath, "As they are so eager to celebrate the *puja,* you may officiate as priest." Preparations were made and a statue procured. When the ceremony was to begin, Ma sat down to perform the *puja.* Gurupriya Devi reports,

> After performing the puja for a little while, she suddenly got up, and looking at Bholanath, said, "I shall sit, you do the puja!" She laughed loudly, and in a trice [a split second] swept though the crowd and sat leaning against the

image of Kali. . . . In a moment the cloth on Ma's body slipped down. Her tongue protruded. Father started calling out loudly, "Ma, Ma!" Bholanath, seated on the asana for worship, was offering flowers with both hands. In a moment's time, the tongue went in and Ma lay down with her face to the ground. . . . saying "Everybody shut your eyes. . . . " After a long time, on Bholanath's command, everyone opened their eyes and saw that Ma was sitting near the image of Kali. What a divine, blissful countenance, glorious like the Queen of all goddesses! Her entire body was covered with flowers. Bholanath was worshipping Ma with flowers and bel leaves. A little later the puja was finished.[180]

Early the next morning, Ma arranged for the sacred fire, which normally would have been extinguished, to be tended in Kali's room. She said, "The fire of a *Mahayajna* [Vedic sacrificial fire] will be lighted from this fire," which it was in Varanasi in 1946, twenty years later. Ma initiated another change in the conventional *puja*: The statue of the goddess, which is normally immersed after the *puja*, was retained at Ma's request and remained intact although it was moved five subsequent times.

During this same period of time, Ma displayed less and less interest in her physical body. She needed people to keep watch on her and explained, "See, I cannot differentiate properly between fire and water. If you people can look after this body, it will remain, otherwise it will be destroyed."[181] So look after her they did. The self-imposed regulations in Ma's diet changed from day to day. For a period of time, she would eat only two or three grains of rice a day, or she would eat only fruit which had fallen from the trees, or only food eaten off the floor. In January 1926, Ma was feeding Gurupriya Devi, or Didi, as she was affectionately called, some fish curry off her plate and laughingly said, "Today I have fed you. In the future you will feed me." Some weeks later Ma's "eating with her own hands stopped once and for all." She had been eating a meal at the house of a devotee and "felt that her hand was not going towards her mouth but was bending downwards."[182] The task of feeding her from this day forward usually fell to Didi.

Caring for Ma, however, was not always a straightforward task. Sometimes she would eat normally for a few days, and then she would eat nothing at all for a while. She would say, "Do not put any food into my mouth. If you do, it will be harmful to you."[183] She continually placed restrictions on what she would eat or drink. Once Ma went without even drinking water for twenty-three days.[184] Another time Didi forgot to take the bones out of some fish that she was feeding Ma and Ma obediently ate the fish, bones and all. Didi reports that it always seemed "as if she were absolutely unaware of whom I had fed and what she had eaten."[185] Sometimes she would eat enormous quantities of food without stopping. Once when a devotee feeding her finally asked Ma if she wanted still more, Ma said, "First you ask me to eat, but no sooner do I start than you tell me to stop! What am I to do?"[186]

Indeed, there were times when Ma went into such states that her devotees gave up all hope for her life. One day in 1926, Didi reports that Ma was sitting in *samadhi*, and her body turned black and no pulse could be felt. Didi remembered Ma had once said, "If the *kheyala* to return into the body is not present when the body is in that state, the whole game may be over, therefore it is only your intense yearning which makes me return. . . . If such a state occurs, then keep your hand on any part of my body and repeat the name of God mentally." Didi did that, and Ma eventually returned. Other times, she and Bholanath resorted to vigorous rubbing of Ma's body to bring her out of unnatural rates of breathing or stiffness of the body.[187] One time Ma demonstrated her detachment from the body by placing a hot coal on her foot and reporting, "I was not aware of any pain. It looked like nothing but fun; with great joy I watched what the poor coal was doing on my foot."[188]

By the end of 1926, the "sadhana phase" of Ma's life was coming to a close. She was beginning the life of ceaseless travel which was to characterize the last fifty-six years of her life, following her *kheyala* as it took her all over India. Her travels began with a trip to Deogarh in Bihar in May 1926. In the early spring of 1927, the Kumbha Mela festival[189] was being held in Haridwar, Uttar Pradesh. Ma, accompanied by Bholanath, her parents, and a party of devotees, traveled to the festival by way of Calcutta and Varanasi, where many new people took her *darshan*. While in Haridwar, Ma ordered Didi and her father to stay there for three months to do *sadhana*. When Ma returned to Shahbagh, the crowds continued to increase.

At the end of April 1927, on the occasion of Ma's thirty-first birthday, Bhaiji suggested performing a special *kirtan* and *puja* in her honor. This set the precedent for the celebration of Ma's birthday, which continues to this day. Meanwhile, Ma's devotees were beginning to realize that her *kheyala* might take her away from Shahbagh any time. Indeed, in July 1927, Ma traveled to Vindyachal in Uttar Pradesh, and in August she visited her birthplace in Kheora. Didi reports,

All of us requested Dadamahashaya to show us the spot where Ma took birth. But the house had been changed so drastically, that neither he nor Didima could point out the spot. Ma was walking here and there looking at the plants and trees and was talking about incidents of the olden days. I . . . said, "Ma, do show us your birthplace, please!" A little later Ma went and stood at a place at the back of the house near a mound of cowdung. Ma picked up a handful of earth from where she was standing and began weeping loudly. Later we came to know from Ma herself that that was her birthplace. . . . After some time Ma became calm, called the Muslims and told them, "Look, if you keep this spot pure, it will be for your own welfare. If you come here and pray with a pure mind, you may hope for the fulfillment of your desires. Do not ever pollute this place."[190]

Early in 1928, Bholanath lost his job at Shahbagh. Bholanath, Ma, and Ma's parents rented a house in the Tikatuli district of Dacca. Ma was continually being asked by new devotees to visit this or that town, which she often did. In the meantime, a room had been built on the site of the platform at Siddheshvari, which may be called the first ashram. It was here that Ma's thirty-second birthday was celebrated with great festivity in May 1928. "The people gathered around Mataji who was lying in an inert heap on the ground in a state of *samadhi*. The devotees arranged the accessories of the *puja* in front of her motionless body. In deep devotion the assembled [devotees] watched Bholanath offer *puja* to the deity most dear to their hearts."[191]

In September 1928, Ma traveled to Varanasi. It had been three years since Ma had told Usha Didi that someday many people would call her Ma, and it was in Varanasi that this prediction became a reality. In Varanasi, "from early morning til late at night, there would be a constant stream of men and women passing in and out of the house [where Ma held *darshan*]." Bholanath, feeling overwhelmed, tried to persuade her not to agree to see so many people day in and day out, but Ma responded, "Now you are not to say anything to me. When there was the time, I warned you, but you did not heed my warning. Now you cannot turn the tide back."[192] Indeed, Ma met some of her most important devotees during that stay in Varanasi, including the famous Sanskrit scholar Gopinath Kaviraj.

The time in Varanasi was remarkable in other ways. Ma sat for the first time in an open gathering, talking freely to a group of strangers. "She spoke on many matters and people listened. Some people asked questions."[193] The quality of these gatherings set the tone for the gatherings of the future. While Ma continued to be seen in states of *samadhi* and deep *bhava*, she also interacted more with people as a spiritual guide and spoke of spiritual matters with authority, all the while maintaining that she was just "a little girl." Also in Varanasi, Ma received people privately in what came to be called "privates," one-on-one meetings in which individuals would ask Ma for personal guidance.

Once back in Dacca, Ma continued to be inundated by people coming to have her *darshan*. One day in December 1928, Ma left the rented house for Siddheshvari, expressing the *kheyala* not to return. She and Bholanath took up residence at Siddheshvari in relative discomfort, initiating Bholanath's formal life as a *sadhaka*, or spiritual seeker. Ma instructed Bholanath to live and do practices in the small room of the Kali temple while Ma stayed in the single room of the ashram, attended by a cook. Devotees came for ten-minute visits. One evening Ma announced to visiting devotees that Bholanath, who was observing silence, would be leaving the following day for an unknown destination. Ma and a few devotees saw him off the next day. For the first time, Ma and Bholanath were not traveling together. Ma's father stayed with her as her guardian.

After a few days, Ma, escorted by a male devotee, boarded a train to join Bholanath in Tarapith, an ancient sacred site where ascetics practice meditation in the cremation grounds. When Ma was seated on the train, Didi reports, she was "gazing at all the people and they in turn were craning their necks and looking at Ma endearingly. A few moments before the train left, Ma suddenly began to cry terrifyingly loudly. I had never witnessed Ma cry in this way when going anywhere. Seeing Ma weep, all the people present had tears in their eyes."[194]

A few days later, Didi and her father were asked to join Ma and Bholanath at Tarapith and Didi found that "a very blissful atmosphere had been set up since quite a few days. . . . Father and I sat up at night and listened to many stories from Ma and Bholanath."[195] Ma and Bholanath reported that when Bholanath was practicing *sadhana* at Siddheshvari, he had had a vision of a headless Kali. When he told Ma about it, she had instructed him to go to Tarapith. Ma knew nothing about Tarapith, but when Bholanath arrived there, he found that the image of Tara Ma there had a detachable silver head, which was removed when the statue was being bathed. Bholanath "had attained to a very exalted state" in Tarapith, and it seemed that his life as a serious *sadhaka* had begun in earnest.[196] Soon thereafter, Ma instructed Bholanath to stay in Tarapith for one day every year, along with many other places of pilgrimage.

A Pattern of Future Life Emerges (1928–1938)

By the time of Ma's birthday in May 1929, a small ashram in Ramna, near Dacca, had been completed that included a small cottage for Ma to stay in. The festivities themselves were carried out in Siddheshvari. However, on the final day, Ma, accompanied by devotees, went to the newly completed ashram in Ramna. There was *kirtan* and *prasad,* and Ma gave *darshan.* As devotees were doing *pranam* in front of Ma,

> Ma turned towards Bholanath and asked him laughingly, "You have not done *pranama?*" Bholanath shook his head to say "no." Ma laughed and told all those present, "He often does *pranama* when we are alone in the house. Here it seems he feels shy to do so before all of you." We all burst into laughter when we heard Ma say this. Bholanath also laughed. Maroni [Bholanath's great-niece] was then a little child. She spoke up, "Yes, I have seen Grandpa prostrate before Grandma." This sent Ma, Bholanath and all of us into peals of laughter again. The whole night was thus spent in various kinds of divine sport.[197]

Immediately after the celebrations, Ma suddenly said, "All of you must let me go. I shall leave Dacca today." The assembled devotees began to protest. Ma began to "weep like a small child and said, 'You must not put obstacles in my way. If you don't let me go, I shall leave the body right here and go away, but go I must. . . . When Bholanath comes, explain to him that he should not try to stop me.'" When Bholanath arrived, Ma asked his permission to leave, and when he "expressed his mild displeasure, Ma declared, 'If you stop me, this body will be given up right here at your feet.' Bholanath agreed, though saying, 'If you do not stay with me, people will criticize you.' Ma rejoined, 'I shall never do anything which people can criticize. Father is going with me. Will anyone still criticize me?'"[198]

Ma left Ramna that night and traveled throughout northern India as far as Haridwar. When she returned to Dacca nearly a month and a half later, she was increasingly unable to perform household tasks. She seemed unable "to clasp or hold things. Her hands were uncoordinated like those of a child."[199] Bholanath, feeling frustrated and somewhat pressured by relatives, decided to assert himself and ask Ma to cook meals and take care of the house as she had once done. But, as Ma reports, "I had no objection and it made no difference to me. Since he asked me, I made an attempt but evidently it was not to be. Bholanath fell ill after a few days and then I myself was ill. So it did not come to anything after all."[200]

In October 1929, Ma was again in poor health, and she asked Bholanath to leave his bed in the middle of the night so that she might sleep in it instead of in her usual place on the floor. Bholanath willingly assumed Ma's place on the floor. Within a few days, Ma had Bholanath's bed taken apart and she returned to sleeping on the floor.[201] In early 1930, Ma asked Bholanath to practice his *sadhana* at Siddeshvari. Bholanath lived in relative solitude there for two months. "He experienced special *bhavas* while he was there and while in *bhava* he rolled on the ground in ecstasy. In the afternoons, he sometimes came to Ramna Ashram, where his body underwent various *kriyas*. He initiated brahmacaris and also gave initiation to a few other people, while he was in that state."[202]

Meanwhile, Ma continued her life of travel, receiving learned, professional visitors wherever she went. In August 1930, accompanied by Bholanath and a few others, she traveled to southern India for the first time. During 1931 her *kheyala* took her away from Dacca to visit many places of pilgrimage such as Puri, Orissa. Always, however, she returned to her home base in Dacca.

In May and June 1932, Ma's birthday was celebrated in Dacca, with *kirtan* that continued for twenty-one days. At the end of the celebration, on the night of June 2, 1932, Ma informed Didi that she would be leaving Dacca permanently. Anticipating Didi's response, she said, "Do not get upset. Haven't I gone out several times before? I have returned knowing you all get so disconcerted. Let me go my own way. If you obstruct me, I am not able to go."[203] Thus, accompanied only by Bholanath and Bhaiji and carrying no baggage, Ma left Dacca, leaving instructions for no one to follow her. Although she returned three years later for a few days, this departure marked the beginning of a lifetime of ceaseless travel, the reflection of Ma's complete detachment and renunciation.

Within a few days, Ma, Bholanath, and Bhaiji reached Raipur, a small town near Dehradun in the foothills of the Himalayas. During their six months in Raipur, Ma inspired Bholanath and Bhaiji to share the ascetic life with her. Ma cut her hair, Bholanath took a vow of *mauna*, or silence, and the three of them lived very simply in a dilapidated Shiva temple. Bholanath and Bhaiji engaged in intensive *sadhana* while Ma sat or walked by herself. In October and November, Ma and Bholanath traveled to Tarapith and, in December and January, to Nalhati. There, after much pleading on the part of Bholanath, Ma agreed to notify the longing devotees in Dacca of their location, and many of them came to join them. After two weeks, however, Ma ordered them all back to Dacca and returned to Raipur.

This pattern of travel back and forth in northern India continued through 1933. In August 1933, Bholanath trekked alone to the Himalayan pilgrimage sites of Badrinath, Kedarnath, and Uttarkashi. By the end of 1933, when devotees from Dacca were granted permission to visit Ma in Raipur, they found her speaking Hindi and surrounded by countless non-Bengali devotees.

During the next few years, many prominent people, Bengali and non Bengali alike, had the opportunity to meet Ma and number themselves among her devotees. In 1933, Kamala Nehru, wife of Jawarharlal Nehru, met Ma and became her devotee. Kamala's daughter, Indira Gandhi, would come to seek Ma's spiritual guidance throughout her life. Other well-known Indian devotees who met Ma during this period include the former presidents and vice presidents of India, wealthy industrialists, professors, and performing artists. Within the ensuing decades, European visitors to India had Ma's *darshan* and became devotees. Ma's foremost foreign devotees include Adolphe Jacques Weintrob, a French physician, now Swami Vijayananda, British photographer Richard Lannoy, and the French film producer Arnaud Desjardins.

The years after 1933 were characterized by spontaneous pilgrimage punctuated by "an unending procession of religious festivals, *kirtans* and *satsangas*."[204] Ma never stayed in one place longer than two weeks. She would arrive at the train station with various numbers of devotees and simply board a train followed by those devotees who were available to travel with her. Everywhere she traveled, from the Himalayas to the tip of Kerala, across the breadth of India, she attracted new devotees.

Ma continued to direct the *sadhana* of those closest to her. In March 1934, she instructed Didi's father, Shanshanka Mohan, to take *sannyasa*. In 1936, according to Ma's *kheyala*, Didi and Bholanath's grandniece, Maroni, were invested with the sacred thread, previously worn only by males. "There was no precedent in this matter. . . [however] Pundit Gopinath Kaviraj, when appealed to, declared that Mataji's *kheyala* itself was enough, no further corroboration about its legitimacy was required."[205] In 1937, Bhaiji and Bholanath accompanied Ma on a pilgrimage to Mount Kailash, the sacred abode of Lord Shiva in present-day Tibet. On that trip Ma informally conferred *sannyasa* initiation on Bhaiji and the monastic name Swami Maunananda Parvat.

On April 13, 1938, at the Kumbha Mela at Haridwar, Bholanath performed by himself the rituals of adopting the life of *sannyasa*, "in pursuance of some conversation he had had with Mataji, earlier."[206] Ten days later, Ma predicted that Bholanath would be seriously and inevitably ill. Ma proceeded to instruct those close to her to leave her alone with Bholanath. Indeed, Bholanath died of smallpox, with Ma at his side, on May 7, 1938.[207]

Ma Tends Her Garden (1932–1982)

By 1938, the pattern of Ma's play in this world had been fully established. Thus, life after Bholanath's death continued relatively unchanged. Ma's *kheyala* took her all over India, as she tended to her old devotees and attracted new devotees in great numbers. In 1939, Ma's mother, Didima, took *sannyasa diksha*[208] and became the primary person to whom devotees came for initiation, since Ma did not give initiation herself.[209] She remained in service at Ma's side until her death at the age of ninety-three on August 8, 1970.

As the number of Ma's devotees grew, the spontaneous travel typical of the earlier years became curtailed.

> Programs were announced beforehand and Shri Anandamayi Ma's travel itinerary fixed so that people might meet her or know where to go on these special occasions. Provision was made in those towns which she visited regularly for permanent rooms for her to stay in. Ashrams were built all over the country so that she would not be obliged to stay in inns.[210]

As ashrams sprang up around the country, there was a need for a central administrative organization. In February 1950, the Shree Shree Anandamayee Sangha was established in Varanasi. Although Ma had no involvement with this governing body or with the administration of any of the ashrams, the Sangha established two Sanskrit schools, one for boys and one for girls, a quarterly journal called *Ananda Varta,* and a charitable hospital. In 1973, the Shree Shree Anandamayee Charitable Society, based in Calcutta, was established to take over some of the many projects of the Sangha, particularly the publication of books about Ma. There are twenty-seven ashrams around India at present. At the time of the opening of each ashram and project, Ma came to offer her blessings.

Although Ma was not involved in the running of any of the institutions founded in her name, she was responsible for founding the annual Samyam Vrata, a week-long retreat held each year in a different location. Devotees from all over India and the world gather to perform a *vrata,* or vow, to fast except for one light meal a day, to attend spiritual talks and meditations, and to refrain from gossip, quarrels, smoking, engaging in sexual relations, and drinking tea, coffee, and alcohol for the week. From 1952 until Ma's *mahasamadhi* in 1982, the Samyam Vrata was held at different locations each year, with each day culminating in a *satsang* with Ma. Since 1982, the Samyam Vrata has been held at the Kankhal ashram.

The Kankhal ashram was to become Ma's final resting place. In July 1982, Ma's health began to deteriorate seriously. On Sunday, July 11, Ma gave public *darshan* for the last time. As she weakened day by day, her devotees encouraged her to eat and drink, but she resisted. They implored her to "have *kheyala* on Her body,"[211] but she continued to reply, "There is no *kheyala*. Whatever God does is alright."[212] On July 23, she instructed people to shift her from her cottage at Panchavati to Kishenpur ashram in Dehradun. She never left her second floor room there, although prayers and chanting continued uninterrupted in the hall below. On August 27, 1982, Ma breathed her last in the room right below the one in which Bholanath had died in 1938. The next day, in accordance with Ma's wishes, her body was taken in procession from Dehradun to the Kankhal ashram, the route lined with mourners who hoped to have their last darshan of Ma.[213] On Sunday, August 29, Anandamayi Ma was buried as a realized being, and her shrine has become a place of worship and pilgrimage renowned for its spiritual power.[214]

Summary

Thus concludes the life story of Ānandamayī Mā, although the story of the community for which she is the religious focus continues to be written to this day. We have seen that the emphasis in the story of Mā's life upon her first forty years, in particular, her childhood, her early marriage, and the "*līlā* of *sādhana*," draws the reader into the establishment of her extraordinary nature. Once this nature has been established, as well as the pattern of the second half of her life as renunciant and spiritual master, there seems to be a withdrawal from a story line *per se* and an emphasis on her timeless, ahistorical interactions with her devotees. The "story" of importance becomes the story of those who were transformed by contact with her. In this way, the autobiographies of the members of Ānandamayī Mā's community enhance and complete the biography of its founder.

THREE

Ānandamayī Mā as a Woman

mukhyo dharmah smritishu vihito bhartrishushrūshanam hi
strīnām etat pitur anumatam kāryam ity ākalayya
tat kurvānābhajata vapusho bhartur ardham himadreh
kanyā sā me dishatu satatam dharmamārgapravrittim

Obedient service to one's husband is the primary religious duty
enjoined by sacred tradition for women. When the daughter of
the Himalayas (Pārvatī) realized that this duty was endorsed by
her father, she put it into practice and so assumed the form of
half the body of her husband. May she always show me how to
follow the path of *dharma*.

Tryambaka's *Guide to the*
Dharma of Women, Verses 1–4[1]

OST OF ĀNANDAMAYĪ MĀ'S devotees would regard the title of this
chapter as an oxymoron because they do not consider Mā to be
a woman. Ironically, however, although they insist that Mā was
not a woman, they maintain that she was "the perfect wife," ever devoted
and obedient. For example, Narendranath Bose, a young male householder
devotee, told me, "The fact that Mā left her body in Dehradun is no
coincidence in my mind. Her husband, Bholanāth, left his body in the
same ashram. And being the dutiful wife, even to the last, she lived by his
example. She wanted to leave her body in the same place her husband left
his body."[2] The claim that Mā was not a woman and that she was "the
perfect wife" raises problems and challenges for the interpreter and scholar.
We first focus on the latter claim, assuming that Mā was a woman and, as
such, can be evaluated as to her conformity to Hindu ideals of womanhood.
Certainly, at first glance, Mā's extremely unconventional life and marriage

55

seem to reflect nothing at all of the paradigm of the perfect wife. Although in the very beginning of her marriage she cooked and cared for her husband, it is maintained by her biographers that she never engaged in sexual contact and that within a few years her husband was caring for *her*.

In this chapter we look at the story of Ānandamayī Mā's life in light of the paradigm of the ordinary Hindu woman, which is the paradigm of the perfect wife. Within the Hindu context, the ordinary norm is that traditional code of conduct intended for the majority of religious people, in which one's goal in life is the pursuit of *dharma*, or righteousness, in order that one might improve one's position within the cycle of birth and death.

The Hindu Ideology of *Strīdharma*

The Epic period in India (ca. 500 B.C.E.–500 C.E.) saw the development of an important genre of religious texts called *smriti*, literally, "what has been committed to memory," a vast category of Sanskrit scripture whose authority in theory is secondary only to *shruti*, or the Vedic corpus. The class of *smriti* texts equivalent to law books were called *dharmashāstra*, or treatises on righteous behavior, or *dharma*. *Dharmashāstra* texts such as the *Laws of Manu*, compiled around the turn of the common era by brahman men, were to become a religiously sanctioned standard by which to measure one's behavior as a Hindu for centuries to come. A Hindu ideology of *strīdharma*, or the righteous way of life for the Hindu wife, was set forth in such texts.

As powerful as such texts may have been in shaping women's experience, they have not provided the only paradigm on which Hindu women have drawn. As Katherine Young warns, an approach that is dependent on an analysis of Sanskrit texts "that have a prevailing Brahman, masculine and North Indian bias" provides "little access to understanding how women may have contravened, ignored or redefined the ideals, nor does it help us understand those lower-caste or tribal women who were not centrally influenced by Brahmanical values, thus making a largely 'silent history' of women even more silent."[3] To reconstruct women's lived experience throughout the centuries, we must read texts written by men more critically, as well as draw on contemporary fieldwork on the religious lives of ordinary women.[4] Since women's rituals belong to an oral tradition passed down from women to women, "text" should be defined more broadly to include stories that are sung, danced, and ritualized. At this point, however, we will lay out a classic *dharmashāstra* model of "the perfect wife." Although it may not have been normative for all Hindu women, it undoubtedly has had a powerful influence on the formulation of Hindu conceptions of the righteous woman, along with its mythical and literary counterparts.

The *Laws of Manu*, or *Manusmriti*, spells out the brahman conception of a way of life that not only reflects *dharma*, or righteousness, but also upholds it, thus maintaining the universe. Its male-inspired articulation of the *dharma* of women, in particular, seems to reflect, on the one hand, an idealization of women and, on the other, a powerful need to control them.[5] Its idealization of women can be seen in verses such as chapter 3, verses 55 and 56: "Women must be honored and adorned by their fathers, brother, husbands, and brothers-in-law, who desire [their own] welfare. Where women are honored, there the gods are pleased; but where they are not honored, no sacred rite yields rewards."[6]

The need to control women in the *Laws of Manu* is reflected in three critical verses. In chapter 9, verse 3, the text says of a woman, "Her father protects [her] in childhood, her husband protects [her] in youth, and her sons protect [her] in old age; a woman is never fit for independence."[7] A woman's lack of independence is ensured by defining a wife's spiritual practice as worship of her husband. In chapter 5, verse 155, it is stated, "No sacrifice, no vow, no fast must be performed by women apart [from their husbands]; if a wife obeys her husband, she will for that [reason alone] be exalted in heaven."[8] In other words, a woman's husband is to be her god, and her liberation is linked to her performance as an obedient wife. Finally, in chapter 5, verse 165, the text articulates the promised reward: "She who, controlling her thoughts, words, and deeds, never slights her lord [her husband], resides [after death] with her husband [in heaven], and is called a virtuous [wife]."[9]

The powerful ideology of *strīdharma*, as formulated by texts such as the *Laws of Manu*, was elucidated in commentaries and *dharmashāstra* digests throughout the following centuries. One such text is the eighteenth-century digest, *The Strīdharmapaddhati* of Tryambakayajvan discussed by Julia Leslie in *The Perfect Life*.[10] This little-known Sanskrit text, which describes the proscribed life for Hindu women, was written by an orthodox pandit in Muslim-dominated southern India and was designed to inspire the high-caste Hindu ladies of the court to live a life of *dharma*. Although we have no way of knowing how seriously it was taken by its audience, it mirrors the expectations of orthodox texts such as the *Laws of Manu* and describes a way of life for women admired as ideal by traditional Hindus even today. Because of its detail and relative contemporaneity, it may provide further insight into an orthodox brahman Hindu ideology of *strīdharma*.

Its ideology is distilled in Tryambaka's opening verse, which he repeats in his conclusion: "Obedient service to one's husband (*bhartrishushrūshanam*) is the primary religious duty enjoined by sacred tradition for women."[11] Thus the *pativratā*, or devoted Hindu wife, is she who lives a life of selfless service to her husband, her god, as her primary religious duty. Her husband's word is to be equated with the word of the guru (*guruvacana*) and is to be obeyed unquestioningly, even if it involves action that is unlawful or potentially life-threatening. The text explains that this obedience to her husband includes obedience to his elders, who take the place of her father and mother, and she must salute them each morning (*gurunām abhivādanam*). In addition, "nothing should be done independently (*svātantryena*) by a woman, either as a child, a young girl, or an old woman, even in her (own) home."[12] She must consult her husband for his permission in everything she does.

The *pativratā's* daily duties (*strīnam āhnīkam*), described in detail from dawn until bedtime, are seen as "the signs of her religious path, that of devotion to her husband."[13] It is a life of selfless service in which the *pativratā* awakens before her husband and works tirelessly all day until she adorns herself to go to bed with her husband, where "treating her beloved in a way that gives him pleasure (*āhlādasamyuktam kritvā*), she should engage in sexual intercourse (*sammyogam ācaret;* i.e. she should make love to him)."[14] Tryambaka describes a variety of penalties which may be imposed on a wife who refuses to make love.[15] Although Manu explicitly states that a wife's main purpose is to be the bearer of sons for her husband's family,[16] we can infer this nearly universally accepted Hindu assumption as stated by Tryambaka.

Household tasks (*grihakrityam*) required of the *pativratā* include preparation of food, keeping things clean and pure, saving and spending money, and paying homage to guests (*atithipūjā*). There is particular emphasis on the preparation and serving of food and that "the wife (*patnī*) should eat what is left (*ucchishtam*) after her husband has eaten."[17] His leftovers become her *prasāda*, blessed food. According to Manu, a prime source for Tryambaka's text, "mistakes in this sphere (*annadoshāt*) are among the four main causes of death to brahmans."[18]

Of particular interest is Tryambaka's list of the six actions that cause women to fall into hell: the recitation of sacred texts (*japa*), the performance of austerities (*tapas*), going on pilgrimages, renunciation, the chanting of mantras, and the worship of deities.[19] In addition, the good wife "should stay well away from festivals and public gatherings"[20] and should never associate with female renouncers or religious mendicants.[21] Leslie points out that Tryambaka's injunction to *pativratās* to avoid contact with female renunciants is a reflection of his more all-encompassing prohibition against women other than widows becoming renunciants.[22] According to *dharmashāstra*, the householder path is the only *āshrama* open to women, and to have contact with a female renunciant might lead to a wife's fall from *dharma*. Only through the proper performance of *strīdharma*, in fact, can a woman erase the mark of bad conduct that led to her birth as inferior.[23]

Finally, Tryambaka, in accordance with the *dharmashāstra* tradition, outlines two possible paths for the *pativratā* who dies after her husband: suttee, referred to in Sanskrit as *sahagamana*, literally "the going with"; and the life of the celibate, renunciant widow, living at home, stripped of her auspiciousness and authority. *Sahagamana* is recommended (*prashastah*) as the best option. He reminds women that at a wedding the brahmans chant, "May you be one who accompanies her husband, when he is alive and even when he is dead!"[24] He argues that *sahagamana* cannot be considered suicide any more than the religious suicide of an ascetic who kills himself at a sacred place in order to go directly to heaven.[25] He admits that *sahagamana* is an act to be performed voluntarily for the purpose of reaping its great rewards and blessings, but his description of the alternative life for a widow "makes his own opinion on the question abundantly clear."[26] Tryambaka, in line with Manu, outlines in great detail the practices of the virtuous widow, which include tonsure (shaving of her head), self-mortification, avoiding social gatherings, and worshiping her dead husband by means of a portrait or a clay model.[27] Tryambaka concludes that three kinds of women deserve to be considered *pativrata*: the wife who dies before her husband and patiently waits for him to join her; the wife who follows her husband on the funeral pyre; and the wife survives her husband and assumes a life of asceticism and celibacy until she dies.[28]

In summary, Tryambaka states that women, excluded from initiation, or *upanayana*, should consider their marriage as their spiritual initiation. A *pativrata* who wishes her husband to live a long and happy life must see her selfless service to him as her spiritual path and "assist her husband in his religious obligations rather than pursue any religious commitment of her own."[29] In life as in death, she should embody the selflessness of a servant devoted to her lord. As Leslie remarks, "The religious role allotted to women [in *stridharma*] is defined in terms of their relationship not to God but to men."[30]

To evaluate the applicability of the *dharmashastra* paradigm within the Bengali context, however, we should consider available ethnographic material on women in Bengali society. There are two such studies; *Bengali Women* by Manisha Roy and *The Gift of a Virgin* by Lina Fruzzetti.[31] Roy's study is the result of anthropological fieldwork spanning the 1950s and 1960s with "middle and upper middle class" married women in educated Calcutta families. Fruzzetti conducted her field research between 1971 and 1973 in the rural town of Vishnupur, West Bengal, with women "of different residential sections," different classes, and different castes.

Both studies focus on the centrality of marriage and childbearing in a Bengali woman's life, and each study offers relevant material to our inquiry into the relationship between Mā and Bholanāth. Roy, who includes the *Laws of Manu* in her references, maintains that even among middle and upper-class Bengali women in urban society the ideal is that

> the wife must consider her husband as her god whom she worships as she worshiped the god Shiva in her *Shiva-rātrir brata* [her vow to obtain a husband on Lord Shiva's night].[32] She must obey his wishes without question. She must love and respect him irrespective of his behavior and without the expectation of any return of love and respect from him. . . . She must follow him in every way and sacrifice her own interests and life if necessary to insure his safety and well-being. She must also be chaste and faithful.[33]

Although this ideal "looms large in its difference from reality," it has been "complimented and often heavily reinforced by other kinds of cultural, as well as religious influences, tinting expectations with romantic colors."[34] Roy discusses these influences, which we can assume might have been a part of Ānandamayī Mā's socialization, especially in that her upbringing would undoubtedly have been even more traditional than that of a daughter of the urban middle class.

Roy's description of the socialization of a Bengali girl begins with examples of how even the smallest girl comes to understand the centrality that both marriage and bearing a son will play in her life. Her grandmother is likely to have criticized her parents' attempts to educate her, repeating such aphorisms as "*Swāmi putrer ghar karte hobe,*" or "She will [only] have to make a home for a husband or a son." According to Roy, such sayings "are often used to express the message that a girl's future is only justified if she becomes a homemaker for her husband, sons, and her husband's family."[35] The value of devotion to one's future husband is further instilled when a girl is exposed at about ten years old to the stories of the "great virtuous women of the epics," such as Sītā and Sāvitrī. Sītā, the wife of Lord Rāma, is extolled in the *Rāmāyana* as "the ideal wife who was supposed to have reached the heights of conjugal love, consisting of unconditional obedience, self-sacrificing love, and tolerance. The ideal wife must accept her husband's wishes and remain faithful and devoted to him irrespective of his behavior."[36] The story of Sāvitrī, indelibly etched in the heart and mind of every Bengali girl, centers on her devotion to her husband, devotion that brings her victory over Yama, the god of death. Roy's interviews reveal that the story is popularly interpreted as demonstrating that "a good and faithful wife has superhuman power."[37]

As a young teenager, the Bengali girl is exposed to stories such as the story of Shakuntalā, immortalized by the playwright Kālidāsa, in which the notion of romantic love in marriage is introduced. In particular, Roy found that every father and daughter in Bengal is familiar with the passage in *Shakuntalā* in which her father, the sage Kanya, sends Shakuntalā back to her husband. In this remarkable statement of a *dharmashāstra* ideal, Kanya says,

> Listen, then, my daughter. When thou reachest thy husband's palace, and art
>   admitted into his family,
> Honor thy betters, ever be respectful
> To those above thee, and should others share
> Thy husband's love, ne'er yield thyself a prey
> To jealousy; but ever be a friend,
> A loving friend, to those who rival thee
> In his affections. Should thy wedded lord
> Treat thee with harshness, thou must never be
> Harsh in return, but patient and submissive
> Be to thy menials courteous, and to all
> Placed under thee, considerate and kind;
> Be never self-indulgent, but avoid
> Excess in pleasure; and, when fortune smiles,
> Be not puffed up. Thus to thy husband's house
> Wilt thou a blessing prove, and not a curse.[38]

In addition to learning to identifying with classical heroines, Roy says the Bengali girl is also watching her female elders performing *vratas*, or ritual vows based on medieval literature, in which the desirability of motherhood and the virtue of sacrificing oneself for the welfare of one's husband are emphasized.[39] She listens to *katha* (tales told by older women) about Shashthī, the much-loved goddess of fertility, and about Behulā, the devoted wife of Lakindar, stories whose message is that "it is good to have children and to love one's husband."[40] Finally, according to Roy, the Bengali girl is influenced by the poems of Chāndidās, Govindās, and Vidyāpati, the local *bhakti* poets of the fifteenth century, which speak of the passionate love between Rādhā and Krishna. She also witnesses the saffron-robed wandering Vaishnavīs coming to the door for alms, young widows who have become *sādhvīs*, or holy women, symbolically married to Lord Krishna.

Fruzzetti's study of women in rural Bengal reinforces Roy's thesis that marriage and devotion to her husband are the focus of a Bengali woman's life, but it emphasizes the importance of a virtuous wife's bearing children. It focuses on women's rites related to the marriage ceremony that ensure the fertility of the marriage, because "children represent the wealth of the *bangsha* [family line]."[41] In all the marriage rites performed by women, there are "symbolizations of women as 'containers,' 'holders,' 'vessels,' and 'carriers.'" An empty vessel symbolizes a barren woman.[42] Through elaborate ritual, the new wife is introduced to her new family as "a deity, a wife and a future mother."[43] For Bengali women, says Fruzzetti, "the ability to bear children is the sacred gift of all women."[44] Childbearing, while a sacred gift, is also seen as a responsibility, and the young bride is in an inferior position until she bears her first child.[45] Fruzzetti concludes that throughout their lives women spend a great deal of time performing rituals, almost all of which are for the protection and health of the woman's husband and children.[46] Although Roy, in her study of urban women, concludes that "no woman is more unfortunate than one who is unable to bear a child,"[47] she describes an alternative, socially condoned path for barren middle-class women in Calcutta of taking a guru and engaging in full-time religious activities.[48]

In conclusion, the ethnographic material of Roy and Fruzzetti confirms that there are many ways in which the *dharmashāstra* ideal of the virtuous wife, or *pativratā*, is alive and well in Bengal today. Rather than learning about this ideal of the selfless, obedient wife who worships her husband as her god and happily bears him sons from *dharmashāstra* texts such as the *Laws of Manu*, however, it seems more likely that women imbibe the ideal from listening to classical stories and by watching and later performing rites handed down from woman to woman.[49]

Bholanāth and Ānandamayī Mā: From Husband and Wife to Disciple and Guru

We turn now to an examination of the Ānandamayī Mā as an ordinary woman. As we have mentioned, in spite of the fact that Mā's devotees for the most part do not considered her ordinary or a woman, her most influential sacred biographies maintain that she was the perfect wife. While Bithika Mukerji describes Gurupriya Devi, Mā's close disciple and caretaker, as having "categorically refused to follow the conventional path of marriage and housekeeping,"[50] she says of Mā that Bholanāth "received from her the untiring and selfless service of a devoted and dutiful wife." She states unequivocally that "throughout the lifetime of Bholanāth, Mataji never did anything without his consent and permission."[51] In other words, according to Mukerji, Mā never strayed from strīdharma in her bhartrishushrūshanam (obedient service to her husband), consistent with Tryambaka's decree. In her detailing of Mā's life while Bholanāth was alive, however, Mukerji describes many incidents and behaviors which contradict her statements about Mā's perfect performance of strīdharma. Mukerji's books rely heavily on the diaries of early devotees, and it is unlikely that she herself witnessed Mā's behaving as the perfect wife.

Most of Mā's other biographers echo Mukerji's statements about Mā's fulfillment of strīdharma, perhaps in less absolute terms. Gurupriya Devi, who met her in 1926, seems to place Mā's unquestioning obedience in the context of time. Of Bholanāth and the twenty-one-year-old Mā, she says, "At that time Mā would do anything Bholanāth asked her to do."[52] Later, when Mā was around thirty, Didi writes, "As far as possible, she never failed in her service of Bholanāth. I have never seen such unwavering devotion to the husband anywhere else. She obeyed him like a child—she never tried to reason with him."[53] What follows, however, are Gurupriya Devi's firsthand observations of countless incidents between Bholanāth and Mā in which Mā does exactly what she wants to do and, in fact, orders or manipulates Bholanāth into following her commands.[54]

Bhaiji, one of Mā's oldest devotees, who met Mā in 1924 and traveled extensively with her and Bholanāth, contradicts Mukerji. He gives the impression that Mā directed the relationship according to her kheyāla, or spontaneous manifestation of divine will. Furthermore, Bhaiji asserts, Bholanāth surrendered to Mā's kheyāla: "During all the extraordinary happenings in Her life, Pitājī [Bholanāth] would often show great anxiety about their final outcome. But in spite of all criticism and speculation, he never stood in Her way as regards any of her actions."[55] Mukerji's biography, however, seems to be favored by devotees and my contributors echoed her conviction that Mā was "the perfect wife."

In order to examine this claim, we must certainly consider the degree to which Mā was obedient to her husband. However, there are many other requirements of the perfect wife according to orthodox strīdharma—having no independent religious life other than devotion to her husband, not traveling or attending gatherings, cooking for her husband, and eating his leftovers, working tirelessly to keep the house in the proscribed manner, engaging in sexual relations, bearing sons, avoiding the company of ascetics or renunciants, and following her husband into death or assuming a subservient role at home as a widow-ascetic—that we need to consider. Although Mā lived forty-two years after her husband's death, since her devotees emphasize her identity as a perfect wife, we must look carefully at the period of her marriage.

Chapter 2 tells us that on February 9, 1909, in the tiny village of Kheora in the interior of East Bengal, what appeared to be a most ordinary brahman wedding took place.[56] The stars had been consulted. The groom, Ramani

Mohan Chakravartī, a clerk in a police department, probably in his mid-thirties, and Nirmalā Sundarī, then twelve years and ten months old, were considered well-matched. Ramani Mohan no doubt considered himself fortunate to have found a bride from a revered family, who was, despite her young years and apparent simplicity, quite beautiful. There was no way for him to foresee that this shy village girl, hardly literate, was to become one of the most powerful and revered saints of modern India, leaving behind thousands of mourning devotees at her death at eighty-six in 1982. Neither could he imagine that he himself would be numbered among her devotees, having forsaken the life of a householder to wander with her as an ascetic until his death in 1938.

The story of the wedding, as told by Brahmacharini Chandan, however, contains three details that foreshadow this remarkable relationship and challenge what I believe to be the myth that Mā was the perfect wife. First, Nirmalā's youngest uncle withholds that part of her horoscope which predicts that she will "never be tied down to family life."[57] It is not surprising that a relative would not want to share this kind of astrological reading, which would be considered highly inauspicious from the perspective of dharmashāstra. There is no place in the Laws of Manu or any related text that describes a dharma for a woman other than that of a wife. Leslie goes so far as to say that, from an orthodox male point of view, "the concept of a 'female ascetic' is itself an anomaly." From the point of view of dharmashāstra, marriage is an inevitability, and a woman may never renounce the life of a householder unless her husband asks her to join him in a life of renunciation, although after her husband's death a life of renunciation is possible and even, in some cases, strongly prescribed.[58]

Second, the wedding rites are performed strictly according to scriptural injunctions, except that, when the time comes for the exchange of the auspicious glance, Nirmalā does not look at her husband because she is too busy looking at spiritual entities floating overhead.[59] While this establishes Mā's advanced spiritual state at a young age, it also interjects a second note of inauspiciousness. Brahmacharini Chandan goes on to say that between 1914 and 1924, when "Mā was deeply engaged in Her play of sādhana with absolute indifference to the world," Bholanāth occasionally mentioned the absence of the auspicious glance to friends, who remarked, "Yes, yes, really it is so; perhaps all this is due to this reason—the family life has not functioned with the normal bond."[60]

Third, the pandit who performed the fire oblation told Ramani Mohan that someday he would know what a jewel Nirmalā was, and the pandit's son said that she was "not an ordinary person [a human being]." Again, we have here the foreshadowing of Mā's extraordinariness, this time by learned brahmans and, therefore, sources of orthodox authority.

Chandan's is the only spiritual biography that describes the wedding in this detail, and most of her information came from conversations with Didimā, who was Chandan's guru. Other biographers, choosing to emphasize Mā as the perfect wife, might have glossed over details of the marriage ceremony that foreshadowed an unconventional marriage.

The relationship between Ānandamayī Mā and Bholanāth seems to have had four somewhat distinct phases. During the first, which begins in 1910, a year after the wedding ceremony, Nirmalā Sundarī *appears* to be the perfect young bride, although she is not yet living with her husband. The second phase begins in 1914, when she joins her husband in Ashtagrama, and continues through their tenancy at Bajitpur and Shahbagh. It can be seen as the period in which Mā's "true identity" as an exceptional woman is revealed. It can also be characterized as a period in which Mā attempts to fulfill her role as a wife, while serving as Bholanāth's and other devotees' guru. During the third phase, which begins in 1928, Mā appears completely unable to fulfill her role as wife and grows into the role of guru, leading her husband and others on pilgrimages around India. The final phase of their relationship begins in 1932, when Bholanāth follows Mā to the Himalayas, fully embraces the ascetic life, and, with Mā as his guide, lives out the last six years of his life as a *sādhaka*, or spiritual practitioner, taking the vows of *sannyāsa* a month before his death in May 1938.

The first phase is set in the house of Nirmalā's brother and sister-in-law in Shripur, 1910 to 1914. The stage is set for Nirmalā's faithful performance of her duties as a sister-in-law by the reported conversation prior to her departure from her parent's home, when Didimā instructs her daughter to "implicitly obey the orders of her husband and the elders of his family." It is clear from the description of Didimā's marriage that she modeled the obedient, ever patient, selfless wife and mother. We are further told that Ramani Mohan, himself, instructed his thirteen-year-old bride to "carry out the commands of all elder members of his family, especially [those of] his eldest brother Revati Mohan and his wife." Nirmalā, obedient to her husband's command (*guruvacana*), would thus be expected to tirelessly perform the daily duties of the *pativratā* as modeled by her sister-in-law.

Indeed, every account of this period emphasizes Nirmalā Sundarī's extreme adherence to the dharma of the new bride. She is said to have taken full responsibility for "carrying out all household duties, including looking after the children. Thus she completely relieved Her sister-in-law from all housework." Her willingness to perform household tasks cheerfully, even those normally done by others, is described by many as extreme. It is said that she "worked like a machine,"[61] seemingly oblivious to fatigue or physical discomfort. The description of Nirmalā's daily routine of *grihakrityam*, or household work, closely parallels Tryambaka's prescription: rise before dawn, boil milk to serve to the eldest brother-in-law, light the kitchen fire, cook breakfast, grind spices, cut vegetables, take care of children, cook the noon-meal, perform handicrafts, make *parāthas* (fried bread) in the afternoon, cook the evening meal, clean the kitchen, take her own meal, work on an embroidery of Shrī Krishna, cook Revati Mohan's assistant's meal at 10 P.M., and, finally, at 11:30 P.M., wash the floor and plaster it with mud and cow dung.[62] Nirmalā Sundarī is said to have performed these tasks with complete cheerfulness and efficiency and to have been much loved and appreciated by all members of the household for her "spirit of seva [selfless service]."[63]

It is not clear whether Nirmalā Sundarī was aware of the particular *dharma* described in the *dharmashāstra* texts of a wife whose husband is away (*proshitabhartrikādharmāh*). According to Tryambaka, "The woman whose husband is away should abandon playing, adorning her body, attending gatherings and festivals, laughing, and going to other people's houses."[64] Chandan notes, "Under pressure of work, She could not have the *kheyāla* (the impulse) at all to take food, comb Her hair, keep Her body tidy—to do all this in time." This sentence may indicate that Mā was following the injunction not to adorn her body while her husband was away, but it seems more likely to reflect her lifelong disinterest in her body and her appearance.

During this period the only occasional cracks in the picture of the perfect wife are interpreted as "spells of absentmindedness" or "sleepiness." Every once in a while, we are told, someone would smell burning food and find Nirmalā inert on the kitchen floor. But all was forgotten when she apologized and repaired the damage. Nirmalā's relatives remained impressed and grateful for her attitude of loving obedience. However, up to this point, Nirmalā had only had to perform part of the duties of the perfect wife, those of the ideal sister-in-law. The true test of perfect wifehood was yet to come. In the next phase of the relationship between Ānandamayī Mā and Bholanāth, in fact, we see that Nirmalā Sundarī was more suited to fulfill the *dharma* of the daughter-in-law whose husband is away, which is similar to that of Vedic student who tirelessly cares for her guru and his wife (in this case her in-laws), than to fulfill the *dharma* of the *pativratā*.[65]

Phase two of the relationship between Ānandamayī Mā and Bholanāth, in which Mā's extraordinary nature began to manifest itself and she became less able to fulfill the requirements of *strīdharma*, began in 1914 at age eighteen, when she went to Ashtagrama to live with her husband for the first time. It was there that the picture of the perfect wife truly begins to crack. We are told that when Nirmalā left to join her husband at Ashtagrama, her mother repeated her parting instructions: to look upon her husband as her guardian and to obey and respect him just as she did her own parents. Before we fully examine the devotees' claim that Mā never did anything without Bholanāth's permission, however, we consider the apparent lack of sexual relationship between Mā and Bholanāth, its implications for Mā's identity as the perfect wife, and the mystery of Bholanāth's acceptance of an asexual marital relationship.

Although there are indications that from time to time Bholanāth came to visit his young bride at Revati Mohan's house in Shripur, there is no mention of a sexual encounter between the two of them during the years 1910 to 1914. Because continuation of a husband's *bangsha*, or line, is the aim of a Hindu Bengali marriage,[66] and girls are assumed eligible for the consummation of a marriage after the onset of menstruation,[67] it would have been unusual for Bholanāth not to have initiated sexual contact before this time, since Nirmalā was, by then, already eighteen. Nirmalā's own mother was married at age twelve and had her first daughter at sixteen. According to Roy, on the first night in the husband's house, a Bengali girl is expected to participate in the ritual night of consummation, called the "night of flower bed," in which the couple's bed is adorned with flowers and they are expected to have sexual relations for the first time.[68]

There is some intimation that, while Nirmalā was living with Revati Mohan and his family, Bholanāth did not often stay long with his brother, not only because he was looking for a job but because Nirmalā had not "won him over."[69] It is not clear whether this phrase refers to Nirmalā's indifference to her husband or to the lack of sexual activity between them. It is simply reported that Nirmalā's sister-in-law suggested as a remedy that Nirmalā write him a letter. In the face of Nirmalā's resistance, it is said that her sister-in-law wrote a letter for her to copy which spoke of her unhappiness since her husband's departure and asked when he would return.[70]

The first mention of the subject of sexual contact between Nirmalā and Bholanāth in any of the biographies occurs in the description of the years after Nirmalā joined her husband at Ashtagrama. Gurupriya Devi makes no mention of the subject except to note that "at that time Mā would do anything Bholanāth asked her to do." Bithika Mukerji, however, broaches the subject of the "unusual consequences of the marriage" by quoting Mā as saying, "From the beginning Bholanāth was just like a father to me."[71] She goes on to say that "when the time came for them to make their home together, the young husband found a spiritual aura around his wife which precluded all worldly thoughts from his mind. He accepted her as he found her: gentle, obliging and hardworking but without a trace of worldly feeling or desire." Mā herself, says Mukerji, later referred humorously to this phase of her life in the following way, "In the beginning he used to say, 'You are very young and childlike—it will be alright when you grow up'—but it seems I never grew up!"[72]

Mukerji's description of the early marriage does not mention Mā's role in the lack of sexual contact, other than that she projected a "spiritual aura." Later, however, she introduces a quote from Mā which implies that Mā played a more active role. She quotes Mā as saying to Gurupriya Devi after Bholanāth's death in 1938:

> There was never any shadow of a worldly thought in Bholanāth's mind. He made no difference between me and little Maronī when we lay near him at night. You will remember that many times when you were going away at night, you laid me down near him when this body was in a *bhāva*. He was never troubled by any self-consciousness. . . . He guarded and looked after this body most confidently and unselfconsciously. Once or twice, when there was an inkling of a worldly thought in him which was so unformed that he was not aware of it, this body would assume all the symptoms of death. He would feel frightened and do japa, knowing that he could reestablish contact with me by that method alone.[73]

Alexander Lipski claims that the young Nirmalā fended off her husband's sexual advances even more aggressively: "When [Bholanāth] first tried to approach Her physically, he supposedly received such a violent electric shock that he put for the time being all thought of a physical relationship out of his mind."[74] Curiously, there is no reference to this violent rejection in any of Mā's other sacred biographies. Lipski read about this incident in the first edition of *Autobiography of a Yogi* by Paramahamsa Yogananda, published in 1946. In this edition, he relates a conversation he had with Mā in Ranchi between March and September 1936, about two years before Bholanāth's death. Bholanāth was apparently standing near Mā at the time of the conversation, although he was observing his fifth year of practicing *mauna*, or silence. Yogananda asked Mā, "Please tell me something of your life," and Mā replied with the famous words that are nearly mantra to every devotee:

> Father there is little to tell. . . . My consciousness has never associated itself with this temporary body. Before I came on this earth, Father, "I was the same." As a little girl, "I was the same." I grew into womanhood, but still "I was the same." When the family in which I had been born made arrangements to have this body married, "I was the same."

In later editions, Mā goes on to close with the famous lines, "And Father, in front of you now 'I am the same.' Ever afterward, though the dance of creation change around me in the hall of eternity, 'I shall be the same.'" However, in the first edition, Mā is reported to have said,

> And when, passion-drunk, my husband came to me and murmured endearing words, lightly touching my body, he received a violent shock, as if struck by lightning, for even then "I was the same." My husband knelt before me, folded his hands, and implored my pardon. "Mother," he said, "because I have desecrated your bodily temple by touching it with the thought of lust—not knowing that within it dwelt not my wife but the Divine Mother—I take this solemn vow: I shall be your disciple, a celibate follower, ever caring for you in silence as a servant, never speaking to anyone as long as I live. May I thus atone for the sin I have today committed against you, my guru." Even when I quietly accepted this proposal of my husband's, "I was the same."[75]

The quote then concludes with the traditional, "And Father, in front of you now. . . ."

Curiously, this part of the conversation between Mā and Yogananda was deleted from later editions.[76] The entire chapter remains the same except for this passage. Since this version of the conversation is not mentioned in any of Mā's other biographies, we wonder if devotees asked that it be omitted in the future because it was inaccurate or because it was offensive in some way. We can question its accuracy from one perspective. Bholanāth was certainly not practicing *mauna* throughout their marriage. Gurupriya Devi reports that Bholanāth was so distressed at Bhaiji's death in 1937 that Mā had to silence him to prevent him from breaking a six-year vow of silence.[77] That would place him in the fifth year of *mauna* when Mā was conversing with Yogananda in 1936.[78]

There is no way of establishing whether Mā referred to her husband as "passion-drunk" in her conversation with Yogananda or whether she claimed to have given him an electric shock.[79] It is hard to imagine that Yogananda would have fabricated such a long piece of her response to his question about her life, but we have no way to establish its legitimacy or to reject it.

What we do know is that this description of a rejected sexual advance resurfaced in the most contemporary of Mā's biographies, Alexander Lipski's, published in 1977, five years before Mā's death, a biography which was recommended to me by many devotees. Thus, it lives on as a part of Mā's life story.

Second to blind obedience to her husband, a *pativratā*'s most important duty is to perform sexual intercourse with him and produce children, particularly sons. The texts do not detail consequences for wives who refuse to have sexual intercourse with their husbands, probably because it seemed unthinkable. Consequences for wives who do not produce offspring, however, are described in some detail in the *Laws of Manu*, chapter 9, verse 81: "A barren wife may be superseded in the eighth year, she whose children (all) die in the tenth, she who bears only daughters in the eleventh, but she who is quarrelsome without delay."[80] Thus, a woman who offers her husband "her service, her care, her well-cooked food, her aesthetics of pleasure, and her capacity for children" could expect his protection and his economic support.[81] If a barren wife is in danger of abandonment, a wife not willing to engage in sexual relations at all is surely at risk. According to Roy, even a contemporary Bengali man believes he is entitled to "sexual union whenever he wishes."[82]

There are intimations in Mukerji that Nirmalā's indifference to sex presented a substantial challenge to Bholanāth's family.

> The members of Bholanāth's family, however, were not very easily reconciled to Nirmala's way of life. With the gradual unfoldment of her personality, it became clear to them that it would never be possible for Bholanāth to lead a conventional life with her. Although Nirmala had endeared herself to her husband's family, they thought it their duty to urge Bholanāth to separate from her and marry again. Those who have known Bholanāth, will readily understand that he could not have given any serious thought to this suggestion.[83]

It is likely that the "conventional life" refers to the "normal bond," or sexual activity leading to the continuation of the family line.

Both Mukerji and Brahmacharini Chandan mention pressure on Bholanāth from family and friends to leave his wife or take another and describe Bholanāth as someone who would never consider such a thing. According to Chandan, in Ashtagrama between 1914 and 1918,

> Joy Shankar Sen's wife [the wife of the landlord] and others used to talk amongst themselves about [Bholanāth]. Their opinion was that though [Bholanāth] and his wife were so simple and good natured, [Bholanāth] should marry again. Everybody observed that Ma's body was physically so tender that the slightest indisposition affected Her health."[84]

She writes that when Bholanāth saw the devotion that his young wife extended toward him and his family, he

> remained charmed, feeling always as if a small girl was near him. He was extremely simple-hearted, but did wonder as to what was this strange

phenomenon! Why was there not the least evidence of any worldly inclination at any time in Her? Externally, at the same time, no deficiency of growth in any part of the body could be observed. Often such thoughts would recur in his mind then. On the other hand, a childlike obedience was noticed by him in Ma all the time. That made him quite lost in it, as it were, simple-hearted and self-forgetful as he was. When Ma's play of *sadhana* began and continued on an intensive scale, Bholanāth. . . was filled with a feeling of compassion as on a child. So he could not offer the least hindrance in Her *sadhana*. All the time he was under the influence of some invisible power, not knowing what it was and having within himself a feeling of reverence as well. But sometimes, upon being influenced during talks with his friends and companions, his mind would question as to why it was like that.[85]

Several interesting threads woven into this passage address the question of Bholanāth's acceptance of an asexual marriage. Chandan and, most likely, Didimā project Bholanāth as a simple, compassionate, and even selfless man, touched by his wife, who evoked fatherly impulses in him. Seeing her spiritual states, he felt sympathetic toward her and chose not to interfere with her *sādhana* by putting worldly expectations on her. He was also, Chandan proposes, under a kind of spiritual spell from Mā's "invisible power" that kept him from pursuing his doubts about her. Yet, he was human and was occasionally provoked by friends and family to wonder why she was not responsive.

Anil Ganguli, a foremost Calcutta devotee, tends to spiritualize this even further.

To [Bholanāth] Nirmala was, from the beginning, a mystery—a wonder of wonders. His mind was puzzled by a conflict of ideas. She was completely unresponsive as a wife. [He] hoped she would be all right in the course of time. But that time never came. He often wondered: "Is she the goddess in human form?" And how was he received by Nirmala? . . . She saw in her husband not only the *guru* but the embodiment of Gopal (child Krishna). . . . She instilled into Bholanāth spiritual fervor which ultimately transformed him into an ascetic. From the very beginning theirs was a unique relationship poised on a spiritual plane beyond the comprehension of ordinary humanity. It reminds one of the relationship between Thakur Sri Sri Ramakrishna Paramahamsa and Mother Sarada Devi. Let us approach the subject with reverence.[86]

Most accounts of the relationship between Bholanāth and Mā are highly spiritualized, with hardly any suggestion of the doubts and frustrations a husband might have when faced with a platonic marriage. The concept of a spiritual, celibate marriage had been glorified by this time in Bengal in the spiritual biographies of Shrī Ramakrishna and his wife, Sarada Devi. Isherwood says that Ramakrishna's disciple, Saradananda, concluded that Ramakrishna "married in order to show the world an ideal," the ideal of a sexless marriage.[87] There is almost no material on Bholanāth himself, even though some devotees received their initiation from him and considered him their guru.[88] We have little or no information about his life before he married Mā, nor do we know how he felt about anything, except for the little that others, including Mā, have said about him.

Later we explore a paradigm that explains the community's lack of emphasis on Bholanāth and his surrender to an asexual marriage, a Shākta paradigm in which a woman is seen as a manifestation of the goddess and her husband considers her his guru. For now, however, we conclude that, from the perspective of orthodox Hindu *strīdharma*, Ānandamayī Mā can hardly be considered the perfect wife if she refused to engage in a sexual relationship with her husband and produce children. In fact, from the perspective of orthodox *strīdharma*, one might say that a Hindu woman who refuses her husband cannot be called a "wife" at all; a marriage without sex is not a "marriage."

During the second stage of their relationship, Nirmalā seems to be cheerfully fulfilling her role as a Hindu wife in ways other than as a sexual partner, such as cooking, cleaning house, receiving guests, and honoring and obeying her husband. However, she becomes increasingly absorbed in her relationship with the Divine and is portrayed as beginning to reveal her "true identity" as an exceptional woman. At Ashtagrama we hear that she was so devoted that she ate Bholanāth's leftovers as *prasād*, or blessed food, and did *pranām*, or bowed in reverence, to the water with which she washed his feet and then drank it. At the same time, she is first being recognized as a "spiritually exalted woman" as a result of her ecstatic behavior during devotional chanting, or *kīrtan*. During this phase she began her own spiritual practice, asking permission of her husband to perform *Harinām*, the repetition of God's name, in the evenings after all the household work had been done, although use of mantra and performing spiritual practice other than worship of one's husband is forbidden by *dharmashāstra*. At Ashtagrama, her first devotee, Harkumār, called others' attention to her ecstatic states of the body and invited musicians to her house for *kīrtan*.

It was at that *kīrtan* that others first saw Nirmalā in *bhāva*, or divine ecstasy. This is remarkable because, according to the rules of purdah, wives were supposed to be cloistered, listening through a crack in the wall, but Nirmalā apparently became so overcome with spiritual energy that Bholanāth, accompanied by the other men, was called to help revive her. According to *strīdharma*, it would be highly inappropriate for any man other than Bholanāth to see Nirmalā in such an unusual state. After the first incident, Bholanāth is quoted as saying, "What is all this? I feel ashamed to face people," but others convinced him that they should hold a second *kīrtan*, at which the same thing happened.[89] Nirmalā's parents got the news that she was suffering from hysterical fits, and they wrote to Bholanāth about it, but he is said to have replied "that the rumor was quite unfounded and that there was nothing to be worried about."[90]

The events that continued to unfold in this second phase of their relationship, however, certainly gave Bholanāth occasion to worry. When Nirmalā joined him in Bajitpur in 1918, what is referred to as the "*līlā* of *sādhana*," or the play of spiritual practice, is said to have formally begun.

Devotees refer to this period as a "*līlā*" because they believe that Mā, God-realized from birth, merely went through the motions of spiritual practice for the benefit of her devotees. While at first she continued to cook for Bholanāth and guests, she became increasingly absorbed in mantra and meditation and was in trance much of the day. During most of the day she remained "the serene and pleasant-spoken housewife," but at night "she was the devout and dedicated spiritual practitioner fully occupied with the manifestations of the inner life."

Although some say that Bholanāth was "awestruck in Her presence and soon enough ceased to look upon her as wife proper,"[91] other accounts point to his increasing concern about her.[92] Lipski says that, "Bholanāth was placed in an awkward position, experiencing the pressure of friends and neighbors to put an end to the improper behavior of his wife. He felt compelled to summon several *ojhās* (spirit exorcisers) to 'cure' his wife."[93] One such *ojhā*, upon touching Nirmalā in a state of *samādhi*, is said to have fallen on the floor as if possessed. Bholanāth reportedly asked his wife nervously, "Please do something to pacify this man!" which she is said to have done. This incident is particularly interesting because, initially, Bholanāth succumbs to pressure to make his wife more "normal," either out of his own concern or a desire to pacify concerned friends and family; then, in the middle of the crisis, he assumes that his wife might have the power to "cure" the *ojhā*, just as she might have created his condition; finally, he implores her, rather than orders her, to help the *ojhā*. Bholanāth seems to have been trying to understand what was happening to his wife. Also, when Nirmalā apparently healed a friend's son, Bholanāth went to a holy man for reassurance.[94]

In 1922, when her spiritual activity intensified and she neither ate nor slept much, it became impossible for Nirmalā to attend to household work. Bhaiji reports that she was in such a constant state of *samādhi*, or absorption in the Self, that she sometimes forgot how to laugh or talk or how to distinguish between different articles of food or drink.[95] Mukerji says, "Bholanāth watched over her as best he could. . . . [A young maidservant] quietly shouldered all the extra work which [Nirmalā] could not do."[96] At this point we have to consider that the picture of the perfect wife has surely cracked. For Nirmalā to have become so Self-absorbed as to be unable to oversee the household and care for her husband, and for the roles to have become reversed, we have to consider that Nirmalā had abandoned her *dharma* as a wife.[97] Bholanāth, we are told, did assert himself on at least one occasion, when he became angry that Nirmalā was reciting a Vaishnava name of God instead of a Shākta one, and she happily agreed to change the name of God that she was reciting.[98]

Bholanāth's apparent concern over his wife's unsupervised spiritual activity, along with that of his family, led him to suggest that Nirmalā be initiated by a guru as soon as possible.[99] One month later, Nirmalā performed *svadīkshā*, or self-initiation.[100] According to Mā, Bholanāth did not learn of the initiation until her cousin, Nishikanta Bhattacarya, entered the house to find her deep in meditation and asked her who she was. She responded,

"I am Mahādevī and Mahādeva [Goddess and God]." Bholanāth then asked her what she was doing, When she told him she was performing the practices of an initiate, he challenged her. She replied, "I conferred [initiation] on myself the night of Jhūlan Pūrnimā."

At this point the tables turn in the relationship. Bholanāth does not respond in anger to Nirmalā's presumption that she could initiate herself, something very rare within the Hindu tradition,[101] but asks her a question one would only ask one's guru, "When should I take *dīkshā?*" It appears that something was communicated to him at this point either by Nirmalā's extraordinary state or by her report of her self-initiation. Nirmalā then gave him the exact date upon which he should be initiated five months hence and told him that she herself would perform the initiation. Bholanāth accepted her instruction. Within minutes he was directed to sit in front of her, she touched him, and he fell into a "deep trance," foreshadowing the conscious relationship between guru and disciple that would begin at Bholanāth's initiation.

Indeed, five months later Nirmalā performed Bholanāth's *dīkshā.* According to Mā's account, Bholanāth tried to avoid it, but she "sent for him" at the office. Such an act is obviously unthinkable within the confines of orthodox *strīdharma.* After the initiation, Nirmalā went into a three-year *mauna,* or silence. Again, if no sacrifice, vows, or fasts should be performed by women apart from their husbands according to orthodox *dharmashāstra,*[102] certainly a lengthy period of *mauna* is cause for anger if not abandonment. The perfect wife could never become so self-involved as to refuse to speak. In fact, a sweet voice is traditionally important in a good wife.[103]

In 1924, while Nirmalā was still in silence, she and Bholanāth moved to Dacca, where Bholanāth had procured a job as manager of the Shahbagh Gardens. Their four years there served as a transition to the third phase of their relationship. Nirmalā was becoming less and less functional from the standpoint of *strīdharma* and was attracting "a lot of public attention as a young housewife who was in a state of constant spiritual exaltation."[104] Bholanāth, though becoming more reconciled to his role as devotee and more surrendered to Mā's *kheyāla,* or spontaneous action of divine will, was still experiencing the struggle of letting go of his concept of married life. Her states of *bhāva* were interfering more and more with her work. She seemed in real danger of being scorched when cooking or of drowning when bathing, and her trancelike states seemed to manifest without warning. Bholanāth "began to worry about her physical well-being," and so he asked his widowed sister, Matarī, to stay with them.

The years at Shahbagh were characterized by the rapid growth of a circle of people devoted to Mā, as they had begun to call her. By 1926 her intensive *sādhana* seemed to be over, and more and more people came to have Mā's *darshan.* Bholanāth not only welcomed people who came to see Mā but also invited more and more people to see his extraordinary wife. Although she remained veiled, Bholanāth encouraged her to speak to those gathered. So many people were apparently coming that Mā was moved to warn her husband, "You must think twice before opening the doors to the world in this manner. Remember that you will not be able to stem the tide when it becomes overwhelming."

It seems clear that at a certain point Bholanāth moved from the role of husband to that of disciple and became the person who mediated between Mā and her potential devotees. It is difficult to imagine that this role was not deeply satisfying to him and a source of pride and status. We hear of scores of the intelligentsia of Bengali society coming to Shahbagh for Mā's darshan, all by Bholanāth's invitation. In 1925, Mā performed the first of her yearly public Kālī Pūjās; Bholanāth was able to host a *pakka* brahman *pūjā*,[105] something a poor caretaker of an estate would never have been able to perform on his own. The following year, Mā asked Bholanāth himself to perform the Kālī Pūjā, certainly an honor. At this *pūjā* Mā allowed herself to be worshiped as Kālī in public for the first time, certainly a significant move from wife to saint or *avatāra*. The same year, Mā's birthday was celebrated publicly for the first time. With more and more public gatherings focused on Mā, Bholanāth, who is usually portrayed as someone without a profession, moving from job to job, seems to have found his vocation as Mā's protector and manager. As more and more people saw her as worthy of worship, Bholanāth spent more time in his new "job," which must given him a sense of purpose as well as public acknowledgment. His new role as Mā's most intimate devotee certainly compensated for the loss of "the perfect wife."

We are told that after 1926 Mā stopped feeding herself and that, if Gurupriya Devi was not present, Bholanāth often fed Mā. Because of Mā's bodily indifference and passivity, getting Mā to eat became the daily concern of all her devotees, including her husband. From the perspective of *strīdharma,* refusing to eat unless fed by another, rather than feeding one's husband and taking what is left over for oneself, is nothing short of anathema. Yet in the sacred biographies, Bholanāth, as well as Mā's other devotees, appear to have taken it in stride. In fact, by 1926, Bholanāth seems to have ceased to think of Mā as his wife.

Mā's "aimless wanderings" around India moved by her *kheyāla* also bring into question her role as the perfect wife. Mukerji says after 1926 Mā often called herself an *udā pākhi,* a bird on the wing, and describes travel with Mā as follows:

> [Sometimes] a suggestion would be made to go on a pilgrimage; a party would assemble and the journey would take place. [Mā] on such occasions always took along with her such men and women of her or Bholanāth's family who by themselves would never have had the chance to travel out of their villages or towns. Wherever she went, she was always the central figure of a large crowd of men, women, and children. She managed with ease to hold together without tension the life of a thoughtful and kind matron of a large family and a mendicant's life of aimless peregrinations. . . . For many years her mode of travel was something like this: she would arrive at a railway station and suggest that they board the first train available. This decided the direction of the journey. [On these occasions] companions were not chosen

or selected deliberately. All who wished to go with her went along if they were in a position to do so.[106]

For the first two years, Mā traveled accompanied by Bholanāth, although later she was to challenge *strīdharma* even more by traveling extensively without him, "no longer covering her face with the folds of her sari."[107]

It is significant that one of Mā's first trips in early 1927 was to the Kumbha Melā festival in Haridwar, Uttar Pradesh, the gathering of ascetics and yogis from all over India at one of four sacred sites every six years. Traditionally, the Kumbha Melā would certainly not be an appropriate destination for a thirty-year-old wife in purdah. *Dharmashāstra* texts prohibit women from attending festivals of any kind but would be particularly concerned about this one, as they warn of the dangers of keeping the company of renunciants. That Bholanāth allowed his wife to travel to the Kumbha Melā is another sign of his surrender to her. It also foreshadows her later attendance there as an honored spiritual leader.

In 1928, Bholanāth lost his job at Shahbagh, and Mā instructed him to start living in a small room of the Kālī temple at Siddheshvari and to become engaged in *sādhana*. A few months later, she sent him to meditate at one of the most sacred sites for worshipers of the *shakti*, or divine feminine, the cremation grounds at Tarapith. When he returned from Tarapith, Mā arranged for his bed to be taken apart; he would have to sleep on the floor, as she did.[108] This symbolic move, unparalleled for a wife, heralds the period in which Bholanāth truly became Mā's disciple. While he intensified his *sādhana* under her instruction, Mā began to travel, often without him, all over India. Symbolically and literally, she left the householder life and became a full-time wandering ascetic. Bholanāth followed her lead and began his transformation from disciple into *sannyāsin*.

By the time Mā was thirty-three years old, Mukerji reports,

> Mā now tried to cook meals with the help of Didimā and Pisimā but was unable to do so. Mātājī had said to Didi in Shahbagh one day in a different context that human beings do not have to forsake anything willfully. When the time comes, all distractions fall away by themselves. Now when Mā tried to help with the housework, she would not be able to clasp or hold things. Her hands uncoordinated like the hands of a child. She had, at one time, accomplished single-handed the entire work of a big family—the same hands were now powerless to do anything.[109]

Mā's words to Didi are the words of a renunciant, not a wife.[110]

On the night of June 2, 1932, Mā told Bholanāth that it was her *kheyāla* that they leave Dacca permanently and travel to the Himalayas. He reluctantly agreed. Accompanied by Bhaiji, they departed by train that night, instructing everyone else to stay behind, taking no baggage, and leaving behind home, family, and friends. Thus began the fourth and final phase of the relationship. Bholanāth came to surrender completely to the ascetic life and fully put his faith in Mā as his spiritual guide. Though he continued to care for her, he did so as one devotee among many, although her close disciple. Until his death in 1938, Bholanāth engaged in intensive sādhana, often in solitude, separated from Mā, who moved independently according to her *kheyāla*.

At Raipur, they "settled down to a routine of daily life in the manner of ascetics."[111] They lived in a *dharamshālā*, a rest house for pilgrims. Bholanāth and Bhaiji followed their own routines of *sādhana* under Mā's guidance, and Bhaiji bought or begged for food and cooked for the three of them. Mukerji tells us, "Bholanāth looked like an ascetic now. Mā was also looking different. The erstwhile housewife could hardly be recognized in the young, boyish-looking pilgrim dressed in white."[112] One wonders if Mā cut her hair in the manner of women ascetics. It is likely that at this time Bholanāth was instructed by Mā to take a six-year vow of *mauna*.

As a community and an ashram began to develop around her at Dehradun, Mā moved into the role of spiritual master. Mukerji says that when she returned to Dacca in 1935 for a visit, "The transition from a house-wife to a recognized Teacher who spoke unhesitatingly about spiritual matters had been so gradual as to be quite unremarkable."[113] Mā had mastered Hindi to communicate with her new non-Bengali speaking devotees. She would usually stay at one place for a few days and then move on, often returning to Dehradun. Meanwhile, Mukerji reports,

> [Bholanāth's] outgoing personality immediately made him welcome to all the devotees of Dehradun. They received him with respect and began to address him as "Pitājī [dearest father, the parallel term of affection to Mātājī, dearest mother]." Very soon he acquired a position of great affection in their midst as a dear friend and well-wisher.[114]

Devotees did not see him as "husband" but as "spiritual father."

By now, Mā was providing intense spiritual direction to many others, such as Gurupriya Devi, or Didi, her father, and Bhaiji. For example, in 1934, she instructed Didi's father, Shashanka Mohan, to take *sannyāsa*, at which time he received the name, Swami Akhandananda.[115] In June 1937, accompanied by Bhaiji, Bholanāth, and Didi, Mā went on a pilgrimage to Mount Kailash, the sacred abode of Lord Shiva in Tibet,[116] a pilgrimage destination that involved a terrifically challenging trek through the Himalayas. When Bhaiji met Mā in 1924, he was married and had a family. In the years that followed, he withdrew more and more from his family and worldly life, much to the dismay of his wife, who blamed Mā for her eventual abandonment.[117] In a radical departure from the traditional woman's role, at the base of Mount Kailash, Mā conferred *sannyāsa* initiation upon Bhaiji, along with a spiritual name, Swami Maunananda Parvat, or "the bliss of the silence of the mountain." Bhaiji died soon thereafter, in August 1937.

In reading accounts of Bhaiji's death and comparing it to accounts of the death of Bholanāth soon thereafter, we can learn more about Bholanāth and Mā's relationship to him. Gurupriya Devi relates,

> Mā sat calmly wiping [Bhaiji's] forehead. We were weeping. Mā said, "Khukuni, [Mā's nickname for Didi] sing the Name." I wiped my tears and sang the name of Mā. A little later he said, "How beautiful! . . . A few

moments later he raised one finger and said, "All are one; there is nothing other than the one. . . . Ma and I are one, Baba and I are one. There is nothing other than the one. He then began reciting the *sannyasa mantra* very clearly. . . . Gradually he began losing consciousness.[118]

Didi says that Mā displayed a detached calm right after Bhaiji's death. Later, however, she took to her bed in *bhāva* for days, to the great alarm of all who were with her, who feared that she might leave her body to join Bhaiji. She also details the reverence with which Mā spoke of Bhaiji at his death, referring to him as "no ordinary man" but "an *avadhūta*," or one who has reached the highest state of spiritual life.[119] The community, too, was reportedly devastated by his passing and to this day refers to him as Mā's closest or model disciple. Mukerji even says,

> There was nobody to take his place and mediate Mātājī's *kheyāla*. And exemplary identification with Mātājī's *kheyāla* was unique to him. Mātājī herself has said that many times [Bhaiji] would do things or deal with people according to her *kheyāla*, without the necessity for her to speak to that effect.[120]

It is Bhaiji whose words on Mā's teachings have been immortalized in *Mother as Revealed to Me*, one book which all devotees of Mā said was essential to read.

There are three accounts of the death of Bholanāth: that of Joshi, who was present, and those of Mukerji and Gurupriya Devi, who were not. One month before his death, in April 1938, the Kumbha Melā was again held in Haridwar. On the final day, Bholanāth went to the sacred bathing spot for the ceremony of the bath. Mukerji reports, "Unknown to others, Bholanāth, while bathing in the holy river, performed by himself the rituals of adopting formally a life of renunciation. This was in pursuance of some conversation he had had with Mātājī earlier."[121] Mā soon thereafter gave him the name of Swami Tibbatananda Tirtha, or "the bliss of the sacred pilgrimage place of Tibet."[122]

A few weeks later, Mā predicted that Bholanāth would become seriously ill after traveling again to Haridwar to accompany a male devotee who intended to take vows of *sannyāsa* there. A male renunciant devotee told me the story this way:

> Yes, Mā used to see all these things. Even about her husband. . . . Mātājī told him, "Don't go. You stay with me. Don't go just now." Bholanāth says, "No, I'll go." Mā told, "This body thinks this is not a good thing." Bholanāth says, "I will go." Mātājī was telling devotees, "He'll come back with this very bad business." And then devotees say, "Mā shall I go and tell him what you know?" "You can tell," she said, "but he won't come back." And Mātājī said, "This time your going to Haridwar will not be good. You will come back with some disease." And Bholanāth said, "Oh, this is nonsense. I will go." Then Bholanāth went and when he came back he had smallpox. And that was it— that was the final attack, the final and he died. He was gone. In fifteen days he was gone.[123]

Ironically, Bholanāth apparently died as a result of not obeying the command of his guru.

Hari Ram Joshi describes Bholanāth's death:

> He died in Kishenpur Ashram after a protracted illness of about three weeks on May 7th, 1938, at 9 P.M., while Mātājī was sitting by his side. . . . [At the end] Mātājī placed Her right hand over the top of his head (Brahma Tālu) and directed us to recite *Mā Nāma Kīrtana* [the name of Mā] as was the earnest desire of Pitājī. It seems that while Mātājī touched the top of Pitājī's head, his *prāna* (life force) left the body through his *brahmānda*. . . . after Pitājī's death, Mātājī was always seen in a calm and serene mood with the usual smile on Her face just as had been observed after Bhaiji's death.124

Mukerji says that Mā later reported that

> Bholanāth had been calling out to her, "Mā," like a child in distress and [she] had responded to his call naturally and spontaneously. . . . Sitting by his bedside on the last day of his life Mātājī asked him, "Are you in great pain?" Bholanāth replied that he was but that he could not quite locate where the pain was. . . . He was lying on his side facing her and Mātājī was seen to pass her hand over his entire body, from head to toe and seemed to perform some *kriyā* [yogic gesture] over it. After some time, in answer to a question, Bholanāth replied that he did not have any pain and was completely relaxed. Since the beginning of the illness, this was the first time he was at peace. He murmured "Ānanda."
>
> At one time he said, "I am going." Mātājī responded by saying, "Why do you think so? There are no goings and comings, but a presence only in which there is no room for such things." Bholanāth seemed to agree, saying, "Yes, so you have always said."125

Unlike Bhaiji, who spontaneously experienced the supreme teaching of Advaita Vedānta that All is One on his deathbed, Bholanāth appeared to remain a student in need of direction; Mā, as always, displayed her characteristic combination of compassion and detachment. It is said that her response to Bholanāth's death was to say, "What is the occasion for grief? Do you feel sad when you are obliged to go from one room to another?"126 Bholanāth's body was immersed in the Ganges, and Mā had a Shiva temple built in his honor on the shore.

It is interesting to compare devotees' attitude toward Bholanāth after his death with their eulogizing of Bhaiji. Joshi says,

> An impartial study of Pitaji's life, especially the period from his marriage in 1909 until his death in 1938, will be very illuminating to the future devotees and admirers of the Divine Universal Mother, Anandamayi Ma. Only due to Pitaji and Bhaiji, the two foremost devotees of Mataji, so many *sādhakas* were able to come in such close contact with Mataji and receive Her guidance in their various *sādhanas*. In this life as well as in the previous one, Pitaji was a *sādhaka* of a very high order. Mataji, in Her *bhāva*, showed him the spot at Ramna, Dacca, where the *samādhi* of his previous life had been. She had also

shown [such a place] to Bhaiji. . . . Pitaji was a great *tapasvi* (ascetic) endowed with the capacity to recognize Mataji's Divine Nature. Yet, in spite of being helped so much by Her, he could not shake off his ego completely. Fortunately, while suffering from smallpox, Pitaji at the end of his life realized his mistakes and in the early morning of his last day prayed to Mataji to forgive him for all his shortcomings. At his request, Mataji then with Her own hand put Her *prasāda* into his mouth. . . . It is certain that by Mataji's grace he achieved the final goal of Self-realization. . . and merged his identity with the Universal Mother, as had been the case with Bhaiji.[127]

Initially, Joshi puts Bhaiji and Bholanāth in the same category as "the two foremost devotees of Mataji." Yet he goes on to talk about Bholanāth's limitations as a human being and a disciple and concludes with more a hope than a certainty that Bholanāth might have transcended his ego in the end to merge with the Universal Mother, as Bhaiji is said to have done. Thus, he and the rest of the community seem to be saying that Bhaiji was best able to align himself with Mā's *kheyāla* and undoubtedly attained Self-realization.

Mā, as well, speaks of Bholanāth, not with reverence as an *avadhūta,* but as a human being who was an extraordinary seeker. Her nicknames for him—Bholanāth, which is a name for Shiva in his naive and even simple-minded form, and Gopāl, which is the name for the child Krishna—may reflect a warm but slightly patronizing attitude. Mukerji reports a talk in which Mā reminiscences about Bholanāth:

> Bholanāth's self-control and sense of dignity were always extraordinary. I have never known him to make a light or frivolous remark or an improper joke. . . . All the years I was with him I did not have an inkling of the desires which trouble mankind. . . . Bholanāth was very fond of his family also. At that time he came under the influence of his worldly-minded relations. He always had great faith in me, but he was at times blinded by his anger which clouded his judgment. . . . All of you know that Bholanāth was prone to fits of great anger. It is said that even Rishis were subject to the emotions of anger. Not that I am saying Bholanāth was a *Rishi.* If I did, people would think I was praising my husband. But you have all seen for yourselves that he led an extraordinary life of self-denial and rigorous asceticism.[128]

While Bhaiji's life and experiences with Mā have been published and widely distributed, nothing has been written about Bholanāth's life or realizations.[129] It is ironic yet significant that Bhaiji, the man who left his wife and children to pursue Self-realization under his guru's guidance, is nearly sanctified by the community, while the man who remained with his wife, despite the fact that she had abandoned that role, is seen as a good-hearted, yet flawed seeker.

Having surveyed the twenty-nine-year relationship between Ānandamayī Mā and Bholanāth, we conclude this section with the initial question: In what ways was Mā "the perfect wife" described in *dharmashāstra* and in what ways did she present a radical challenge to this paradigm? It certainly cannot be said that Mā's life was one of selfless giving to her husband as her god. Mā's first allegiance throughout her life was to her relationship with the Divine. It is more problematic to say whether Mā was engaged in obedient service to her husband. Clearly devotees repeatedly describe her as obedient from early childhood on. But it seems clear that when it came to a choice between her *kheyāla* and the word of her husband, Mā found a way to follow her *kheyāla*. As Lipski says:

> Her mother had enjoined upon Her, "Now you must look upon your husband as your guardian and obey and respect him, just as you did your own parents." Initially she obeyed him in all matters and carried out Her household duties promptly and efficiently. But when her *kheyāla* inspired her to act in a certain way, She would brook no opposition [to her *kheyāla*]. Formally She would always ask his approval before any undertaking, but if his approval was not forthcoming, She would find means to bring about his assent.[130]

It appears that to Mā her *guruvacana* was not the word of her husband but the instruction of her *kheyāla*.[131]

Most interestingly, as Lipski intimates, once Mā began to live with Bholanāth, she began to teach him that, while she wanted to be an obedient wife, the consequences of not following her *kheyāla* would be disastrous for both of them. For example, when he would not grant his approval for something, she would become ill with a fever or threaten to stop eating until he relented. In 1928, when it was her *kheyāla* to leave Dacca with her father, she told her devotees, "Please explain to Bholanāth when he comes. Tell him not to say 'no' to me." Then, when she asked Bholanāth for his permission, before he could express his displeasure, she said, "If you say 'no,' I shall leave this body at your feet just now." Needless to say, Bholanāth was silenced. Mukerji says, "He was the last man to call into question the truth of her statement. Mā had never before expressed her *kheyāla* so forcefully."[132] Apparently he had had enough experience with the consequences of obstructing Mā that he took this threat seriously and backed down.

Swami Krishnananda told me the following story, which took place right after he met Mā in 1927 and which illustrates the mystifying decision-making process that took place between Mā and Bholanāth:

> So I thought Mother was born in Dacca and we were going to Dacca. So I told Bholanāth, "I should be fortunate to see Mother's birthplace." He said that her birthplace was not in Dacca, but in Kheora, a remote village in East Bengal. He told Mother and Mother immediately said, "It *can* be done!" Bholanāth was adamant against it. He said the whole program would be upset. Now Mother did not speak much against Bholanāth. So what was decided was that a small party would go via Kheora to Dacca and Bholanāth would take a large party straight there. So even though Bholanāth did not agree, somehow it was decided that we will go to Kheora and won't stay there for long.[133]

We can conclude that Mā almost always asked Bholanāth's permission to do something and that Bholanāth learned to give his permission. Thus, if devotees such as Mukerji define "the perfect wife" as someone who always asks for her husband's permission, technically speaking Mā can be said to have done so. In this way, Mā and Bholanāth participated in a "*līlā* of marriage." They came to an understanding that *both* of them needed to follow Mā's *kheyāla*.

However, it would be a stretch to substantiate that, as Mukerji and others say, Bholanāth "received from her the untiring and selfless service of a devoted and dutiful wife."[134] Clearly, as their relationship developed, Mā became more and more independent, even though she went through the motions of asking Bholanāth's permission. Furthermore, by the age of thirty-three, she had completely stopped performing the daily duties of the *pativratā*. She no longer cooked, served food, or did household chores. Most important, she never fulfilled her duty to have sexual relations with her husband or to produce sons. Finally, when we look at Tryambaka's list of things to avoid, lest one go to hell, Mā seems to be the epitome of the woman who has fallen from *dharma*. She recited and chanted sacred mantras, went on pilgrimages, became a renunciant, worshiped deities, and presided over festivals and gatherings. Even appearing in public unveiled and with her hair loose marked her as unorthodox.[135] She talked to and was worshiped by men other than her husband. Not only did she not follow her husband into death but also she lived an independent life, displaying no apparent remorse or grief over his death.

So if Ānandamayī Mā was not the perfect wife, why did her devotees insist on seeing her in that light? Let us consider several possible explanations. First, the story of her life as woven by the community of her devotees is based on the assumption that, although Mā was not a human being, she incarnated in a body and went through the motions of human life for the edification of her devotees. Therefore, she played all human roles to perfection: obedient child, devoted wife, and one-pointed spiritual aspirant and renunciant. Gurupriya Devi says, "On reflecting over Ma's past life, it appears that Ma has already performed *līlā* with total perfection."[136] For example, when Mā completed her *līlā* as a householder, fulfilling her role as devoted wife perfectly, she became the perfect ashram dweller.[137] This way of envisioning Mā's life confirms her identity as an *avatāra*. If, conversely, one were to say that Mā never adapted to married life and could live only as a renunciant or a *yoginī*, then, by implication, one would be saying she was (merely) a woman born to pursue her spiritual life who inevitably failed in the life of the householder.

Second, as Carolyn Heilbrun points out in *Writing a Woman's Life*, the patriarchal paradigm is so powerful as to preclude what she calls the "quest plot" and renders it eccentric at best. While stories of men's lives encourage men to live the quest plot, stories of women's lives focus on the only narrative available to them, the conventional marriage plot.[138] In Ānandamayī Mā's case, this phenomenon may be compounded by what Max Weber first recognized as "the routinization of charisma," a process by which the community that grows up around a charismatic religious figure transforms the leader into the holder of traditional institutional authority.[139] In any case, this story of a young woman too ecstatic to function in the day-to-day world and too focused on the call of the divine to pay attention to her husband becomes the story of "the perfect wife." It could be said to reflect a taming of the script to render it less charismatic and more traditional.

Third, as Lynn Teskey Denton has pointed out, the most familiar adoration of a living woman as a manifestation of the Holy Mother among Bengalis is of Sarada Devi, the wife of Sri Ramakrishna Paramahamsa, and perhaps Mā's devotees and even Mā herself emphasized the perfect wife aspect of her life story to follow that example, even though it did not fit.[140] Although there are many reversals in the two couples—for instance, the male in one couple is considered the *avatāra* while the female in the other is—Sarada Devi is renowned for her selfless service to her husband, in spite of his abandonment of and apparent lack of interest in her. Certainly the differences between Mā and Sarada Devi far outweigh the similarities, but Sarada Devi's more stringent performance of *strīdharma* may have helped inspire the perfect wife label for Mā.

Fourth and finally, the claim that Ānandamayī Mā was at once "the perfect wife" *and* "the perfect renunciant" resolves an age-old tension within the Hindu tradition between the *dharma* of householder and the *dharma* of the ascetic or *sannyāsin*.[141] David Lorenzen points to a similar phenomenon in the spiritual biographies of Shankarāchārya, the ninth-century philosopher credited with establishing an elaborate network of renunciant orders still in existence today. The account of his life by his successor, Mādhava, includes an unusual incident in which Shankara learns through his yogic powers that his mother is ill. He levitates to her side, and she asks him to honor his vow to perform the rites of cremation for her when she dies. While all sons are expected to perform this rite, a *sannyāsin* like Shankara is exempt because when he took vows of renunciation he died to his old life and is therefore no longer a son. In the story, however, after giving his mother teachings and praying for her, Shankara kindles his own fire and performs the ceremony. Lorenzen concludes that, although Shankara's visit to see his mother and his performance of the rites is illegal, it resolves "the conflict between the ascetic individual-outside-the-world and the householder man-in-the-world."[142] Although the tension between the life of the ascetic *woman* and the life of the perfect wife is more extreme, the story of Mā's life told by her devotees seems to resolve it.

Summary: Alternative Paradigms

If the relationship between Ānandamayī Mā and Bholanāth does not fit the paradigm of the orthodox Hindu wife, are there other paradigms against which to measure it? How was Bholanāth able to withstand the severe family criticism of his surrender to the unorthodox lifestyle that Mā dictated?

The key may lie in the seldom mentioned fact that Bholanāth was a Shākta. There are two major religious sects in Bengal, the Shākta and Vaishnava sects, the former focusing on the worship of the Absolute as the feminine principle, or *shakti,* and the latter focusing on the worship of the Absolute as incarnations of Vishnu, such as Lord Rāma and Lord Krishna. Related to Shāktism is the practice of *tantra,* which involves attaining union of the male and female principles, Shiva and Shakti, through ritual practice with its locus in the body. Mā's biographies emphasize that Mā herself came from a Vaishnava family. Bholanāth's Shākta roots are only briefly mentioned. Gurupriya Devi calls Bholanāth "a great believer in the Shākta faith,"[143] Mukerji mentions that Kālī was the presiding deity of Bholanāth's family,[144] and Sri A. K. Datta Gupta relates the story in which Bholanāth orders Mā to use a Shākta mantra.[145]

Bholanāth's Shākta roots would incline him to be receptive to the possibilities of the Goddess manifesting as a woman on earth and of a woman as spiritual preceptor. The works of Sanjukta Gupta, Catherine Ojha, Lynn Teskey Denton, and June McDaniel confirm a Shākta acceptance of the possibility of incarnation of the Goddess on earth and an ancient tradition of Shaiva/Shākta feminine asceticism and guruhood.[146] In tantrism, in fact, there is a preference for women gurus.[147] It is known that Bholanāth had tantric friends on whom he called for spiritual advice.[148] Bholanāth's lifelong reverence for Kālī certainly put him in a position to make sense of the spiritual states he witnessed in his wife as an indication of her identification with the Goddess. His familiarity with tantric women ascetics and gurus certainly predisposed him to accept his spiritually powerful wife as his guru. This background, coupled with Bholanāth's apparent spiritual sensitivity, enabled him to consider replacing the goals of the householder life with the goals of the yogic life, in spite of the pressures of family and friends.

Contemporary representation of the phenomenon of an ordinary Bengali woman being recognized as an the incarnation of the Goddess can be found in Satyajit Ray's classic film, *Devī,* made in 1961, based on a story by Rabindranath Tagore. In this poignant story, the father-in-law, a devout Shākta, has a dream in which he sees his son's wife, Dayāmayī, as an incarnation of the goddess Kālī. He interprets the dream as an answer to his prayers that the Mother reveal herself to him. Within a day, Dayāmayī becomes the focus of worship for the family, and soon thereafter, when people hear that she has cured a sick child, crowds begin to come for her blessing. Her husband, who has been away studying for an exam, returns to find that his wife has become a living deity. The parallel ends here because the film's skeptical, Western-educated husband never accepts her divinity, maintaining to the end, "She is human. I know it!" However, the film does confirm that traditional Bengali culture has well-developed criteria for recognizing a human incarnation of Devī and, once she has been recognized, welcomes her with open arms.

In the world of Shāktism and *tantra,* then, a paradigm exists in which a husband can develop into the disciple of his wife. Catherine Ojha says, "Wherever the influence of Tantric literature and practices is found, women have been in a position to play key roles in religious spheres otherwise closed to them."[149] Likewise, where there is intense devotion for the Mother, there are women elevated to the status of the Goddess. Ojha herself sees Ānandamayī Mā as a self-made *sannyāsinī*, or female renunciant, who was elevated under Shākta influences to a position in which her husband, along with her other devotees, might worship her as an incarnation of the Divine Mother.[150] Lynn Teskey Denton, by contrast, says that Mā reflected the *brahmachārinī* paradigm in maintaining caste purity and pollution regulations but reflected the Shākta paradigm in manifesting the spiritual superiority of women.[151] According to both Ojha and Denton, Mā also fits the paradigm of the Varanasi *gurumā*, or guru-mother, who, having begun life as a spiritual genius, was nurtured by her Bengali family that boasted of a lineage of *yoginīs* and *pandits* into her adulthood as a "remarkable woman."

A related phenomenon can be seen in Kathleen Erndl's profiles of women's bhajan groups in the cult of Sheranvālī and the lives of several *mātās*, or Goddess-possessed women.[152] For example, in her profile of Kamlā Devī of Chandigarh, she describes a fifty-nine-year-old housewife, mother of six, who is considered a living *mātā*. Her husband is described as "reconciled to her possession."[153] He is, of course, a Shākta. In addition, his reconciliation, like that of Bholanāth's, must be influenced by the fact that his wife's reputation in the community contributes to the support and status of the family. Unlike Mā, Kamlā Devī chose to restrict her possession to Friday nights, because, as she explained, "if she did this every day, she would get the *chanki* [possession] everyday which would interfere with her family obligations."[154] We do not know what would have happened if Kamlā Devī had refused from the beginning to have a sexual relationship with her husband and had abandoned *strīdharma* seven days a week. Another of the *mātās*, Gumtivāle Mātā, never married because she believes "celibacy makes it easier to maintain the purity necessary for a vehicle of the Goddess."[155] However, many of the other *mātās* married and mirror, to some extent, the relationship between Mā and Bholanāth.

June McDaniel interviewed Bengali ecstatic holy women and found relationships that paralleled Mā and Bholanāth's. She concluded from her interviews that most Bengali ecstatics are married and accept their marriage. The paradigm seems to be living with husbands for a period of time, then leaving and periodically returning, eventually turning their husbands into holy men. For example, there is Lakshmī Mā, a sixty-five-year-old mother of five originally from Dacca, whom McDaniel calls "the celebrity of her Calcutta street." Lakshmī Mā said she was obsessed with the goddess Kālī from childhood and that she exhibited states of divine madness early in her marriage. Her husband apparently cared for her during those times and later followed in her footsteps and became a holy man and a worshiper of Kālī. Another Bengali holy woman, Yogeshwarī Devī, however, had been married and the mother of five but described leaving husband and home "when my relatives wanted the gifts from my disciples."[156] Both Lakshmī Mā and Yogeshwarī Devī are Shāktas, as were their husbands. Unlike Ānandamayī Mā, however, neither had celibate marriages.

One final paradigm, from which we might understand the relationship between Ānandamayī Mā and Bholanāth, remains that of the *yoginī* and the *yogī* as discussed by Hawley in relation to the medieval saint-poet, Mīrābāi.[157] Hawley describes the early hagiography of Mīrābāi as putting forth a paradigm of a new form of sacred marriage between *yogī* and *yoginī*. He presents poems in which "yoga and marriage, those impossible bedfellows, meet in an explicit way."[158] Mīrābāi, says Hawley, was envisioning, even experiencing, a marriage between herself and Krishna as her yogi-husband. This paradigm may hint at a relationship that Mā may have conceived as possible between herself and Bholanāth. Certainly, from the conventional point of view, she saw Bholanāth as a flawed human being, who was transforming himself into a yogi and pursuing liberation. Possibly from the ultimate point of view, however, she saw Bholanāth as her Gopāl, her Krishna, although it seems unlikely that she identified herself with Rādhā, longing for union with Krishna.

A story in Mukerji's spiritual biography suggests that Mā may, have viewed her relationship with Bholanāth as a relationship between Shakti and Shiva. One night in 1931, the arm of an image of Kālī installed by Mā in the temple at the Ramna ashram at Dacca was broken off by thieves. The event was foreshadowed that same night, when Mā, walking on the beach with some devotees, complained with tears in her eyes of severe pain in the same arm. The next day, when she was consulted for guidance as to how to dispose of the damaged statue, she replied, "Let it be repaired. An accident of this kind would not prove fatal to a living person. If a beloved person meets with an accident, we don't throw him away." She asked Bholanāth to do the repair and perform the *abhisheka*, or rite to reinstall the deity into the statue, which he did. Thereafter, once a year, the doors of this temple were opened and devotees participated in a *pūjā* to the statue. In 1938, several months after Bholanāth's death, this annual practice came to an end. When the day for the *pūjā* arrived, the arm was found to be broken again. The *pūjāri* telegrammed Mā in Dehradun for guidance. She replied, "Let this form of the image of Kālī become invisible now. There is no need to perform *pūjā* to a broken image." She explained that she had seen a vision of Kālī with no Shiva under her feet.[159] "Now why should there be no Shiva as is usual?" she asked.[160] Perhaps Mā and Bholanāth saw themselves on the cosmic level as Shakti and Shiva.

We conclude in agreement with Hari Ram Joshi that "it is not very easy to understand the secret of the relationship of Pitājī. . . with the Divine Universal Mother."[161] We leave Mā with the final word. In Banaras in 1968, thirty years after the death of Bholanāth, Mā made the following statement regarding the purpose of her marriage to Bholanāth:

> Yes, you people performed the marriage. You did it from the worldly point of view. But actually, what it was done for did not happen. You did perform the marriage, but he calls me Mā and this body calls him Gopal. When man and woman marry, they are called a couple. This couple starts *grihastha āshrama* [the householder stage of life]. But this body does not own any house, so

who will make me a slave to it? Someone asked this body, "Mā, where is your house?" I replied, "*Brahman ghar, Brahman* is my shelter." But . . . then he asked again. I replied, "*Ātmāmanda*, the bliss of the Self." So this body does not have a house which would enslave it. No *grihastha*. . . . And that is why Bholanāth had to take *sannyāsa*, because he was wedded to this body and when he saw there was no *grihastha*, he started calling me "Mā." He saw that the best way to serve this body was to take *sannyāsa*. Now think of this, you arranged the marriage but it resulted in Gopāl and *sannyāsa*!"

See the marvel, the coincidence! Had you not arranged this marriage, I can't think what would have happened to this body. This marriage came as a boon to me. It helped me during those days of *bhāvas* and *kriyās*. This body was very young, very beautiful, who else could have protected it then? See, when Bholanāth took hold of me, people would just reconcile that the husband was holding me. Thus, this marriage protected me from so many unwarranted things. . . . I was so helpless. Who else could have saved me from all those unruly things had I not married Bholanâth? He held me in his arms just as a father holds a falling child. . . . To hold and handle a young woman in public when she is out of her senses is not a small thing. Nobody else could have done it.[162]

Ironically, this statement contains the suggestion that, at least on the conventional level, Bholanāth served as Mā's protector, just as Manu might have prescribed.

FOUR

Ānandamayī Mā as Saint

I had instantly seen that the saint was in a high state of *samādhi*.
Oblivious to her outward garb as a woman, she knew herself
only as the changeless soul; from that plane she was joyously
greeting another devotee of God. She led me by the hand to
her automobile. "Ananda Moyi Ma, I am delaying your journey!"
I protested. "Father, I am meeting you for the first time in this
life, after ages?" she said. "Please do not leave yet." We sat
together in the rear seats of the car. The Blissful Mother soon
entered the immobile ecstatic state. Her beautiful eyes glanced
heavenward and, half-opened, became stilled, gazing into the
near-far inner Elysium. The disciples chanted gently: "Victory
to Mother Divine!"

I had found many men of God-realization in India, but never
before had I met such an exalted woman saint. Her gentle face
was burnished with the ineffable joy that had given her the
name of the Blissful Mother. Long black tresses lay loosely behind
her unveiled head. A red dot of sandalwood paste on her forehead
symbolized the spiritual eye, ever open within her. Tiny face,
tiny hands, tiny feet—a contrast to her spiritual magnitude!

Paramahamsa Yogananda
in *Autobiography of a Yogi*[1]

I N THIS PASSAGE FROM *Autobiography of a Yogi*, Paramahamsa Yogananda
uses the term "saint" to describe Ānandamayī Mā. Until recently, his
chapter on Mā was one of the sole vehicles for Westerners to come to
know about her. Undoubtedly his positive evaluation of her stature as a
holy person influenced many seekers from the West to seek her *darshan* in
India. Although Ānandamayī Mā's close devotees are uncomfortable with

labeling her as a saint because they believe that she was an embodiment of God rather than a human being, many Hindus and Westerners identify her as Yogananda did, as "an exalted woman saint," an extraordinary human being.

We in the West seem more than vaguely uncomfortable with the idea of an extraordinary person. Our culture is both fiercely individualistic and based on a presumption of the basic equality of all people. The stories of our saints and spiritual teachers are on balance the stories of human beings who struggle with the ultimate questions of life and through their angst and devotion discover an intimate relationship with the divine. Western saints are almost by definition no longer alive, since what qualifies them as saints are the miraculous events that have taken place since their death. The Roman Catholic Church has a well-defined process of canonization, through which a person is identified as a saint after his or her death.

When I tell Western people about my research on Ānandamayī Mā, they usually ask, "Oh, what century did she live in?" They are shocked to find that Mā, like most other saints and gurus of India, was considered by many to be a saint within her own lifetime. I tell them that, like many proclaimed Hindu living saints, Mā enjoyed this status because of what people perceived as her supernatural state and its effect on others. For Hindus, signs of a special intimacy with God are observable states of ecstasy or divine madness and the ability to perform miracles. Those who possess these qualities are considered worthy of reverence. In fact, I tell them, when you travel in India, an acquaintance is as likely to recommend that you visit a certain saint who possesses certain powers and performs certain miracles as to recommend that you visit a certain famous site.[2] Hindu culture revels in its living holy people and considers the extraordinary quite ordinary.

I first heard of Ānandamayī Mā through such a recommendation when I was in India in 1978. I was told that an amazing woman saint was traveling around northern India and that I should be sure to find her and have her *darshan* because her state of bliss and union with the divine was contagious. The person who was giving me this tip compared Mā with other saints I might have heard of to give me a sense of where she stood in the annals of extraordinary beings. In this way, spiritual personalities in India are constantly being evaluated and ranked by both spiritual seekers and proclaimed saints.

In this chapter we explore the complex landscape of sainthood within the Hindu tradition, enumerating the extraordinary qualities that Hindus claim their saints display and measuring them against the claims of the devotees of Ānandamayī Mā.

What Is a Hindu Saint?

There has been considerable scholarly interest recently in the subject of sainthood. Richard Kieckhefer and George Bond have edited an overview of the phenomenon of sainthood in the world religions, *Sainthood: Its Manifestations in World Religions*. John S. Hawley has edited a comparative study of saints as exemplars, *Saints and Virtues*.[3] Kieckhefer notes in his introduction that sainthood is a problematic notion in two ways: First, it means something different in each culture, and second, there is a tension between the "immitability" of a particular saint and his or her "utter distinctiveness from normal humanity."[4] Yet, as Hawley points out, the collections of exemplary lives vary significantly from one religious community to another but "bear family resemblances that are often striking."[5] Perhaps most important is their tendency to present a saint as exemplifying "something deeper than ordinary morality,"[6] a supernatural standard designed to inspire and transform.[7] He notes that in many cultures there appears to be a double standard in the way audiences are expected to react to the lives of its saints. The lay audience would be more likely to "appropriate his [or her] virtue less as moral canon than as charismatic power" to be drawn on for worldly blessings, while the clerical or monastic audience would be more likely to emulate his or her deeds.[8] This distinction between those seeking a power to be tapped for assistance within the wheel of *saṃsāra* and those drawing on the power of the saint for their own progression toward sainthood or liberation will be apparent as we become more familiar with the community of Ānandamayī Mā.

Before we examine some of the qualities of sainthood within the Hindu tradition, we must enumerate and discriminate between the multitude of Sanskrit and vernacular terms that might be considered synonymous with the English term "saint." We can conclude from the extensive list of terms which follow that the Hindu tradition has a highly developed and valorized institution of renunciation and "sainthood." The most general term for a holy man is *sādhu* (female, *sādhvī*). The root of the word is *sādh-*, "to accomplish or to succeed" and it means "a good and virtuous man." It is used to describe a person who follows a certain spiritual practice in order to realize an ultimate ideal. A *sādhu* or *sādhvī* is usually an ascetic mendicant. The term *sannyāsin* (female, *sannyāsinī*) comes from the root *samny-*, "to throw down or cast off." It refers to a renouncer, one who has taken formal initiation in which he has cast off his worldly *dharma* and taken new birth as a celibate ascetic in a particular order of monks. Thus, while a *sannyāsin* is considered a *sādhu*, a *sādhu* is not necessarily a *sannyāsin*. Although neither a *sādhu* nor a *sannyāsin* is necessarily a saint, a Hindu saint is someone who embodies the true spirit of the *sādhu* and the *sannyāsin*.

Although their etymology is considered unrelated, the word that is most often translated as "saint" is *sant*. The term, literally "good" or "true," actually refers specifically to a group of northern Indian devotees of God, such as Kabir and Nanak, who worshiped God without qualities. In *Darsan: Seeing the Divine Image in India*, Diana Eck describes the important distinctions between the *sant*, the *sannyāsin*, and the *sādhu*

> The saints (*sants*) are not the same as the *sādhus*, the "holy men." Perhaps the most notable distinction between them is that the saints of the *bhakti* movements were, to a great extent, anti-establishment figures who often championed the downtrodden and the untouchables and despised brahmanical

ritualism, while the *sādhus* and *sannyāsins* represent the brahmanical establishment, even in transcending it by casting off their worldly *dharma*.[9]

The term *bhakta* usually refers to a saint of the *bhakti* movements, such as Mīrābaī or Tulsidās, who worshiped God with attributes. Thus, both *bhakta* and *sant* refer to God-intoxicated people.

Many terms describe different kinds of religious practitioners. Many of these terms developed within sectarian contexts and later became more universalized. The terms *yogi* and *yoginī* refer, respectively, to male and female practitioners of *yoga*, the ancient practice of self-discipline and mental purification, the classical form of which was codified by Patanjali about the turn of the common era. A *sādhakā* is a man who is accomplished and disciplined in his practice of *sādhana*, originally Shākta or Shaivite tantric *sādhana*, and a *sādhikā* is such a female practitioner. A practitioner of *tantra* may be called a *tāntrika* (female, *tāntrikā*), especially in Bengal. *Jīvanmukta* is the term used in Upanishadic philosophy to designate one who is completely liberated while in the body. The term *siddha*, again from the Sanskrit root *sādh*, "to accomplish," used first in the Nāth and Buddhist tantric yogic contexts, usually refers to those who have perfected themselves through spiritual practice. In Bengal, a holy woman who is seen as an embodiment of Shakti may be called a *bhairavī*. Finally, but not necessarily completely, the term *avadhūta*, which originated in the Nāth yogic cults, usually means one who has reached the highest stage of spiritual life.

Although "saint" itself is a Christian category, in recent centuries it has been applied by Westerners and other English-speaking peoples to certain figures in the non-Christian religious world. Since English has been spoken for two hundred years in Bengal, the term "saint" has come to be commonly used there. The community of Ānandamayī Mā, although pan-Indian, is predominantly English and Bengali speaking. Thus, among the devotees of Ānandamayī Mā, the word "saint" might be slipped into an otherwise predominantly Bengali conversation. Because most of my interviews were conducted in English, the term "saint" was often used to refer to other Hindu religious figures, such as Ramakrishna or Ramana Maharshi, as well as to refer to what Mā was *not*. Yet, these Hindu terms are also part of the fabric of holiness in which Mā participates. Therefore, it is appropriate to look at the ways in which she embodies the spirit of different aspects of Hindu sainthood.

The phenomenon of sainthood within the Hindu tradition has been widely studied for decades,[10] and scholars have attempted to list the qualifications for being considered a saint within the tradition. This task has been complicated by the usually unacknowledged multitude of equivalent terms for "saint," as well as their variations of region, class, and gender.[11] However, there are common themes that can be applied to our investigation of Ānandamayī Mā as a Hindu saint.

Lawrence Babb distills the phenomenon of Hindu "sainthood" by concluding that in the life of a Hindu saint or holy person, there is a fusion of the moral and the powerful "in a way that generates a unique glow of spiritual energy." Hindu saints, Babb maintains, "are focal points of spiritual force-fields," contact with which is believed to lead to transformation of the lives of those with whom they come in contact.[12] For the sake of our discussion, we will adopt Babb's framework, envisioning that a Hindu saint's "moral presence," or exemplary lifestyle, might include his or her renunciation of the world, shedding of the ego with its accompanying unity awareness, and intense devotion to the Absolute, whether formless or in form. The saint's renunciation usually includes the pursuit of an itinerant lifestyle, along with the practice of forms of asceticism or *tapasya*, which include intense meditation, periods of fasting, and occasionally self-mortification, long periods of isolation, and silence. The shedding of the ego may be accompanied by a sense of a mission to serve others. The unitary vision that is said to result from renunciation and spiritual practice, which replaces self-centeredness, may lead to a rejection of and even an abhorrence of caste and a welcoming of devotees, regardless of caste or gender. Finally, the saint's moral presence is characterized by an intense devotion to God, whether as the formless Absolute or possessing form.

The second element of the fusion which leads to the transformative energy field of the saint is his or her powerful presence as expressed in his or her *bhāvas*, or the ecstatic states that come with direct experience of the divine,[13] and in his or her miraculous powers, or *siddhis*. June McDaniel, in *The Madness of the Saints: Ecstatic Religion in Bengal*, claims that in Bengal it is *bhāva*, not yogic knowledge or ritual skill, that determines saintly status.[14] Her claim is based on Bengali theological texts, biographies of ecstatic Bengali saints, and interviews with living ecstatics.

Within the larger Hindu context as well, the presence of *bhāva* also seems to determine whether a person is considered to possess the charisma of sainthood.[15] Certainly the spiritual biographies of Hindu saints from the seventh century to the present contain vivid descriptions of ecstatic states of divine absorption on the part of men and women saints, and their devotional poetry can be read as a manifestation of that ecstasy. For example, the ninth-century Tamil saint-poetess Āntāl was so absorbed in ecstasy as a result of her devotion to Lord Krishna that she sang the thirty verses of the *Tiruppāvai* while completely identified as one of the *gopīs*, or cowherdesses of Lord Krishna. Lalleshwarī, the fourteenth-century saint-poetess of Kashmir, is said to have left her husband and wandered around northern India half-naked, dancing in ecstasy, and singing of her complete identification with God.[16] In a more contemporary context, there is much documentation of the *bhāvas* of the Bengali saint, Ramakrishna (1836–1886).[17] Stories abound of Ramakrishna's states of *bhāva*, in which he did everything from decorate himself as the Divine Mother to put himself to bed next to Kālī's image.[18] Hindu saints are renowned as extraordinary persons who display a madness for God. Moreover, this madness for God and its accompanying bliss and ecstasy are believed to be contagious.[19] Thus, one is encouraged to spend as much time as possible in the presence of saints in states of *bhāva*.

Stories of the saints of India are also replete with tales of miraculous powers. S. D. Gupta says that "occultism is associated with religious beliefs and practices since the time of the Atharva Veda."[20] The possession of miraculous powers is seen as a second important indicator of charisma.[21] Shrī Aurobindo, considered a saint in his own right, describes a yogic process whereby "the gross body begins to acquire some of the nature of the subtle body and to possess something of its relation with the life-energy" that leads to the cultivation of extraordinary powers.[22] In other words, the development of miraculous powers is the logical outcome of successfully completing the path which its scientists of "inner technology" have developed and refined.

Hindu and Buddhist schools of yoga have overlapping lists of supernatural powers that can be attained through yogic practices. Patanjali's *Yoga Sūtras* provides the classical list of *siddhis*, or yogic powers,[23] enumerating twenty-six *siddhis* that a yogi can attain through the perfection of *samyama*, which is the threefold practice of concentration (*dhārana*), meditation (*dhyāna*), and stasis (*samādhi*).[24] For example, Sūtra 3.16 says, "By making *samyama* on three kinds of changes, one obtains knowledge of the past and future."[25] Other *siddhis* include knowledge of one's past lives,[26] invisibility and inaudibility of the body,[27] the ability to give joy to everyone one meets,[28] the ability to enter into the body of another,[29] the ability to walk on water and to die at will,[30] and the acquisition of the "lightness of cotton fiber" and the ability to fly through the air.[31] The list culminates in the acquisition of omnipotence and omniscience. Other *siddhis* attributed to Hindu saints and holy people are the power to be in several locations at once, including being in the dreams of devotees, the power to cure illness, the power to manifest wealth in the lives of devotees, and the power to take on the karma of devotees.[32] The tradition, however, while acknowledging these powers, cautions against attachment to them. Patanjali says, "By giving up these powers, the seed of evil (ignorance) is destroyed and liberation follows." Swami Prabhavananda explains, "The yogi who has held even these powers within his grasp and nevertheless renounced them, has rejected the ultimate temptation of ego. Henceforth, he is freed from bondage."[33]

It is the fusion of the *moral* presence of the Hindu saint and his or her *powerful* presence that leads to spiritual transformation in the lives of those who come in contact with him or her, transformation that is discussed more fully in chapter 5 on Ānandamayī Mā as guru. It seems that almost all Hindu gurus are considered saints, but that not all saints are considered gurus. A guru consciously takes on disciples through an initiation process that involves an awakening of spiritual energy and guides the unfolding of that energy, while a saint may be so immersed in *bhāva* as to hardly notice those who come to him or her for *darshan*.

Ānandamayī Mā in the Context of "Sainthood"

We begin by considering Mā as an embodiment of a "moral presence," exploring the degree to which she embodied the qualities of renunciation, egolessness, and devotion to God as we ask: Was she a *sannyāsinī*? Was she a *sādhvī*? Was she a *sādhikā* or a *yoginī*? Was she a *bhakta*, or a *sant*?

Renunciation

The Sanskrit word for renunciation is *sannyāsa*, literally the "casting off." The Vedic system of *caturvarnāshrama*, or the four stages of life, describes movement from the first stage, in which the celibate youth studies with a guru (*brahmacharya*); into the second, the householder stage (*grihastya*), in which he performs the Vedic sacrifice and upholds society; into the third stage, the forest dweller stage (*vanaprastha*), in which, with one's wife, one practices meditation and lives like a hermit; and finally, into the fourth stage, the renouncer stage (*sannyāsa*), in which one has no fixed abode, no possessions or attachments, and devotes oneself solely to the Absolute. In practice, many men and an occasional woman throughout the centuries have chosen to take *sannyāsa* initiation right after *brahmacharya* and have been initiated into renunciant orders without ever having been married.

In the *Sannyāsa Upanishads*, the *sannyāsa* rite is described as symbolically dying to one's former life and taking up the symbols of renunciation, such as the staff, the water pot, the loincloth, and the garment, usually a yellow or orange cloth.[34] The customs and rules of *sannyāsa* are described in great detail. Broadly speaking, they entail living an itinerant lifestyle, in which one is *aniketanah*, or "no longer having his own dwelling place,"[35] abandoning all possessions and existing by begging, and performing spiritual practices and austerities (*tapasya*).[36]

Although Ānandamayī Mā never took *sannyāsa* initiation, she may have reflected the spirit of *sannyāsa*. It seems from her behavior that Mā deeply embraced the logic of homelessness. We have been told that she called no place home yet seemed comfortable everywhere. We have heard of her leaving Dacca in 1932 with no baggage to begin what was to be fifty years of constant movement; she described herself as a "bird on the wing." It is said that she never committed herself to any definite plan, or "programme," as it is called in India. In fact, Mā followed the ethic of homelessness more stringently than is dictated in the *Sannyāsa Upanishads*, staying in one place no longer than two weeks, never resting for the four months of the rainy season.[37] Her commitment was to follow her *kheyāla* wherever it took her. In response to devotees of a certain place expressing grief at her departure, she would say,

> I see the world as a garden. Men, animals, creatures, plants, all have their appointed places. Each in its particularity enhances the richness of the whole. All of you in your variety add to the wealth of the garden and I enjoy the multiplicity. I merely walk from one corner of the garden to the other. Why do you grieve so if I am not visible to you for a while?[38]

In addition to her usual practice of homeless wandering, accompanied by devotees who would notify others of her whereabouts, Mā went through periods in which no one knew where she was. Devotees said, "At that time

Mā was *ajnātva*," or "not known." Subodh Chattaraj, a male householder, said, "Mā used to come to Calcutta in *ajnātva*, or in disguise. But it so happened that I accidentally met her traveling in my car. I followed her car and got her touch."[39]

Devotees told me that Mā refused to stay in the house of a householder. In the early days, she would stay in a temple, a *dharamshālā*, or guest house for spiritual practitioners, or on the veranda of a building. Later on, she stayed in ashrams built in her honor or in small *kutirs*, or cottages, built for her to stay in, should her *kheyāla* direct her to, in the gardens of devotees. I was proudly shown four such *kutirs* by devotees in Calcutta, Bombay, and Allahabad. I was unable to determine exactly when Mā stopped staying inside a house or why. Some conjectured that she realized that devotees would compete to have her stay with them and she was trying to circumvent that conflict.[40] Others believed it was simply a reflection of her commitment to renunciation.

The second custom of *sannyāsa* is the abandonment of all possessions to exist by begging. Clearly Mā fulfilled the ideal of having no possessions. She wore the simple garb of a *brahmachārinī*, or celibate woman, a white cotton sari. As a young bride, her white sari often included the traditional Bengali thin ribbon of color at the bottom hem, but later on her saris were pure white *dhotis*, yards of white fabric wrapped and worn by men in the place of pants. Often she is pictured with a yellow cotton towel around her shoulders and neck; yellow also signifies *brahmacharya*. Mā usually wore her hair loose, also a sign of renunciation. Very occasionally, she allowed devotees to dress her more elaborately as Devī, the Goddess, Shiva, or Krishna. However, no matter how many possessions were given to Mā by well-meaning devotees, she gave them all away.

It is more difficult to say whether Mā lived by begging. She rarely asked for anything to eat and simply ate what was fed to her. Wherever she went, she was provided for by devotees—train fare, lodging, food. However, there was never any question of excess or any intimation that Mā, like many gurus who have come to the West, became more materialistic as she became more famous. Although surrounded by wealthy devotees and the focus of elaborate *pūjās*, her personal lifestyle remained bare and simple throughout her life.

The third custom of renunciation is the performance of spiritual practices, or *sādhana*, and austerities, or *tapasya*. Although devotees claim that she never *needed* to practice *sādhana*, Mā spent several years apparently engaged in intensive *sādhana*. After 1932, while she directed devotees in their *sādhana*, she herself did not appear to be engaged in a personal spiritual practice. However, she did lead devotees in chanting scriptures such as the Bhagavad Gītā and in singing the names of God.

Mā practiced many forms of austerity throughout her life. According to Ghurye, Chāndogya Upanishad, 8 v.5, lists the three kinds of austerities *sādhus* and *sādhvīs* are expected to follow as celibacy (*brahmacharya*), silence (*mauna*), and noneating (*anāshakāyana*).[41] We established that Mā observed life-long celibacy. Gonda maintains that the practice of chastity, or brahmacharya, which literally means "devoting oneself to Brahman," has been central to the Hindu tradition from Vedic times.[42] During the early Vedic period, a young boy or girl was initiated into a period of celibate study, called brahmacharya, in preparation for the subsequent householder period, or grihastya, in which one's duty was to perform the fire sacrifice foundational to upholding the cosmic order. According to Olivelle, with the development of cities and the breakdown of kinship networks around sixth century B.C.E., an individualistic spirit developed that paved the way for renunciant orders practicing lifelong celibacy, or naishthika brahmacharya.[43] Since the Upanishadic period, within the Hindu yogic context, sexual abstinence, or in tantric traditions the retention of one's sexual fluid, has been considered a requirement for self-realization because the sublimation of sexual energy is believed to lead one into higher states of consciousness.[44] Mā was a naishtika brahmachārinī, a lifelong celibate.

Two male swamis in Mā's ashram in Kankhal provided insights into the importance of strict celibacy for serious yogis. Swami Jnanananda was speaking about the tremendous sexual desire that can arise after one's spiritual energy has been awakened through shaktipāt initiation.[45] He said, "I was in a position that I would rather die than yield to sexual desire. Only then can you withstand it. If there is the smallest idea in your mind that you could end your celibacy, then it won't work." I asked why was it so important for a serious seeker to maintain celibacy. He replied,

> They will waste it all on a sexual relationship. They will waste it. They will fall down. The sexual urge in the mūlādhāra [the lowest chakra] must be sublimated. . . . Mā's path is the path of purity, vishuddha mārga. . . . Mā told me in only one word, you see. She said in Hindi, "Jabardastī mat karo," which means don't fall. That's the only thing and it helped me a great deal."[46]

Swami Krishnananda said that one day, long before he met Mā, when he was a young, unmarried, celibate man, he was called to sit beside the famous saint, Meher Baba:

> [Meher Baba] was silent and he used to speak on his board. So the interpreter was rapidly interpreting. He said, "Baba says be very careful regarding women." I said, "I am already careful." He said, "If you touch a woman, wherever you are, wherever I am, I'll shoot you and I'll commit suicide. Two lives will be lost." Now I was a boy of twenty, twenty-one and he gives me a warning like this. Then, you see, he saw I was worried. He said, "Don't worry. The mind is like a pig and it loves shit. Don't let the body go with the mind." This appealed to me very much. Later Mother once asked me about this brahmacharya matter. I said I was very worried about this. I said, "At any time he will shoot me." She said it is great grace that this thing happened. Otherwise it is very difficult to keep.[47]

The second form of tapasya that Mā observed was mauna, or silence, for example, during the three-year period after she initiated Bholanāth. Devotees describe many other periods when Mā took formal vows of silence. Gurupriya Devi says of the year 1926, Mā "sometimes suddenly took a vow of silence. At that time we felt very sad. At first she spoke a few words to Bholanāth while maintaining silence, finally she did not do even that. Neither did she make any signs. Her face and eyes remained expressionless."[48] When devotees mention that Mā "was *maun*" at a certain time, they often say that if asked something, she replied indistinctly. Even in times when Mā was not practicing *mauna*, her speech was restrained and occasionally cryptic. She herself often referred comically to her cryptic speech as "*tooti-phooti*," glossed by Brahmacharini Chandan as "an incomplete expression revealing secret matter," *tooti* meaning broken, incomplete, or discontinuous and *phooti*, from the root *phūtna*, meaning "revealing a secret."[49]

The third form of *tapasya* is severe restriction of food, with extended periods of fasting, or *anāshakāyana*, more commonly referred to as *upavāsa*. Gurupriya Devi writes at length about Mā's relationship to food, her fasting, and her eventual refusal to feed herself.[50] Indeed, her refusal to feed herself and her lack of interest in food are cited by all her devotees as a sign of her extraordinariness. It is fascinating to compare Mā's relationship to food to that of the female Christian mystics Carolyn Bynum profiled in *Holy Feast, Holy Fast*. Bynum says that in the Middle Ages self-starvation was considered more basic to renunciation for women than sexual abstinence or vows of poverty. Furthermore, failure to eat ordinary food and the seemingly related failure to excrete ordinary fluids, such as sweat or menstrual blood, are considered signs of sainthood in the medieval Christian context.[51] Significantly, the time when Mā ceased to menstruate is mentioned in Gurupriya Devi's account,[52] and countless devotees reported to me that, although Mā rarely bathed, her body exuded an intoxicatingly sweet smell.[53]

Emphasis on self-denial around food as juxtaposed with the charitable distribution of food provides a further parallel between Mā's life and the lives of medieval Christian women mystics.[54] Mā is renowned for having fed people generously who came for her *darshan*. The distribution of *prasād*, or food blessed by Mā, was a central part of every public gathering. I have seen videos in which unbelievable amounts of food are being amassed for Mā's birthday celebrations, to be distributed at the end. Whenever I left the site of Mā's *samādhi* shrine, I was given fruit that had been previously offered there.

Within the Hindu yogic context, fasting is recommended for purification of the body and mind.[55] One of Hinduism's most famous contemporary *brahmachārīs*, Mahatma Gandhi, was convinced that self-discipline regarding food supports sexual continence. He said, "Control of the palate is the first essential in the observance of the [*brahmacharya*] vow." On the basis of his experiments on the relationship between food and *brahmacharya*, he concluded that "the *brahmacari*'s food should be limited, simple, spiceless and, if possible, uncooked."[56] The food served in Mā's ashrams is close to that. During the yearly Samyam Vrata, a week-long retreat initiated by Mā in 1952 and still held in Kankhal ashram every November, celibacy and food restrictions are observed. Participants fast for the first thirty-six hours, drinking only water. After that, they take only one meal a day, rice with boiled vegetables, and a glass of milk in the evening. Many of Mā's householder devotees observe weekly food *vratas*, or vows, such as not eating onions or garlic on Thursday, Mā's birthday.

We turn now to Mā's seemingly unique refusal to feed herself. One of the requirements of a *sannyāsin* or a *sannyāsinī* is to take only that food acquired by begging,[57] but a renunciant is expected to eat such food with his or her own hands. According to Ghurye, a classical text on ascetic practices maintains that one who eats with his mouth without using his hands, called a "cow-mouthed one," can be considered a *tuñyātīta*, literally, one who has gone beyond the fourth and highest state of consciousness: "He has no belongings, wanders naked, and regards his body as a corpse."[58] While other Hindu saints and *sādhus and sādhvīs* are said to have fasted for long periods and to have only begged for food, I have been unable to find reference to another Hindu saint renowned for a lifelong refusal to feed herself. Regardless, such indifference to food represents a dramatic form of austerity, renunciation, and disidentification with the body. Finally, Mā's refusal to feed herself made her a virtual *mūrti*, or statue, of a deity. *Mūrtis* are symbolically and ritually fed by hand, and their leftovers given away as *prasād*.[59]

Did Mā participate in forms of self-mortification for which *yogis* and *yoginīs* are renowned? It does not seem so, although there are countless anecdotes that illustrate her imperviousness to pain and refusal to receive treatment for injuries or illnesses.[60] She always slept on the floor or ground with only a thin covering and encouraged her men and women renunciant followers to do the same. Sita-Ji Aunty, a *brahmachārinī*, told me a story in which Mā playfully tried to wean the students and teachers at the Sanskrit school for girls from sleeping on a mattress with a pillow.

> Mā would not let you live with attachments. She would say, "Why do you have to keep these things? The less luggage you have, the happier Mother will be with you. For a *sādhu*, a mat in the summer, no pillows." One day we found our thick mattresses and pillows had been removed. Then a doctor said the girls should have pillows. So Mā blessed all the pillows.[61]

Thus, while she did not take the formal initiation into *sannyāsa*, Mā fully manifested its spirit in her life. She was *aniketanah, one* who no longer has her own dwelling place and travels without possessions from place to place. She practiced formal *sādhana* for a short time, but, her devotees maintain, it was superfluous in her case since she existed in a permanent state of absorption in the divine. Mā also practiced the three primary forms of asceticism—celibacy (*brahmacharya*), silence (*mauna*), and noneating (*anāshakāyana*)—throughout her life and led a life of relative austerity. We must note, however, that Mā's devotees do not use the term *sannyāsinī* to describe her.

Egolessness

Every book written about Mā and nearly every devotee I interviewed contend that Mā had no ego. The first thing cited to illustrate this is Mā's way of referring to herself simply as *ei sharīra,* or "this body." It is difficult to determine exactly when Mā began to use this term in place of the personal pronouns "I" or "me." Almost all devotees I interviewed, including the four who met Mā as early as 1926 or 1927, mentioned her use of the phrase when they related personal conversations with Mā. For example, "Mā said to me, 'It is very good that you have turned towards God. But there is nothing this body can do. Your parents want you to get married.'" They would add, "You know, Mā always referred to herself as *ei sharīra,* this body." Gurupriya Devi, in her first volume, says that once in Bajitpur in about 1918, young Nirmalā was sitting in a back room with other women listening to the *kīrtan* taking place in her landlord's house. She began to feel a *bhāva* coming on and called her hostess to her, saying, "I do not know what my body is doing," at which time she was escorted home.[62] Perhaps she began to refer to herself as "this body" shortly thereafter, reflecting the bodily detachment she was experiencing.

Devotees maintain that Mā had no struggles with "inner enemies," the obstacles to enlightenment listed in the Patanjali's *Yoga Sutra* as ignorance (*avidyā*), egoism (*āsmita*), attachment (*rāga*), aversion (*dvesha*), and the desire to cling to life (*abhinivesha*).[63] Even as a small child, she is portrayed as having "no emotion of her own," referring particularly to the emotions of anger, grief, envy, or any kind of attachment. According to Lipski,

> There seems to be general agreement that [Mā] does not exhibit what is normally considered ego consciousness. No personal likes or dislikes, cravings or aversions are apparent. At no time did She have to face the agonizing struggles, conflicts, temptations and doubts occurring in the lives of even the greatest saints. She is totally devoid of fear and anger. Whenever She displays moods it is clear that She is acting in that manner to bring home a certain point, to teach a lesson.[64]

Swami Jnanananda, a European, put it another way:

> [Mā] is a being who has gone beyond the ego, there is no ego. She was giving herself to everyone. She was one with everybody. Normally, you love one person, you love the nearest person to you and you love yourself much more. But if everybody is your own Self, your love naturally flows to everybody. I think that is the way. She had no ego, no limited personality.

I asked, "So how did you know that she had no ego?" He responded,

> First thing, she did not have these basic defects—anger, sexual desire, *any* desire, greed for money—you see? She did not have these things. And then when you get angry at her, she does not get angry. On the contrary, she laughs and smiles. She doesn't feel wounded when she's insulted. That is the second thing. And the third thing is that she has told us that she is fully realized and according to the tradition fully realized means absence of ego, you see? It means you have no personal center. The center of the realized person is everywhere. She can identify with everyone who comes to her. She becomes yourself and has your problems at the very moment and can help you from inside, do you follow?[65]

Jnanananda seems to be saying that Mā was fully identified with the universal Self, beyond ego.

Devotees also maintain that "instead of being the captive of common human motivations and impulses, [Mā] follows what She terms her *kheyāla*."[66] *Kheyāla* in Bengali comes from the Persian, its first meaning referring to a musical form. Its second and colloquial meaning corresponds to the English "thought, notion, spontaneous desire, or whim." The statement, "I had the *kheyāla* to drop out of school" conveys that this action was unconventional, individualistic, even quirky. However, Mā and her devotees have defined *kheyāla* as the spontaneous impulse of the Divine Will, implying that Mā's every action or thought was divinely inspired. For example, when someone asked Mā to do something, she might have refused, saying, "This body does not have the *kheyāla* to do that."

It is difficult to say when Mā or her devotees began using the term *kheyāla*. Bhaiji's *Mother as Revealed to Me* (1937), first published in Bengali, does not use the term or have it in the glossary. Gurupriya Devi's journals, the first volume of which was published in Bengali in 1942, appear to introduce the term. Her glossary defines it, as she says Mā does, as "the incomprehensible acts of the Supreme, as for instance His dividing himself in creation . . . a spontaneous upsurge of Will, which is divine and therefore free."[67] Ganguli's *Anandamayi Ma: The Mother Bliss-incarnate* (1983) devotes an entire chapter to the phenomenon of *kheyāla*.

> So far as Mā is concerned, the question of the existence of an individual will, apart from the Divine Will, does not arise at all. An ordinary individual, however, lives in duality. His will arises from his personal desires. So far as Mā is concerned, she has no individual life. She is in a state of uninterrupted oneness. Naturally, there is very definite difference between Mā's *kheyāla* and an ordinary man's wayward will or whim or caprice.[68]

Mukerji's "Śrī Ānandamayī Mā: Divine Play of the Spiritual Journey" (1989) defines *kheyāla* as "a sudden spontaneous thought arising not out of any need in her but because it was just the right idea for the time, place, and people around her." Mukerji goes on to say that it connotes a "conscious and benevolent intent" and that in following it Mā "did not contrive to bring about results, but once expressed, it became irresistibly operative."[69]

We can draw two implications from these definitions. First, Mā fulfills the saintly requirement of being someone beyond ego, evidenced by the fact that her will was aligned with the Divine Will and, thus, her actions were divinely inspired. While devotees of many Indian saints have claimed that their master *attained* the state of egolessness in which his or her will had become one with the Divine Will, the emphasis on *kheyāla* in the stories of Mā, is on the absence of ego in her *from the beginning*. Therefore, the second implication is that Mā never had an ego, that she did not need to work for her state of egolessness, and that her *kheyāla* was interchangeable with God's *kheyāla*, not because she had become a clear vessel but because she was God.

This concept of *kheyāla* establishes that anything Mā wanted or any action she initiated was seen as arising out of her divine nature and, therefore, needed to be responded to. For example, Malini-Di, a *brahmachārinī*, told me,

> If Mā had the *pakka kheyāla* [*pakka* usually means fully cooked, but I think here it implies correct or perfect] of doing something, then nobody dared interfere with it. But sometimes Mā would just play around with us, you know? One thing I know, Mā did not like us contradicting anything she said. Because she became quiet after that. That was the only time she became like that. And then we faced our own product. Suppose Mā said to me, "This body does not have the *kheyāla* to take you anywhere with me. You stay here." But I would cry and say, "No, I want to go with you!" Maybe Mā would change her *kheyāla*, but I might have to face the consequences, which could have been avoided if I had obeyed Mā.[70]

In other words, not only does Mother (as God) know best but also what she wants for you, as one devotee put it, is not coming from "the urge of ego" but from the "divine current."[71] Vasudha-Di, another *brahmachārinī*, says:

> People used to write to Mā and she would reply. So one day two of us were reading letters to Mā and those letters were serious, with some spiritual questions, some feelings. Mā was listening. And suddenly Mā said, "You people read letters and this body replies. You think that this body has listened to the topic and is replying according to that. It is not so. This is what happens generally, but this is not what happens with this body. What this body does is by the Great *Kheyāla* [*Mahā Kheyāla*] and when it comes you think this body is replying according to your letters. This is not so." So Mā's point, as far as I can grasp it, was this: Mā's *kheyāla* was the Great *Kheyāla* of that One. There was nothing conditioned involved, like you read the letter and write the answer. Mā's response was unconditioned. Mā's every move was unconditioned. So it was that Great *Kheyāla*. It was a great thing Mā was telling. And I'm not able to explain it to you.[72]

Even Mā's death was considered a conscious act of Divine Will. Naren Bose, a young Calcutta businessman, told me,

> She lived through many illnesses. I say illnesses as they appear to the ordinary eye. But we have seen many manifestations which suggest they were states of the body at a particular time that manifested themselves as illnesses. But although she would go through periods of what seemed like very, very critical illness, they would turn around like magic. The only reason she left her body was because she didn't have the *kheyāla*, you know the expression *kheyāla* or spontaneous will, to retain her body. She had no more *kheyāla* to do that.[73]

Scholars have often linked the egolessness of saints in many religious traditions with an ideal of altruistic generosity.[74] In the Hindu tradition, the shedding of the ego is sometimes but not always linked to a sense of mission to serve others. The range of saintly expression in India includes celebrated saints who have lived solitary, even antisocial lives, their "mission" defined as inspiring ordinary and extraordinary people to pursue an experience of the divine. However, in the past two centuries, more Hindu saints have become associated with charitable work.[75] Some scholars hold that the nineteenth- and twentieth-century impulse on the part of religious figures to enact social reform and do charitable work has been the result of Christian and Western influence.[76] Whatever the contributing factors, around the turn of this century, a spiritual movement, now called the Ramakrishna Mission, was formed by renunciant devotees of Shri Ramakrishna for the purpose of committed involvement in educational, medical, and welfare projects. Swami Vivekananda, Ramakrishna's best-known disciple, developed and taught an ideal of service, which, Carl Jackson maintains, breaks with traditional Hindu views based on the doctrine of karma in its advocacy of human aid. Jackson says that while Ramakrishna himself "tended to show little sensitivity to and, on occasion, outright contempt for humanitarian efforts, Vivekananda proclaimed that Hinduism should be based both on 'renunciation' *and* 'service.'"[77] Later in the century, Mahatma Gandhi, widely considered a saint, was admired as a model of altruism and social service.

Ānandamayī Mā is said to have been the embodiment of love and compassion. Every devotee I interviewed expressed this point in one way or another. Yet, as in the case of many Hindu saints, her compassion seemed largely directed toward alleviating the spiritual ignorance of humanity rather than its physical suffering. According to Lipski, Mā's diagnosis of the human condition reflects the traditional Hindu view: alienation from one's true Self is the basic cause of all suffering. Her prescription is to welcome suffering, to detach oneself from the world of duality, and to turn within to experience the immortal Self which cannot suffer.[78] Mā said, "The search after Truth is man's duty, so that he may advance towards immortality."[79] If we look at Mā's seven famous aphorisms, Bengali phrases that she repeated over and over, we see little emphasis on serving others. As translated by Anil Ganguli, they are as follow:[80]

1. *As the intention, so the reward*
2. *One cannot be sure of the next breath*
3. *Take an about-turn* (from looking outward to looking within)
4. *With God's name on your lips, engage in your work in the world*
5. *The suffering of life is a blessing in disguise*
6. *Whatever happens is equally welcome*
7. *As you play, so you hear*

These aphorisms primarily direct individuals to see suffering as an impetus to pursue a life absorbed in *sādhana*. Mā seems to have defined "selfless service" as taking up a life of spiritual practice, seeking God-realization.

However, Lipski includes a quote of Mā's that speaks of selfless service in the more conventional sense.

Widening your shriveled heart, make the interests of others your own and serve them as much as you can by sympathy, kindness, presents and so forth. So long as one enjoys the things of this world and has needs and wants, it is necessary to minister to the needs of one's fellowmen. Otherwise one cannot be called a human being. Whenever you have the opportunity, give to the poor, feed the hungry, nurse the sick. . . do service (*seva*) as a religious duty and you will come to know by direct perception that the person served, the one who serves and the act of service are separate only in appearance.[81]

While Mā's devotees in ashrams and those living in households might see the importance of consecrating one's activities to God, selfless service, or *seva*, directed toward suffering humanity does not seem to be a dominant theme in the community. Although charitable institutions have been set up in Mā's name—for example, a charitable hospital, a Sanskrit boarding school for girls in Varanasi, and one for boys in Dehradun—Mā is said to have had nothing to do with their establishment. By contrast, there are twenty-eight ashrams and many informal centers established in Mā's name all over India, places where devotees and newcomers alike can go to participate in spiritual practices. The devotees I met were by and large either renunciants involved in a life of spiritual practice or householder couples, with the husband a businessman, civil servant, or scholar, and the wife a housewife. I met few devotees whose spiritual practice translated into service work in the larger community. In my interviews, the only context in which service was mentioned was in reference to serving Mā. For Mā and her community, as for many Hindu spiritual communities, the definition of *seva* is limited to dedicating your daily activities to God and seeing God in each other; it does not necessarily extend to charitable activities.

Ānandamayī Mā and Caste

The egolessness of a Hindu saint and the accompanying experience of the unity of all beings are often reflected in a saint's rejection of caste differences. The *bhakti*, or devotional, movement, which began to flower in southern India between the sixth and ninth centuries C.E. and had swept north by the fifteenth century, posed a challenge to the brahmanical hierarchy by teaching that anyone can have unmediated access to God through devotion.

Many famous Hindu *bhaktas* and *sants* were critical of the caste system—Appar, Kabir, Tulsidās, and Eknāth, to name a few. Caitanya, the sixteenth-century Bengali Vaishnava ecstatic, completely rejected caste. Some *bhaktas*—such as the Shaiva *nāyanmār*, Nandanar, the Vaishnava *ālvār*, Tiruppān, and Ravidās of Banaras—were untouchables. Appar, the seventh-century Tamil *nāyanmār*, or Shaiva saint-poet, reflects the unorthodox doctrine of the *bhakti* movement and its challenge to caste, singing,

> Were they to offer me both treasures
> of Kubera's world,
> and give me earth and heaven itself to rule,
> the wealth of decaying mortals
> would be as nothing to me,
> when those who gave
> were not single-minded devotees of our great Lord.
> But the leper with rotting limbs,

the outcaste, even the foul *pulaiyan*
who skins and eats cows,
even these men, if they are servants
of him who shelters the Ganges in his long hair [Shiva],
I worship them, they are gods to me.[82]

The religious communities inspired by these *bhakti* saints have, in some cases, given their founders' ideals institutional form.[83] As Hawley points out, however, the equality espoused by *bhakti* saints has often remained a spiritual reality instead of a social one in order for *bhakti* to coexist with brahmanical Hinduism.[84]

The issue of caste in relationship to Ānandamayī Mā is extremely complicated. We need to address three questions: What part did caste play in the running of Mā's ashrams while she was alive, and what part does it play today? What did Mā say about caste? What does Mā's behavior tell us about her attitude toward caste?

I became interested in the subject after my first interview with Mā's devotees, Elizabeth Walters, an American, and her Indian friend, Chandra Srinivasan, near Boston in 1989. During the interview they told me that Elizabeth, a long-time devotee of Mā, had been unable, as were most Westerners, to live in any of Mā's ashrams and was fed separately when she attended functions at any ashram. This segregation had caused Chandra and her sister, Rupa, whom I interviewed later in Kankhal, much distress. They had both taken up the subject with Mā while she was alive and, since her death, with the ashram authorities.[85] They gave me the impression that it was not Mā's policy to treat Westerners as untouchables or to encourage only high-caste devotees to surround her, but that she had accommodated the desires of her brahman devotees. I was determined to find out more.

In India, although I was welcomed with great love by Mā's devotees both in ashrams and private homes, I, too, was unable to stay in an ashram. When I was served a meal there, it was in a separate room on a disposable leaf plate. Although I initiated the subject of caste in relation to Mā and her ashrams with my contributors only three times, seventeen of forty-four interviews contain a significant reference to caste. We can, therefore, assume that caste was an issue for Westerners trying to have access to Mā and was often an issue for some of her devotees or that they had dealt with it in conversations with other Westerners and had assumed that it was on my mind as well.

Contributors related various kinds of stories about caste. Westerners who were not devotees often juxtaposed Mā's spiritual power and generosity with the unwelcoming behavior of her devotees. The most dramatic story was told by Swami Shivananda, a Western *sannyāsin* of a different guru, who describes his visit to Mā in 1971:

What I noticed was it was a little difficult to get close to Ānandamayī Mā. She had a cadre of brahman ladies who were very protective of her, and for good reason. She was quite old and frail. But not only that, they didn't like to have foreigners around. Word got around India that a foreigner was not very welcome in that circle. So I remember, the first day I was very hungry and I asked for lunch. So they said, "Yes," and they brought very delicious food, but they brought it outside of the dining room, put the food on the floor on some leaves. I sat out there but I didn't know why. It was only later that I realized that I was being treated like an outcaste. It never bothered me because what I received from Ānandamayī Mā was much greater than the treatment that people around her would have given me.

Shivananda said that a few days later, after a powerful personal encounter with Mā, he had returned to his tent and found that two "handsome men dressed up in coat and tie with two huge thick sticks were waiting for me. They said, 'You had better leave right now or you are in trouble.' " Although he told them he had permission to stay, they escorted him out the gate of the ashram. On the train the next day, he fell into a deep, ecstatic meditation and began to feel an intense longing for God. Shortly, he found a guru who welcomed Westerners. He concluded, "Ānandamayī Mā, it seems to me, was a saint that came to serve the Hindu *dharma*. She was a saint for India, for the Hindu upper castes. It was their good *karma* that she was there."[86]

Other conversations tried to offer an explanation for the caste restrictions in the community. In two separate interviews, renunciant devotees of Mā brought up the subject and offered stories of the origin of the restrictions. Vasudha-Di, a Bengali *brahmachārinī*, said,

> When Mā was in her early days in Dacca and people were gathered together, we used to say, "Mā is Mother" so we are all her children. We are one, no caste, no nothing was considered. And Hindus and Muslims, they lived like one family. And what happened, there were some devotees, Gurupriya Didi's eldest brother and some others, and they said to Mā, "We are not observing these caste rules." Then Mā said, "Baba, this body has nothing to do with caste, Hindu or Muslim. But this is for you to decide. For this body, everything is the same." Then they decided and they said, "Oh, no, Mā, we are not on that level. We can't be so generous. So we can't take your *prasād* if you take everybody's things and mix them all up like this. It will disturb us. We can't break the rules not because of you but because of us." So the rules were observed. Mā said, "This is your ashram. This body has got nothing to do with this ashram. This body never ordered this ashram to be made."[87]

Swami Jnanananda, the European *sannyāsin*, said that he was the only Westerner allowed to live in the Kankhal ashram and that he and Mā had spent many hours talking about caste. He told a slightly different version of the story.

> Mā told me that she is not a reformer. She was born into this surrounding and she continues in that form, you see? Then she told that actually in the beginning, she didn't mind and even once she wanted to eat with a dog but they prevented it. She did not mind, you see? But at a certain point in the very beginning, her close devotees assembled all together and told her, "Mā, whatever you eat becomes *prasād* for us. If you eat impure food, so do we

brahmans." So Mā didn't reply. Then she said, "All right, let us see what will happen today. That will be the rule for the future." That day one big pandit came. She didn't tell me the name, but I thought it was Gopinath Kaviraj, [and] she asked him about this question. And he told her, "These rules are good for the Kaliyuga. People go astray, so it is good to keep up the discipline." So from this day after, she kept the rule. And everything Mā did, she did in fully, not half way.[88]

Several conversations focused on Mā's indifference to caste. Rupa Bose, a *brahmachārinī* in Calcutta, said that Mā's grace did not depend on caste. She once waited outside Mā's door for six hours while a Western monk, a devotee of another guru, had a "private" with Mā. She complained, "Mā, Kriyananda is so lucky. We are with you for the last twenty years. You don't give us five or six hours at a time." Mā replied,

When the lotus opens there are frogs under the pond, there are other insects. But suddenly a bee comes and sits on the open lotus and sucks out the honey from the lotus, the epitome of essence that the lotus produces, and flies away. But all the frogs all day long go, "Ga, ga, ga," and the insects fly around but don't know where the honey is. . . . So you don't know how to take the honey out, but Kriyananda, a foreign *brahmachārī*, has come for two days, but he has got that capacity of holding this body for six hours private.[89]

Swami Gitananda, a *sannyāsinī* in Kankhal, told about an event she witnessed in Varanasi in which "Mā's grace descended on those who were pure and simple." An illiterate, poor, woman (she implied low-caste) had lost her beloved cat. She entered a gathering of important devotees at the Banaras ashram uninvited and unannounced. She reported that she had been on a boat in the middle of the Ganges intending to commit suicide when she saw Mā's ashram on the shore and decided not to. According to Gitananda, "Mā gave the same importance to the poor woman who had lost her cat as she gave to these great scholars." After letting the woman tell her story, Mā invited her to move into the ashram saying, "From today, this body is [I am] Gopāl [Lord Krishna as a child] *and* your cat. You will stay here and serve this body!" For the next three years, she cooked for Mā and fed her. When devotees complained, Mā said, "Well, you do not approve of anyone who stays near this body! They have to do what you like or you don't approve of them!" After three years, the woman asked to go back to her guru's ashram, and Mā was pleased and said, "For three years there was still this latent suicidal tendency. Now she has gotten over it."[90]

Abhijit and Mira Chatterji, an elderly couple in Calcutta, emphasized that Mā's grace was always available to everyone. According to Mira,

Mā used to love everybody. She knew everyone in her own way. You didn't have to speak. Language was not important. God knows all languages. Whatever you wanted, you got it. Europeans, Indians, from so many countries. Even the poor, the poorest person coming from Chitrakut. When the car was passing, there were old ladies with bundles of vegetables and Mā was smelling them. Mā went into one lady's house. People say she only belongs to the rich. No, she belongs to the poor, to everyone. No, everyone was near and dear, everyone. She used to tell people, "Don't stop people from coming. Let them come near this body."

Abhijit added, "There is a saying that Ānandamayī Mā walks in the pockets of only rich people. It is not true, we happen to be brahmans, but not everyone was brahman. Where else can in ill person come besides a hospital? Mā said, 'This body is like a hospital, let anybody come who wants to get cured.' "[91]

According to most of her devotees, Mā was oblivious to caste, but she deferred to her brahman devotees to encourage them to be near her. As a result, she has been called "a saint for the Hindu upper classes." Certainly, since her *samādhi*, residents in her ashrams have been primarily brahman. A devotee told me that, although theoretically any Indian can come to the ashram in Kankhal, for example, in reality, all will not be welcome. Everyone living there is either brahman or *kayastha* (a nonbrahman high caste), with the exception of a few *vaishyas* and perhaps one *sūdra*.

When I asked Rupa Vishvanathan why Mā allowed her brahman devotees to dictate caste regulations in the ashram, she resorted to the "piety of indeterminacy," the assumption of the unknowability of the divine, saying,

> It is very difficult to know Mā. We have known her for nearly forty years . . . and I think there are certain things we do not understand. Mā [said] she has come to accept everything and not to destroy it. That is why. . . Mā didn't tell them, "Oh, *ātman* is one. Why do you observe these things?" and things like that. She said, "Yes, you can do what you like." You know, she accepted everyone from their own understanding, on their own level. And that is difficult for us to understand. We think as a great person she should have guided them and made them do certain things. But that was not her method of teaching. She wanted them to evolve on their own.[92]

As one might expect, Mā's actual words on caste indicate that on the ultimate level there can be no distinctions of caste. For example, in Dehradun in 1974, she said,

> See the people doing *dandavat pranām* [prostrating like a stick in obeisance in front of Mā]? Why? Because they think that their soul is different from the one to whom they are paying homage. But in fact both are one and the same. This is the attitude of "mine" and "thine" which is causing all this fighting, quarrel and massacre. . . . But actually there is He alone. . . . Why then this "untouchability?"[93]

In Brindavan in 1975, Mā said,

> Some people follow *sanatana dharma* [the orthodox caste system]. But for a person who is *ātmasthā* [abiding in the Self], who has attained *mukti* [liberation], there is no such discrimination based on caste or creed. There is no caste or creed for a person who is free from the point of view of place and time.[94]

As a young bride, Nirmalā Sundarī, later known as Ānandamayī Mā, began to withdraw more and more from everyday activities into states of spiritual ecstasy. Her husband, Bholanāth, while bewildered and frustrated at first, became convinced that his wife was a manifestation of the Goddess. (Photo courtesy of Matri Satsang.)

In the early years in Dacca (1924–1928), Ānandamayī Mā's radiant presence drew thousands to have her *darshan*, or the auspicious sight of a deity. (Photo courtesy of Matri Satsang.)

Ānandamayī Mā directed the
sādhana, or spiritual practices, of
many of her close devotees,
beginning with her husband,
Bholanāth (right) and her first
devotee, Jyotishchandra Ray,
affectionately known as Bhaiji
(left). The three of them traveled
extensively together throughout
northern India in the years
between 1928 and 1938, according to the instructions of Mā's
kheyāla, or divine will. (Photo
courtesy of Matri Satsang.)

Upon meeting her for the first time,
Paramahamsa Yogananda said of Ānandamayī Mā, "Oblivious to her outward
garb as a woman, she knew herself only
as the changeless soul. . . . Never before
had I met such an exalted woman
saint. Her gentle face was burnished
with the ineffable joy that had given
her the name of the Blissful Mother."
(Photo courtesy of Matri Satsang.)

Hindu saints are known by their states of absorption in the divine. Ānandamayī Mā said, "What is suffering? To feel that God is far away. If one starts feeling God's presence in everything in the world and sees the world to be His play, one will never feel any sorrow." (Photo courtesy of Matri Satsang.)

Ānandamayī Mā displayed classical *bhavas*, or ecstatic states of immersion in the divine, throughout her life, especially during the chanting of *kirtan*, or devotional songs. (Photo courtesy of Matri Satsang.)

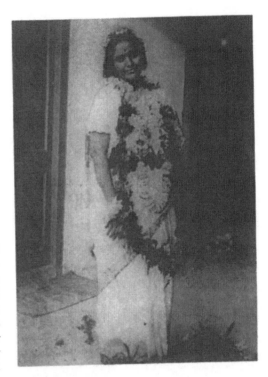

Always willing to respond to the desires of her devotees, Ānandamayī Mā was often the focus of ritual worship, known as *pūjā*. Here she gracefully wears garlands offered her by her devotees. (Photo courtesy of Matri Satsang.

Occasionally, Ānandamayī Mā's devotees requested her to dress as a certain deity, at which time they would worship her as God in that form. Some devotees tell stories of dancing with Mā dressed as Krishna, taking part in Krishna's spontaneous *līlā*, or play. (Photo courtesy of Matri Satsang.)

Devotees of Ānandamayī Mā often describe her contagious laughter and the joy they felt in her presence. (Photo courtesy of Matri Satsang.)

Ānandamayī Mā said, "You may want to banish this body from your mind. But this body won't leave you for a single day—it does not and never will leave your thought. Whoever has once been drawn to love this body will never succeed in wiping out its impression even despite hundreds of attempts. This body rests and shall remain in [her] memory for all times." (Photo courtesy of Matri Satsang.)

Yet Mā chose to defer to her brahman devotees. She relates a poignant story about an Austrian woman devotee, Atmananda:

> Let me explain it with a living example. You know Atmananda? She has been with me for thirty years. She is a life-long celibate. . . . One day she said to this body, "Mā, how is it that the cat goes everywhere, even in your house? Does it spoil the purity? I cannot go everywhere. I cannot eat sitting with others. I cannot sit with everybody. Why is it so?" I said, "What can I do? It is all the things of the *shāstras*. They say it like that. One has to go towards God from the place that one lives. Do not be perturbed." Atmananda said, "Mā, cannot the Mother Ganges purify me?" I said, "Go ask this question to the pandits and do as they say." But she said, "Why should I listen to them? I touch you. That is enough for me." Then one day she came back and said, "I shall go to the ashram of Ramana Maharshi. There is no untouchability practiced in that ashram. All sit together and eat." I told her, " Go to that ashram. Even if you go there, nothing will change as far as this body is concerned. My door is ever open for everybody. You will find it open when you come back. You can come back any time. This body shall take anything from your hand."
>
> What happened, this body went to Almora. After a few days Atmananda came there. I said, "Hello, are you here? Didn't you go?" She replied, "How to go, Mā? I can't. Whatever be the case, I must be here only." I thought, "Oh, my Lord! Oh, my Goddess! You have come in the form of this woman to live with me!" Her cottage was made in the ashram and now she lives in it and cooks her own food.[95]

Mā, in her unity awareness, clearly made no caste distinctions. Like the *bhakti* saints of the past, she renounced caste and invited all people to take refuge in her. Yet, within her ashrams, she complied with the enforcement of caste restrictions that contracted the inclusiveness of her vision and limited her accessibility.

Devotion to God

A saint in the Hindu tradition is intensely devoted to God. There is no need to equivocate about Mā's absolute, one-pointed devotion to God. Mā implored everyone to become absorbed in God. In Suktal in 1962, Mā said, "What is suffering? To feel that God is far away. If one starts feeling God's presence in everything in the world and sees the world to be His play, one will never feel any sorrow."[96] In the same *satsang*, Mā described how to come closer to God, the method of many saints in the *bhakti* tradition:

> What is the method? Recite the name of your beloved you like best. That is all. You have to call your beloved. Do that in whatever way you want. You can recite the name of God at any time you want. You can remember him all the time. And just as your beloved is always there in your heart, you can still try to have that Lord awakened in your mind through meditation and *japa*. There is one simple way—just call him.[97]

Many of her devotees told me that everything Mā said and did reflected her total absorption in the divine. Subodh Chattaraj said, "You could be talking about anything—your business, the weather, the marriage of your daughter—and Mā would bring the subject back to God. Very subtly. But soon you would realize you were talking about God."[98] Others told me about how much Mā loved *kīrtan* and how she could sing for hours, completely absorbed in the name of God. Mā's absorption in the divine also took the form of spontaneous *līlās*, or devotional plays, with a small group of women devotees. Her unquestionable devotion to God included different states of ecstatic absorption. Vasudha-Di told a story of how she and Nirmala Chatterji, a famous devotional singer and also one of Mā's celibate devotees, were called to respond to Mā's God absorption in the following way:

> It was Mā's birthday celebration when we do the *kīrtan* of "Mā, Mā." In the morning Mā had the *kheyāla* to ask me, very privately, to make three sets of frocks and ornaments, one for Shiva-Pārvatī, one for Rādhā-Krishna, and one for Sītā-Rām. She said, "Don't tell anyone." So I made them in the basement of Kishenpur ashram. That night when we started our *kīrtan*, one by one Mā was calling us up away from the *kīrtan*. She called two Kanyapith girls for Shiva and Pārvatī, two for Sītā and Rām, and then she called me and dressed me as Rādhā. Finally she called Nirmala-Di out of the *kīrtan*. She pointed to me and said, "Look, you like this Rādhā?" We were all laughing like anything, enjoying. And Mā decorated Nirmala-Di and fixed her hair like Krishna and put on the frock and the ornaments. Then she made us, Rādhā and Krishna, sit in the center. She switched off the lights in the hall. Then she turned on the lights, like a play. And she herself did the *ārati* [waving of the lights in worship], around and around. After the *ārati*, she took me as Rādhā and she danced with me. Then she took hold of Nirmala-Di and danced with her as Krishna. She danced like the *Rās Līlā* [dance of Krishna and the *gopīs*]. She was in full *bhāva*—drunk with God. She went round and round. Then she took Shiva and she placed him like Natarāj [dancing Shiva]. The *bhāva* was wonderful. And no one was watching. Mā would never have allowed.[99]

It is clear, then, that Ānandamayī Mā displayed all of the elements that establish the moral presence of the Hindu saint; renunciation, egolessness, and intense devotion to God.

Mā's Bhāvas as Evidence of Her Powerful Presence

According to Babb, the transformative field of the Hindu saint is created when the saint's moral presence is fused with his or her powerful presence, as expressed in his or her *bhāvas*, or ecstatic states of immersion in the divine, and in his or her miraculous powers, or *siddhis*. June McDaniel maintains that *bhāva*, defined as "spiritual ecstasy," is "the major criterion for female saints and holy women in Bengal."[100] Religious ecstasy and divine madness have been criteria for identifying saints of the *bhakti* tradition since its flowering in southern India between the sixth and eighth centuries. In the *Bhakti Sūtra* of Nārada, a classical text on *bhakti* thought to have been composed between 900 and 1100 C.E., the author describes one who has realized divine love as intoxicated or mad (*mattah*), fascinated to the point of losing the power of independent action (*stambhah*), and immersed in the bliss of the Self (*ātmārāmah*).[101] Later he speaks of the signs of *bhakti* as a choking voice (*kanthāvarodha*), the thrilling of body hair (*romāncha*), and a flow of tears (*ashru*).[102] Within *bhakti* circles in Bengal, these signs would be considered manifestations of *bhāva*,[103] in both the Vaishnava and the Shākta traditions. Ānandamayī Mā was Vaishnava by birth and Shākta by marriage, so both are relevant. Vaishnava *bhakti* has two elaborate listings of *bhāvas*, enumerated in the *Bhaktirasāmritasindhu*: *anubhāvas*, indicators of *bhāva* within the mind, and *sāttvika bhāvas*, spontaneous organic manifestations of emotions originating in pure spirit.[104] *Anubhāvas* include dancing, rolling on the ground, singing, screaming, roaring, and wild laughter. *Sāttvika bhāvas* include immobility, thrilling of body hair, sweating, crying, changing skin color, and loss of consciousness. In the Shākta tradition, a devotee might be ecstatically absorbed in the worship of the Divine Mother and exhibit divine madness for her, as did Sri Ramakrishna Paramahamsa, or relate to the sacred feminine as the *kundalinī*, the serpentlike spiritual energy of the subtle body. The ecstatic symptoms, sometimes called *kriyās*, or involuntary yogic activities include waves of bliss, visions of lights and deities, hearing mantras, involuntary yogic postures (*mudrās* and *āsanas*), trembling of the body, involuntary deep breathing or cessation of breath, a feeling of spirit possession, and feeling as if dead or paralyzed. In both traditions, various degrees of *samādhi*, or deep trance, are considered a form of *bhāva*.[105]

In the community of Ānandamayī Mā, *bhāva* seems to be an important indicator of Mā's extraordinary "personality." As described in chapter 2, spiritual biographers describe Mā as having experienced states of spiritual ecstasy from early childhood. In interviews, fifteen devotees reported having witnessed Mā in states of *bhāva*, in answer to my request to talk about experiences that would show who Mā was. Many more mentioned her *bhāvas* as an indication of her extraordinariness. Both the spiritual biographies and the interviews describe Mā's frequent states of *samādhi* with varying degrees of withdrawal from the body.

According to Mā's spiritual biographies, Nirmalā was seen in states of ecstasy even as a toddler, especially during *kīrtan*, with symptoms that included immobility, spontaneous devotional singing, and crying, all recognized Vaishnava *bhāvas*. As she grew older, *kīrtan*, and especially the sound of the drum, continued to affect her in the same way. She also fell into trancelike states at other times, such as in the middle of performing chores, playing, or eating. As a young girl of perhaps nine or ten, while participating in an annual Kumārī Pūjā, she "fell into a trance and began to recite some mantras," technically a Shākta yogic *kriyā*. Furthermore, relating to nature is said to have brought on *bhāvas* in young Nirmalā. She is described as "leaping and jumping in the air, dancing and singing, surging in exaltation and exhilaration,"[106] when communing with trees and flowers, again signs of Vaishnava *bhāva*.

When Nirmalā went to live with her husband's family after her marriage, although she was the model sister-in-law and worked her fingers to the bone, she did have "a few instances of trances which were by and large interpreted as 'spells of absentmindedness' or 'sleepiness.'" But, significantly, Mā's spiritual biographies associate the revelation of her "true identity" with the public revelation of her states of *bhāva*, beginning at Ashtagrama, where her first devotee, Hārkumār, called attention to her ecstatic states and where Nirmalā was observed in *bhāva* for the first time by those outside her family. At the second *kīrtan*, Mā is described as first rolling on the ground and quivering with her hair standing on end, then laughing and crying, and finally sitting motionless. Her face is described as "bathed in a radiant glow," possibly referring to the change of skin color listed among the *sāttvika bhāvas*.

This pattern of ecstatic response to *kīrtan* is said to have continued for many years, certainly through 1928. I heard three firsthand accounts of incidents in later years by older devotees who described a very similar pattern. The first one took place in Solan in 1936, when Sita Gupta, a householder devotee, was eighteen. It was confirmed by Abhijit and Mira Chatterji. Sita Gupta says,

> In the evening Mā came. The *kīrtan* was almost over. Everyone was getting more enthusiastic and an echo started resounding. Mā started dancing in a circle. We all caught hands and made a circle around Mā. Mā took five to six rounds. Suddenly she lay on the floor and started rotating, like the earth moves around the sun, like a dry leaf. The *kīrtan* came to an end. Everyone was gazing at Mā, amazed. Mā was still rolling. After ten minutes, she sat up. Her face looked like the sun, there was such a reddish glow, and her eyes had an eternal gaze. She started reciting verses, in something like Pali, something close to Sanskrit. It was as if she were listening to some very sweet melodious music very far off. Then she said some mantras for five or ten minutes. Then gradually she started to come back. At that time everybody touched her feet. Didi took her inside her room.[107]

The second incident was witnessed in 1942 by Gauri and Sharada Chatterjee, who were twelve and thirteen years old at the time.

> So people would make a pedestal in the middle with photographs of Rām and Krishna, decorated with flowers and such. And they would sing *kīrtan* and circle around from sunrise to sunset. And this time, when the *kīrtan* was almost over, Mā also joined in. And she was also going around like that. They were chanting, "*Hare Krishna, Hare Rām.*" And Mā—her hands were going like this [her arms up the air], just like that. And after some time, her head was hanging back and it was touching there [her waist in the back]. I'm not exaggerating. It's very hard to do. It really happened. And we were crying loudly because we were young and we thought there was something wrong with Mā. And no one was supposed to touch her like that, only Swamiji and Gurupriya Devi. They were allowed. And her voice! And then she fell like a leaf on the ground. She was rolling. Her whole body rolling like a dry leaf! After that her face was glowing, just like it was two thousand light bulbs

inside her mouth. And she couldn't even talk. You couldn't understand her speech. But Gopinath Kaviraj, afterwards he said it was Pali, a kind of Sanskrit. And her eyes were half-closed. And tears were coming out, unending tears. It was terrible and it was wonderful![108]

The phenomenon of rolling "like dry leaves" was described by Leela Mitra, a householder devotee in Calcutta, who reported seeing it when she was ten: "I saw her. It was always the same thing—rolling on the ground around the house. Mā described it herself, saying, 'Dry leaves, this body rolls like that. When the wind comes, the dry leaves move in the road. As the dry leaves roll, so does this body.'"[109]

These states often included *attahāsi*, or "laughter like thunder," as described by six devotees and mentioned by several others. Swami Gitananda referred to it as "the laughter that goes on at all eight levels" and said,

> When I saw Mā, the first thing that struck me was her *attahāsi*. Such joyful laughter reverberates out of all the pores of Mā's body. The laughter and supreme bliss was coming out of her, radiating unlike any human being. I felt both wonderment and joy. I wondered to see such a person. No human being can laugh like this.[110]

According to Gita-Di Bose, a female householder devotee in Calcutta, "When Mā used to laugh, your hairs would stand on end. Everyone was electrified. This laugh was not of this world!" When I asked if it had been frightening, she replied, "No, it was exciting. The sound went into your body. It is a very particular feeling in your body."[111]

Before 1918, the beginning of Mā's *"līlā of sādhana,"* most of her *bhāvas* were, as described previously, Vaishnava *bhāvas,* usually in response to *kīrtan.* Between 1918 and 1924, however, during her period of practicing *sādhana,* Mā began to display classic *kundalinī* yoga *kriyās.* After Bholanāth went to bed, we are told, Nirmalā "would sit in a perfect yogic posture on the floor in the corner of the room and repeat the name of God." Her body would then assume spontaneous yogic postures, *āsanas,* and hand gestures, *mudrās.* She performed spontaneous *kumbhaka,* or deep breathing, and other forms of *prānayama,* or breath control. Mā reports that after she was instructed by Bholanāth to start using a Shākta mantra, "the yogic postures performed by this body became even more intricate."

When Sanskrit mantras and verses began to flow from Nirmalā's lips in the presence of outsiders, Bholanāth hired an *ojhā,* or spirit exorcist, to "put an end to the improper behavior of his wife." McDaniel notes that in Bengal, recognition of *bhāvas* in women saints is usually preceded by accusations of madness,[112] and four of five Bengali women saints she profiled were accused of being mad before being recognized as exhibiting *bhāvas.* Many were treated by either exorcism or Ayurvedic medicine, but the treatments usually backfired.[113] That was certainly the case with Mā, since the *ojhā* ended up falling to the ground and moaning, "Mā, Mā," finally recovering, and then referring to Mā as "Bhagavatī herself." Mā's states of *bhāva* began to interfere with her duties as a housewife, and within a few years she was unable to cook and care for the household. Although some scholars have maintained that certain women within both the Hindu and the Christian traditions have managed to escape their traditional role as caretaker and food preparer by exhibiting abnormal behavior, which was then labeled as divine ecstasy,[114] it is difficult to imagine that Mā was feigning states of divine ecstasy out of that motivation.

Devotees maintain that Mā's *bhāvas* became less frequent over time. Gauri Chatterji told me that Mā predicted that that would happen. She said, "Mā used to say, 'My behavior will gradually become more and more normal.'"[115] Although Mā may have appeared *more* normal, there is still evidence of dramatic states of *bhāva* and *samādhi* in the later years. Brahmacharini Chandan, for example, describes an incident during the celebration of Mā's birthday in 1981, when Indirā Gandhi was about to visit:

> The Prime Minister was informed that on the morning of this particular day, Mā was not found in a normal state. . . . On learning this, [she said she would come] at 1:30 in the afternoon and remain in Mā's proximity as long as it was possible. In order that Indirāji might have Mā's company in her normal state, we all combined our effort, repeatedly calling Mā to make Her get up and sit. . . . We tried to rub the soles of Her feet and palms of Her hands quickly. . . . It was observed that Her entire body, starting from the toes, was a lump of flesh. . . . The entire body was unnatural. . . . Then she suddenly turned from one side to another. There followed many other changes, strange as they all were. I am unable to describe the changed contours of Her face. To say that it was like that of a small child—this analogy too is inadequate. The eyes turned steadily upwards, it seemed as if they could not be directed by any means. Then slowly, She looked, with eyes turned reddish in hue, and the manner of Her first look, I cannot describe in any language. In fact, all these were beyond description.[116]

In her *satsangs* with her devotees, Mā herself emphasized *bhāva* as an indication of spiritual depth and sincerity.

> Do you know what real worship is? The expression of man's love of God. When something is boiled in a closed vessel, there comes a stage when the vapor will push up the lid and, unless force is used, the vessel cannot be kept covered anymore. In a similar manner, when, while being engaged in *japa* or some other spiritual exercises a wave of ecstatic emotion surges up from within, it becomes difficult to check it. This ecstatic emotion is called *bhāva*. It emerges from deep within and expresses itself outwardly. At first it arises only for brief spells but by spiritual practices it is gradually strengthened. For *Mahābhāva*, the supreme source of divine love and inspiration is present in every human being and, given the opportunity, it functions freely and spontaneously. [To the degree] that this state of divine love becomes more constant, the aspirant is vouchsafed a glimpse of his Beloved. Religious practices carried out mechanically, without *bhāva*, are like artificial flowers: very beautiful to look at, but devoid of perfume. *Kīrtana* may be performed in great style, the hall almost breaking with the throng of the congregation,

but if the singing is without *bhāva*, there will be no response from on high. The deity answers only to the call of the heart.[117]

In another conversation, Mā indicates that divine madness is an intrinsic part of realizing God.

Go forth to realize God, try at least. This is the genuine madman. Madman (*pagol*) means *paoya gol* (to reach the goal), signifying unlimited Enlightenment. When one becomes obsessed by this madness, the madness for the world of duality takes flight. Some people are crazy over another's body. By this sort of insanity, falling prey to infatuation (*moha*), one ruins one's body. Turning into a madman after God will not spoil one's body.[118]

Yet I observed among Ānandamayī Mā's community a certain aversion to states of ecstasy. For example, I was invited by two devotees whom I had interviewed to a *kīrtan* session at the home of another devotee in Varanasi. The group of twenty or so sat in front of the family altar, which held a picture of Mā, a picture of the family guru, and pictures of ancestors. Alternating harmonium players led us in a series of chants, some dedicated to Mā, some to Krishna, some to Shiva. A middle-aged woman sitting next to me began to fall into states of ecstasy while chanting the name of Lord Krishna. She was exhibiting *bhāvas,* which included dancing, shivering, and falling into a sort of trance in my lap. After the evening was over, she apologized and told me that for a minute, she thought I was Lord Krishna. When I left with my friends, several people made a point of disassociating themselves from the woman, saying, "She is not a regular devotee." She was the only person I witnessed in a truly ecstatic state in my time with Mā's Indian devotees. At most *kīrtans* and *āratis*, worship services where Mā is honored with offerings, people seemed relatively controlled and rational. The only signs of absorption I saw were occasional clapping, closing of eyes, and swaying.

Like the domestication of Mā's life story, devotees' disassociation from *bhāva* might be explained by Weber's concept of the "routinization of charisma," which Hawley and Juergensmeyer define as "a process whereby personal magnetism is transmuted into institutional authority." They point out that Kabir, the iconoclastic fifteenth-century saint-poet of northern India, is now worshiped as a deity in orthodox services.[119] Likewise, despite Mā's valorization of *bhāva* and divine madness, there seems to be a tendency to elevate her to deity and worship her in an orthodox way, rather than imitate her ecstasy.

A second way to understand Mā's devotees' aversion to displays of *bhāva* might be Mā's apparent contextual shift from Bengali Vaishnava to Bengali Shākta to northern Indian Neo-Vedānta or Advaitin. Within the Advaitin context, it is *jñāna,* or knowledge, not *bhāva,* that is the important indicator of spiritual attainment. As mentioned in chapter 3, Neevel has shown how the devotees of Shri Ramakrishna "Vedantafied" his life story and his teaching, deemphasizing his ecstatic Shākta and tantric characteristics and experiences and emphasizing his Advaitin orientation. We might be observing the same phenomenon within the community of Ānandamayī Mā.

Besides displaying states of *bhāva*, the powerful presence of a Hindu saint performs miracles based on miraculous powers, or *siddhis*. Within the Hindu tradition, as within the Christian tradition, there is a certain ambivalence toward miracles. Christianity has often expressed disdain for miracles and held that demonstration of one's moral presence and virtue is more important than performance of a miracle, for "even demons can work wonders."[120] Within the Hindu tradition, although "miracles seem to define the biography of a saint as opposed to that of a secular hero,"[121] there is a sense that one should not focus on mere phenomenal miracles but rather on the saint's power to transform people's lives. In addition, one should not covet *siddhis* or get attached to them. Mā once said:

> Wonderful powers are acquired [as a consequence of successful *sādhana*]. [But] all that the spiritual aspirant should do is to watch. Once he indulges in playing with those powers, he misses the chance of reaching the destination and gets stuck up on the way. Supposing you are bound for the railway station from the ashram. On your way you will come across many buildings, the college, etc. You will be able to reach the railway station only if you proceed onwards without caring for what you see on the way. If, on the contrary, you get interested in the college, enter in to the building and enjoy what you see there, there will be no certainty as to your arrival at the railway station.[122]

This teaching mirrors the instruction given by Patanjali as he concludes his list of siddhis: Having gained the mastery of the mind which yields fantastic *siddhis*, a yogi should renounce them and covet only God realization. In both Hindu and Christian contexts, then, there is a recognition that extraordinary people perform extraordinary acts, as well as a warning that one should not focus on either developing them or valuing them too much.

John Carman wonders whether debate over the existence of miracles is a relatively contemporary phenomenon that parallels the shaping of the Western concept of "miracle" over the last two centuries: to name that which cannot be explained by science. In India, such a definition is still largely unnecessary, and few words correspond to "miracle."[123] One reason the concept of "miracle" has not taken root in the Hindu context is the belief that the proper practice of yoga inevitably results in the acquisition of *siddhis*, or extraordinary powers. A *siddhi* simply reflects a yogi's command of the laws of nature as they are understood within the yogic paradigm. For example, the *siddhi* of *laghiman*, or the lightness of body which enables a yogi to fly through the air, is described by Patanjali as the result of achieving concentration, meditation, and absorption on the relationship between the body and the ether.[124] Swami Krishnananda, a *sannyāsin* devotee in Kankhal, a man in his eighties who had once walked the length of the Ganges and back with no possessions, very matter-of-factly described this *siddhi*:

I would be walking and suddenly I would see that the body is going very fast like a thing up in the air. And then I would get a shock [when I looked down] but something said, "Don't try to stop it. If you stop all your bones will go and be dispersed if you fall." So then I would just carry on with my work and at the moment I was conscious that the body was moving fast, it gradually slowed down.[125]

Krishnananda did not see this as a miracle, but as a *siddhi*, which is the result of the successful performance of *sādhana*.

In *Autobiography of a Yogi*, Yogananda Paramahamsa devotes an entire chapter to "The Law of Miracles," in which he describes the science of yoga. He says that a yogi, through perfect meditation, merges "his consciousness with the Creator and perceives the cosmic essence as light. . . . The law of miracles is operable by any man who has realized that the essence of creation is light. A master is able to employ his divine knowledge of light phenomena to project instantly into perceptible manifestation the ubiquitous light atoms."[126] Thus, according to Yogananda, a yogi can manipulate the environment in extraordinary ways.

A second aspect of the Hindu worldview that renders the word "miracle" irrelevant is the tradition's valorization of a "piety of indeterminacy." If someone performs an act which cannot be understood with the rational mind—for example, appearing in two places at the same time—a traditional Hindu is likely to assume a holy or divine association with that act before he or she would question that the act actually occurred. A Hindu guru, Shrīmat Ānandāshram Swami, explains it this way:

That lives of saints teem with miracles is a fact known to you all. . . . It is not the purpose of today's discourse to declare our views as to whether such incidents are probable or are products of mere poetic fancy; whether they are useful even if they are probable; and whether it is necessary, as contended by moderns to expunge them from lives of saints and to make such lives simple and understandable like those of ordinary men. . . . If the faithful explain such incidents in one way, moderns may explain them in another. Nevertheless, this does not affect the view that seemingly wonderful things do occur in this world. The power of Paramātman is unbounded. It can bring about strange occurrences. Hence if a miracle takes place, it is in consonance with the nature of that power, and is, therefore, natural. Similarly, there are ever so many laws of nature not yet known to us, and it is possible that incidents which appear miraculous to us are in harmony with such laws. Accordingly when a seeming miracle occurs, we can only infer that it must be in accordance with a law of nature not yet known to us, and it will not be right to deny it merely because it does not fall within the compass of our limited experience.[127]

Devotees of Ānandamayī Mā told countless stories of occurrences that fall outside "the compass of our limited experience" when asked about who Mā was. These stories were reported to me by primarily Western-educated devotees, some of whom were scientists. They challenge our sense of what is possible because they cannot be considered hagiographic accretions on the story of a saint of the past; they are events devotees actually witnessed, experiences they actually had. Often in the course of an interview, devotees would throw up their hands and say, "Who can understand Mā?" Rarely did they try to explain the experiences.

Forty-three of forty-four interviews contain stories of "miraculous" events devotees associated with Mā. Eleven interviews contain twelve incidents of miraculous healings attributed to her. Thirteen relate nineteen incidents of Mā's reading devotees' minds. Thirty-one interviews contain fifty-eight stories of other kinds of miracles associated with Mā, such as her appearance in dreams or visions, her protection of devotees, her fulfilling devotees' desires, and even her intervention in global conflicts. There were many stories demonstrating her *siddhis*, such as her knowledge of the past, present, or future; her materialization of objects; and her omniscience. Six devotees brought up the subject of miracles and offered some explanation of the role of miracles in the phenomenon of Ānandamayī Mā.

My first encounter with such a story was during the first interview I conducted in India, which happened to be with a nondevotee. I was invited to the house of Mahendranath Dev, a middle-aged brahman Sanskrit pandit, to whom I had been directed by professors at Banaras Hindu University. They said he could "tell me a story about Mā, although he was not a devotee of hers." Talking with a nondevotee seemed like a good way to begin the interviewing process. I arrived at a small adobe house, where I was greeted very warmly by Mahendranath Dev, who introduced me to his wife and his four beautiful young daughters. He spoke little English, so a colleague of his was to translate. I turned on my tape recorder and asked him to tell me about his experiences with Mā. He seemed shy, and I had to ask him to speak up to ensure that his voice would be heard on the recording. He said,

> I met with Mā in 1981. She was performing a *yajna* [a fire sacrifice] at that time. It was called the *Atiyuga Yajna*. Here in Varanasi. From time to time we used to assemble with Mā to discuss the method of performing the *yajna*, how and when and in what way. We had the best opportunity to see the Mother, even in seclusion, when nobody was allowed to see her. It was a private meeting. It has been heard by so many persons that Mā has got the *shakti* [spiritual power] and she has got *siddhis*. I saw one of her *siddhis* one day.
>
> Mā was taking rest in her room one day alone. I went to her with two or three of my friends with very urgent work. She used to take much interest in the performance of the *yajna*. Therefore she used to see us in her room. She was lying in her bed and her mouth was covered with a cloth. We saluted the Mother and sat beside her. She said after a few minutes, "Be seated with me and I will show you something, but please don't get afraid." She got up and sat on her bed and she removed the cloth that had covered her mouth. The face of the Mother had become very ugly. The lower lip and the chin were hanging down. They were swollen. They hung three to four inches below. We were wonderstruck to see this. Mother said, "Don't worry, I'll just make myself normal."

Within a few seconds Mother made her face normal as if she were chewing something. And then she said, "Now you can talk about the matter you came with." We talked but we still had some curiosity to ask her about her face. We asked her, "What was happening to your face?" She said, "This is the fruit of karma that this body bears and it is also the fruit of the karmas of devotees that it has taken on." She had the power to imbibe the karmas of the devotees. She said everyone has to bear the fruit of the actions he has done, past or present. The fruit that she is bearing is the fruit of the actions of her devotees. When her devotees touch her feet, she takes it on.[128]

This story propelled me into the extraordinary world of Ānandamayī Mā. It was made all the more remarkable by the matter-of-fact quality of its delivery by the shy, unassuming nondevotee. The *siddhi* referred to in this story is the power to take on the karma of one's devotees, which, although it is not listed among Patanjali's classic yogic powers, is a *siddhi* attributed to many Hindu saints and gurus. Lawrence Babb says of the Radhasoami sect:

When the sant satgurus of the Soami Bagh line were living, offerings from devotees to their gurus were a central feature of the congregational life. . . . An implicit idea in this pattern seems to be that what a devotee gives the guru carries something of himself or herself with it. . . . [Thus] an offering to a guru would appear to be, among other things, a possible vehicle through which the offerer can deliver up impurities, his or her "sins," which are taken by the guru into or onto himself. This concept has a deep paradigm in Hindu mythology. When the gods and demons churned the ocean in order to obtain ambrosia, Shiva swallowed the residual poison, holding it in his throat and thus becoming the "blue-necked god". . . . When the infant Krishna killed the stinking demoness Pūtanā—who had tried to kill him by offering him a poison-smeared breast—he did so by sucking her life from her body. When her body was burned, the smoke was sweet in smell; she was purified, for in sucking away the poison, Krishna had destroyed her sins.[129]

The twentieth-century Hindu saint Neem Karoli Baba is said to have occasionally imbibed enormous amounts of food given by devotees as an offering in an apparent attempt to eat their karma. A devotee explains that "a very high being can work with subtle vibratory patterns and can take from devotees patterns with which they have been stuck for this lifetime or many lifetimes. . . . In India, such karmic healers often work with things the devotee gives them."[130] Sai Baba of Shirdi, a nineteenth-century saint of Maharashtra, would take coins given to him by devotees and handle them, supposedly extracting from them negative karma. According to Charles White, he would then process this karma through yogic processes.[131]

Two of the twelve stories of miraculous healings associated with Ānandamayī Mā contained this element of "taking on of karma." For example, Gita-Di Bose, a Calcutta housewife and lifetime devotee, told a story about Mā's healing a deadly boil or tumor on her infant brother's head.

My brother, a few months after he was born he got a big boil, behind his ear, big like a double head. The doctors said they could not do anything about it because he was too young to operate and he would die either way. My grandfather was so upset, he went to Mā and said, "I am leaving this boy to you. If you wish him to live, save him. If you wish him to die, leave him." So he came back to the house and the baby was screaming like anything, the whole day and night. So next day Mā came and from the door she looked at my brother and she took him in her lap and fed him some milk. From that day my brother had no pain. She stayed the whole day and he was sitting on her lap, nothing else. In the evening she came in and entered the room where my brother was sleeping with my mother. She asked everyone to leave the room and told my grandfather, "Just stand behind me and don't try to look at what I'm doing." And after that what she did nobody knew. She just told my mother, "Tomorrow morning you will get up, have your bath, and go to that certain tree and near the roots just pull out whatever comes into your hand. Grind it and make a paste and put it on the boil." So my mother did that and this boil burst, the blood drained and it healed.

And then after many years, forty-five years, we all went to Mā. And Mā was sitting in Banaras and many people were sitting. All of a sudden Mā said, looking at my brother, "I have a mark. One of the marks of his body is on this body." You know, at that time, he was supposed to die, but Mā scratched her own hand with a pin, on this side of her hand. And there was a very thin mark on her hand. And still she said, "This body did not do this. It was Mā Kālī who saved him, not this body."[132]

Another story which reflects this pattern was told by Rupa Bose, a *brahmachāriṇī* devotee in Calcutta. When she and another *brahmachāriṇī* were serving Mā, Mā broke her toe in the bathroom, seemingly just placing it on the floor. Rupa-Di was feeling some responsibility for having left a bathmat in Mā's way and felt bad about it, but her friend said, "Someone has fallen down or some big accident has been averted by Mā's taking this on in her own body." That evening, around midnight, a telegram came from Brindavan ashram saying that a swami close to Mā had suffered from a burst appendix and was in critical condition. Rupa-Di jumped up and said, "He would have died but Mā has taken it on her toe and he is still alive!" Apparently Mā did not contradict this assertion. Rupa-Di said that after the surgery, an American doctor at the mission hospital said his survival was a miracle because the appendix was gangrenous and the patient should have died. She ended the story, "So that day Mā took that on."[133]

Ten more stories of healings associated with Mā do not explicitly mention her physically taking on an illness. One, however, claims that Mā directed an exchange to take place in which the mother of a young man who was dying of tuberculosis would herself vomit blood once, and her son would recover. According to Gauri and Sharada Chatterjee, sisters from Varanasi, their father was the young man's honorary uncle, and he begged Mā, saying, "Please take my life and save Prahlad's! You have to do it!" The doctor said, "There is no chance he will survive the night." That night, the young man's mother vomited blood, and his condition started improving. Many years later in Varanasi, Mā told Prahlad, "You are here because of your 'uncle.' He saved your life!"[134] In this story as in others, Mā deflected credit for the healings. When thanked by devotees for saving friends and relatives, she usually replied, "No, no, no! This body didn't save him! God saved him!"

The rest of the healings attributed to Mā include a uterine tumor, diabetes, arthritis, a tumor on the spinal cord, and an ulcer. Several stories emphasized that medical doctors at first held out no hope and later admitted "it must have been a miracle." In the case of Shashi Bhushan Mitra, whose son-in-law was cured of encephalitis and tubercular meningitis, a doctor is reported to have said, "I didn't do anything! I didn't do anything! It is only Mother that did everything!"[135] Such statements reflect a culture in which even scientists believe in the possibility of divine intervention by extraordinary individuals.

Most "miracle stories" attest to Mā's alleged *siddhi* of mind reading. In nineteen stories, devotees said that Mā read their unspoken desire and fulfilled it. Five such stories were about desires for material things. For example, Malini-Di, a *brahmachārinī* who had been with Mā from birth, told me,

> There was this *Bhāgavat saptah* [chant to Lord Krishna]. . . . So Mā was distributing the *Shrīmad Bhāgavatam* to all the ashram girls. So she had given to everybody, almost. So I was standing [there]. . . . and a very childish thought came into my mind that, "Mā has given everybody the *Bhāgavat* and she hasn't given me one. And maybe she wants everybody's salvation but mine." You know, it was a very sincere thought and suddenly I turned and she looked at me. . . . So soon after that she went to her room and one of the girls was feeding Mā. . . . So I went to see what Mā was doing, and as I peeped in, the girl had just put a sweet in Mā's mouth, you see. So she couldn't speak. Mā did like this, "Mmmmmmm," to call me. Then the girl turned around to see who it was. So she came out, and she said, "Mā is calling you."
>
> So I went in and the first thing Mā said is, "Malini, it's not like that." And she held out two *Shrīmad Bhāgavatam* books in front of me. One was an old hardbound book and one was a new paperback. She held both of them in front of me in two different hands and she said, "Okay, now choose which one you would like to take. . . ." So I chose the old hardbound one [because it will last longer]. And Mā was extremely pleased. And she said, "I had run out of these books. That is the reason why I couldn't give it to you."[136]

A second story of material needs being fulfilled was told by Parvati Banerji, an elderly householder devotee in Calcutta.

> I was once at the Banaras ashram and a devotee of Mā's said, "You have to serve people their lunch." So I started serving, but then I started feeling very, very hungry, in fact so hungry that I said to myself, "I cannot serve anymore." You know tears nearly sprang from my eyes. Then I set the bucket down and sat down and I was talking to myself, berating Mā, saying, "You are a mother, aren't you, can't you see that I am hungry?" And at that instant, just from

upstairs someone called to me, saying, "Please give Parvati her lunch immediately, because she's very hungry!"[137]

Other stories in this category also involved reading devotees' desires for gifts and for food or drink. They seem to be saying that Mā's compassion extends beyond the spiritual into the mundane. Devotees believe that Mā cares about all of their needs, however trivial. Classic texts on the guru say that gurus give their devotees everything, both worldly riches, bhukti, and spiritual riches or liberation, mukti.[138]

Three stories of "mind reading" involved devotees' desiring Mā's darshan. For example, Krishna Bhattacharya, a householder devotee from Varanasi, told this story:

> One day something was going on in Puri, some kind of religious exposition of religious kings. Mother was sitting silently. And all of a sudden she stood on her feet and ran down the ashram and ran to some place. And everybody was saying, "What has happened? Mother is running so speedily!" Then we all came to know that a small girl who could not walk because of polio, she was weeping to see Mother, sitting silently in her house, weeping all the time. And Mother went to her and put her in a wheelchair, and took her to her place. Mother did not know this girl. And this girl, from the age of three could recite all the verses from the Bhagavad Gītā, at so small an age.[139]

This story emphasizes that Mā answered the call of someone who was not a disciple. It implies that she was able to hear this longing because the girl, herself, was somewhat extraordinary.

Four "mind reading" stories were about devotees who secretly wished to touch Mā, which was technically not allowed. In fact, nondevotees often remarked that there seemed to be an army of brahman ladies around Mā repeating one mantra over and over, "Don't touch Mā!"[140] Lalita Kumar, a householder devotee in Kankhal, told two stories about this, one involving her and one another devotee:

> There is one thing I don't know if I should tell you or not. But one day in Banaras I had this feeling. I said to myself, "You know, we call her Mother, and yet we can't run and put our arms around her, put our heads in her lap, do all the things we want to. We are always doing *pranām* [bowing in respect] at a distance." So I was sitting outside Mother's room in Varanasi ashram and one of the girls was inside. She came out and Mā was sitting on her cot and she looked out like this through the doorway and she motioned me in like this. So I went in and then she motioned to me to close the door. So I closed it and, you know, she put her arms around me like this, and I put my head in her lap and she put her arms around me and she hugged me tight. Then she smiled at me and said, "*Aap tik hai?* Everything is alright?" It was such ecstasy, I can't tell you.
>
> There was a Swiss girl. She had seen a flash of Mother's photograph on television and came rushing to India to look for her. And I happened to be in Kanpur when she came for the first time, in her tight jeans and sweater,

looking very hip. And she said to the translator, "I have seen this picture of Mother and I want to be accepted by Mother." And you know, somebody started translating and mother told them to stop. She looked deep into her eyes and she took off the garland she was wearing and threw it so casually to land around her neck. And the girl had tears streaming down her face when she said, "Am I accepted?" And Mother did this [patting her head]. And after a few months she wanted a name. And Mā gave her the name Krishna Priya. And she wanted to touch Mother's feet, she told me later. And nobody is allowed to touch Mother's feet. And Mā was walking up and down the veranda and she came and she put her foot out and said, "Nurse, there is something in my foot." And then there sat Krishna Priya, holding her lotus feet in her hands. Mā said, "If you really want something, it doesn't take a moment to get it. It is in the wanting."[141]

In these two stories we again see that Mā circumvents ashram rules when the devotee's desire is strong enough. In the story of the Swiss woman, Mā seems to be saying that she is compelled to respond to her devotees' earnest desires. Put one way, Mā's *kheyāla* responded to a pure longing for God.

A final mind-reading story, related to the prohibition against touching Mā, was told to me by an elderly *brahmachārinī* woman who ran up to me at the Kankhal ashram when I was about to leave to catch a train to Varanasi. She said, "I must tell you this story before you go!"

One day when I was a young woman, I was drawn to meet Mother. I went to where she was staying in Brindavan and as soon as I saw her I was filled with devotion. I began to throw myself at the feet of Mother. It was natural. But some girls near Mother chastised me, saying, "No one is allowed to touch Mother's feet." That night I had a dream. In the dream Mā was sitting so sweetly on a cot in a beautiful garden. When I approached her, she garlanded me with a *mālā* of flowers and motioned for me to touch her feet, which I did. I awoke with a beautiful feeling. It was so sweet. Many years later I was preparing for Mā to visit the house of my elder brother in Calcutta. When Mā arrived, she seated herself on a cot in the midst of my brother's beautiful garden. Mā beckoned me forward. She took the *mālā* from around her neck and placed it around my neck. Then Mā said, "Isn't there something else you long for?" She pointed to her feet. I pranāmed to touch Mā's feet. I was full of amazement.[142]

Nine miracle stories involved Mā's appearance in dreams to initiate devotees, console them, or give them direction, considered one of the indicators of sainthood within the Hindu tradition. Two devotees told stories of being given mantra initiation by Mā in a dream and then checking with Mā afterward and having her confirm that she had indeed given it to them and that they should repeat the mantra. In the second case, Rupa Visvanathan, a householder devotee, told of receiving a mantra from Mā in a dream, but she told herself that it was simply her subconscious wanting to be close to Mā, and ignored it. Nine years later she had a second dream in which Mā chastised her for not repeating the mantra. This dream moved her to talk to

Mā about both dreams. Mā asked if she had been repeating the mantra, and she replied that she had not because she already had a mantra from another guru, and she had thought the dream was just her subconscious longing. Mā said, "No, I came to you and I have given you a mantra. It was wrong of you not to have chanted it. You had better start doing it."[143]

It seems that Mā, as well as her devotees, took her appearance in their dreams seriously. According to Wendy Doniger O'Flaherty, Indian thought typically considers events which occur in dreams as real and objective as the "hard facts of waking life," and some Indian philosophers consider dreaming *more* real than waking.[144] Another story reinforces this impression. Rupa Bose, a *brahmachāriṇī* from Calcutta, while reading a book on Ramakrishna, had a dream in which Mā and Shrī Ramakrishna stood near her window. Ramakrishna told Mā something, and Mā began embracing Rupa. "Mā was embracing me in her bosom, a very close embrace that I had the feeling of the touch of Mā also," she said. She wrote to Mā of the dream, and when she visited Mā in Calcutta, Didi told her that Mā had responded to Rupa's letter by saying, "Didi, this body has given a special embrace to Rupa and this is the first portion of her spiritual awakening." When she saw her, Mā said, "Now, you remember this incident every day four times, once in the morning, once in the afternoon, once in the evening, and once before you go to bed. Now don't forget that." Rupa told me, "But it would be a lie if I say that I always remember. . . . I try to remember at least once at night but sometimes I forget."[145]

Four interviews contain stories of Mā's appearance in visions, thus being in two places at once. Two women saw Mā in their bedrooms at night, and one man saw her at his father's deathbed. A classic story of Mā's ability to be two places at once was told by a eighty-two-year-old woman, Aparna-Di, a householder devotee in Kankhal ashram.

> I was very fashionable. I had gone to Europe in 1938 with my husband, Dr. Subosh Altekar. He had gone only to meet professors there. I used to see many shops. I had gotten some books in Delhi. I was a very literary person. I don't know how Mother did this. In my heart, I loved to dress well. This was Mother's work. When people used to come to visit me, they would say, "Do no *mahātmas* come to this district?" I said, "I would like to know that myself." One Ayurvedic doctor came and said "One Mātājī has come." I asked, "Can you arrange for me to get there?" He told me it was across the river but he could arrange it. My husband said, "What has happened to you? You want to change your clothes?" But it was all arranged.
>
> It was a very difficult trip. Crossing the Ganges was alright, but on the other side it was not a proper road. The last seven miles were by bullock cart. It was bumping and lurching. I thought I would fall. I was thinking, "Such a hard trip. I am having pain. Is the *mahātma* that great?" Then I noticed a lady walking in the front of the cart. She was holding onto the cart, steadying it with her hand. As soon as we reached the proper place, no lady was there. I had only seen her from the back.
>
> Mātājī gave me time at 11 A.M. I went to her and she asked me, "You

want to talk about something?" I didn't have anything to say, but in my heart she told me to say, "Yes, Mother, I want to say something." When I started to talk, she said, "Come in the back room." She turned and asked me to follow. When I saw her from behind, I recognized that she was the lady who had steadied my cart. I said, "Mā, I saw you from behind, catching my chariot." She said, "Did you see that?" I said, "Yes, you are the same person." I began to cry and I said, "I have seen you catch my cart. Did you?" She said, "Yes. How did you recognize me?" Tears came to my eyes. There were only tears. I was feeling very pure and fresh. Then Mother said, "You are staying here for some time?" I said, "Yes, some days." From that day I never liked comfortable living. I only wanted to reach there to be with her.[146]

Most interesting are the miraculous events associated with Mā after her death, including her appearance in dreams and other manifestations of her presence. One of the questions that I asked most of the devotees I interviewed was "How have things been since Mā's *samādhi?*" This question evoked "miracle stories" related to her presence in dreams or visions since her death, discussions of how nothing had changed, and, less frequently, stories of loneliness and despair.[147]

Several stories relate Mā's appearance in dreams and through her pictures since her death. Narendranath Bose, a young businessman devotee who had known Mā since birth, said the house in which I was staying was in the process of being built when Mā took *samādhi.* He was a student in Boston at that time. Soon after Mā's death, he said:

I was in Boston and had no knowledge of what our new house [in Calcutta] looked like inside, much less what my bedroom was going to look like. But I had a dream that I am in a home which today resembles our home, but at that time I had no idea. And in the dream we were having the *griha pravesh,* you know, the housewarming, the blessing. And I was in that house and there was this really little woman who kept following me. She was wearing her sari over her face and she's following me. I go over the whole building and come into my room and sit on the bed. She follows me and comes in and sits next to me. And it's pretty unusual in India for a woman to do that and I say, "For God's sake, why are you following me? Don't you have any shame?" And as I turned my face toward her, this woman took off her veil and it was Mā, Mā as she was in her thirties and forties. And she looked at me and smiled. What I remember distinctly from the dream was the pattern on the marble floor and where the bed was placed. Today if you walk into my room, the marble floor and the bed are exactly the same.

What can you say? You cannot relate it to the subconscious because it is not an experience that I have had before. My explanation is this. You know, this was her way of showing me that what she meant was eternal and, just because she was not able to be present in her physical manifestation, did not change anything.[148]

Swami Samatananda, an *āchārya,* or teacher, at Mā's ashram in Calcutta, told me that Mā's picture is full of her presence since her death.

This photograph has worked wonders. . . . If you keep this picture in your house for one month, praying "Mā, let me see some miracle," I give you my word, you will see some miracle. It is working wonders. There was a little boy of nine years. He keeps Mā's photograph and tells Mā things and Mā laughs with him. Mā talks to him and gives him guidance. . . . All from the photograph."[149]

Two stories claim that Mā's scent and her energy manifested after her death in the home of a devotee. One story related Mā's alleged appearance since her death *in person* two months before the interview. Rajkumar Roy, a successful Calcutta businessman, met with me in a building he had constructed in his garden in preparation for a visit from Mā in 1974. Shrī Roy said that since Mā's *samādhi*, devotees had been continuing to gather for Samyam Vrata in Kankhal every November. This past November, however, his family and ten or twelve others had decided to spend the time in retreat in his country house an hour outside Calcutta, which has a large *kutir* built for Mā where Mā had stayed in 1975. Mā had promised to return there but had not. The story goes that one morning on the fifth day of the *vrata* the group was meditating in Mā's hall in the *kutir*. A young woman cook, Mena, who was a friend of the family but had never met Mā, was sitting and preparing vegetables on the floor of the veranda attached to Mā's *kutir*. She heard a woman's voice asking, "What are you doing?" and replied, thinking that it was Shrī Roy's wife, "I am cutting vegetables." The woman spoke again, saying, "Come with me. I will take you there." Mena didn't look up, still thinking it was Mrs. Roy. Then the woman said, "Do you hear? Get up. I'll take you there. Come with me." Then Mena saw the woman's feet were not Mrs. Roy's feet, and she realized that Mā had come. She grabbed Mā's legs, crying "Mā, Mā, Mā!" Mā took her arm, lifted her up, and took her to the *kutir*. Rajkumar Roy and the group meditating heard a big bang at the door, and Mena entered, fell down on the floor, and crawled with her arm extended as if trying to grab something. She seemed in a trance. When she came out of it, she told everyone that Mā had brought her in and then had moved toward her photograph at the front of the hall and vanished into the picture.[150] Shrī Roy believes that Mā thus kept her promise to return and demonstrated to her devotees that death could not come between them.

Within the context of the extraordinary abilities of a Hindu saint, it is considered quite ordinary to hear of saints whose presence is felt as strongly or more strongly after their death. It is as if physical death does not inhibit the saint from making his or her presence known and, in fact, may free them up to do transformative work. From the perspective of the science of yoga, it is a commonplace occurrence that can be explained. In *Autobiography of a Yogi*, Yogananda relates a conversation between himself and his dead guru. Yukteswar explains, according to the science of yoga, how he can now materialize and dematerialize his astral body at will.[151]

The remaining stories of miraculous events associated with Mā are stories of protecting devotees from danger, demonstrations of the *siddhi* of knowing the past, present, and future of her devotees, materializing objects, and helping devotees find things that were lost. In nine stories, Mā is said to have protected devotees from danger. For instance, she is reported to have saved one devotee from being eaten by a tiger, another from being bitten by a snake, and two others from being killed on a train, and she protected others from being raped, killed in war, or drowned. Four of the stories claim that Mā knew that these catastrophes were happening and intervened from afar. For example, Swami Brahmananda, who told of his brush with an enormous snake, said, "Mā was in Puri at the time with her mother. There Mā was telling two others, 'I am seeing one of the boys has been attacked by a snake, but he is alright.' Of course, this is a miracle, no doubt, because these things are thousands of miles away. But still, she had an eye, she could tell whatever you are doing."[152] In the other three stories, Mā said that she saw the disaster as it was happening or indicated later that she knew about it. The latter version occurs in a story by Pushpa Banerji, a housewife from Calcutta:

In the year of 1964, my husband and I and two children and mother-in-law and sister-in-law went to the ashram at Ranaghat by car to have our first darshan of Mā. Mā was coming there the next day. We were asked to cook because we were brahmans and all the people will come and have Ma's darshan the next day. So we prepared the meal. . . . The next day, Mā [was very pleased] and called me and my family inside and gave a mālā [a garland] to all five of us. After that Mā left that place.

My mother-in-law asked if she could go to Navadwip. We went there. When we were returning from there, we stopped and my husband went to find the boatman. Then the car slipped down the bank into the water. My husband, daughter, and the driver came out of the car. My mother in-law, eldest daughter, sister-in-law, and I remained in the car. We were stuck inside the car. My mother-in-law said, "We are going to drown!" But I said, "Ma's mālās are here. We cannot drown." A boat came by. The pilot saw the sunken car. So he came near by and my husband who could swim under water swam to the car and opened the door and pulled out my daughter's body and my sister-in-law's body, my body, and his mother's body. We were all filled up with water.

After an hour we regained consciousness. How can the people who have been under water for an hour not be dead? I thought, "We can't die, no harm will come to us. Ma's mālās are with us." After we all gained consciousness, we couldn't move because we didn't have any saris on. So we stayed the night in that village. We were sick and vomiting for two days. We sent a message to the priest, he went to Mā, and Mā said that we were supposed to die. My mother-in-law was very angry because while coming from Mā it happened. Mā went to visit us after three days but my mother in-law didn't allow me to see Mā! *I* wasn't mad at Mā.

So after that I met Mā in 1970 and at that time Mā said, "You were the lady who was drowning in the car? You said, 'Ma's mālās are here. We cannot drown.'" Now I had never told anyone that I had said that thing. Mā said,

"Who saved you?" I said, "Who else but you." Mā said, "I didn't save you. Bhagavān did." Mā never used to say that she had done it. She always used to say, "Bhagavān has done it, not me."[153]

Finally, eight stories claimed that Mā had the *siddhi* of knowing the past, present, and future of her devotees. The most dramatic was of a French woman devotee to whom Mā revealed that she had known her in a past lifetime. Rupa Bose relates:

Now Denise is the wife of Arnold Desjardins, they came from Paris in the year 1964. Now Denise, we just knew that she was a very devoted person ....At that time I was given the charge of all the foreigners who used to be with Mā because I had the privilege to speak fluently, French and English. In Banaras ashram Mā told me, "They have been coming and going, why don't you feed them once. You know how to make special dishes for restaurants. They can't take spicy food." So I made separate dishes. So I brought a *thali* [a large platter] with small cups, and Mā followed me to see how I was serving Denise, just to make sure they were served properly. They had sat down on mats. And I was coming. Mā was behind me. Denise, seeing Mā, stood up and within a flick of a second she just fainted. Denise fainted and Mā called out to another girl to bring water and then Mā went near Denise. Then Mā asked Denise if she would be able to eat, but Denise said, "I want to rest." So Mā went upstairs and asked the girl to bring orange juice to her.

I was sitting in Denise's room and a little later Denise told me, "Rupa, I had a reminiscence of my past life. I felt that in my past life I had begged alms from Mā in Dacca and I was a beggar, a Bengali beggar woman, who ate in the street asking for rice, asking, '*Anno dayi*.' And I could see in a flash that Mā came out with a bowl of rice cooked and she poured the rice in my platter as I was walking and when I saw you coming and Mā behind you with this rice placed in the center of the platter, that past picture came to me and I fainted."

So I went to Mā later and I said, "Mā, Denise is about my age"—at that time it was about 1964, I would be thirty-eight or thirty-nine. So Mā said, "Denise was right, when this body was about twenty-five years old and this body was in Dacca in some small village, there was a beggar woman, very slender, very frail looking, black hair, who came shouting, '*Anno dayi, anno dayi*, give me rice, give me rice' and this body was cooking and came out with the cooked rice and poured it in her platter. So in this life Denise in the form of Arnold's wife was brought to this body after so many years. This body is now aged but Denise in her second life has the good *samskāras* to visit it again. And that platter of rice that you were bringing to Denise—I had never followed you when you serve foreigners—but I had a special *kheyāla* that when rice is served to Denise she will remember her past life." So Mā followed behind me and Denise just fainted getting that shock, the remembrance of her past.[154]

This story, like many others, emphasizes that when Mā admitted that a miraculous thing had happened in association with her, she either attributed the power to her *kheyāla*, which we know refers to God's will manifested through her, or, in the case of healings, said, "Bhagavān did it." Ganguli says,

Mā has made one thing perfectly clear. The exercise or non-exercise of occult powers attributed to her depends not on her volition but on *kheyāla* (Divine Will working through Mā). She completely resigns herself to *kheyāla*. In fact she makes no effort to perform any miracle nor to resist any event due to happen as a matter of course. Thus, she is supremely indifferent to this aspect of spiritual life, vis. miracle-working.[155]

Ganguli is not questioning here that Mā had "occult powers." He is simply pointing out that she never used them out of her own will. Swami Jnanananda, one of Mā's closest *sannyāsin* devotees, put it this way,

The miracle came spontaneously, as a channel from the Divine. That means she actually did *not* do it. And she *knew* she had not done it. She knew it was the Divine Power, which acted through her. . . . When the sages say, "I am doing nothing," it is not humility, they really believe it. . . . It comes from the *bhāva* of people, from their core. It is people who drag it from the saint."[156]

Swami Turiyananda put it in another way: "Mā never performed any sort of miracle. When a pitcher is very full of water, it can spill. These incidents, you call them supernatural things or miracles, these come from within spontaneously when the guru is full. There is no reason why Mā graced this person or that."[157]

Yet, even though forty-three of forty-four interviews contain at least one story about Mā's extraordinary and miraculous powers, devotees concur that Mā's "*real* miracle" was her "ability to transform the heart of people."[158] Swami Vijayananda speaks of the spiritual transformation in his life:

What does it matter to me if a certain Yogi has walked across the water or flown through the air? The real miracle is when that which one needs, which one desires keenly or feebly, comes at the very moment it is needed. And still better when it comes, not only as one desired it, but as one would have loved to see it in the innermost depth of one's heart. It has been for me as if I were guided on a path beset with obstacles by the hand of the most loving mother, an all-powerful mother. As you advance, she removes all the thorns, all the stones from your path and, when it is necessary, she lifts you across in her arms. And all circumstances adjust and adapt themselves with a marvelous precision, without hurt. "Coincidence" I thought at first. But a coincidence that goes on repeating itself daily cannot be called so any more. And all this happens without apparently violating the laws of nature—for the Lord has no need to break any laws. He is the Law. Should I give examples? No, for those who do not know her will not believe me and those who have lived near her have already understood.[159]

The spiritual transformation alluded to is that which is believed to inevitably arise out of the transformative energy field created by the fusion of the moral and powerful presence of the Hindu saint. In chapter 5, as we discuss the category of guru in relationship to Ānandamayī Mā, we address the phenomenon of spiritual transformation attributed to gurus in general and Mā in particular. Although the Hindu saint's presence is considered transformative for devotees and passersby alike, the specialty of the Hindu guru, considered a saint and more, is to guide initiated disciples from within and from without on a path to become like him or her.

Summary

In conclusion, it is true that although her devotees reject the category of "saint" to define her, Ānandamayī Mā, as she represented by her devotees, participates in the moral and charismatic context of Hindu sainthood. In terms of her moral presence, although she did not fulfill the ritual cutting of the ties, she was in spirit the paramount renouncer, or *sannyāsinī*. She fulfilled a lifelong vow of *brahmacharya* and was, therefore, a *brahmachārinī*. Steeped in unity awareness, completely disidentified with the body, and totally one-pointed on God, she could be called a *siddha*, one who has realized the Absolute. In terms of her powerful presence, Mā's *bhāvas* are well documented, reflecting, even epitomizing, the Bengali conception of religious ecstasy. Thus, she could be called the paramount God-intoxicated *bhakta* or *sant*, absorbed in God as both the form and the formless. Finally, according to the stories of devotees, Mā displayed the miraculous *siddhis* attributed to Hindu *yogis* and *yoginīs*. As such, she could be considered the supreme *yoginī*.

Yet, as we will see in chapter 6, Mā's devotees choose not to delimit her by describing her in these terms, since all of these terms refer to human beings who have become perfected. Ānandamayī Mā, say her devotees, was an incarnation of God who, unlike a saint or a guru, always possessed divine qualities. So while those as estimable as Yogananda may refer to Ānandamayī Mā as an "exalted saint," her devotees implore us to consider her as much more than that.

FIVE

Ānandamayī Mā as Guru

If your desire is intense, it is quite impossible that the Light should not come to you. The question of whether the path is long or short must not be allowed any room in your mind. "Realization will have to be granted to me," this should be your determination. . . . In order to be liberated from constant coming and going, the round of births and deaths, one has to seek the support of the guru.[1]

In order to find a *sadguru* (true guru), genuine endeavor is needed. When your aspiration becomes pure, you are bound to find a *sadguru*. Look, when a child keeps on crying, "Ma, Ma!" writhing in pain, can the Mother remain indifferent? She will hasten to him with alacrity. Pine for a guru with equal intensity and he will most certainly come to you.[2]

The relation between *guru* and *shishya* (disciple) deserves to be called eternal only when the *guru* is possessed of divine power and can and does communicate this power to the latter at the time of his initiation. This power being eternal, the relation between *guru* and *shishya* as thus established is also eternal.[3]

—Ānandamayī Mā

ALTHOUGH ĀNANDAMAYĪ MĀ SPOKE frequently of the indispensability of the guru, or spiritual master and guide, on the spiritual path, she did not apply the term to herself. Instead, in her public statements, she encouraged people to find a true guru, take initiation, and "try your utmost to carry out fully the guru's orders."[4] Similarly, Mā's community rarely refers to her as a guru, officially maintaining that she was not a guru because she did not give *dīkshā*, or spiritual initiation. In this chapter, we look beneath the public statements to the experiences of Mā's devotees and to Mā's informal conversations to determine the ways in which Mā served as a guru to her close devotees, or disciples. As we encounter the many levels on which Mā and her disciples perceive themselves as eternally bonded in a transformative process which began either at their first *darshan* or at their initiation, we ask why the community insists on saying that Mā was not a guru. Keeping in mind that the guru serves as a model of the human being who has successfully followed the path to God, we conclude the chapter by examining whether Mā was an exemplar for her devotees. We ask, "Did Mā's devotees model their lives on her life, striving as the disciple of a guru ideally does to become like her?"

Who Is a Guru?

In many Hindu families in India even today, to have a family guru is considered as commonplace and as necessary as it is to have a family doctor or lawyer. People explain, "Just as one needs a specialist in the physical body when one is ill, a specialist in the law when one has a legal problem, in the same way, one needs a guru to guide one along the spiritual path. You need an expert who has already arrived where you wish to go." In someone's home, it is common to see photographs of the family guru on the wall or on an altar, along with pictures of the family ancestors. One might even be invited to see a special room for used for worship, or *pūjā* room, in which there are pictures of the guru and statues or photos of the deity or deities worshiped by the family. Although the classical Hindu guru may have been conceived of primarily as a guide on the path to liberation, the contemporary family guru often serves as both a spiritual and secular mentor. He or she might be consulted about a myriad of concerns, from the mundane to the sublime. In fact, no question might be considered too trivial for the guru, whether about diet, career, or marriage problems. The guru is seen as both a spiritual mother and father, regardless of gender.

The word "guru" in Sanskrit means "teacher or highly respected person." As an adjective, "guru" means "heavy, weighty, or venerable." However, hymns of praise to the guru, which can be found in Hindu scriptures from Vedic times to the present, usually describe the guru more grandiosely as the one who takes the seeker from ignorance to knowledge or from darkness to light. In the *Shree Guru Gita*, a text chanted in praise of the guru, it is said, "Salutations to Shrī Guru, who, with the collyrium stick of knowledge opens the eyes of one who is blinded by ignorance."[5] Within different strands of the Hindu tradition, the guru is envisioned in slightly different ways. Within the *bhakti* tradition, the guru has become totally and perfectly absorbed in his love for the beloved as God. In the tradition of Advaita Vedānta, the guru has realized the Absolute, or Brahman. Within the tantric tradition, the guru has had a direct experience (*anubhava*) of both the unity and the multiplicity of Brahman. In all three cases, the guru has lost his or her identification with the ego and is, therefore, one who *knows* God experientially. However, to qualify as a *sadguru*, or true guru, and not simply a saint, one must possess the capacity to guide his or her disciples to the same state of awareness. The *sadguru* is considered to be in a highly contagious state of consciousness, out of which she or he is able to transform an ordinary disciple into an extraordinary person, in fact, into a guru just like himself or herself. In this way, the *sadguru* is often defined as the grace bestowing power of God. This transformation begins at initiation and, as White says, "creates an indissoluble bond between master and disciple described by Hindus as the closest of all human relationships."[6]

Scholars of the Hindu tradition have been somewhat slow to recognize the significance of the phenomenon of the guru within the tradition throughout history. Nearly two decades ago, David Miller, on the basis of his research on Hindu monasticism, called for scholars of the Hindu tradition to stop making sense of sectarian Hinduism by classifying sects according to the three major theistic divisions, Shaivite, Vaishnava, or Shākta, and to begin to see the "dynamic, sacred centre of Hinduism" as the enlightened guru, "whose charismatic leadership creates the institution for philosophical, religious, and social change."[7] While the guru may not be *the* sacred center of the Hindu tradition, he or she continues to play a formative role in shaping the religious experience of many Hindus. Yet, while there have been some important scholarly works that discuss the centrality of the guru within the Hindu religious context,[8] relatively few scholars have undertaken studies of particular gurus.[9]

The path of the guru, or *guruvāda*, which is widespread across sectarian divisions, maintains that the means to liberation is not a particular theistic or philosophical orientation but surrender to a true guru. This path maintains that only through the guru-disciple relationship can the seeker shed his individuality and attain God-realization. Shashibhusan Das Gupta concludes that the path of the guru "may be regarded as the special characteristic, not of any particular sect or line of Indian religion ... [but] rather the special feature of Indian religion as a whole."[10]

The belief in the indispensability of the guru can be traced from Vedic times through Hindu scriptures and sacred literature. A very early reference, here referred to by the Sanskrit term *āchārya*, or teacher, is found in the Atharva Veda, 11.5.3, dated by scholars to between 1200 and 900 B.C.E.

The master (*āchārya*), welcoming the new disciple into his bowels, takes the celibate student.
Three nights he holds and bears him in his belly.
When he is born, the Gods convene to see him.[11]

While *āchārya* is used in the Vedas to refer to the spiritual teacher, the term "guru" is used for the first time in the Chandogya Upanishad, 8.15.1,[12] believed to have been composed around the middle of the first millennium B.C.E. The Upanishads include countless references to the indispensability of the guru and his initiation. The Mundaka Upanishad describe the qualities of a true guru, the most important of which are being well-versed in the scriptures (*shrotriya*, having "heard" much) and being fully established in the Absolute Reality, which is the nondual Brahman (*brahmanishta*).[13] The Taittirīya Upanishad describes the guru as the embodiment of Absolute knowledge, and the disciple as its latent form.

> Now with regard to knowledge, the teacher is the prior form,
> The pupil, the latter form,
> Knowledge is their conjunction,
> Instruction, the connection.[14]

The Chandogya Upanishad maintains that the guru-disciple relationship is a necessity for gods and human beings alike if they are to transcend the world of duality.[15] Thus, the guru is one's spiritual parent and is to be served as a god. The Shvetāshvatara Upanishad, 6.23, says,

> To one who has the highest devotion (*bhakti*) for God,
> And for his spiritual teacher (*guru*) even as for God,
> To him these matters which have been declared
> Become manifest [if he be] a great soul (*mahātman*)—
> Yea, become manifest [if he be] a great soul![16]

The Upanishadic dialogues make it clear that one of the most essential qualities of the true guru is the ability to adapt the teachings to the individual needs of each disciple. This quality (which the Buddhist tradition ascribes to Gautama Buddha, calling it *upāya kaushalya*, or skill in means) is the ability to assess the capacity of the disciple, to perceive the obstacles to an understanding of the truth, and to present the teachings in such a way as to remove these obstacles. The teaching methods for a particular disciple may include thought-provoking riddles, similar to the *koans* of Zen masters, or physical or mental austerities. The disciple, for his or her part, must approach the guru with complete faith, or *shraddhā*. [17]

In the epics and Purānas that developed around the turn of the common era, the guru continues to be portrayed as essential to spiritual life. The doctrine of the grace, or *prasāda*, of the guru is introduced in the *Mahābhārata* when Agni grants the seer, Gaya, the power to know the Vedas without study through renunciation and the "grace of the gurus."[18] We see the increasing deification of the guru in a story in which Ekalavya, a low-caste boy who, when rejected by the famous guru, Drona, because of his caste, makes a clay image of the guru, worships it, and, as a result, spontaneously receives the instruction.[19]

In his commentaries on the Upanishads, which form the foundation of Advaita Vedānta, the ninth-century philosopher and guru Shankarāchārya reinforces the *gurum eva*, or the "teacher alone" doctrine, maintaining that there is "no pursuit of wisdom independent of the guru."[20] The Vedantic guru is he who embodies the truths of the Upanishads and whose experience these truths articulate,[21] he who, having had the bandages removed from his eyes by his guru, has loosened the bandages from the eyes of his disciples.[22] Such a man is worthy of both reverence and devotion, for he is not merely godlike but one with the divine.[23] We note that, for Shankara, both guru and disciple, regardless of class, are men who have made a lifelong commitment to monkhood, or *sannyāsa*.

Shankara and his disciples delineate two other essential elements of the *guruvāda*: the importance of a *sampradāya* [teaching tradition] and its *paramparā* [the lineage of gurus], and the existence of the guru as *antaryāmin*, or inner controller, as first articulated in the Upanishads.[24] Shankara views the guru as one who sustains and transmits lineage to the degree that "repeating the line of teachers serves as mantra which heightens consciousness and becomes a source of power."[25] Shankara describes the *antaryāmin*, or inner guru, as the Higher transcendent Brahman, who, when conditioned by *māyā*, becomes immanent in the world as the inner ruler, residing within the heart.[26] From this concept evolved the idea of the guru principle, that grace-bestowing power of God which is beyond the personality of a particular guru.[27]

The doctrine of the indispensability of the guru reached its height in the Hindu tantric traditions, in the schools of Kashmir Shaivism, Pāñcharātra Vaishnavism, and Shāktism, and came to its pinnacle in the tenth and eleventh centuries. Tantrics of all schools have traditionally placed an extraordinary emphasis on the authority of the guru, considering him or her the embodiment of *shakti*, or divine power. A seminal verse of the *Shiva Sūtras*, verse 2.6, says, *Gururupāyah* or "The guru is the means." In the commentary on this verse, Kshemarāja says that a guru is one who is able to "throw light on the virility or efficiency of mantras" and that the "power of grace inherent in the mouth of the guru is greater than the guru himself."[28] According to Muller-Ortega, the guru literally "represents the embodied wholeness that is the goal of the *sādhaka*" and through the transmission of her or his *shakti*, or *shaktipāt*, the guru as mantra enters the disciple and guides him or her from within. Thus, this verse also translates as "the means (transmission of *shakti* as mantra) is the guru."[29] Because tantra equates the guru, the mantra, and God, the initiation process which "consists of the transference of the guru's vital energy to the adept"[30] in the form of a mantra, marks the beginning of the disciple's transformation into a divine being like his guru.

The guru is further idealized and divinized by medieval saint-poets such as Kabir, Nanak, and Tulsidās, in the Vaishnava sect of Chaitanya (1485–1533), and in the Nāth cults of Bengal and Maharashtra. Traditional hagiographies of the *sant* Kabir (1440–1518) emphasize the primacy of the guru. Kabir, certain that his would-be guru, Rāmānand, would not accept him because of his low caste, rolled himself up next to the steps leading to Rāmānand's bathing place on the Ganges. When Rāmānand, walking in the dark, accidentally stepped on Kabir, the guru yelled out "Rām," one of the names of God. Kabir took this as mantra *dīkshā* and considered Rāmānand his guru from that day forward.[31] The *Guru-Māhātmya*, or song of praise, to the guru of the school of Kabir equates the guru with God and says that those who do not honor the guru will fall into rebirths. Likewise, in the *Rāmcaritmānas* of Tulsidās, no one can save a person with whom the guru is angry.[32]

The guru Chaitanya was considered an *avatāra* of Krishna and Rādhā, setting the stage for devotees to claim that their guru, too, was an *avatāra*.[33]

In the Nāth yogic tradition of Marathi *siddhas*, or perfected masters, the doctrine of *guruvāda* reaches great heights, emphasizing the grace of the divine guru, and his unity with God and with the disciple who serves him perfectly. One of the most widely used Marathi Nāth texts, the *Guru Charita*, extolls the lineage of the Vaishnava saint, Dattātreya. Like the *Guru Gītā*, or Song of the Guru, it is a collection of Vaishnava and Shaivite *shlokas*, or verses, taken from sources such as the Upanishads, the Tantras, and the Purānas. Both proclaim the guru's primacy, even over God, as the guru can transform a disciple into a God-realized person. Verse after verse of the *Guru Gītā* says *Na guroradhikam*, or "There is nothing greater than the guru."[34]

Thus, as Gonda says, "the tradition of profound respect for the guru. . . grew, especially in the later centuries, not rarely to exaggerated dimensions," and the guru "became the vital center of the religion."[35] Klostermaier lists one of the ten Vaishnava sins against the name of God in the *Bhaktirāsāmritasindhubinduh* as "thinking that the guru is a mere human being," a sin which cannot be atoned for.[36] In Hindu ashrams in India and the West even today, devotees sing their guru's praises by chanting,

Tvameva mātā ca pitā tvameva
Tvameva bandhushca sakhā tvameva
Tvameva vidyā dravinam tvameva
Tvameva sarvam mama devadeva.

You are mother, you are father, you are brother, you are friend. You are knowledge, you are wealth, you are everything, O god of gods![37]

Certainly this elevation of the guru has created many opportunities for less than egoless gurus. Sacred texts that describe how to discriminate a true guru from a false guru have been consulted by would-be disciples for centuries. The teaching of Gautama Buddha, "Be a light unto yourself," was one response to a system of spiritual authority that had its limits. Abuses of power by contemporary gurus considered to be divine and infallible are documented in a new genre of literature, critiquing the authoritarian structure of the guru-disciple relationship, especially in a Western context.[38] In reevaluating the guru-disciple paradigm, one must consider its historical roots, as well as its triumphs and abuses.

Before we begin our analysis of Ānandamayī Mā as guru, we should review some of the ways in which the Hindu guru is conceived, particularly within the Bengali Shākta context, which has strong tantric elements. First, the true guru is one who gives *dīkshā*, or initiation.[39] This initiation is called *shaktipāt*, literally the descent of power from the enlightened guru into the disciple, the *shishya*. Shākta texts define initiation by the guru's touch, or *sparsha dīkshā*, initiation by the guru's word, or mantra, or *vāg dīkshā*, and initiation by the guru's gaze, or *drik dīkshā*. They also describe initiation into spontaneous knowledge that can arise from the guru's look, speech, or touch, called *shāmbhavi-dīkshā*.[40] The most common form of initiation, however, is by mantra, which is considered alive with the enlightened guru's *shakti*.

However, regardless of the form, *dīkshā* is the moment when the guru ignites the dormant spiritual energy, or *kundalinī*, at the base of the disciple's spine, which begins to transform the disciple from within. It is often seen metaphorically, and even literally, as the planting of a seed which, given the proper conditions, will grow into a tree. Muller-Ortega says that in Kashmir Shaivism "there is a sense in which [the disciple] is 'infected' with the germ of infinity, with the 'seed,' which will sprout into the acquisition of the state of enlightenment."[41]

Second, the true guru has the ability to guide the awakened spiritual energy of the disciple from within and without. The internal guidance comes from the inner guru, known as the "serpent power" or supremely intelligent *kundalinī*, whose task it is to remove all inner obstacles to realization of one's divine nature. The external guidance takes the form of teachings and guidance that make the disciple aware of the goal and the obstacles to reaching it.

Third, the true guru possesses "skill in means," or the ability to guide each disciple according to his or her own needs, aptitudes and *samskāras*, or impressions from past lifetimes. If the guru is genuine, no two disciples receive the same instructions. As Baumer says,

> The teaching and the method are always adapted to the actual spiritual stage of the disciple which can only be recognized by the true master. There is no place for make-believe and also no place for mass instruction in the spiritual field, for everything depends upon the capacity of the disciple to receive.[42]

This capacity is connected to a fourth quality, one that is particularly apparent within the tantric tradition: the commitment to secrecy, or *rahasya*. Brooks says that tantric teachings and practices are not secret because "they are restricted and limited both in transmission and in accessibility to outsiders" but "because without initiation one is not fully empowered to use or comprehend them." Tantric secrecy, he says, is a "complex religious category that binds tradition (*sampradāya*) and lineage (*paramparā*) together into a socio-religious community."[43]

Fifth and finally, the true guru follows and/or creates a tradition and a lineage. Traditionally, a guru becomes a guru by being the perfect disciple. The Swaminarayan religion, a contemporary Vaishnava movement originating in Gujarat, subcribes to a the doctrine of *akshara* or the abode of the supreme person: The supreme devotee serves his guru as the abode of *purushottama*, or the supreme person, and thereby partakes of his essence, thus becoming the guru (and abode of God) that he serves. In this way, they say, a lineage has developed from their founder, Sahajānand Swami (1731–1830), down to the present guru, each guru grooming certain disciples from which he chooses a successor to carry on the lineage.[44] Many Hindu gurus centuries ago founded a lineage or a philosophical school that continues to the present day, for example, Shankara, Abhinavagupta, and Rāmānuja. As Vail notes, the members of a lineage are linked through successive initiations to their founder in a substantial way.[45]

The Bond between the Guru and the Disciple

In order to evaluate the guru-disciple relationship between Ānandamayī Mā and her devotees, we need to better understand the substantial link, the "indissoluble bond," between the guru and the disciple, or guru-to-be. Anthropologist McKim Marriott, of the ethnosociological school, offers one language in which to frame it. According to Marriott, the Hindu concept of a person is that of an unbounded "dividual," in contrast to the Western concept of the person as a bounded individual. "Individuals" do not exist in the Hindu world because persons, like everything else, are "divisible into particles that can be shared or exchanged with others."[46] The Hindu worldview sees everything as permeable substance—a person, ideas, the land, karma, the guru—and in a constant state of interaction and flux. As Val Daniel, one of Marriott's disciples, writes in *Fluid Signs: On Being a Person in the Tamil Way*, "A person is not an 'individual.' A person includes his wife, his children, his kinsmen, his *jāti* fellow (members of his sub-caste), and even extends to include his ancestors and ancestral deities."[47] Thus, transactions, whether between different castes or between guru and disciple, can be seen as involving exchanges of substance that are either compatible or incompatible, resulting in differing degrees of substantial equilibrium or disequilibrium. Not only is the saint or guru's state considered "contagious" but also everyone's state is contagious.

Using transactional language, the guru might be seen as a "dividual" who has been spiritualized by contact with the substance of his or her guru, who, in turn, has become one with the substance of God, or Brahman, whom Marriott refers to as "Number One, the constant, who is *nirguna* (without attributes), whose process is consciousness and non-relationality."[48] The guru, in planting a seed of her or his God-realized substance within the disciple, is sharing his or her substance with the disciple. When the disciple nurtures the seed, reinforcing its substance with spiritual practice in proximity to the guru while renouncing the stuff of the material world, his or her substance becomes more and more like the guru's.[49] The guru, by contrast, having become established in the substance of God, cannot be depleted through transmission.[50]

The understanding that people interpenetrate each other over time can help to explain the belief that Mā, like other gurus, took on the karma of her devotees, as seen in miracle stories such as the one in which Mā reportedly took on a devotee's karma, became disfigured, and had to digest it. It is the guru's job to take on the negative karma of her devotees, process it, and thus reduce obstacles in the way of the liberation; the disciple, in turn, receives the grace of spiritualized substance. In Bengal, God is usually envisioned to be both *saguna*, with attributes, and *nirguna*, without attributes. From this perspective, only Mā's *saguna* form—that form possessing changing, subtle properties—could be affected by karma, which Mā could normalize by digesting it. Because Mā was established in a *nirguna* state as well, her unchanging formless presence could not be injured.[51]

Most of Mā's devotees maintain that she was not a guru and explain that she did not give *dīkshā* and that she herself said that she was not a guru. When I began this study, I assumed this was true. Like my friend, the scholar Bettina Baumer, who met Mā a number of times, I believed that Mā "did not have the impetus to give people *sādhana*, to make them do something."[52] Rather, she appeared to be more a passive focus for her devotees' devotion, almost like a *mūrti*, or statue of a deity.

However, eight devotees referred to Mā as such, including Bhanumati Ganguli, who referred to Mā's grace, or *kripa*, as *gurukripa*, or guru's grace[53]; Swami Samatananda, who referred to himself as *āchārya* and Mā as the "real guru"[54]; Swami Turiyananda who said that Mā was the kind of guru who, like Lord Krishna, had a magnetic personality and was full of compassion and love, yet was so powerful that once you got in her grip it was "like being in the jaws of a tiger";[55] and Swami Jnanananda who articulated many ways in which Mā fulfilled the qualifications of guru.[56]

Did Mā Give Dīkshā?

We begin by asking whether Mā performed the central function of the guru: to bestow initiation that awakens a disciple to the spiritual life. When I first read that Mā did not give *dīkshā*, I suspected this was a technicality, that while Mā may never have actually given *dīkshā*, she was often present, and devotees must have felt connected to her as the overseer of the initiation. However, in my interviews, I was presented with the reality that Mā gave *dīkshā* indirectly and directly, many devotees marking that moment as the beginning of their spiritual awakening and considering that Mā resided within them from that time on.

The discrepancy between official statements and reality became apparent in one of my earlier interviews.[57] I was telling two devotees that, although I knew that Mā never gave *dīkshā*, I was interested in whether she gave spiritual instruction. One devotee said,

> Although Mā had a question and answer period nearly every evening in which people could ask questions about their *sādhana*, she rarely volunteered specific instructions unless a person asked for them. Mā gave *dīkshā* only when a person was ready and asked for it. Mā touched people in three ways: through dreams or visions, by calling people to her, or by waiting for people to approach her for *dīkshā*. In the case of the third way, a person would contact [someone] in the ashram and say, "I want to be initiated," or "I want to have a private," which meant a private meeting with Mā in which she gave initiation. In my case, Mā sent for me to give *dīkshā*. [She laughs] I was content just to sit in Mā's presence but Mā said emphatically, "No, you must have a private!" It was during the private that Mā gave specific instructions to each devotee. Unlike the general instructions for the public, such as practice ceaseless prayer, read the Bhagavad Gītā, the specific instructions Mā gave an

initiated disciple in the "private" entailed much more responsibility. It was to be understood that these instructions were to be followed for life, as a vow. If there was a time when one thought, "Gee, should this continue?" then one must ask Mā if it was time for a change. When you go into this private, these subtle things come out. She looks at you and says, "Do this for one year." In a year she may say drop it, because now it has become part of you. You see, these are very intimate private things which are told only you when you have this private session.

They went on to tell about the common elements of the *dīkshā* ceremony: the preparatory practices of a purificatory bath; fasting; gathering gifts of flowers, fruits, and nuts; and sometimes the reading of a certain text. Then Mā asked, "Who is your inspiration?" and gave an appropriate mantra, her instructions for daily practice to be done three times a day, and finally, her instructions not to tell anyone from whom they received *dīkshā*. They explained that before 1970, Mā had given *dīkshā* to only a few people, but mostly she had her mother give it. Didimā died in 1970, and in the early 1970s Mā started giving *dīkshā* and initiated many people. One devotee added, "It was always denied that Mā gave it. It was denied in all the books." The other said, "Mā told us when we were asked, just say 'Isvara is my guru. He gave it to me.' Mā tells you it is the Supreme who is giving it to you, because at that moment, she is That."

At that point in the interview these devotees added, "Of course, you cannot tell anyone this." I was aware of the esoteric level of the conversation, but I had assumed that if they were revealing this information with the tape recorder running, they had decided it was for inclusion in this study. One devotee explained, "You cannot convince people about *dīkshā*. There are certain spiritual things which you may write about, but they won't accept it. The mystical aspect, it's not for the general public." The other conjectured that Mā might have told them not to tell out of a concern that it would become a fad among people, especially Westerners, to "join up." By the end of the interview, both devotees had softened on the issue of confidentiality. Eventually, they decided that only Mā could say if this was important information for my study and advised me to consult Mā on this question, listen for her guidance, and decide for myself.

I postponed this decision until I had completed all the interviews. Nineteen of forty-four interviews contained stories about *dīkshā*. Although seven devotees claimed that Mā did not give *dīkshā* and told me of their initiation from Didimā, Bholanāth, Bhāskarānanda, or Nirvānānanda, four other devotees did lower their voices to tell me in veiled language that Mā had initiated them herself. Others admitted that Mā gave *dīkshā* herself "on special occasions when her *kheyāla* moved her to."[58]

Two devotees told of *dīkshā* directly from Mā in the 1950s and one in the 1960s, all before Didimā'a death. One said, in the ambiguous language that typified all four revelations: "No, there was nobody in between. I think it would be wrong for you to write that Mā gave me the *dīkshā*, but Mā arranged for me to get the mantra. But I didn't want *dīkshā* from anybody but Mā. She gave me what I needed." Another said, "I must not comment on whether she initiated people directly or not, but she used to govern the whole thing. Mā told me to tell people that it was Nārāyaṇa who gave." I asked a devotee to tell me who gave *dīkṣā* to her for Mā, and she replied, "For me? That I don't want to express. Mā made all the arrangements. Didimā was alive, but she was not present. Not even Bhāskarānanda was there. Nobody was there." In each case, there was a reluctance to say unequivocally that Mā gave them initiation. It seems that she told them not to tell who gave it to them, while giving them the understanding that no one was between them and God.

The interviews also reflected that devotees received *dīkṣā* from Mā through three different processes: through dreams and visions, by being invited by Mā to take it, and by approaching Mā with a request for *dīkṣā*. Five devotees spoke of having received a mantra from Mā in a dream. All five of them went to Mā later to confirm that this was, indeed, their initiation. Mā told all five of them that the dream was to be taken in that way and asked two of them to take formal *dīkṣā* after that.

Even if Mā only occasionally gave formal *dīkṣā* directly, the interviews show that she orchestrated the initiation of her close disciples from beginning to end. Keshab Bhattacarya, a young male devotee from Varanasi, told me that when he asked Mā for initiation at the age of eighteen, Mā responded, smiling, "Well, there are many specific rules of this ashram. One rule is that this ashram never invites people to take initiation. And on the other hand when somebody has come with a wish to take initiation, this ashram can never say no."[59] However, according to the *dīkṣā* stories in my interviews, Mā invited at least as often as she waited to be approached. Eight devotees told stories in which Mā forcefully urged them to take initiation, only two reported asking Mā for initiation. Five whom Mā asked to take initiation resisted but eventually surrendered when Mā either ordered them or persuaded them by eliminating every excuse. For example, Bhanumati Ganguli said:

One day Mā suggested that I take *dīkṣā*. I said, "Why should I take *dīkṣā*?" Mā replied, "It will make you stronger." So at that time there was no opportunity. But soon we decided to go see Mā in Lucknow and come back in the evening, because we had work the next day. So my own mother was there and as soon as I got there she said, "You have not taken *dīkṣā*. Mā suggested it to you. Why have you not taken it? Take it. Mā is here." I told my mother that I have not thought it over. . . . Immediately Mā called me and said, "Do you want to take *dīkṣā*?" I said, "Yes, but just me. My husband will not want to." Mā told me, "No, no, it will be good for you to take it together." So I came out and told my husband what Mā said. He said alright. Then I said to Mā, "We have no clothing or bedding for the night. We were going back to Kanpur." Mā said, "You go spend the night with your mother in her bed, and sari, that's no problem. You come to me after two o'clock and the problem will be solved." She arranged everything—sari, *dhoti*, everything. And she told me to go to bed and come in the morning having bathed. And next day she made all the arrangements.[60]

In spite of the fact that Mā did give *dīkshā* directly and indirectly, some interviews addressed the question of why Mā did not do so. Bettina Baumer, an Austrian scholar who, though not a devotee, had taken Mā's *darshan* many times, said, "The fact that she was not anxious to initiate people herself is the sign of a real saint. She wasn't out to catch anybody. You had to really want initiation."[61] This assumption was challenged by stories in which Mā tricked, persuaded, or ordered reluctant devotees to take *dīkshā*. Sita Gupta said that Mā did not give *dīkshā* directly because "people couldn't take it." The three times Mā gave it (to Bholanāth, Bhaiji, and Didimā), "the three of them took *sannyāsa* and soon after that they passed away."[62] Jogendranath Bhattacarya gave me a theological explanation he credited to Gopinath Kaviraj, saying, "Mā cannot be the initiator [the guru] because she is the *ishta* [the deity]. . . . Mā is the end. It is quite impossible to think of her as the means. Mā as an end cannot initiate." In other words, Mā is God; she is the end; therefore, she cannot be the guru.[63]

The most illuminating remarks were made by Nirmala Chatterji, a renunciant devotee who spent many years with Mā.

> In *satsang* great learned *sādhus* used to ask Mā, "Why don't you give *dīkshā*? People are devoted to you. They want their *dīkshā* from you. And we are fortunate to have you among us. You are available. So why don't you give it?" And Mā would say, "*Dīkshā* is of five types. It is not only that you utter the mantra in someone's ears. That is one type. You can give *dīkshā* by touch. You can give *dīkshā* by giving things to people." Mā was saying that the simple fruit she gives has her *shakti*. She said, "You can have *dīkshā* in a dream. You can have *dīkshā* through a word." You know, so many people, Mā uttered something and somebody took that as *dīkshā*.[64]

By way of Nirmala-Di, Mā seems to be revealing that she *was* giving initiation in a multitude of ways, thereby awakening the *shakti* of her devotees. Even when Bholanāth, Didimā, Nirvānānanda, or Bhāskarānanda was giving the mantra, she was in close proximity, transmitting her *shakti* through touch, speech, or an object permeated with her *shakti*.

Indirect Dīkshā:
The Touch, the Gaze, and the Word

Most devotees reported that during their initiation Mā sat on one side of them and the person giving the mantra on the other. Many relate that Mā went under a towel with them and had her hand on them the whole time, either on their head or on their back, thus giving *sparsha dīkshā*, or initiation through touch. The description of Narendranath Bose's *dīkshā* at age twelve is a perfect example:

> I have certain special things that happened during the *dīkshā*. I don't know how to convey it. When I received my *dīkshā*, the mantra was and is always on this leaf, this *bel patra*. You know, she never gave *dīkshā*, you know that? She at all times had her hand on my head, on the center here. And I always

felt as if electric current was going through. And the other thing I will never forget is after I received the mantras which were written in sandalwood on the leaf, she rubbed that sandalwood off on my chest with her own hands. And there were these sandalwood stains and she then rubbed these off with her own hand, like that. And that vibration, oh my God, I can't explain it . . . . It was like an electromagnetic sort of therapy. I cannot tell you.[65]

Naren is describing classic *shaktipāt dīkshā* in which the guru's vibrational substance is said to enter the disciple, while maintaining that Mā did not give him *dīkshā*. It is accurate to say that Mā did not give him mantra *dīkshā*, but rather gave him *sparsha dīkshā*. Another example of substantial transmission, or *shaktipāt*, is given by Shashi Bhusan Mitra of Calcutta: "When Mother touched me, I had some feelings. It was like this spark from down inside and it is going up to my head. Yes, from down here. [He points to the base of his spine.] I told Mother and she said, 'Good, very good.' She had touched me back here on my head. She woke me up!"[66]

Twelve interviews describe receiving initiation from Mā, usually outside the formal setting, through her look, or *drik dīkshā*, which often occurred during their first *darshan* with Mā.[67] Swami Nirmalananda described his father, who had abandoned his family to be a *sādhu*, in meeting Mā for the first time in 1936. He said, "So my father went to see her and from that first look, that is called *vinīdrishtividhi* (the ceremony performed by looking), my father was struck down." From that moment, his father followed Mā's every instruction, which began with her demanding that he return to his wife and send his eight-year-old son, whose image came to Mā in that moment, to her school for boys. Mā told Swami Samatananda's parents, "This boy is a saintly figure and will not live in the world."[68]

Three devotees who received this kind of initiation are at present prominent swamis of Mā. Two received *drik dīkshā* and decided within days to stay with Mā. Their stories bear a remarkable resemblance to each other. Swami Jnanananda, the former French physician, describes his initiation as a classic *shaktipāt* experience, during his first *darshan* with Mā in 1951:

It [meeting Mā] was not something very important to me, very secondary . . . . So I went to the ashram and just then Mā Ānandamayī came out and she looked at me. You know, she had this special look. It looked at you, inside you, and through you to beyond you. Like seeing your past, your future, your destiny. . . . I felt something strange inside. . . . So instead of going away, I said, "Let's sit a little more." So I sat and there was *kīrtan*. *Kīrtan* I like very much. Then I went back to my hotel, to my room. And there was an inner explosion, a revolution within myself, you see? A feeling of unearthly love, unearthly love. And the solid conviction, without a shadow of a doubt, that this was the guru I was looking for. . . . And it lasted, it didn't go away. Next morning I came to the ashram, asked permission to stay in the ashram. She agreed and since I'm there.[69]

Swami Brahmananda, described his first meeting with Mā, at the age of forty-three.

It was a Friday. There was no one in the ashram at the time. Mā was sitting. Hardly ten heads were there. Mā's face was like this, with eyes closed, but at that moment her eyes opened. The moment I saw her, face to face, eye to eye, I got something in meditation which I had never had. Not even ten minutes I was there. The next day I came again. The third day she asked about us. Monday we had a private. That evening I came and joined the ashram.[70]

Swami Turiyananda described a dramatic spiritual awakening from Mā's look in 1944, which culminated in his joining the ashram a few years later:

I had a job at the time. But I was in the habit of having the *darshan* of saints and reading books on the saints. I selected Mā's book. And by just reading it I was full of yearning, to know that there is something more, to know the Absolute. In three days Mā was coming to Bombay. You may call it coincidence but the time was right. It was five o'clock in the afternoon. There was heavy traffic. When I got to the station, I inquired about her train. I saw some people, I was running. I found the compartment. There was Mā. I had her *darshan*. She looked at me—her look was full of compassion. Something you cannot describe. And that started transforming my world, my inner being. She just looked at me. For some months I couldn't take food or water. I was thinking that my *samskāras* (impressions from past lifetimes) and inner things were breaking away just like a river can break away part of a mountain. I was feeling something that I cannot describe. I lost fifteen to twenty pounds. I was full of consciousness. I had no other thoughts other than thoughts of the Absolute.[71]

This story parallels classical tantric texts of the spontaneous insight and inner purification said to result from the unfolding of the awakened *kundalinī* after *shaktipāt*.

Significantly, three stories of the power of Mā's look came from nondevotees. Melanie, already a devotee of another Hindu guru, met Mā in 1978 in Brindavan. She said,

She looked over at me with one of her looks that just melted your heart and I burst into tears. And then every once in a while she would just look back over at us and smile this very gentle smile and it was like her whole heart would open and you would feel her enter you with this beautiful caress that was sweet, sweet, sweet. She would just open and she would enter instantly into you. I felt this melting, melting into a puddle of love. I guess unconditional love like that I'd never seen in a woman before. . . . And we left and we were in a very, very beautiful state.[72]

Since that time she has seen Mā's face in meditation. Siddharth Sharma, a renowned pandit in Varanasi told me, "Her gaze was amazing. If you looked at her, it was as though you were looking at something divine. All the thoughts inside you when your eyes met ceased. You were one-pointed in gazing at her. In her presence all anger and lust would subside and you would be in a state of divine happiness."[73]

Other stories refer to Mā's look as an "x-ray look," with which she sees everything inside. One devotee said, "Just one look was sufficient in order to spend twenty-four hours in *ānanda* (bliss)."[74] Two *brahmachārinī* devotees separately described being small children around Mā and having her "stare nonstop" at them. Both said they found that they could not move and wanted to stare back forever; they ended up pursuing a lifetime vow of *brahmacharya*.[75] Two devotees described the powerful impact of Mā's look from her picture. Tara Banerji told about a European woman who was watching a television program about holy people in India. When Mā's picture came on the television,

> She felt that Mā was coming out of the television toward her. She was so impressed by her look that she could not forget her. The picture haunted her. She drove to India in a van, searching all over for Mā. She found out where the ashram was located and Mā was just waiting there for her. She went to Mā and fainted.[76]

Swami Samatananda maintained that since Mā's *samādhi* people have been "having many experiences" from looking at Mā's picture; "Mā's photograph is working wonders."[77]

Two other nondevotees describe an experience of Mā's *shakti* from a combination of initiation modalities. Swami Shivananda, the European who was kicked out of Mā's ashram, received a spiritual awakening from a combination of Mā's touch, look, and speech:

> When she passed me, her clothes rubbed against my chest. Suddenly she turned to me and looked me straight in the eye and said, "*Hari, Hari*." At that very moment I felt that something open up in my heart. Then some energy went in and them my heart kind of closed upon itself and contained that energy.

For a week afterward he experienced ecstatic spontaneous meditation that he attributed to Mā's *dīkshā*.[78]

Rupali Frank met Mā in Brindavan in 1978.

> Mā was just sitting on the bed cross-legged. I was standing at the foot of her bed. With her eyes, Mā started at my feet and worked her way up. When she got to my eyes, she let out this incredible, "*Aacha*! (Ah!)" At that moment, it sounded to me like the Universal Sound. I fell to my knees and pranamed. I hit my head on the mattress. . . . I gave Mā an orange. She took it. Then she gave it back to me. . . . God gave me that experience. One word, one look, and she has been in my being every since. I can feel her touch all over. I met my Divine Mother. Her "*Aacha*" still resonates in my being. I just have to think of it. The experience is not in my head. It is in my heart.[79]

The concept of a transmission of *shakti* from guru to disciple, which seven devotees referred to as *shaktipāt*, existed as a concept in the minds of devotees, and they believed they had received it from Mā. It was usually described with the analogy of the seed. I asked Swami Jnanananda if Mā gave *shaktipāt*. He said, "She tried to, yes. . . . It is like putting in a seed, you see? You put it in the earth and in due time it may sprout. . . . But very few people can bear the real *kundalinī* awakening. Really, very few. . . . But she planted the seed. Maybe next lifetime. Almost all people had at least some awakening in the heart."[80] Swami Turiyananda explained it this way:

> Some came to Mā out of curiosity. But after seeing her once, that seed is planted in the causal body. I see it as a time bomb. There is no time limit of one or two births. The time will come when everyone will have this intense longing for this God relationship. So it will slowly transform. Mā is always changing and transforming the causal body, the *karan sharira*. But it takes time. When you go to the river to take water, the dirty water comes first and after a while the pure water will come. Mā said, "It is a cleaning process. These impurities will come up and be passed off and the inner purity which is there will be able to come forth."[81]

Swami Samatananda said,

> There is a connection that we are talking about. Mā is here. And she is inside you, inside everywhere. So there is a place where Mā used to uplift the soul of man and then give, in Bengali, *anubhūti*, the current of real love. . . . You go to Mā and outwardly Mā will laugh with you, give you some fruit, some flowers, ask you some ordinary worldly thing. But she is trying to buy time for the real thing which is going on on a higher plane. She is injecting the real influence of her spiritual power, the real *shaktipāt*.[82]

Thus, the theme of spiritual contagion and the language of substantial transmission pervaded thirty-one of the forty-four interviews. Rajkumar Roy talks of Mā's ten-day stay in his garden in Calcutta, referring to her touching his *ajna chakra* (third eye) three times every morning as "charging the battery."[83] Many devotees talked of the value of being in any kind of proximity to Mā's physical body. Swami Samatananda spoke with envy of women's advantage of being in physical contact with Mā,[84] and countless women devotees confirmed the tremendous advantage of being a woman because that could feel the thrill of touching Mā's body. Six women spoke of the privilege of being asked by Mā to sleep under or next to her bed; Rupa Bose said that while she slept near Mā she had a powerful experience of spontaneous mantra repetition, which Mā confirmed as "a second spiritual awakening."[85]

The Guru's Presence, in Death as in Life

Most of Mā's devotees indicated that the substantiality of the bond established between guru and disciple is unaffected by death. Mā's devotees believe that Mā is not "dead,"[86] that she dwells literally in their hearts and speaks through her pictures. As Rupa Vishvanathan said, "The guru–disciple relationship is eternal. She is not going to let you down until you reach your goal."[87] I asked twenty-one devotees if they felt a difference in Mā's presence after her *samādhi*. The overwhelming response of seventeen devotees was that nothing has changed since Mā left her physical body, and "there is no question of thinking that she has departed."[88] As Sita Gupta said, "I am closer to Mother now. The longer the body is gone, the more we meet her."[89] The *samādhi* shrine in Kankhal is experienced as particularly full of Mā's *shakti*; it is considered to be alive, or *chaitanya*. Swami Brahmananda explained that the purpose of having the *samādhi* shrine full of pictures and artifacts is to attract visitors to linger there. "They get interested in the pictures," he said, "meanwhile the vibration will go within him."[90] Mā's alleged appearance in Calcutta in 1990 shows that devotees believe that "Mā is still alive and can still assume form and talk to us just as she used to do."[91]

However, six devotees said they had difficulty feeling Mā's presence since her *samādhi*. Three said they could not bear to go to the *samādhi* shrine. Two explained, "Although we realize she is still with us, protecting us, we have no access to her."[92] The other said, "We have lost Mother and we have lost everything. I am totally devastated."[93] The most despondent devotee said, "Time is not passing since her *samādhi*. . . . In those days we felt the physical presence of Mā everywhere. Now we feel helpless. . . . Mā's love, Mā's support, Mā's umbrella is not there."[94] Swami Jnanananda and I wondered if devotees who had a primarily external relationship with Mā, as the personality, seemed to suffer the most. Those who through intensive *sādhana* had established an inner relationship with her seemed to suffer the least.[95] However, for the *bhakta*, the physical form of God is paramount, and thus many of Mā's devotees would agree with Malini-Di, who said, "Nothing has changed. Her presence is still here, but 'Oh, for the touch of the vanished hand and the sound of the voice that is still!' "[96]

We have seen that the question of whether Mā gave the mantra to devotees during a formal *dīkshā* ceremony is irrelevant. The fact is that countless devotees envisioned that at a particular moment or in successive moments Mā entered them and they become hers. Whether that moment was when they were sleeping under Mā's bed, receiving her *prasād*, hearing her laugh, being touched by her body, meeting her in a dream, or receiving formal initiation, devotees became disciples as a result of what they experienced as a transmission of her *shakti* into them. Businessmen spoke of losing interest in material things from that moment on, housewives spoke of forgetting about fancy clothes, one man said he stopped losing his temper, another said he learned to play the harmonium and to sing devotional songs, and, as we have seen, eighteen disciples of those whom I interviewed committed themselves to a life of renunciation and rigorous spiritual practice. Swami Turiyananda said, "Mā's capacity was for transformation. When people came to Mā, they were feeling that eternal bliss and peace was not to be found in this world. And simply by contact they were filled with that peace. If your inner being is ready for this, it opens for you."[97]

The Guru as Personal Guide on the Path of Sādhana

Mā awakened spiritual energy in her disciples through a transmission of her own *shakti*. A guru must also be able to guide a disciple from within and without, taking into account the disciple's needs and the *samskāras*, harnessing the power of secrecy, or *rahasya*, when giving personal instruction and initiation. Thirty devotees spoke of receiving personal instruction from Mā in "privates" and of her *siddhi* of knowing at any given moment what they needed to progress in *sādhana*, although they did not reveal the content of the instructions. Keshab Bhattacharya explained the relationship between individualized instruction and secrecy this way:

> Mā used to caution us, saying, "Look, whatever I am telling you, this is for you. This will not profit others." And a very popular saying was, "Mā is having a private with someone." Because from person to person, everything is different. Mā never believed in a standardized kind of relationship or teaching. And she had that immaculate power to see each and every person with eyes open—what had happened to this person in many lifetimes, their *samskāras*. So Mā used to say, "Look, these are very private." Because if Mā was telling me to do *japa*, that is for me. If I come out and tell some other person, they may be on a level where *japa* is of no value. That is why these things are so esoteric, or secretive, so private. Because there is no other way. I am not on the level of teaching, so why share and hurt another's path of *sādhana*.[98]

All devotees agreed that no two people received the same teachings from Mā, according to Bettina Baumer, "a sign of a very great being."[99] Swami Samatananda said, "Mā had the greatest capacity to know the heart of all people. She is the greatest teacher. She is the greatest physician. Because she knows every individual."[100] Lalita-Di said of Mā's instructions, "She never forced anybody to do anything which was not within their means or capabilities. She was so practical."[101]

In general, Mā encouraged both householders and renunciants to "be true to your *āshrama* [stage of life]. Do it well."[102] She also asked all devotees around the world to meditate for fifteen minutes every night at 8:45.[103] Many devotees were asked to perform *samdhyā*, or spiritual practice of mantra recitation, recitation of a sacred text, and/or worship of a deity, three times a day, at sunrise, high noon, and sunset.

The overall directive for householder *sādhana* was to fulfill the *āshrama* of householder to perfection, to be a *sadgrihasta*, a true householder. According to Sita Gupta, this meant living a "dharmic, controlled life, the wife treating the husband as God, the husband treating the wife as Gaurī, and both treating the children as Gopāl."[104] I asked householders if Mā expected them to be celibate in their marriages. The answer was a resounding "No." Lalita-Di said,

> No, I'll tell you. It's that you do not have or you do not even *think* about having *extra*-marital sex. Within the rules of the *shāstras*, if you and your husband cleave to each other, then you are as good as someone who is celibate. Mā always said, "Celibacy is of the mind. If you are celibate with your body and in your mind you are lusting after somebody else, then that is not celibacy."[105]

Despite the secrecy of individual instructions, I did get a feel for the range of possibilities. Some householder women spoke of Mā's compassion for their plight as young wives and mothers. Lalita-Di told me how as an overwhelmed young wife she had said to Mā, "How will I do all this?" Mā had replied, "Why ten minutes is not such a big thing!" Mā then told her that if she tried to sit for longer, she would only be thinking about boiling milk. "Later," Mā said, "you can chant the name in your mind when you're working."[106] Sharada Chatterjee said,

> The fact is I was not the type to do *sādhana*. I was very close to Mā. When I was with Mā, Mā asked me to look after guests. It was more *karma yoga* than *dhyāna* or *jap* or anything like that. Mā asked me when I was away from her to sing *bhajan* every day for a few minutes and think I am singing to her. This I can do. I know that Mā will do the rest for me. Because I depend on Mā.[107]

Then again, some householders were given extensive instructions. Gita-Di Bose, my hostess in Calcutta, was involved in *pūjā* several hours a day. At her *dīkshā*, Mā instructed her to do *pūjā* morning, afternoon, and evening to the *Shrī Yantra* she had given her family.[108] Bhanumati Ganguli did four to five hours of practice a day according to Mā's instructions.[109] Most people, however, were somewhere in the middle. Mā instructed Shashi Bhusan Mitra to chant a chapter of the *Chandi*, a Shākta text, and the Bhagavad Gītā every day, followed by meditation on Kālī.[110] Keshab Bhattacharya showed me the *pūjā* room in which he worships three times a day the Gopāl Mā blessed at his *dīkshā*. Couples like Sita Gupta and her husband received *dīkshā* together and were instructed to sit together for *japa* and meditation daily at four A.M.; others, like Shashi Bhusan Mitra and his wife were instructed to sit successively in the *pūjā* room.

Mā had two levels of instructions for renunciants, it seems, one somewhat standard and the other individual and private. The life she established for renunciants was rigorous. Swami Turiyananda said,

> When Mā first takes anyone, she makes you her own through her love and compassion. Then we have to do *sādhana*. When the fish is in the pot, then . . . . If you are a brahman, you do the *Gāyatrī* [mantra]. You must not take food from the market. Whatever your caste, you must follow that particular life. Mā was very particular about these things. Mā gave each person instructions to follow very carefully. So once we did *Gāyatrī*, it has twenty-four words, and we did twenty-four *lakhs* of japa. And it took longer than two and one-half years. And then there was a bath three times a day in the Gangā. Even at four o'clock in the morning at Haridwar. And we would have to do everything ourselves—washing, cooking—in one month rotation. And you had to complete the *japa* before twelve. And after twelve you would worship Lord Shiva. The whole day was so busy. And Mā was saying, "Four and a half *krores* of japa." All these inner things. It was purifying.[111]

Swami Brahmananda described how Mā used to test the *sannyāsins*:

> Within a few days of our being accepted into the ashram, she asked us to go somewhere to do *bhiksha*, to live only on begging. Now if we were able to

do that for years, then she would ask us to do something else. In this way she examined us. Once in Banaras we came on the veranda where Mā was and there were two bells used during the *pūjā*, one triangular and one round. They showed us how to play these, each one different, very difficult. And Mā watched carefully to see how much concentration we have got because concentration is needed for *sādhana*. She used to keep us writing, whatever is on our minds, and after seven or fifteen days you would read that to her and find how much progress you are making.[112]

The path for *brahmachārinīs* at Varanasi ashram was described by Sita-Ji:

Mā's path was *shuddhāchārya*, the teaching of purity. She asked us not to eat outside the ashram, to do *pūjā* early in the morning, go to temples, do *japa*, *dhyāna*, *kīrtan*. At 10:15 we were asked to recite the Gītā. We sat for *satsang* four times because Mā said, "You will find me in *satsang*." This we still do.[113]

At Kankhal ashram the schedule for *brahmachārinīs* is slightly different, according to Malini-Di, but equally rigorous: 4 to 6 A.M. individual practice according to Mā's instructions, serving in the temple for the morning *pūjā*, *kīrtan*, at 8 A.M. recitation of Bhagavad Gītā and *Vishnu Sahāsranāma*, at 10 A.M. Bhāgavat *ārati*, in the evening, *Rāmāyana* recitation and two *āratis*.[114]

To Be a Householder or Renouncer:
Mā's Hand in the Decision

Another kind of instruction that Mā gave certain devotees that dramatically shaped their *sādhana* was the instruction to marry or not to marry. According to Swami Premananda, "Bhaiji has written that whatever Mā says is for your own good. Whatever she says, you should follow it. If someone is a *sādhu* and Mother says he should marry, he must do that. If she says to a householder, 'You must leave it,' then they must leave it. Whatever she says is not for her own good, it is for your good."[115]

Two devotees told stories in which Mā ordered a devotee bent on a life of renunciation to live as a householder, and seven told stories in which Mā suggested, encouraged, or even ordered them to become renunciants. Mā ordered Swami Samatnanada's father to return to his family in exchange for sending his son to her to become a renunciant. Sharada Chatterjee, the wife of a wealthy Bombay businessman, said when she was twenty Mā sent her away to Bombay, much against her wishes. She believes that Mā picked out her husband and arranged for her to meet him there.

Even after I met him, I told Mā that I'm not going to marry. I don't want to marry. She forced me to marry him. I wanted to be free to spend time with Mā. But if Mā asked me to marry, anytime, anyone, I would. I had experienced what could happen if you went against her will. Then she will stop taking care of you!

Later Mā said, "Do you know why I got you married? Because you were quite good looking and you had talents, and I knew that so many people would be after you. And you would not be able to save yourself. If you were going out to teach in the world, you needed protection." Sharada concluded, "Mā was right. Besides, my husband always let me spend time with Mā."[116]

More commonly, Mā chose a life of renunciation for young devotees. Keshab Bhattacharya, when he was about fifteen, went to see Mā in Brindavan with his grandmother. Mā said to him, "*Aaj se hum bandhu*," or "From today we are friends, remember." He explained that Mā's "friends" were her celibate, renunciant disciples. Although she called all children *bandhu*, if she said, "From today we are friends," it was considered a command to live a celibate life.[117] When Rupa Bose was about to leave for study in America, Mā shocked her by saying,

> "You are going. I have given you permission to go, but you be careful. You don't mix with boys or don't go into some action that is not proper in a life of a *kumārī*, a virgin girl." The next advice she gave me was, "You are my friend. I call unmarried boys and girls my friends. Be my friend all your life. Don't get married ever." That was a very point-blank instruction given to a very modern smart girl who had all hopes for a future career and life.[118]

There were other ways that Mā communicated that a devotee should live the life of *brahmacharya* or *sannyāsa*. A few months after Swami Jnanananda came to be with Mā, she gave the name Jnanananda; a name ending in "*ānanda*" usually indictes a *sannyāsin* in the Sarasvatī order of monks. Twenty years later she gave him ochre-colored clothes to wear.[119] Mā gave Swami Krishnananda the name Krishnananda within days of his initiation from Bholanāth.[120]

Sometimes Mā's wishes interfered with the intention of parents or tampered with an already established marriage. Nirmala Chatterji's translator said of Nirmala:

> Mā performed so many *līlās* with her. Mā danced with her. Mā decorated her. Mā took her when she was sixteen or seventeen. You see, she went to Puri with her parents. And there Mā asked her father, "Please give this daughter to me." Her parents—there were seven brothers and sisters but she was the favorite one of her parents. So how could they give her like this? So then Mā asked her to stay one night in her room. The next day Mā asked her father to dedicate this daughter to her. He did not say no and she was dedicated. Whatever Mā told, it was done.[121]

Bhaiji's wife apparently felt a great deal of anger toward Mā for luring him away from his family responsibilities into the life of *sannyāsa*. In Bhaiji's journal he apologizes to his wife for hurting her, but talks of the irresistible lure of "a new world." Mukerji reports that a few years after Bhaiji's death his wife "became reconciled to Mātājī," realizing that she could have gone to live with him while he did his *sādhana*.[122]

Vasudha-Di told of Mā's persuading a married person to take vows of *brahmacharya* in spite of her resistance.

One day in 1974 Mā was giving a few girls during the Kumbha Melā yellow *dhotis* to wear [traditionally, a color of *brahmacharya*]. There was one girl married to a long time devotee of Mā's who was a musician. It was an arranged marriage. One son had been born and died. The husband was living in the ashram and the wife came to visit him. Mā called the wife and handed her a yellow *dhoti*, saying, "Here, take this." This girl was fond of saris and ornaments. She said, "Oh, no, I'm not taking!" She was very frank with Mother, like a daughter to a mother. "I'm not taking. I don't like this. Yesterday you took my ornaments and now you are giving me this! What are you thinking?" And she was afraid maybe her husband was going to die or something. So she said, "You have made me stay in the ashram. I could have stayed in my family's home." Then Mother scolded her, saying, "You are a *sādkikā* [female holy person]. You have come to this body. You are supposed to do *sādhana*. You are staying in the ashram. Don't you want to leave everything and do your meditation? Why have everyone looking at you?" Mā scolded her like this. The girl said, "Well, I'm not taking this anyway. You may scold me but I'm not going to change my dress any more." Then Mā said softly, "Listen, this body likes to see you in this *dhoti*. So what to do? So you take this and go into this bathroom and change, just for a few minutes, to show this body." Then she took the *dhoti* and she changed into it and came to show Mā. And Mā said, "Oh, how pretty you look in this! Anyhow, you can change and do whatever you like now." This was Mother's approach. Now this girl is staying there in that ashram and is wearing a white sari, of course.[123]

Three interviews contained stories in which female devotees wanted to be with Mā as *brahmachārinīs*, but their families wanted them to marry. Mā seemed to remain neutral, but devotees indicated that Mā manipulated circumstances to enable them to stay with her. For example, Malini-Di said,

> I decided not to marry when I was about thirteen years old. But nobody is going to listen to things from a thirteen year old. When I finished my B.A., I became even more irritated with the superficiality of society. One day I went to Mā and said, "I don't want to get married. I want to stay with you." I was about twenty-one then. Mā said, "No, you are the only daughter. Your parents want you to get married. You should do whatever they say." So the arrangements for the marriage were made and Mā was consulted as she was about everything and she agreed. I was in Calcutta with my mother. Suddenly I began to run a very high fever. I was hospitalized. The doctors said I had pericarditis and it was very serious. Mā found out that I was very ill and had five fruits sent to me. After I ate the five fruits, my temperature miraculously went away. But I was weak and under treatment for so many months. The groom's family gave up. The critical marriage age passed. When I got well and went to Mā, she said, "Who broke off the marriage?" My mother said, "I did." I told Mā, "Mā, I want to stay with you." Mā asked my parents and they said, "Mā, whatever is good for her, you do." So I am here.

Malini-Di believes that Mā arranged the whole illness to give her parents the impression that they chose the outcome.[124]

Thus, according to her devotees, Mā fulfilled the function of guru in that she guided her disciples lives from within and without. No two disciples appeared to receive the same instructions, yet she told each disciple exactly what spiritual practices to do, and when and how to do them. Her sphere of influence extended even into her disciples choice of lifestyle—householder or celibate. These instructions were given privately, maintaining the secrecy common in most esoteric guru-disciple relationships, as well as the power of her intimate connection with each disciple.

By giving instructions in a "private," Mā seemed to be doing at least two other things. She enabled each disciple to move along his or her path according to his or her particular needs and abilities without creating a common standard of comparison. She also created an esoteric private community of disciples within the larger public community of devotees. Those privileged to know the private Mā undoubtedly felt a stronger sense of commitment to both their *sādhana* and to the community than others.

The Sampradāya of the Guru

The final qualification of a true guru is creating or being part of a teaching tradition, or *sampradāya*, and a lineage of gurus, or *paramparā*. In this area Ānandamayī Mā does not appear to have functioned as a traditional guru. First, Mā did not have a guru, having performed *svadīksā*, or self-initiation. This was consistent with the claim that she was not a human being. Thus, Mā did not inherit a *sampradāya*.

It is unclear whether Mā *established* a *sampradāya*, if *sampradāya* is defined as a religious order or sect which shares the teachings and form of worship of, and belief in, a founding spiritual personality. She did create an esoteric, inner circle of disciples completely devoted to her teachings and, ultimately, to worshipping her. She demonstrated her religious authority by personally conferring *sannyāsa dīkshā* on Bhaiji and Bholanāth. She also arranged for ten to fifteen other disciples to take *sannyāsa dīkshā*, thus establishing certain official teachers for the community. She authorized five or six of them to give *dīkshā*, and they still do. Mā gave the sacred thread to ten or more women, beginning with Bholanāth's niece, Maronī, in 1936.

However, a fundamental aspect of Hindu *sampradāya* is the guru *paramparā*, the succession of gurus, which is one of the first things a disciple learns to recite. The guru is to be succeeded by another guru, usually but not always selected by the previous guru before he or she dies.[125] As Swami Samatananda said, "I am the *āchārya*, she is the guru"; the teachers appointed by Mā are only representing Mā. Mā died without a successor, and no one has come forward since.

Most devotees seemed horrified when I asked if there had been any suggestion of a successor and indicated that Mā was in a category so far above even the purest or most self-realized *sādhu*, that it would be absurd to contemplate. Swami Jnanananda said that Swami Paramananda was "practically the successor. Mā didn't need to say it," but he was senile by the time Mā took *samādhi* and "not capable of transmitting anything."[126] Today when Swami

Nirmalananda and the other teachers give *dīkshā*, they make it clear that *Mā* is the guru and they are but the teachers.

Several devotees revealed the relative instability of the community since Mā's *samādhi*, a phenomenon well documented in literature on leaderless post-charismatic movements.[127] There seems to be considerable tension and jockeying for power within the community. Lakshmi Shrivastav said that since Mā's *samādhi*, without Mā as "the head of the court of appeals," there are endless unresolved arguments among the women.[128] Swami Premananda said that, although a committee runs the ashram, people argue over how it should be run: "Everyone thinks he is the most important person and Mā confided the most in him. They think they are the heir to Mā and that whatever they do is the best for the ashram. There is no compromise."[129] Several Calcutta devotees said that some infighting had come to litigation. One devotee, accused of mishandling money from the charitable hospital in Varanasi, raised support among lay devotees to sue swamis who managed an ashram for mismanagement. This case was scheduled to be heard soon after I left India. Most people, however, such as Swami Jnanananda, said, "Oh, administratively. . . . It goes quite well, I think."[130]

Two devotees alluded to a different kind of succession, claiming that Mā promised to return again, referring to her identity as an *avatāra*. In an interview with Sita Gupta, her translator, Rupa Vishvanathan, interrupted to say, "Excuse me, but Mā has said herself that she is going to take birth again here in Haridwar." Sita-Di cut her off, saying, "I don't believe that. No proof, nothing. Don't write that."[131] I was planning to ignore this claim, until Swami Brahmananda, the head of the ashram, told me something similar.

> Somebody went to Mā and told her, "You are building this building and everything, what is the future for it?" Mā told them that in the third generation someone is coming. In this room, Mā has told me this. Now which is the third generation? That I don't know. But in the Krishna *līlā*, Kalki is the *avatāra* to come in the future. So in Mā's *līlā*, there may be another to come in the future.[132]

The lack of concern with *sampradāya* around Ānandamayī Mā reflects Mā's complete indifference to institutions. When devotees suggested various projects from publishing houses to hospitals, Mā reportedly turned it back on them. For example, Bhaiji had a vision of a Sanskrit boarding school for boys in the ancient *gurukula* tradition to be established at the Kishenpur ashram. At his death, his friend, Hari Ram Joshi, approached Mā about the project. She said,

> If you wish to undertake a work of this order, you are certainly free to go ahead with it. I have nothing to say in this matter. As you know I have no *kheyāla* for undertakings of this kind. . . . All of you are as a rule engaged in work for your own selves, so it is desirable that you should become involved in altruistic work also to take you out of the narrow limits of self-centeredness. However, one must constantly remember that unflagging endeavor is to be directed towards the realization of Truth alone. . . . Enterprises which help

one toward God-realization are alone worthwhile. Similarly anything which proves to be a distraction is to be rejected. Discrimination is required. All action must be undertaken with a view to increasing and expanding the sphere of God-remembrance.[133]

Mā's one-pointed mission was for each of her disciples to attain Self-realization, not to set up institutions, even to carry on her teachings.

At this point we must explore whether Hindu women religious figures have historically founded *sampradāyas*. A. K. Ramanujan has pointed out that although *male* Hindu *bhakti* saints often founded their own sects, female *bhakti* saints have not usually been considered gurus and have not founded sects, even though their poems of devotion to their Lord may become liturgy in the *sampradāya* of which they were a part.[134] In contrast, women within the Shākta paradigm have not generally taken part in divine marriages and have often become gurus. However, only a few of them founded *sampradāyas* and chose successors.[135]

Mā's indifference to institutions and organizations may reflect the inclination of most Bengali holy women. McDaniel maintains that many Bengali holy women are recognized by their *bhāva* and do not depend on religious institutions for their authority; in the same way, they may not be inclined to create such institutions.[136] While they may have disciples, they may not think in terms of their "tradition" being carried on by successors. The women gurus of Varanasi profiled by Ojha and Teskey Denton may refuse to live according to social norms, but they do not often question the established order by creating a new order or envision their teachings being carried on through succession.[137] The Shākta *mātās* researched by Erndl, believed to embody the Goddesses *shakti* during *chauki*, or possession, may have devotees, but most live relatively normal lives as housewives when not possessed. *Mātās* around whom a cult or institution has grown are more likely to be deified, even after their death, than be thought of as founders of a *sampradāya*.[138]

Mā on the Guru

Mā herself acknowledged the rareness of *shaktipāt* and of the guru who can give it, and said, "Gurus who give *dīkshā*, also may give *shaktipāt*. This *shaktipāt* by a guru is a very significant thing. The *jagadguru*, the guru who saves his disciple from the world, is very rare, only one in two to three million."[139] Mā sometimes used a metaphor of awakening in which the guru cuts through some barrier within the disciple and lights a light waiting to be lit. For example, she said, "In *shaktipāt*, the knot is cut and the *kundalinī* is awakened, opening the way for attainment of God."[140] Once this knot is cut, "there is a great change in a person's talking, dealing, speaking, seeing and in all the movements in his life. He is totally changed, his self begins to melt to become Self."[141] She also used the metaphor of the transmission of the spiritualized substance of the guru into the disciple, explaining that this *shaktipāt* occurs only once because, "once the *shishya* (disciple) has been endowed with the power, there is no problem left. In the real *dīkshā*, the spiritual seed is sown. It produces a tree and there are manifested the fruits on it. One knows that it has happened when one feels the current of the guru's *shakti* flowing in him."[142]

As during the *dīkshā* ceremony, when Mā maintained that God was the guru, her public words usually deflected guruhood from herself to another guru or to God. In the second volume of *Mātri Vāni*, Mā says, "Many tell Mā, 'You are my guru.' And Mā always declares, 'Whatever you may say is all right.' Mā also says, 'The one who is all-pervading, who is variously called *Parabrahman*, *Paramātmā* or God, He verily belongs to all.'"[143] Occasionally, however, Mā admitted to her role as guru. For example, once a disciple asked Mā if the state of realization could be achieved if a *mahātma*, or great soul, casts his glance upon a devotee (*drik dīkshā*) and she replied, "Yes, when a *mahātma* casts a particular glance, it enables the devotee to see the light." The devotee said, "Mā, then cast your kind glance over all these children, please." Mā replied, "You have not instructed me in a correct and perfect way."[144] On another occasion a devotee said to Mā, "You are our guru. Now, please tell us. . . ." and Mā interrupted to say, "There is no case for the guru-*shishya* relationship if the *shishya* is not there. The guru will only speak if the *shishya* is genuine and true." The devotee asked, "Now, you tell me how to become a true and good *shishya*." And Mā replied, "By acting as his guru tells him."[145] In both dialogues, Mā seemed to say that, while she had the capacity to perform the function of guru, only a true disciple could invoke her to fulfill that role.

Mā also spoke of herself as equipped to diagnose each disciple and minister to each according to her or his needs and capacities. Even brief encounters were an opportunity to redirect people's lives according to their particular capacity. Mā narrates:

> I met two *seths*, rich people [on a train]. I asked them to give *bhikshā* (alms), saying, "What can you give?" They were afraid. They thought I was asking for money. They said, "We want to leave right now." I said, "But you said that you want to hear something spiritual from me. I did not ask you to come here. You have come on your own. You asked me to speak and I started speaking. You said you will do as I say. Now when I started talking about alms you are talking of leaving." Both were looking dumbstruck. They were caught in their own words. . . . "What do you want?" one of them asked, "Beans, rice, flour? Whatever you need I shall give you." I explained, "Remember Him who has created you. That is the only alms I want from you." Then he listened to me with great attention and interest and said after listening to me, "I shall surely do as you say. The truth is that we are rich people and we are engaged twenty-four hours a day in these things alone." I said, "At least take off fifteen minutes for Him a day." I thought, "Everybody is busy with this world alone. There should be some efforts to return to their real home."[146]

Thus, Mā functioned as a guru for an inner circle of disciples, giving them *dīkshā* directly or indirectly and guiding their *sādhana*. She exhibited "skill in means" in giving individualized instruction and teachings. However, she did not establish an ongoing lineage to carry on her teachings.

Summary

One of the messages of the Hindu *guru-vāda*, path of the guru, is "Follow me and I will make you like me." The extraordinary guru, a full-grown tree of wisdom and consciousness, takes a disciple, implants within him or her a seed of his spiritualized substance, and nurtures the seed through his teachings, until the disciple grows into his or her own guruhood. Depending on the particular school, this process may be believed to take many lifetimes, or it might be considered possible in one lifetime. But when the seed has been planted and the eternal guru-disciple relationship has been alchemically forged within, it is only a matter of time. Having considered Ānandamayī Mā as both saint and guru, we conclude by asking whether Mā served as an exemplar for her devotees. Did Mā inspire her devotees to follow her example and become like her?

Mā's devotees perceive that Mā's life fell into three fairly distinct stages: the *līlā* of the householder, the *līlā* of *sādhana*, and the *līlā* of the "bird on the wing." Mā, they maintain, fulfilled each consecutive role—that of householder, *sādhikā*, and renouncer—to perfection for their sake. The implication seems to be that Mā was offering models to inspire her devotees. Indeed, although Mā's instructions, particularly to disciples in "privates," were highly individualized, she seemed to direct her devotees according to two broad paradigms: the householder paradigm and the renunciant paradigm.[147] In fact, each of these paradigms can be subdivided by gender because male and female householders often received different advice and male and female renunciants certainly lived out different *sādhanas*.

There is little evidence that Mā wanted all her disciples to follow in her footsteps as a renunciant, although she encouraged or even ordered some disciples to choose the path of renunciation. Most of Mā's devotees and even most of Mā's disciples are householders. Of those devotees I interviewed who were close to Mā, twenty-six were householders and seventeen were renunciants. Here I am referring to both *naishthika brahmachārīs* and *brahmachārinīs*, as well as *sannyāsins* and *sannyāsinīs*, as renunciants.[148] Thirteen of the twenty-six householders were women, and ten of the seventeen renunciants were women. While these numbers may not reflect the proportions among devotees in general, which I suspect would be much higher on the side of householders, I believe they do reflect the division among close disciples. I believe that almost half of Mā's inner circle chose a life of renunciation.

Certainly, the fact that about forty percent of women around Mā chose a life of renunciation, whether formally initiated into it or not, is remarkable, given the pressure on Indian women to marry. However, my interviews indicated that these women did not choose the renunciant life to model themselves on Mā as much as to spend more time in her spiritualizing presence. Most renunciant women managed to avoid an arranged marriage, with or without Mā's help, in order to live full-time with Mā and "serve her." I asked a number of women whether Mā was a model for them. Most of them could not relate to the question and either ignored it or simply said it was impossible to see her as a model. For example, Malini-Di responded, "No, you see, to model yourself on Mā was very, very difficult because Mā was the embodiment of perfection." I asked, "But you had somebody to look up to?" Malini-Di replied, "Really look up to. Way, way up!"[149] Again, Mā is considered beyond the extraordinary and beyond emulation.

From the beginning of my research, I had assumed that women devotees would have been inspired by Mā's life story to take on a life of renunciation in imitation of Mā. Yet the "otherness" attributed to Mā has apparently inhibited that process. I asked Gita-Di Bose, a lifelong disciple, if she ever considered not getting married and taking *brahmacharya*, on the theory that most old, close women devotees had followed Mā into the renunciant path. She responded, "No. I never thought about it. Because I don't believe in that. I believe that I can do everything being here in *samsāra*."[150] Likewise, I asked Malini-Di if she ever thought about getting married as Mā had. She replied, "No. We had accepted Mā as supreme, that whatever Mā did, she had her own reasons for which I had nothing to question."[151] It seems that women devotees did not see Mā's life choices as relevant to them. What was more relevant was what Mā wanted for them.

A few devotees responded in the affirmative to my asking whether Mā was their model. Yet most of their explanations still reflected the same view of Mā as "other." For example, I asked Sita-Ji Aunty, the *brahmachārinī* head of the girls' school in Varanasi, "Who is your model?" She replied, "Mā, she is our model. But she is not a human being. She is above that. Mother and Truth and Reality are One."[152]

However, several people did indicate that Mā was an inspiration to them, if not a model. Vasudha-Di said, "You know, Mā never used to say, 'I.' This is such a great thing that Mā had shown us by her expressions how to be egoless."[153] Narendranath Bose said of Mā,

> She always taught by example. She was one person who always practiced what she preached. Take, for example, simplicity. She wore only white and a yellow towel. What was her bedding? Her bedding was one durrie, one straw mat, and a white sheet on top. She never liked to waste anything. Once in the Kanyapeeth they had washed some rice to be cooked. And in that little place where they washed it, Mā, in her very inscrutable and inimitable way, was going up to her room and noticed three grains of rice, three grains, Lisa, on the floor. She picked them up, washed them and put them inside her mouth. She didn't say anything else. Teaching by example. She used to say in Bengali, "*Pīth karano*," or "Make this a temple." This meant that the rice that you get here is what people give out of charity and should not be wasted here.[154]

Swami Premananda, talking about Mā during her *līlā* as a householder, said, "After fulfilling her household obligations, Mā would sit for meditation. Mā has shown us the ideal. An ordinary human being cannot be like that. But that is the ideal. When she sat for meditation, she had no worldly ties."[155] He seems to be expressing a subtle but important difference between a model and an ideal. People hope to model themselves on a model, becoming like them, while people are inspired by an ideal.

Only two devotees spoke unequivocally about a disciple's potential to become like Mā. I asked Rupa Vishvanathan if she thought that people felt that Mā was beyond imitation. She replied, "No, if you read the Bhagavad Gītā, you know that we are made in the image of God. We must aspire to these qualities. Anyone who reads the Gītā knows that Mā wanted us to be like her." I then asked her, "So can we ever hope to be like Mā?" She replied, "Yes, why not!"[156] A Sanskrit pandit in Varanasi, Gautam Shrivastav, expressed a desire to attain *samādhi* like Mā's:

> We read about *samādhi* in the *shāshtras*. But by seeing Mā in that state, we saw that it was a practical reality. After seeing Mā in that state, I felt an outpouring of love and kindness in my heart. I also wanted to experience that state. So I asked Mā, "Even though this state is so high, if I want to know that state, can I do it?" Mā said, "Baba, if the Lord wishes, it will happen." This was a very common answer. I was silent for a while. But finally I said, "No, Mā, let me know something. Tell me something at least." Then Mā said, "Look, even though that state of *kriyā* is very high, if you earnestly want that state, nothing is impossible." After that, with great kindness, she told me, "This state of *samādhi* can only be reached through *prānayam* (controlled breathing). That is the first step." So now I do *prānayam* according to her instruction.[157]

I imagine that this second set of remarks in particular would raise doubts in the minds of most devotees about the speaker's seriousness as a devotee. They might feel that he was arrogant to imagine himself attaining Mā's state or spiritually materialistic to want to. As already mentioned, there is a sense in which Mā's charisma had been institutionalized in the community so as to make ecstatic states her sole propriety.

Although it seems difficult to determine whether she intended her devotees to emulate her, Mā clearly had a vision of their attaining Self-realization. She was untiring in delivering her prescription: be receptive to her powerful presence, turn within, follow her teachings, do the practices. She said:

> When the burning desire to know Truth or Reality awakens in man, he has the good fortune of meeting a Saint or Sage. The Holy and Wise must be approached with a pure heart and a steady mind, with genuine faith and reverence. Much greater benefit will be derived by sitting still and meditating in their presence than by discussing or arguing. The behavior of saints is not to be copied by ordinary people. But one should endeavor to carry out in one's life the teaching or advice received by them. Otherwise it would be

like sowing any number of seeds without allowing a single plant to grow. This would indeed be a matter of deep regret.[158]

Mā seems to raise the question here of whether her devotees had what it takes to pursue *sādhana* seriously enough to grow into a full plant. This theme is echoed in the following statement Mā made in *satsang*:

> The *kripa* (grace) of God is always there. He is showering the *kripa* just as the clouds rain. Not only *kripa*, but his *shakti* (power) is also raining inside. Three things: *kriyā* (action), *kripa*, and *shakti* are raining inside. Those who keep their vessels upright, fill them with that *kripa* and *shakti*. But if the vessels are kept upside down, these things flow away. But since it is raining all the time, if one holds his vessel the way he should, he gets it.[159]

In the course of my interviews with Mā's devotees, seven people said that Mā may have been disappointed with devotees who were unable to be serious disciples, holding their vessels up. Vasudha-Di reported that most people wrote to Mā only for worldly things.[160] Mira Chatterji confirmed this, saying, "Naturally persons in the household world want money, children, that kind of thing. So Mā says, 'Don't waste time in this way. Ask for something great.' But we didn't ask for something heavenly."[161] One swami praised Swami Jnanananda: "He has taken whatever Mā wanted to give; we have taken only worldly things. Mā can give the spiritual world, but we are interested only in good living and good food."[162]

Others, like Lakshmi Shrivastav, put it more dramatically, speaking of Mā's statement to the head of the northern Shankaracharya sect that it was not her *kheyāla* to get well because of "the call of the unmanifest":

> Another thing, I think Mā was quite disheartened. Even those people who were very close to her were not very truthful according to her standard. And no one was prepared to take the truth from her. She told Bithikaji, 'I have so much to give, but there's no one to take it. . . . Even those who asked for philosophical things, they didn't go as deep as she wanted them to go. She understood those who only wanted materialistic things. But she did not find anyone who could go as deeply into the truth that "There is only One" as she did.[163]

Rupa Vishvanathan told me that Mā's disappointment in her disciples was revealed to her in a dream.

> Mā herself said it in my dream. Mā came in my dream. There is a narrow path going along a hill, dimly lit. I am just about able to see Mā. Then she comes up to me and she says, "See, you have come up this path. It looks very difficult. But I am telling everyone, 'It won't be difficult if you carry me on your back.'" Those were her words. She means if you take her with you always. But she told me, "Nobody's willing to do it!" She said this. She said, "I'm telling everybody. 'Don't be put off by the path. You just have to carry me with you. It will be made easy!' But they are not willing to do it." Then I tell her—of course, this looks like a little bit of ego—"Mā, I think I will do it." She says, "Oh, will you do it, will you?" She seems so pleased in the

dream! So, Mā was the manifestation of love and compassion. She wants us to pick it up and manifest it, too. The guru expects you to be like him![164]

I asked most devotees, "What is the goal of your *sādhana?*" Several householders either ignored the question or misunderstood it. One person said she "was not the type to do *sādhana*" and told me that her practice was "to remember Mā in every moment. Mā will do the rest for me."[165] However, a surprising number of householders appeared to be devoted to *sādhana*, setting high goals for themselves. Lalita Kumar said that the goal of her *sādhana* was liberation from karma. She added, "A lot of our sins have been washed away by having Mā's *darshan*, Mā's *kripa.*"[166] Sita Gupta told me that the goal of her *sādhana* was *brahmajnāna*, the knowledge of Brahman. She follows a strict regimen of daily practices, which includes *japa* and meditation on Mā, or *gurubhāva*.[167] Rupa Vishvanathan said that she told Mā, " 'I would not mind coming back to this world again, but I have to be with you. I don't want marriage, no children, nothing.' " I only desire to be with her, to serve her any way she wants me to serve her."[168]

Predictably, renunciant devotees were more forthcoming about the goal of *sādhana* than most of the householders. Malini-Di said,

> What we have heard from Mā is that the highest point of *sādhana* is when you and God become one. That is the goal of *sādhana*. . . . Mā used to add something else, "*Apne ko jana, maine apne ko pana. Bhagavān ke jana, maine apke ko pana.*" This means, "And if you realize God, you have realized your Self. If you have realized your Self, you have realized God."[169]

Sita-Ji's answer mirrors Malini-Di's: "The goal of *sādhana* is to realize your own Self. Everything you see outside you is within."[170]

Swami Samatananda's answer to the question blends the goal of nondual awareness with the flavor of Shākta devotion. I think Swami Samatananda articulates the prevalent notion of *sādhana* and its goal within the community of Ānandamayī Mā. He describes Bhaiji's death, in which he reportedly experienced union with Mā. He goes on to say,

> The goal of meditation is to merge inside Mother. Bhaiji is our greatest devotee of Mā. . . . This is our goal, the goal of Bhaiji. By meditating on Mā, by living by her teachings, as the river merges into the sea, we want to merge into her sea. . . . So a child enters into Mā. So the merging beyond duality is this path envisioned as merging with Mā. . . . Mā is the goal and we think that by meditating on Mā we can reach that. If we catch hold of Mā's hand, then Mā will lead us to whatever is needed for us. So we do not have a beautiful idea about the light of consciousness and I'll become this and that. We think we will meditate on Mā and we will love Mā and she will show us. Whatever is good for us, she will give us.[171]

This theme of Mā as the goal of *sādhana* and surrender to Mā as the means is mirrored in my conversation with Vasudha-Di. She said, "In the scriptures we find *moksha*, or liberation, but I myself don't think *moksha* is anything. . . . I don't think about going ahead to reach anything. I don't think I have to do anything. I have got this Mā. That's all. Mā had got a hold on me. So now this is Mā's responsibility to show me how, to keep me or throw me out."[172]

These statements reflect a tension between self-effort and grace, between hard-won knowledge and devotion, a tension we return to in chapter 6. Mā's message to her disciples seems to have been to take their *sādhana* seriously, to take the steps necessary to turn within and "color their lives the color of God."[173] Whether she intended for them to or not, most of Mā's devotees chose to color their lives *her* color, to make her more than their guru, to make her their *ishta devatā*, their chosen deity. Seeing the guru as God is, indeed, part of the *guruvāda* path. However, the *guruvāda* also maintains that a disciple reaches liberation through a perfect balance of grace and self-effort, the two wings of the bird. The disciple nurtures the seed of the guru's realized consciousness, or the guru's grace, by exerting self-effort in following the path that the guru has taken. Ultimately, the disciple becomes the guru.

In the case of Ānandamayī Mā, we see a different phenomenon. Devotees insist that Mā was not a guru because she was not a human being but rather an incarnation of God. Therefore, the theologies of her devotees emphasize grace over self-effort. The goal of their *sādhana* is not to become like her but to remain with her forever. They see themselves less as *shishyas* and more as *bhaktas*, or those devoted to God. Was Mā, then, a frustrated guru who saw her disciples as relying too heavily on grace? Did she wonder why more people were not willing to walk the steep path to liberation, albeit carrying her along with them to help, as Rupa Vishvanathan reports in her dream? Or did *Mā* see herself as "beyond the extraordinary" and encourage her devotees to lean heavily upon her grace? We address these questions as we consider Ānandamayī Mā as deity.

SIX

Ānandamayī Mā as *Avatāra* and Divine Mother

ajo 'pi sann avyayātmā bhūtānām ishvaro 'pi san,
prakritim svām adhishthāya sambhavāmyātmamāyayā.

yadā yadā hi dharmasya glānir bhavati bhārata
abhyutthānam adharmasya tadā 'tmānam srijāmyaham.

paritrānāya sādhūnām vināshāya ca dushkritām
dharmasamsthāpanārthāya sambhavāmi yuge yuge.

Although I am birthless and my self imperishable,
Although I am the Lord of All Beings,
Yet, by controlling my own material nature,
I come into being by my own supernatural power.

Wherever a decrease of righteousness
Exists, Descendant of Bharata,
And there is a rising up of unrighteousness,
Then I give forth myself.

For the protection of the good
And the destruction of evil doers;
For the sake of establishing righteousness,
I come into being from age to age.

Bhagavad Gītā, Chapter 4, Verses 6–8[1]

S O LORD KRISHNA DESCRIBES himself in one of the most famous passages of the Bhagavad Gītā. "Shri Shri Ma Anandamayi: Satsang with the Blissful Mother"[2] a film on Ānandamayī Mā made by several devotees, opens with a panoramic shot of the sun rising over the Ganges in the

Himalayan foothills. Over the background music of a morning *rāga*, a woman's voice recites these verses, which suggest that Mā, like Lord Krishna, is the Lord of All Beings, incarnated on earth for the sake of establishing righteousness. In this chapter we see how and why she is considered divine in origin. In her introduction to *Women Saints East and West,* Vijaya Laksmi Pandit writes that a saint is an example of "the human character at its highest level," a character that is "not a divine gift, but a human achievement."[3] By contrast, the *avatāra* is God who has taken on human form, perfect, birthless (*ajas*), and imperishable (*avyaya*). According to devotees, Ānandamayī Mā's character was not a divine gift or an achievement. It was the perfect, eternal character of the divine itself. Therefore, although most of Mā's close disciples maintain that she is beyond definition, when pressed they use words such as *avatāra*, "Divine Mother", or "God" to describe her.

This chapter begins with a discussion of the history of the Hindu concept of incarnation and a brief overview of the worship of the Divine Feminine within the tradition. It goes on to enumerate the many ways in which Mā is described by her devotees as divine and the evidence presented to substantiate her divinity. The discussion that follows highlights how Mā herself conceptualized the Absolute and her relationship to it, particularly on Mā's role in originating the idea that her periods of spiritual practice were merely a play, or *līlā*, put on for the sake of her devotees. Finally, it tries to determine whether Mā's teaching was primarily that of *bhakti* yoga, with its emphasis on devotion and grace, or *jnāna* yoga, with its emphasis on knowledge and self-effort, and how Mā's devotees responded to that teaching.

The Hindu Conception of Divine Incarnation

There has been considerable interest in the study of the Hindu conception of divine incarnation and in comparative study of Hindu and Christian conceptions.[4] Daniel Bassuk, in *Incarnation in Hinduism and Christianity*, says that "all the world's religions have offered some means of bridging the distance between God and mankind," but in the Hindu and the Christian traditions, there is a common belief that God has taken and may again take human form to serve as a model and savior.[5] Within the Hindu tradition, there are two progressions along the continuum between human and divine. The first progression is the ascending progression from human being to perfected being, for example, *siddha* or *sadguru*, in which matter is considered to have been spiritualized by the will and actions of a human being. The second is the descending progression from God into perfect being, or *avatāra*, in which spirit is seen to have materialized by the will of God.[6] The word *avatāra* itself is composed of the verb root *trī-*, which means to cross over, and the prefix *ava*, which means down, connoting descent of God from the eternal to the temporal realm. Just as there are various levels of spiritual attainment (for example, a *sādhu* or a *sādhvī* [holy person], might progress to be a *sadguru* [true guru] or a *siddha* [perfected being]), there is a notion of degrees of concentration of God in the *avatāra*. The supreme God is called *Avatārin*, or the source of *avatāras*. His embodiment on earth can be full, called *pūrnāvatāra*, or partial, called *amshāvatāra*, embodying only an aspect or portion of the divine.

The concept of *avatāra* was formally introduced around the turn of the common era in the *Mahābhārata* and was developed more fully in the Bhagavad Gītā. Although an *avatāra* is the descent of any deity to earth, in its earliest context it usually referred to the descent of the god Vishnu. The ten classical *avatāras* of Vishnu are Matsya, the fish; Kurma, the tortoise; Varaha, the boar; Narasimha, the lion; Vāmana, the dwarf; Parashurāma, or Rāma with the axe; Rāma; Krishna; Buddha; and Kalki, the *avatāra* of the future. Vishnu's most famous incarnations are Lord Krishna, the hero of the *Mahābhārata* and Bhagavad Gītā, and Lord Rāma, immortalized in the *Rāmāyana*.

That the Bhagavad Gītā is one of the most beloved of Hindu texts is testimony to the power of the doctrine of *avatāra*. In the Gītā we encounter Lord Krishna, called to earth to destroy the wicked and restore *dharma*. We see the formal introduction of the yoga of devotion or *bhakti*, and the doctrine of grace. While it is usually assumed that Lord Krishna of the Bhagavad Gītā is an *avatāra* of Vishnu, Gonda and Hill maintain that Lord Krishna in the Bhagavad Gītā is an *avatāra* of Brahman.[7] Certainly there is a sense in which Lord Krishna is considered the perfect or full *avatāra* in the Gītā and might even be considered *Avatārin*, or source of *avatāras*; many of Mā's prominent devotees maintain that she, too, was greater than an *avatāra*.

The doctrine of *avatāra*, first presented in the epics, became highly developed in the Shri Vaishnava theology of the twelfth-century philosopher Rāmānuja and his successors. In his commentary on the Bhagavad Gītā, 4, verses 4 to 9, in which the opening verses of this chapter appear, Rāmānuja offers a systematic theological statement on the doctrine of *avatāra*. Carman condenses it as follows:

> The Lord comes into our finite world by his own will rather than because of the inevitable consequences of past deeds. Without giving up his own nature as Divine Lord, which includes both his opposition to evil and his possession of auspicious attributes, he takes bodily form appropriate to a particular descent, i.e., he appears to be a god or a man or some other kind of being. . . . The principal purpose of the Lord's coming is to become accessible to those who are seeking him as their refuge but are unable to comprehend him and therefore are in great distress, to allow these virtuous people, who are his preeminent worshippers, to behold him as he is, to see his deeds and listen to his words. The other purposes of God's descent are to destroy the wicked and to restore the declining Vedic religion. . . . If you know that the Lord's birth in an apparently material body is not connected with ordinary matter and that his deeds are his own doing, not determined by past deeds (karma), and that they are intended for the salvation of good people, then you yourself will experience no further births but will attain God.[8]

Although Rāmānuja is, of course, referring to Lord Krishna, several points are relevant to a discussion of Ānandamayī Mā as *avatāra*. First, the Lord descends to earth, as the devotees of Ānandamayī Mā might say, in response to his own *kheyāla*. Second, his body, while real, "consists of a special pure matter unlike ordinary material bodies."[9] Third, his devotees need only, in a sense, recognize his nature as "beyond the extraordinary" to be saved.

Although, Carman reminds us, many Hindus "explicitly reject the idea that God descends to earth and lives out an entire life in an apparently mortal body,"[10] the ideology of *avatāra* has powerfully shaped the religious experience of Hindus throughout the centuries. In the last five hundred years, the concept of *avatāra* has been reinterpreted and applied to many historical Hindu religious figures. One of the first was the Bengali Vaishnava saint, Krishna Chaitanya (1498–1533). Chaitanya, contemptuous of the *bhakti* path as a young man, received a powerful initiation into the worship of Krishna, renounced the householder life, and become famous for his ecstatic states. It is said that three characteristics led to his being recognized as an *avatāra*, although he never identified himself as such: his powerful *kīrtan*, his devotion to Krishna as if he were Rādhā, and his belief that he was possessed by Lord Krishna.[11] At first he was considered an *aveshāvatāra*, one possessed by Krishna and Rādhā, but later he was proclaimed *pūrnāvatāra*, a full incarnation. Dimock says that, according to Krishnadāsa's "Nectar of the Acts," Chaitanya is considered "Chaitanya in overt form, Krishna (and Rādhā) in covert form, and Krishna in essence."[12] Since the "avatarization" of Chaitanya, it has become more common for disciples of holy figures to claim that their master was an *avatāra*.

The second "modern" historical figure considered an *avatāra* was the Bengali ecstatic, Ramakrishna Paramahamsa (1836–1886). Ramakrishna, a temple priest near Calcutta, became mad with love for Mother Kālī and displayed nearly constant states of ecstasy and divine madness. When Ramakrishna was in his early twenties, a tantric holy woman recognized him as an *avatāra*, compared him to Chaitanya, and arranged a debate between two scholars to confirm this identity, which they did. He went on to pursue many different *sādhanas* and to attract a large group of sophisticated devotees, the most famous of which was Swami Vivekananda, who initiated the worldwide Ramakrishna Mission.

Probably the best known list of the characteristics of contemporary *avatāras* is provided by Swami Sāradānanda, one of the foremost disciples of Shri Ramakrishna. Sāradānanda says, first, that *avatāras* are born free; that is, they have no karma to expiate. The implication is that they have never been subject to the law of karma. Second, they have a perfect memory of their former births.[13] Third, *avatāras* discover new religious paths. Fourth, they have the ability to transmit knowledge by touch or will. Fifth, they can perceive the *samskāras*, or past impressions and tendencies, of their devotees. Finally, *avatāras* are conscious of a sense of mission throughout their lives. They have descended to reestablish *dharma*, or righteousness, by their teaching and example.[14] The only characteristic that is not also a characteristic of a *sadguru* is the first one: Although the true guru has performed *sādhana* to burn through his or her karma and develop *siddhis*, the *avatāra* was born perfect and without karma, Self-conscious and Self-realized from birth. Swami Samatananda, Ramakrishna's disciple, maintained: "The incarnations of God are aware, even from their birth, that they are other than ordinary people. And this knowledge gives them immense compassion for all who are in bondage with worldly desires. It is to help them that the incarnation performs his *sādhana*."[15]

Furthermore, according to Isherwood, the orthodox Hindu view is that not only is an incarnation fully conscious of his divinity at every moment but also "whatever he does is only a kind of play-acting (a *līlā*)."[16] This concept of *līlā* has its roots in the Vaisnava tradition and usually refers to the divine love-play between Rādhā and Krishna, activities to be contemplated by the devout. Neal Delmonico clarifies, "Sport *(līlā)* here means all of the activities of the divine couple, none of which can be, almost by definition, anything other than sport or play. In India, the play of a deity is both the proof and the symbol of its divinity. Deities, resting on inexhaustible cushions of power, play; humans work."[17] Beginning with Caitanya, this concept of *līlā* has been applied to historical figures, thereby designating them as divine. We examine later Ānandamayī Mā's devotees' determination to characterize everything she did as *līlā*, particularly her periods of spiritual practice, thereby establishing that she was not a perfected being, but rather of divine origin.

Since Shri Ramakrishna, several others have been considered to possess such qualities and have called themselves *avatāras*. Shri Aurobindo (1872–1950), originally from Bengal but residing primarily in Pondicherry, and his spiritual partner, the French-born Mīrā Richard, or the Mother (1878–1973), declared each other *avatāras* of Shiva and Shaktī and were considered so by their devotees. In 1926, Shri Aurobindo declared that he had experienced the ascent to what he called the Divine Overmind and would begin the corresponding descent of the Supermind, or Godhead.[18] He describes his "descent" in the following poem by the same title:

> All my cells thrill swept by a surge of splendour,
> Soul and body stir with a mighty rapture,
> Light and still more light like an ocean billows
>   Over me, round me.
> Rigid, stone-like, fixed like a hill or statue,
> Vast my body feels and upbears the world's weight;
> Dire the large descent of the Godhead enters
>   Limbs that are mortal.[19]

Shri Aurobindo is reinterpreting the *avatāra* concept to include the descent of the Godhead into a mortal form after a period of intensive *sādhana*.

When Aurobindo went into retreat in 1926, the Mother was placed in charge of Shri Aurobindo ashram. In 1956, six years after the death of Shri Aurobindo, she declared that she had fully evolved as an *avatāra*, articulating a process in which she became the descending Godhead. She describes the moment of her fulfillment as *avatāra* in the following way:

This evening the Divine Presence, concrete and material, was there present amongst you. I had a form of living gold, bigger than the universe, and I was facing a huge and massive golden door which separated the world from the Divine. As I looked at the door, I knew and willed in a single movement of consciousness, that "the time has come," and lifting with both hands a mighty golden hammer I struck one blow, one single blow on the door and the door was shattered to pieces. Then the supramental Light and Force and Consciousness rushed down upon earth in an uninterrupted flow.[20]

Mīrā Richard was regarded as the Divine Mother from that day on. Interestingly, both Shri Aurobindo and the Mother referred to Chaitanya and Ramakrishna as "reputed avatāras," based on their apparent ignorance of their own avatarhood.[21] This reflects a twentieth century phenomenon in which those who consider themselves avatāras reflect on and discriminate between those they consider avatāras and those they think are not avatāras.[22]

Another contemporary of Ānandamayī Mā's who declared himself an avatāra was Meher Baba (1894–1969), who was born a Parsi and is famous for having maintained silence for forty-four years. Meher Baba developed an elaborate theory of avatāras in which he maintained that an avatāra descended every seven hundred or fourteen hundred years. He named seven avatāras: Zoroaster, Rāma, Krishna, Buddha, Jesus, Muhammed, and, finally, himself. He said, "I am that Ancient One whose past is worshipped and remembered, whose present is ignored and forgotten, and whose future (Advent) is anticipated with great fervor and longing."[23] Here Meher Baba seems to be claiming that he is an avatāra in the traditional sense of one who is the perfect Godhead born in an apparently mortal body. He referred to Ramakrishna and Aurobindo as "Perfect Masters," not avatāras. He also held that an avatāra "always incarnates in the the body of a male,"[24] which would exclude both Mīrā Richard and Ānandamayī Mā.

A more recent self-proclaimed avatāra is the miracle-performing Satya Sai Baba (1926–). Sai Baba acknowledges all the mythic avatāras, as well as Shankara, Ramakrishna, Aurobindo, and Jesus Christ, claiming that he himself is a reincarnation of Jesus Christ. While he designates the other historical figures as partial avatāras, or amshāvatāras, he says he is a a full avatāra, or pūrnāvatāra, like Lord Krishna.[25] According to Bassuk, Satya Sai Baba lists seven qualities of a pūrnāvatāra:

> (1) the power to bestow grace on the deserving, (2) the power to bestow grace on the undeserving (aurhetu kripa), (3) the power to awaken new states of consciousness and a new order of society, (4) the power to support what is good but defenceless, (5) the power to destroy what is evil, (6) a form which when recalled mentally invokes the spiritual or physical presence of the avatar, (7) and a name which has divine potency.[26]

Sai Baba spares no words in referring to himself as God descended to earth. In 1963, after recovering from what seemed to be a terminal stroke, Sai Baba said:

Let me tell you one more thing. Nothing can impede or halt the work of this Avatar. When I was upstairs all those days, some people foolishly went about saying, "It is all over with Sai Baba." Some said I was in *samadhi* (communion with God)—as if I am a *sadhaka* (aspirant). Some feared I was a victim of black magic—as if anything can affect me. The splendor of this Avatar will go on increasing day by day. Formerly when the *Govardhanagiri* (a particular mountain) was raised aloft by the little boy, Krishna, the *gopis* and *gopalas* (milkmaids and cowherdsman, friends and companions of Krishna) realized that Krishna was the Lord. Now, not one *Govardhanagiri* but a whole range will be lifted—you will see! Have patience; have faith.[27]

Satya Sai Baba predicts that he will live until the year 2022 and will be reborn as Prema Sai Baba in Karnataka.[28]

Some scholars question what is behind the trend of applying the *avatāra* paradigm to living spiritual leaders. Charles White believes it is motivated by a desire to widen a sect's influence; if the larger community accepts a leader as divine in origin and worthy of worship, the sect will grow in membership and stature.[29] William Jackson says that applying the paradigm to a contemporary pan-Indian religious figure "impresses their importance on reverent minds, enabling the fullest veneration possible."[30] Regardless, spiritual leaders claimed to be divine have been part of the Hindu religious landscape for the last two centuries.

The Worship of the Divine Mother

Sister Nivedita, an English disciple of Shrī Ramakrishna's wife, Sarada Devi, in *Kali the Mother*, says,

> The soul that worships becomes always a little child: the soul that becomes a child finds God oftenest as mother. . . . It is in India that this thought of the mother has been realized in its completeness. In that country where the image of Kali is one of the most popular symbols of deity, it is quite customary to speak of God, as "She," and the direct address then offered is simply, "Mother."[31]

Indeed, worship of God as the sacred feminine is one of the oldest and most continuous forms of religious expression in India. She is called by many names. In her universal form she is called Devī, the Great Goddess; Shakti, the primal creative energy of the universe; or simply Mā, or Mother. In texts that describe her exploits in the world of form, she is called one of hundreds of names, such as Durgā, Pārvatī, or Lakshmī. In the villages of southern Asia, she is called one of thousands of names that express different aspects of her unlimited manifestations, such as Manasā, Māriyamman, or Periyapālayattamman. While she is understood by most of her children to be many, she is also understood to be One.[32] Although most Hindus devote some part of their devotional life to the worship of Devī in some form, those who relate to the Absolute primarily as feminine principle are called Shāktas, or those who are "of the *shakti*."

There has been a great deal of recent interest in the study of the Hindu Devī.[33] Most scholars trace her origin to the pre-Aryan civilization that flourished in the fertile Indus Valley between 2500 and 1500 B.C.E. or to indigenous tribes that preexisted, rather than to the Aryan civilization that migrated into southern Asia during the second millenium B.C.E. Although the Goddess appears sometimes significantly in Vedic texts in forms such as Ushas, the dawn, Vāc, speech, and Sarasvatī, the mother as river, Vedic imagery is heavily masculine, and her appearance in the Vedas and Upanishads has usually related her to the dominant gods. During the epic period, around the turn of the common era, goddesses are prominent in mythology as consorts of the gods but have little or no significance on their own. During the Purānic period, however, from 400 B.C.E. onward, the Goddess as independent, cosmic Mahādevī begins to develop. In the *Devī Māhātmya*, written in the sixth century C.E. and found as part of the *Mārkandeya Purāna*, the Goddess becomes "crystallized," as Coburn puts it, entering the stream of the Sanskritic tradition to become the focus of a legitimate cult.[34] In the succeeding centuries, this cult spread, "both influencing and absorbing various cultic, mythic, and symbolic elements of tribal and local deities."[35]

Sāktism, defined by Erndl as "the worship of the primordial power underlying the universe, personified as a female deity who is the Supreme Being,"[36] developed as a formal sectarian option between the sixth and tenth centuries, influenced by the parallel development of *tantra*, whose Sanskrit texts appeared around the ninth century.[37] *Tantra*, literally "a loom," wove threads of the yoga and wisdom traditions, shamanism, and folklore into the fabric of a spiritual discipline which, once Sanskritized, was to have a major influence on sectarian Hinduism, particularly Shāktism, as it conceived of the liberating energy of spiritual life as *shakti*, the feminine energy.[38]

There are two major approaches in Tantrism, the *dakshinācāra*, or right-handed path, and the *vāmācāra*, or left-handed path. According to N. N. Bhattacharyya, the right-handed tantric path is designed for the "traditional Hindu who believes in the Vedic norms."[39] Called *Devībhakti*, it involves worshiping the Goddess with Vedic rites and engaging in spiritual practices such as *japa* and meditation, often focusing on a *yantra*, or sacred diagram. It may also include internal meditation on the *chakras*, or subtle energy centers of the body. The left-handed path is considered the more esoteric and controversial path. Bhattacharyya says that its followers "are expected to worship the goddess in the traditional way during the daytime, and at night in the special Tantric way with the help of the five M's."[40] The "five M's" are *mamsa* (meat), *matsya* (fish), *mudra* (fried rice), *mada* (intoxicants), and *maithuna* (intercourse outside marriage), all forbidden in brahmanical society but used in the tantric ritual setting for the purpose of transcending duality. Both paths emphasize *dīkshā* from a *shaktipāt* guru, the practices of *kundalinī* yoga, following the guru's instructions for *sādhana* with complete surrender, and the power of secrecy.[41] Ānandamayī Mā served some devotees as a *shaktipāt* guru, yet it seems that Mā's community is overwhelmingly orthodox, and, by and large, devotees avoid the use of the word *tantra* to describe its practices or philosophy. Thus, in this chapter we do not examine tantric texts per se but, instead, use two Shākta texts which are foundational to *Devībhakti*, the *Devī Māhātmya* and the *Devī Bhāgavata Purāna*, to help us understand the theology of Ānandamayī Mā's devotees.[42]

The *Devī Māhātmya*, chanted daily by many Shāktas, is the oldest and most popular of Shākta texts and plays an important role in the yearly celebration of Durgā Pūjā in Bengal. It relates the exploits of the Great Goddess, referred to by fifty different epithets, who was formed out of the light emitted by the gods to come forth and slay the demons who were tyrannizing the three worlds and rendering the gods helpless. It might seem that her creation out of the gods would diminish her greatness; however, when the demon army appears again to be invincible, she herself emits the fierce goddess, Kālī, from her own brow, establishing her self-sufficiency and all-powerfulness. Although the Goddess in this text is associated primarily with Vishnu and secondarily with Shiva, she is clearly envisioned as Ultimate Reality, completely independent and both transcendent and immanent. Furthermore, paralleling Lord Krishna's claim, she promises to incarnate (*avatīrya*) in the future to slay further demons and maintain world order, thus establishing herself as Avatārin, the source of *avatāras*.[43] In the ensuing centuries, many tantric texts offered interpretations of the *Devī Māhātmya*, reinforcing its significance.

The *Devī Bhāgavata Purāna*, an eleventh or twelfth century Sanskrit text, systematizes the Shākta theology of the *Devī Māhātmya*. While the *Devī Māhātmya* emphasized the dreadful side of the Goddess, the *Devī Bhāgavata* stresses the "supremely compassionate side of the Goddess. . . the Mother most herself when at play, rather than at war."[44] It presents Devī as more teacher than warrior. In one section, the *Devī Gītā*, the Goddess emerges out of the mass of light not primarily to slay demons but to teach the gods the deepest truths of Vedānta. This "Vedāntic mellowing"[45] of the Goddess may have set the stage for the further softening of the Goddess seen in the Shākta devotional poetry of Bengali poets such as Rāmprasād Sen, which culminated in the creation of her benevolent, accessible contemporary form as seen in Bengal today.[46] Furthermore, the *Devī Bhāgavata* delineates a devotional path in which the goal of devotion is simply to have the *darshan* of the compassionate Mother. King Subahū of Banaras says,

> In comparing sovereignty of the worlds of heaven and earth, on the one hand, and the vision (*darshana*) of you, O Devī, on the other, there is nothing equal [to the latter]. In all the three worlds, there is for me nothing like your *darshana*. What boon should I choose, when all my goals are accomplished? I only ask this, O Mother, that I may have firm and unswerving devotion to you always.[47]

Along with this emphasis on devotion to the Mother for its own sake, the *Devī Bhāgavata* also articulates a more elaborate theory of Shākta incarnation, more closely mirroring that of the Bhagavad Gītā. While relating the myth of Devī's battles with the demons, it describes her as the defender of *dharma*, having three successive cosmic manifestations related to her three major encounters with the demons. The text names these manifestations as Mahākālī, Mahālakshmī, and Mahāsarasvatī, the goddesses of destruction, preservation, and creation, and thus imposes a theological interpretation on the events.[48] Furthermore, in the *Devī Gītā*, Devī describes her *avatāras* as Satī, daughter of Daksha, and Pārvatī, daughter of Himavān,[49] and her essential forms as Brahman, Īshvara, Brahmā, Vishnu, Shiva, Gaurī, Brahmī, and Vaishnavī. As did Lord Krishna in the Bhagavad Gītā, she also reveals her wondrous cosmic form in a theophany.[50] Thus, the text paves the way for future attributions of avatarahood for women religious figures.[51]

Third, the *Devī Bhāgavata*, unlike its Vaishnava counterpart, the *Shrīmad Bhāgavatam*, offers a positive assessment of the world and of the life of a householder.[52] It attempts to break down the dualism of spirit and matter, espousing a monism that becomes characteristic of the Shākta path, in which "matter and spirit are not differentiated but are a continuity subsumed within *shakti*, the dynamic feminine creative principle."[53] So, rather than point to the commitments of worldly life as fetters, the *Devī Bhāgavata*

> emphasizes that sons, house, wives, and the like are not in themselves what binds; rather it is *ahamkāra* [ego] that binds creatures to *samsāra*. It is the mistaken sense that one has somehow achieved one's wealth, success, and happiness by one's own doing that is the problem. The Devī, like Vishnu, grants wealth and pleasure on a "lower plane." But her higher form of grace does not necessarily deny these creature comforts; rather it provides insight to allow one to enjoy prosperity and good fortune as her gifts without the egocentric delusion of taking personal credit for them. Her gifts are simply to be enjoyed for what they are, the beneficence of the divine mother.[54]

Thus, the goal of spiritual life is the integration of worldly prosperity and liberation, *bhukti* and *mukti*, in which "liberation does not negate or cancel out the temporal order, but exists and is reflected within that very order."[55] Furthermore, selfless devotion toward Devī gives one a perspective on life in which one sees that everything is her doing.

Fourth, the *Devī Bhāgavata* describes the Goddess as both *saguna*, possessing an individual divine form, and *nirguna*, ultimately and eternally existing as formless consciousness or Brahman.[56] It is in her embodied, *saguna* forms that she reveals herself when she grants a devotee her *darshana*. But she rarely reveals her ultimate and transcendent nature as *sāttvikā* (the essence of truth and goodness).[57] For that form to be ultimate, the *Devī Bhāgavata* tells us, it must include both male and female but transcend both. Devī responds to Lord Brahmā's question of her gender by identifying herself as Brahman: " 'One alone without a second,' verily that is the eternal Brahman. That becomes dual at the time of creation. . . . After the creation ends, I am neither a woman, a man nor a eunuch."[58] However, says Brown, although Devī "in her supreme form as consciousness transcends gender," her transcendence is not apart from her immanence, which is feminine.[59]

Mā's Devotees on "Who Is Mā?"

I asked twenty-six devotees and two nondevotees, "Who is Mā?" and, not surprisingly, the answers were as diverse as the devotees themselves. Narendrath Bose explained, "You see, for everybody Mā was a very different person, because she responded to individual vibrations. . . . You will have to draw your own conclusions."[60] The most common reply to the question was "Mā is God." Nearly all devotees were interviewed in English; although some went on to give equivalent Sanskrit terms such as "Parabrahman" or "Devī", the first word that nine devotees used to describe Mā was "God". It is important to acknowledge the inherent complexity of the term "God" as it is used in this multilingual, multicultural context.

The *brahmachārinī*, Malini-Di, spoke poignantly about knowing Mā since her birth, having been born into a devotee family:

> When I was in school, I was about seven or eight years old, the Christian nuns over there, they said that God never comes on earth. And so, I was very upset, because. . . I said, "No, I have spoken to God!" And they said, "You can't speak to God. There is no such thing. God never comes to earth. Only Jesus Christ can and no one else!" They said unless you believe in Jesus Christ, you can never reach God. So I was very perturbed. All these things I was told. And when I came back home I cried and I cried. So my mother asked me, "What is the matter?" So I told her, "They have been telling me that unless I become a Christian, I won't reach God. And I told them, 'No, I have met God. I have talked to her. I have seen her. For on our holidays, we go to God!' How can they say those things?" So my mother said, "Don't worry, they won't understand this. But, yes, your God talks to you."

I asked, "So did your family have an *ishta devatā* [a chosen deity]?" Malini-Di replied, "No, we believe in Krishna and Rām and things like that, but as children we were taught that Mā was everything. For us Mā was Krishna, Mā was Rām, Mā was Shiva, everything. . . . To us, the name of God was Mā."[61] Sita Gupta reiterated this theme when she said, "My children and grandchildren know of no other God except Mother. You say "Rām" or "Krishna" or "Shiva" or "Devī," they think Mā. They don't know these others, just Mā."[62] Naren Bose, who also grew up in a family devoted to Mā, put it this way:

> For me Mā is God. I don't know what God is. I haven't experienced what God is. I have no deep knowledge of the Hindu scriptures or any scriptures. So my conviction in any one established religion per se is not there. All my convictions are what I have seen through Mā. All my belief is only Mā. And God for me is Mā. . . . Mā is my life, very simple. Everything.[63]

Three other devotees put it even more succinctly. Swami Krishnananda referred to Mā as "God himself."[64] Swami Gitananda said, "What does one mean by God? Does God have four legs or arms or what? What is God, who knows? But when you saw Mā, you knew, 'Here is my God!' "[65] Sita

Aunty, the head of the Sanskrit girl's school put it this way, "Mother was God in the form of Truth."[66]

For some people the recognition of Mā's divinity took time. Uma Chatterjee said,

> After I met Mā, I could not immediately associate Mā with God. But after some time, it became Mā and God, the duality. But it took me years to identify Mā with God as One. And it took place because of fantastic experiences and dramatic situations. But for Mā there is no beginning and end to the story. It is all her *līlā*.[67]

However, all devotees faced with this question implied that Mā was not a human being but was the divine in some form. Even other *mahātmas*, or great souls, substantiated Mā's divinity. One of the most interesting stories told about other masters who believed that Mā was God was told by Swami Samatananda.

> There is a great *mahātma*, Swami Chidānanda, of the Divine Light Society. He has hundreds of thousands of disciples. They all believe in Mā. Once he was giving a long lecture in Bangalore, South India. . . . After the lecture was finished a young boy came to him and frankly asked him, "Swamiji, can I put a question to you? Have you seen God?" Such a devotee and hundreds of learned people are sitting there. . . . What is his answer? He was thinking and then he said, "Yes, I have seen God." "Can you show me God?" "Yes, I can show you God." All the audience was spellbound. He said, "Go to Kankhal. Go there and you will see God sitting there in a hall. How much to get to God? Go buy a ticket. Get down at Haridwar station, take a rickshaw to Kankhal and to Mā Ānandamayī Ashram. And the rest of the job will be done by her." It is a real story.[68]

Some devotees spoke extensively of Mā as an *avatāra*. Keshab Bhattacharya presented the most complete theory of Mā as *avatāra*. Being a Vaishnava, he naturally compared Mā to Krishna, whose form as Gopal he worships along with Mā's picture. After Keshab defined *jivanmukta*, a person liberated through self-effort while still alive, he said,

> Then there's another manifestation, *avatāra*. Krishna was *avatāra*, Ramakrishna was *avatāra*. Gauranga was *avatāra*. In *avatāra* there is a definite will, or *samkalpa*. And what is that will? It is the will to do something for the good of humanity. That tremendous will is to do good for people, to shower great compassion, to do *līlā*, to strengthen the bond of others with the infinite. I don't want to utter it, but you must be getting the thing I am hinting at. The *jivanmukta* wants *siddhis*, to achieve great will power, to control things and people. I am not saying the *avatāra* cannot do these things. *Avatāra* has tremendous *siddhis*. Mā had all these things from the beginning. She could control a crowd of five thousand people. People were so eager to see her, a lady of eighty-two years old, they sat in the hot sun waiting for two or three hours. What was it about her? Was it only her physical beauty? No, It was her *samkalpa* that was attracting all humanity and, at the same time, changing the state of people.

Devotees tell, "When I met Mā, my life was changed forever. I started leading a new life." How could that happen? Because of Mā's great will. It was like a strong scent which permeated the whole atmosphere. . . . For a *līlā* you must have a *sangha*, a community, a galaxy of people to play with. . . . And the message she has left, "Understand the Self within you," can go on for a few more centuries. Then there might be some other *avatāra* who might develop it and give it further direction. Or it might cease to exist. But the seeds that the *avatāra* plants, through a succession of lives, will grow.[69]

Many more people spoke of Mā as an incarnation of Devī. Naturally, some of these people were Shāktas. Gita-Di Bose, who spends hours every day worshipping the *Shrī Yantra*, or sacred diagram representing Devī, told of an experience that her grandfather had with Mā during the Shahbagh years:

My grandfather was a doctor from the medical school at that time. There were only ten of them at that time sitting around Mā. All of a sudden grandfather started feeling drowsy. And he thought, "Why am I feeling like that? I just got up from an afternoon sleep." His eyes just closed all of a sudden. And then he opened them forcibly and he saw there was no Mā. And in the place of Mā, there was one of the *Dasha Mahāvidyās*, you know, the ten forms of Shakti. The form he saw was Chinnamastā. You know, the body is here and the head has been severed and she is holding the head and drinking the blood. He saw that form. And the nine other people, they each saw a different form. And one devotee was a judge. He saw all ten forms. And after that the drowsiness went away. And everybody asked each other, "What have you seen? I don't know what to think!" And the judge said, "I saw all ten forms." And they ran to him and said, "You are so lucky!" My grandfather told me this when I was little.[70]

When I asked Rupa Vishvanathan if she thought of Mā as a human being, she said, "I am not to judge. But from my experience no human being can guide you in a dream."[71] The next day she said emphatically, "Mā is an incarnation of divinity, of Devī, being a lady."[72] Swami Premananda also referred to Mā as "an incarnation of the Goddess." Apparently, the girls at the Sanskrit girl's school in Varanasi are taught to see Mā as an incarnation of Devī. Sita-Ji Aunty told me,

If the children make a mistake, they ask for a pardon from Mother. Every day they go in the temple in the morning after the Vedas are recited. They say a prayer in Sanskrit: "*He, Devī*, (O, Devī), with your help may we lead a good life and have a good education that enlightens everyone. With firmness may we stand in the path of Truth."[73]

Swami Jnanananda, however, preferred to describe Mā as an incarnation from the point of view of Vedānta. He said,

The Vedānta does not believe in *avatāra*. In Vedānta we say everybody is an *avatāra*. Everybody is Brahman. I am Brahman. From the point of view of Vedānta, there are two kind of beings, *Īshvara koti* and *manuva koti*.[74] *Īshvara koti* is a being who is the incarnation of God and so is ever free, comes on earth freely and goes away freely. The other being, *manuva koti*, is bound, bound. Mā was an *īshvara koti*. . . . She has said, "You have called me and I have come down to make you work."

I asked Jnanananda with whom he would compare Mā if he were talking to a Westerner. He said without hesitation, "That would have to be Christ."[75]

Other devotees seemed to feel that the term *avatāra* delimited Mā. Gita-Di Bose corrected her son, Naren, for speaking about Mā's former incarnations. "No, no, no," she said. "Not incarnations. Mā says, 'You wanted it, you prayed for it, you got it.' When I asked for clarification, she said that Mā was the Formless Absolute who took form in the physical body when the time was right and when people were calling for her.[76] When I asked Swami Brahmananda if he thought Mā was an *avatāra*, he made a similar distinction:

> No, *avatāra* is too limited. If the Prime Minister of India sends some governors to the provinces, they are limited, their power is limited. The Prime Minister has no such limitations. Mā is unlimited. She is God incarnate. She said once to everyone in Hindi, "We are connected with Mother, we wanted Mother to be with us, to play with us this way, that way. Now when we are no longer attached to this way, that way, she will leave." Now I can tell you, this can be understood by understanding the Brindavan *līlā* of Lord Krishna. . . . Mā's *līlā* and Krishna's *līlā* are parallel, the same. But the ways are different. But the same thing is going on. Mā thinks, "You asked for this body. This body has come." Krishna said, "*Gopī* [cowherdess/beloved] wants, *gopī* gets." . . . Krishna was not an *avatāra*. He was the Lord incarnate. He is the one *avatāra* that was God incarnate. He had the whole world under control as a baby of twelve weeks."[77]

Brahmananda is distinguishing between *avatāra* as an incarnation of a certain god, such as Vishnu, defined as the descent of a part of Vishnu's power, and God, as Brahman, incarnating in his or her fullness.

There had been a tendency in Vaishnava theology to consider Lord Krishna as the one *pūrnāvatāra*, or full *avatāra*. Within Shākta theology, there is also a sense in which Devī is seen as greater than her manifestations. There is a distinction drawn between Devī's *nirguna* form, which is transcendent, and her *saguna* form as manifestations such as Durgā and Kālī. Mā's devotees seem to be saying that Mā is not a part of God, not a representative of God, but God or Goddess himself or herself. Mā is *Avatārin*, or the source from which the descent of *avatāra* is made.[78] Gopinath Kaviraj, the renowned scholar and devotee, unequivocally claims Mā as *Avatārin*, rather than *avatāra*, because of her uninterrupted Self-consciousness:

> The view which accepts Mother's personality as a case of *Avatāra* may be dismissed with a few words of comment. . . . *Avatāras* are self-forgetful Divine emanations. . . . In the case of the Plenary *Avatāra* also, unbroken consciousness of his plenary nature does not appear to exist. A careful study of Mā's utterances and a critical attitude towards her life and activities would perhaps reveal the

fact that Her case is altogether different. She herself has confessed to some that She never loses her Supreme Self-consciousness. *Samādhi* or no *samādhi*, She is where She always has been; She knows no change, no modification, no alteration: She is always poised in the self-same awareness as a Supreme and Integral University, transcending all limitations of time, space and personality and yet comprehending them all in a great harmony.[79]

Swami Samatananda agrees that Mā cannot be considered an *avatāra* for a different reason.

God comes to this world. Why? Because God loves us. We are the children of God. We are the children of Mother. So Mother will come down upon this earth one hundred times. Where her children are playing she cannot leave this earth. So she comes, the Ultimate Shakti. . . . She took form for us. She said, "You prayed for me, you got this body. As long as you want this body, it will stay. If you don't want it, it will vanish." She is not an *avatāra* because *avatāra* has some mission. . . . It means to come upon this earth and show people to love God in this way . . . how to behave. . . . In Hinduism *avatāra* comes for three reasons: to teach the unjust people, many times by killing them and shutting them up, to protect the right people, and to show the path of religion. In Mā's life, there is nothing of that. Mā has not come to show a new religion or a path of religion or to protect people or to save good people. That is not Mā's mission. So we asked Mā, "Why have you come to this world?" Mātājī said very beautiful things. She said, "If you have a beautiful garden. Say you are sitting in the house. In the evening you say, 'Let me go and see my garden.'" Is there motivation to see the garden? There is no motivation. Just an idea. . . . You want to see with your own eyes how your garden is. So Mātājī said, "You are my children. I have come here and I see how my flowers are growing." So there is no motivation and no mission. "And if I see that some flower is not growing well, I pluck it. I do it out of my own affection." So there is no reasoning. So Mātājī saw the whole world as the garden of God.[80]

Gopinath Kaviraj and Swami Samatananda are saying that Mā is greater than an *avatāra*, she is God incarnate. Kavirāj's argument hinges on Mā's apparent unbroken knowledge of her identity as God from birth and Samatananda on her lack of mission.

A common strategy for answering the question of "Who is Mā?" was to give an answer which would encompass many possibilities and then to reside, finally, in the place of a child who knows only that she is Mother. For example, Krishna Bhattacharya said,

Mā is, of course, the guru. Mā is everything. She is *Antaryāmin* [the Inner Knower], that means she knows everything and she is abiding in the heart. I feel this. So many times this has happened. Whenever I have prayed to Mā for something, it has happened. . . . But I think of her as Mother, as Mother and nothing else. She is *Jagatjananī*, Mother of the World. Mā is Mā. She is *ishta* [chosen deity].[81]

Swami Brahmananda said, "Mā is Ātman, she is Māyā. She is my mother, the Holy Mother."[82] In the last analysis, devotees, seeming at a loss to express Mā's identity in a way that they felt would do justice to her, resorted to their own self-identity as her child. Rajkumar Roy said, "I couldn't imagine her like a goddess or some heavenly being. I used to love her as Mother. That's why I couldn't offer her a garland, never in my whole life, as long as I knew her.[83]

Even Gopinath Kaviraj, in a famous article written in 1956 in which he addresses the question of Mā's identity, ultimately surrenders himself to the unknowable and identifies himself as Mā's child. He says that in the early days with Mā, there was a difference of opinion about "the precise status of Mother."[84] Some saw her as the Goddess in human form, Kālī or Durgā, Sarasvatī or Rādhā; others thought she was a human seeker who had attained realization. Some thought she was a *brahmavādinī*, or female Vedic master, others considered her an incarnation of the divine, like Krishna. "That different persons should hold different opinions regarding Her personality is, of course, natural. For in a matter like this, a correct analysis on an intellectual basis is not possible, nor can ordinary human judgement yield any useful result."[85]

Kaviraj proceeds to refute every category one might apply to Mā. He argues that Mā is not a guru or a disciple. She is not a *pratyekabuddha*, a "private buddha," who became enlightened on his or her own but does not spread the teachings, because "she is too sensitive to the sorrows of the world to remain contented with isolated existence."[86] He adds that Mā had no *prārabdha* karma, no previous lives, no future lives and that all her activities were spontaneous and not prompted by will or purpose. She was not, Kaviraj says, a *mahāyogi*, not a *devatā*, a celestial being.[87] Her *sādhana* was a mere *līlā*, to be "an example to ordinary humanity."[88] Employing a method of analysis typical of Advaita Vedānta, in which one says Brahman is "*neti, neti*," or "not this, not this," Kaviraj eliminates all possible classifications that might apply to Mā. Mā, like Brahman, can only be understood by determining what she is not.

Kaviraj maintains that the most viable classification for Mā is the divine in its own perfect form, its *svayam rūpa*, but even then he takes refuge in the piety of indeterminacy:[89]

> Is She then a visible expression of the Absolute Itself? Is She the outer manifestation, within a self-imposed veil, of the Inner Ātma [Self] of the world, of all of us, revealed to us clothed in a human form simply to draw us towards Herself away from the turmoils and tumults of fettered existence? Who can say?[90]

Kaviraj concludes his analysis with a moving demonstration of his own orientation, not as one on the path of knowledge, in spite of his scholarly reputation, but as a *bhakta*, or devotee of God:

> It is therefore a difficult task to describe Mother as She really is. . . . What is really needed is to feel that She is the Mother and we are her children and

that as mere children we cannot be expected to know Her as She is, but only as she shows Herself to us in response to our cravings. It really becomes us to behave as infants crying out in the night and to invoke Mother with an inarticulate language for Her actual descent and benediction.[91]

Two nondevotees to whom I posed the question "Who is Mā?" offered similar answers. After Mahendranath Dev told the story of seeing Mā with a disfigured face allegedly eating the karma of her devotees, I asked him, "After this happened, what was your understanding of who Mā was?" He answered that Mā was "a part of God." He went on to say, "I saw her like the Divine Mother, like a *devatā*." He concluded, "She can be considered to be an *avatāra*."[92] Melanie, who had Mā's *darshan* in 1978, referred to Mā as "the Divine Mother, a manifestation of pure, unconditional love."[93]

Indeed, in spite of the fact that the majority of Mā's devotees are from Vaishnava backgrounds, their theologies, which might be better designated the*a*logies,[94] are predominantly centered on the worship of the Divine Mother. The main spokesperson for Shākta theology among devotees of Mā was Swami Samatananda, the *āchārya* in residence at Mā's Agarpara ashram in Calcutta. As I listened to Samatananda speak about what he called "the Motherly kind of approach," I heard many resonances with the theology of the *Devī Bhāgavata*. In particular, he articulated a devotional path in which all that matters is intimacy with Mā and in which you need not leave the world to attain your goal.

> The first thing is this. The ultimate force, the Absolute, whichever name you may call it, has got two main aspects to its evolution, one is the dynamic aspect, which we call Shakti, the other is the static aspect, or Shiva. If you go high, high up, then the form and the name will vanish. You cannot differentiate who is Shakti and who is Shiva. So the dynamic aspect of the evolution of the world is called the Mother aspect or the Shakti aspect. We prefer this approach because we have to approach from our own side. We are under the influence of our intelligence, our bodies. We have got body sense, mind sense, and intelligence sense. The static force is beyond that, so how can we approach that way? The Motherly kind of approach is simpler. From the very beginning you can understand the Shakti, the dynamism of the whole world, because everywhere there is change. Whatever change goes on, that is the Motherly force. . . .
>
> The goal [of *sādhana*] is to be in the safest place and to enjoy the whole world. Why to say the world is untrue, that there is nothing to the world? No. But you must select the safest place in the whole world. Where you can sit and see the world. What is the safest place in the whole world? It is the lap of the Mother. A child thinks that the lap of Mother is the best place in the world. The most pure, the most protected. So sitting on the lap of Mother you can enjoy the whole world, because Mother will protect you from every evil thing. So this is the Motherly approach, the approach of the Shakti. So they say, "Don't leave the world. Don't go to the hills. Live in the whole world. Enjoy worldly things while sitting in the lap of Mother. Otherwise you will lose. The world will encroach upon you." So this is the Motherly

conception of the world. Whatever creation you see from the trees to the birds to the rivers, everything is here in the form of your Mā. There is no place to go.[95]

This statement reflects what Kathleen Erndl refers to as the "relentless exaltation of the material world" of monistic Shākta *bhakti*.[96]

Love, devotion, and surrender are important themes but are never divorced from a desire for material fulfillment. In the Devī cult, the line between "interior devotion" and "disinterested devotion" or between the transcendental and the pragmatic aspects of religion is not clearly drawn. The worship of the Goddess has many rewards, ranging from good health and enjoyment of family relationships to peace of mind to ultimate liberation.[97]

Mā's devotees, then, follow the example and teaching of her model devotee, Bhaiji. At the time of Bhaiji's passing in 1937, he had assembled a list of twelve "special directions to the devotees of Mā," which the devotees "should always remember."[98] These were issued as a leaflet in 1958 in Calcutta and as a booklet, *Dwadash Pradeep*, or *The Twelve Lights*, on the occasion of Mā's birthday celebration in 1962. Bhaiji's first and foundational direction is this:

Mā is the visible embodiment of the thought image which is perceived while taking the name of God [Bhagavān] or Īshwara. If established in the firm belief that Her physical form, actions, and playful moods are all supernatural and extraordinary, one can in one's thought, feelings and actions, venerate Her as the object of one's adoration. Having enshrined her lotus feet in the heart, the need will not arise for any other support in the path of salvation.[99]

Did Mā agree with Bhaiji's assessment, or did she believe, as she often told her devotees, that she was "whoever or whatever you think I am"?[100]

Mā on Her *Līlā* of *Sādhana*

The biographers of Ānandamayī Mā clearly intend the phrase "*līlā* of *sādhana*" to establish Mā as divine, maintaining that Mā, unlike an extraordinary person, such as a *yoginī* or even a *siddha*, went through the motions of spiritual practice for the sake of her devotees, although she had nothing to attain. I assumed Mā's later biographers, such as Bithika Mukerji and Alexander Lipski, coined the phrase and that Mā herself had never claimed that she was of divine origin. Neither Bhaiji nor Gurupriya Devi, Mā's early biographers both of whom met Mā right after this period, use the phrase. They simply recount "the amazing yogic activities"[101] of the years in Bajitpur. Bhaiji does speak in general about "Mother and Her Līlā," referring to his conviction that Mā's life was a mere *līlā*, or play, that she had no attachments and no desires.[102] However, this is not the primary theme of his work.

The first volume of Bithika Mukerji's spiritual biography, *From the Life of Sri Anandamayi Ma*, published in 1970, systematically introduces the concept of the *līlā* of *sādhana* for the first time. In her chapter, "Bajītpur: The Līlā of Sādhana," she quotes Mā as saying: "One day in Bajītpur I went to bathe in a pond near the house where we lived. While I was pouring water over my body, the *kheyāla* suddenly came to me, 'How would it be to play the role of a *sādhaka*?' And so the *līlā* (play) began."[103] Mukerji goes to describe Mā's yogic trances and movements, interjecting the following interpretation: "At Bajītpur, in the privacy of her cottage Anandamayi Ma enacted the role of a *sādhaka* to perfection. It is to be called a role because even in this she remained self-sufficient, looking to nothing or nobody outside herself. It was in the nature of a manifestation rather than an achievement."[104]

I began to wonder how Mā's devotees developed the conviction that Mā had never performed *sādhana*, that she had no birth and death and had nothing to attain. Was this a reflection of a Hindu trend from the time of Chaitanya to establish that one's master was greater than any other by claiming that he or she was perfect rather than perfected? Did Mā's use of the term *līlā* refer to something more than the Advaitic truth that we are all the deathless Self? I began by examining Mā's famous statement to Paramahamsa Yogananda, mentioned in chapter 3, which is included in nearly every publication, video, or film of Mā.

> Father, there is little to tell. . . . My consciousness has never associated itself with this temporary body. Before this body came on this earth, Father, "I was the same." As a little girl, "I was the same." This body grew into womanhood, but still "I was the same." When the family in which this body had been born made arrangements to have this body married, "I was the same." And Father, in front of you now, "I am the same." Even afterward, though the dance of creation changes around me in the hall of eternity, "I shall be the same."[105]

From the point of view of the Upanishads and Advaita Vedanta, this statement could simply assert, "I am That. I am not this body. I am the eternal, changeless Brahman, the truth sought by all *jnāna* yogis." Countless yogis and saints have come to this realization, through spiritual practice. Had Ānandamayī Mā's devotees, in their earnest desire to see her as "beyond the extraordinary," misinterpreted her words?

Alexander Lipski, in *The Life and Teaching of Sri Anandamayi Ma*, more strongly asserts that Mā herself said she had nothing to attain, quoting Mā as saying,

> Let me tell you what I am, I have been from my infancy. But when the different stages of *sādhanā* were being manifested through this body there was something like superimposition of *ajnāna* (ignorance). But what sort of *ajnāna* was that? It was really *jnāna* (knowledge) masquerading as *ajnāna*.[106]

Again, Mā's use of the phrase "superimposition of ignorance" could be pointing to her realization "I am That," which has been misinterpreted by zealous devotees to mean that she never needed to do *sādhana* to realize it, that she was "beyond the extraordinary" from the beginning.

Superimposition theory, or *vivartavāda*, was put forth in the tenth century by Shankarāchārya and further refined by his followers such as Sureshvara. Eliot Deutsch describes it as the Advaitin notion that ignorance (*ajñāna*) is "the superimposition [*adhyāsa* or *adhyāropa*] on the Self (Ātman, Brahman) of what does not properly belong to the Self (finitude, change) and the superimposition on the non-self of what does properly belong to the Self (infinitude, eternality)."[107] In other words, "It is the notion of that in something which is not-that."[108] Thus, in Mā's quote, we can see how she could be interpreted as saying, "Although I (and you, for that matter) am the eternal Self (*Ātman/Brahman*), because of the nature of this transitory world, there was a superimposition of ignorance and I (like you) had forgotten who I was and needed to remember through spiritual practice."

However, Lipski goes on to relate more of the conversation between Mā and devotees that took place in May, 1941, and was published for the first time in *Mother as Seen by Her Devotees* in 1956. Mā is quoted as saying to A. K. Datta Gupta, Professor Shyama Charan Babu, and Jiten Babu,

> When the different stages of *sādhanā* were being manifested through this body, what a variety of experiences I then had! . . . One day I distinctly got the command: "From today you are not to bow down to anybody." I asked my invisible monitor: "Who are you?" The reply came: "Your Shakti (power)." I thought that there was a distinct Shakti residing in me and guiding me by issuing commands from time to time. Since all this happened at the stage of *sādhanā*, *jñāna* was being revealed in a piecemeal fashion. The integral knowledge which this body was possessed of from the very beginning was broken, as it were, into parts and there was something like the superimposition of ignorance. . . . After some time I again heard the voice within myself which told me: "Whom do you want to make obedience to? You are everything." At once I realized that the Universe was all my own manifestation. Partial knowledge then gave place to the integral, and I found myself face to face with the One that appears as many. It was then that I understood why I had been forbidden for so long to bow to anybody.[109]

If we interpret "the integral knowledge which this body was possessed of from the very beginning" as referring to this lifetime, Mā is implying that she consciously veiled herself for the sake of her devotees. This impression is confirmed in other sources. Anil Ganguli, in *Anandamayi Ma: The Mother Bliss-incarnate*, supports his conviction that "the Supreme Truth has ever been with her from the beginning"[110] by quoting Mā's statement to Gopinath Kaviraj:

> Look, in the case of a *sadhaka* there is aspiration towards a goal. But here [meaning herself], there is no question of goal or no goal, of aim or aimlessness. Every artery, vein and nerve, their functioning and vibration are clearly seen, just as when somebody in a dark room holds a lamp in his hand and throws light on objects one by one—exactly like this. But, for the *sadhaka* who is still on the path, it is impossible to perceive in this matter. He has to advance by

overcoming various kinds of obstacles. Baba, here, there is no question of this. Here, the artery is myself, the vein is myself, the functioning myself and the observer myself. Of course, when saying "myself," it is because some word has to be used. . . . Here change or changelessness, concentration or abeyance of activities—there is simply no question of all these. Baba, here everything is perfectly open and unconditioned. [111]

Similarly, the diary of A. K. Datta Gupta reveals the following statement from Mā:

I may tell you that this body has not followed only one particular line of *sādhanā*. . . but has passed through all the different varieties of practices referred to by the sages of ancient times. This body has successfully gone through *nāma sādhanā*, *hatha yoga* with its various *āsanas*, and through all diverse other yogas, one after another. In order to attain a particular stage along one of those lines of *sādhanā*, an ordinary individual may have to be born again and again, but in the case of this body, it was a matter of a few seconds. Moreover, the different forms of *sādhanā* that this body has been seen to practice, were not meant for this body; they were meant for you all.[112]

This claim is elaborated on in a remarkable conversation also recorded by Datta Gupta between Mā and Professor Sudhir Gopal Mukherji, which took place in 1949, first published in *Ānanda Vārtā* in Bengali in 1953, and republished in English in 1990. Mā is responding to Mukherji's request "to hear how exactly the first manifestations of Guru-power took place within you."[113]

First of all let me tell you: this body is exactly the same now as it was in childhood. There is no such thing as an initial or a subsequent state for this body. I am saying this while sitting on the banks of holy Ganga! (Everybody laughs heartily.) Nevertheless, a play of *sādhanā* did take place for this body: for some time it assumed the role of *sādhaka* and all the conditions and stages that are traversed by a *sādhaka* were fully manifested in this body.[114]

Mā goes on to speak about her states of *bhāva* during *kīrtan* at Ashtagrāma.

But if people become immersed in ecstatic emotion while singing *kīrtan*, this is of a different nature because it is connected with *kriyā* (action) and hence there is a touch of worldliness about it. But this body's condition was not due to any *kriyā*. So worldliness was excluded in this case. Furthermore, the experience of *ānanda* was somewhat different—of its own right.[115]

Next Mā talks about her *svadīkshā*. In response to Mukherji's request to describe the guru from whom she received *dīkshā*, Mā says,

I can say that the Ātmā is in fact the Guru, in other words, this body is itself this body's Guru. Furthermore, about *pūjā* I always say that when a particular Deity is to be worshipped, this particular Deity emerges from this body and after being worshipped disappears again into this body. Thus you can infer something similar in the case of the Guru.[116]

In conclusion, Mukherji says to Mā, "Kusum Brahmachari says your *sādhanā* was no real *sādhanā* because all the obstacles and difficulties that arise from within us when we set out to practise *sādhanā* were non-existent in your case," to which Mā replies,

> Why should this be so? When the play of *sādhanā* commenced within this body, did it not live with a good number of people? This body resided in the midst of Bholānath's large family. Every type of work was performed by this body. But when this body played the role of a *sādhaka*, it assumed every detail necessary for each particular *sādhanā*. For instance, marks on the forehead like *tilak, svarūpa, tripundra,* all appeared one by one. . . . About the *āsanas* [yogic postures] that formed spontaneously I have already told you previously. Some people spend a lifetime in acquiring the art to perform one such *āsana* to perfection. But when this body became a *sādhaka*, it was seen that one *āsana* after another was executed and each of them to perfection. All your questions have now been replied to.[117]

Finally, in the second volume of *Svakriya Svarasamrita*, Brahmacharini Chandan relates the following conversation between Mā and Gopinath Kaviraj:

> GOPINATH KAVIRAJ: Ma, all these behaviors and *sādhanā* of yours which followed in order and system were just *abhinai* [a dramatic performance], isn't it so?
>
> MA: Well, as Bhagavan plays. Indeed, here, the happenings are as He in Himself.[118]

These statements of Mā were not isolated remarks but part of a body of such statements in answer to questions about her *sādhana*. Thus, we must conclude that the concept of the *līlā* of *sādhana* was not constructed by Mā's spiritual biographers but developed out of her own self-description. When Mā said to Paramahamsa Yogananda, "My consciousness had never associated with this temporary body," she was actually setting herself apart and maintaining Self-realization from birth. She described the years between 1918 and 1924 as years in which she temporarily forgot her complete identification with the Self in order to go through the motions of spiritual practice for the edification of her devotees, manifesting "the perfect *sādhaka*" for them. By the end of the *līlā* of *sādhana*, it is implied, Mā had remembered who she was.

Mā on Her State and on Herself as Divine

After I concluded that it was Mā herself who generated and sustained the concept of the "*līlā* of *sādhana*," I decided to look for other statements made by Mā about her state and her identity. In an issue of *Ānanda Vārtā*, Mā alludes to her spiritual power: "Just now something else comes to my *kheyāla*, so I shall tell you about it. Quite often nobody was allowed to touch this body. But the reason for this restriction was not understood by people. This was enforced because they did not possess the power to bear it."[119]

She goes on to describe an incident in which a young man came to touch her feet and pray for a son. Although this was forbidden at the time, he did so and "at once fell down unconscious and therefore could not offer his mental prayers while touching my feet." After more than an hour, he regained consciousness and "even though he had been unable to pray for a son as planned, yet because it had been in his mind while touching me, he later did have children."[120] This matter-of-fact confession of her own power is reminiscent of a comment made by Malini-Di.

> Mā usually behaved with us in a normal manner, a human manner. Because once an incident occurred and somebody said, "But, Mā you know everything!" So Mā said, "If I start dealing with you people like this, you will not be able to stay." Mā was saying that if Mā let us know she was reading every one of our thoughts and revealing it, it would be very difficult for us to stay.[121]

Mā appears to be saying here that she consciously veiled her power in order to protect her devotees and normalize their relationship.

In the second volume of *Mātri Vāni*, "Ānanda Svarupinī," or "Mā on Herself," there are thirty statements by Mā about herself, taken from letters dictated to her devotees in response to requests for personal guidance. The first statement in this section is, "Solely for you all is indeed everything that this body says or does—its actions, movements, its going hither and thither. Whatever is done for your sake through this body at any time, it is you who cause it to happen."[122] Mā intimates here that she has no personal will but has taken birth for the sake of her devotees, in response to their desire for God.

There are several statements in this section in which Mā talks about herself in relationship to her devotees. In the following, Mā alludes to her divinity as it manifests in her omnipresence and oneness with her devotees:

> Wherever they may be, this body is with them at all times. This body does not know how to serve everybody—only what may come about spontaneously at any time: what little they can get done by regarding this small child as their very own, by their love and respect for her while giving *satsang* and *sādhusang*. . . . Here the door is always open; without any hesitation let them come whenever they feel like it.[123]

In response to a devotee's concern that Mā might have "dropped" him, Mā says, "For Mā the question of taking on or dropping anyone does not arise. For Mā there is 'taking on' in 'dropping' and 'dropping' in 'taking on.' At all times and under all circumstances, in inspiration and in dryness, Mā is, remains and ever will remain with everyone."[124] In response to another letter, Mā hints at her divinity in her expression of her complete identification with her devotee. She says, "Your sorrow, your pain, your agony is indeed my sorrow. This body understands everything."[125] Finally, Mā responds to a letter in which a devotee has asked about her health, chastising him for thinking of her as separate from him. She says, "The word "you" is being used because you differentiate between "mine" and "thine." The idea that there is "mine" and "thine" is in fact your illness. In the relationship between the Lord and His eternal servant, however, there is no such thing as "mine" and "thine."[126] It is clear in this case that Mā is identifying herself as the Lord who is one with her devotee. The last two statements point to Mā as God who considers all, devotee and nondevotee alike, as her children. In one she says, "The Ātmā of this body is everyone's Ātmā. It cannot be that anybody, anywhere, is not Mā's very own."[127]

Another source of self-referential statements is the transcribed *satsangs*. Some statements refer to Mā's state of consiousness. In Kankhal in November, 1981, during the last Samyam Vrata before Mā's *mahāsamādhi*, a devotee asked Mā how she managed to keep her hair so beautiful and black. After talking at length about her disinterest in her appearance during the years when she was involved in the "*līlā* of *sādhana*," Mā said,

> One day Udas was combing my hair. After touching it, accidentally her hand touched her lips and she tasted some sweetness on her hand. She thought, "What is this? How are my hands sweet? I did not eat or touch anything sweet." Then she remembered that she had touched my hair. She said, "Mā your hair is sweet." How could I know? Also in those days a lot of ants crept over my body perhaps only due to the sweetness in the body. I didn't care. They became my companions. They started living on my body under the clothes. This body was shelter for them. This body never combed the hair. But even then they were never matted. They remained beautifully arranged, as if they were combed, each and every fibre separate. . . . The color is due to its sweetness. Even inside the mouth so many times I felt that sweetness. I do not say all these things to anyone. Now that you raised this question, I am giving you the details.[128]

There are many examples of Mā's speaking about her state of unity awareness in the *satsang* tapes. For example, in Pilani during the Samyam Vrata in November 1962, Mā says,

> One thing more. As far as this body is concerned, everybody belongs to her, as everyone is the soul only. Therefore this body says that she does not talk with "others," she does not go to "other's" house, does not eat things given by "others," nor does she look at "others" as there are no "others" for her. . . . It is He only everywhere, nothing else. That is what this body thinks and what she thinks is right. That is the reason why she does not hesitate to talk irrelevantly. Whether the "other" thinks alike or not, she thinks all to be her own.[129]

In another conversation during the Samyam Vrata in Brindavan in November 1967, Mā says,

> If somebody asks this body if there is any difference whether a person speaks or not or whether a person sits with closed eyes or open eyes, for me there is no difference at all. I am silent even when I speak with you. I speak even when I am silent. Similarly it does not matter if I sit with my eyes closed or

open. Whether I speak or not, or whether my eyes are closed or open, I am always in meditation.[130]

There are also examples of Mā's alluding to her identity as divine. In Brindavan in January 1975, Mā subtly but directly identifies herself as Shakti, the Divine Mother:

This Shakti is called Mā. That is why the wise person thinks of Mā in the end and repeats the name til the last breath. . . . When Bhaiji went to Almora, someone placed some *prasād* in his hand. He uttered the word of Mā and paced that *prasād* in his mouth. And that was all. He also uttered the word Mā til the last. . . . Bhaiji was in union with God. Why did he utter the name of Mā? You see, your children go on playing. When they see you they become restless to come into your arms. You take them in your arms. They suck your milk and go to sleep. It is just like that. They see Mā and go to sleep in her arms. Her arms give them all comforts. For them there is nothing but Mā. They obtained Mā and they got everything. . . . He saw *pratyaksha* (vision) that Mā was with him so he called Mā just as children call when they happen to see their mother. He felt himself in Mā's union.[131]

In Suktal at the Samyam Vrata in November 1961, Mā says,

Then, naturally he wants to see the image of his *ishta*. He even desires to recite the Name of Mā, keeping her picture with him. Does anyone tell him to do all these things? No, it happens on its own. It comes naturally. The act of meditation upon the One whom one likes, calls, and prays to materializes on its own. Nobody has to show the way or tell the method.[132]

Mā's references to her "beyond the extraordinary" states and her divinity are most remarkable for their lack of self-consciousness and matter-of-factness. While the body of Mā's statements contains only a limited number of self-revelatory statements of this nature, they are unequivocal.

Mā's Humility

What is more typical of Mā's references to herself are statements describing herself as "a small child" and rejecting people's attributions of divinity, deflecting them to the God who is One. On the surface these statements reflect Mā's humility, but in some cases, they seem coded to reveal her underlying power. For example, in 1977, Mā was in Kurukshetra for the celebration of *Shivarātri*, the night of Lord Shiva. There were apparently many *pandits* and other religious figures sitting around Mā. Mā said,

One important thing is there. It is the greatness of these *mahātmas* that they give respect to this little child. This child does not know reading, writing or singing, anything. Still they love me and respect me. By giving so much respect to this innocent, they are manifesting their own good nature. They are manifesting their own Self.[133]

On another occasion, which took place in Delhi in 1961, Mā has just delivered an intricate forty-five-minute lecture to the president of India on the importance of the spiritual life and the difference between *bhakti, jñāna,* and *karma* yoga. She ended the meeting with these words: "This is what this little child wants to say, Pitājī. . . I am grateful for the honor and affection given by you to this child."[134] At some point in nearly every *satsang,* Mā refers to herself as "this child." Even in 1980, two years before her *mahāsamādhi,* Mā responds to a devotee's apparent confession that he did not understand what she had said in the following way: "You could not understand it? Why? This body talks childishly. How can an old person grasp what a small child speaks? It is very difficult to make out the words of an infant."[135]

These statements in which Mā professes her ignorance and simplicity may be understood in two related ways. First, like a tantric master, Mā is speaking at two levels, the most esoteric of which only a true disciple understands. To the uninitiated, Mā might appear simple, but the disciple knows her power and benefits from that knowledge. Second, according to the Vaishnava philosopher Rāmānuja, a devotee need only recognize the incarnate Lord to be saved. Mā may be challenging people to see beyond her presentation as a "little child" to the profundity of her being and her teaching. Her emphatic self-presentation as a child may serve as a kind of test of discrimination, in which those who "love and respect this little child" are believed to qualify for salvation.

Equally common are conversations in which a devotee is trying to entrap Mā into admitting that she is God and she is resisting. In Bangalore in 1979, the following lively repartee took place between Mā and a devotee simply identified as "Baba," or father:

BABA: Please straighten our vessels, Mā.

MĀ: Baba, I shall carry out your orders, but say what I should do?

BABA: They say that if Mā blesses them with her grace, all the obstacles will be removed.

MĀ: All the obstacles will go if God blesses them. Everything is smoothed by Him.

BABA: Are you Bhagavān or not?

MĀ: What I said yesterday stands today also. . . .

BABA: This old question comes up again and again. Either you firmly say that you are not God. . . .

MĀ: That is the difficulty. He lives in "no" as He does in "yes." "Yes" and "no" both are His forms only.

BABA: It means then that you are God.

MĀ: Tell me what you want me to say.

BABA: No, we. . . .

MĀ: Tell me what should I say to please you.

BABA: No, Mā. We do not want you to repeat our words. No, say on your own that you are God.

MĀ: It is God and God alone and nothing else.

BABA: Just tell if you are God or not.

MĀ: Baba, when it is God alone, you, he and I are all God only.

BABA: Then your *darshana* is God's *darshana.*

MĀ: It is just like the *darshana* of all others.[136]

Mā is determined to drive home the point that only God exists. She refuses to concede that she is "more God" than he is.

How Mā Wanted Her Devotees to
Relate to the Divine

If, in fact, Ānandamayī Mā herself claimed to be divine in origin, in spite of her frequent protestations to the contrary, then how did she want her devotees and disciples to relate to the divine and, thus, to her? We begin by considering how Mā described and defined God. Did she teach that God is the formless Absolute or that God has qualities, stories, and forms to be related to, such as the forms of Krishna, Shiva, or Kālī? Was God to be related to as Father or Mother?

Because Ānandamayī Mā never wrote a philosophical treatise or delivered a formal lecture, we turn to the transcription of *satsangs* with Mā to get a sense of the language with which Mā spoke about God and the path to God. In the 104 tapes of *satsangs*, Mā uses every possible name of God to refer to God and defines God in countless ways. She most often refers to God as *Bhagavān* (the Lord, the full manifestation of God, usually Krishna), but she also consistently refers to God as Brahman (the One without Second), *Parabrahman* (supreme Brahman), *Īshvara* (the Supreme Being), *Nārāyana* (a name of the Lord identified with Vishnu and Krishna), and *Mahādevī* (the Great Goddess). She displays a kind of monism in which she considers God as form to be a manifestation of God as formless.

> One thing more, Pitājī! Some people call him *arūpa* (formless) and *anāma* (nameless), which is the subject of Advaita philosophy. If He is said to be nameless and formless, then, what is He? He is *nirākāra Brahman* (the formless supreme). He is the Supreme Spirit, the Supreme *Ātman.* This idea is akin to the idea of water and ice. What is ice? Water only. And what is water? Ice only. The water is ice and the ice is water. The ice is the name of the special formation of the water. Similarly, this *jagat* (world) is akin to the ice. Just like the ice is nothing but water, even so this world is nothing but Hari (an epithet of Vishnu) alone. One should see Hari in the world as he sees water in ice. This world is the *vigraha* (individual form or image) of that Eternal Formless Brahman. *Vigraha* means *vi* plus *graha*, the one that helps one to grasp Him. He himself is nothing but *vigraha.*[137]

Mā uses the simile of water and ice over and over to represent a kind of monism in which the world is a positive manifestation of the Divine. Her sense of nondual awareness includes both the world of form and the personal God with attributes as "special formations" of Brahman. In this passage, she even substitutes Hari, an epithet for the personal God of the devotee, for Brahman, turning a *bhakti-jñāna* distinction on its head.

This kind of philosophical flexibility and translation of formerly sectarian concepts and terms into more universal ones is a hallmark of Mā's teaching, and perhaps of the teaching of other pan-Indian Hindu gurus and saints. We see in the neo-Vedānta of Ramakrishna Paramahamsa and his successors an effort to transcend sectarian and even religious distinctions to accommodate devotees of many different backgrounds, recognizing that for a person to serve as a guru for all of India, let alone for the world, he or she needs to break through the confines of sectarian distinctions and articulate a more universal theology.

In the same way, Mā refers to God as both male and female. She alternates the masculine and feminine pronouns and names of God, always maintaining their nonduality. For example, in Pilani, in November 1962, Mā says,

> It is explained in the Gītā. Everything is from Him only. Another surprise is that He exists in everything. The thing that is called Ātmā? Who is that? It is Shri Krishna Himself, Shri Rāmchandra Himself. It is Bhagavatī Ātmasattā (the Goddess) Herself only. We talked earlier about father, mother, son, husband, etc. They are all none else than Krishna, Rāma, Durgā or Kālī. Everybody is He or She only.[138]

Devotees tried to pin Mā down to stating her preference for God as Mother or Father. Mā would answer as she did in Suktal in 1961: "Call him Mother, Father, or whatever you want. He is one and the same. Just as you are the one who is called husband, father or son, even so He alone is called by all these names. . . Look, there is no Mother without Father and no Father without Mother."[139]

Sometimes Mā talks of God as the Divine Mother, explaining, "There are some who like fathers more. But such people are few. Mostly people like Mā only. It is the God who comes to the children in the form of Mā."[140] She describes the relationship between God and devotee as that between Mother and child:

> Have you seen any mother teaching her child how to walk or swim? What does she do? She makes that child stand at a place and then asks him to walk. When the child starts falling she runs and grabs him to prevent the fall. . . . God is our Mother. She wants us to walk on our own and teaches us. We are all Her children. It is she who is imparting us all this education. There is no doubt about it. She shows us the one light? She only. . . see the forms? They are her forms. The form and the formless, too. . . .Therefore this spiritual pilgrimage which you have started is due to her inspiration only. We are all her children, her eternal children. But we are just infants, innocent kids. The light we have is Her light only.[141]

Mā says it is this Divine Mother at whom we must throw ourselves in abandon.

> Do you want deliverance from the bonds of the world? Then, weeping profusely, you will have to cry out from the bottom of your heart: "Deliver me, great Mother of the World, deliver me!" To obtain Her grace you will

have to shed tears much more abundantly than when you desire things of the world. When by the flood of your tears the inner and the outer have fused into one, you will find Her, whom you sought with such anguish, nearer than the nearest, the very breath of life, the very core of every heart.[142]

However, Mā usually speaks of God as incorporating male and female, as, indeed, incorporating and transcending gender.

You call Mā, only when this body is before you. Who is Mā? Mā means Māyā, the one who is pervading all. All is in Him and He is in all. It is He only. He is the Supreme Mother and Father and everything. Why has He given this body to us? So that we may keep Him in our aim and go towards Him. Let us see Him in the form of Mā and try to obtain His Motherly Love.[143]

Phrases such as "His Motherly Love" abound. Mā takes the dual, the conditioned, that which resides in the world of form, and expands it to include everything, the One in All.

When Mā spoke of God so enthusiastically in the third person, how did she want her community to understand it? Was she expecting the inner circle to read between the lines and translate Bhagavān, Devī, He, or She into "this body"? It is my sense that Mā's close disciples did understand these statements on how to relate to God as statements about how to relate to Mā. I am less clear that Mā intended them to do so, but I think that in many cases she did. When Mā talks about God as the Divine Mother, God as Mā, she seems to be inviting devotees to make that connection. Her use of the third person parallels her use of "this body" to refer to her limited self. Ironically, this deflection of the personal points to her self-definition as greater than an individual, as, indeed, more than human. It is as if she were repeating over and over the Upanishadic truth, "this body" is not who I am; rather, I am That.

Just as Mā did not use one term to refer to God, neither did she promote a certain sectarian orientation. She appeared to be completely indifferent to the sectarian orientation of her devotees and only wanted to encourage them to deepen their practice and their understanding. There are many illustrations of Mā's indifference to sectarian orientation. Lakshmi Shrivastav, an elder *brahmacarinī*, spoke of Mā's acceptance of all forms of devotion.

Mā never said that when you come to the ashram, you only worship this god. She never said that. In Banaras they had Gopāl. At Shivarātri, the Shiva Pūjā used to go on in the temple. So Gopāl was there and the Shiva Pūjā went on in the hut. So there was no difference whether it was Shiva or Krishna or anybody. And when people came for *dīkshā*, Mā always asked, "Who is your *ishta devatā*?" Who is your own. Mā did not tell me that I should have this god or that god. She even asked, "Who is your *ishta devī*, your chosen goddess?"[144]

This policy of asking a prospective initiate who his or her chosen deity is and then giving him or her the appropriate mantra has precedence in Bengal.

The successors of Shri Ramakrishna in the Ramakrishna Mission began soon after his death to encourage initiates to take the mantra of their choice, even a Christian or Muslim one, depending upon their background.[145]

Mā taught that all paths were one and supported devotees in pursuing whatever path fit their inclination. In 1981, a devotee in Kankhal asked Mā, "What is better, to die at Brindavan or at Kāshī?"[146]

> Those who are on the *bhakti mārga* think is it good to die at Brindavan, because they have the *saguna rūpa* (the form with qualities) of God there in the form of Sri Krishna. Those who are on the *nirguna mārga* and want to obtain the God who is *jñāna svarūpa* (the essence of knowledge), *Ātma svarūpa* (the essence of the Self), and *nitya* (eternal) take Kashi as their *mukti kshetra* (place for liberation) because Shiva is there. But where does He not exist? Where is the place unoccupied by Bhagavān? He is everywhere.[147]

In Pilani, in 1962, Mā said:

> A person starts liking a particular *nāma* (name) and *rūpa* (form). Some like the idol of Sri Rāma while others like that of Sri Krishna, Durgā or Kālī or Shiva. Some like to follow the path of yoga, while others like to go on *kriyāmārga* or *karmamārga* (the path of actions and works). Some like worshipping, while others like the Advaita philosophy of *nirākāra-upāsanā* (meditation on the formless God) as they do not want to be involved in *nāma* and *rūpa*. Whatever line one likes, it automatically lays bare within oneself, it opens the way for *shraddhā* (faith) to awaken.[148]

Although Mā insisted that the paths of *bhakti, jñāna,* and karma, are "one in the same,"[149] she did, however, encourage people to pick a path and stick with it. On one occasion Mā was having a conversation with a man about the comparative degree of difficulty of the path prescribed by the Purānas, the path of *bhakti*, and the path prescribed by the Upanishads, the path of *jñāna*. Seeming somewhat exasperated, she said, "Why do you ride in two cars? Go by one. Either Purānas or Upanishads, follow one of them. Then you will not have any confusion. Follow one and do not condemn the other. Do not condemn anyone."[150]

As for the sectarian orientation of the liturgies in Mā's ashrams, most are Vaishnava, presumably because the majority of Mā's devotees who live there have Vaishnava backgrounds.[151] The texts chanted daily are the Bhagavad Gītā, the *Vishnu Sahasranam*, the *Shrīmad Bhāgavatam*, and the *Rāmāyana*. However, the *Durgā Saptashati*, or the *Devī Māhātmya*, is chanted regularly at all ashrams and the celebration of Durgā Pūjā is one of the biggest events of the year.

Mā herself, in her conversations with devotees, constantly alternates language and concepts from many philosophical orientations. In terms of the primary philosophical tension between *jñāna* and *bhakti*, one can find an equal number of examples of her using the language of Advaita Vedānta as the language of Vaishnava or Shākta *bhakti*. Mā could speak the technical language of Advaita Vedānta. For example, in Brindavan, in 1969, Mā says to a devotee,

When the pure *Ātmā* is mixed with *ajnāna* (ignorance), which is the dirt, it becomes dirty and it is called *jīva* (the individual soul). There is a way to make the dirty water clean. We filter it. Similarly, there is a way to change the *jīva* into *Ātma*. Filter it with the help of yoga. Yoga removes the dirt of ignorance and passions from the *jīva* and the pure *Ātmā* starts shining again, it becomes *Parabrahma Paramātmā*.[152]

Mā also speaks the language of *bhakti*. For example, in Haridwar in 1972, Mā says,

> Keep one thing always in your mind. God has come to me in the form of this name. I have achieved Him in this form. I will not leave His company. What is chanting? It is just keeping company with Him. When you will be in His company, it will dye your mind His color. He will dye you the color you need. That is why I say you should never leave His company. Keep Him with you in the form of chanting His name. When you keep on doing it, one day it will "occur" in you. You will attain the state where the name will go on in you without effort.[153]

More typically, however, Mā mixes the language of Advaita and of *bhakti*. It is, in fact, difficult to find a statement in which the language has not been mixed. For example, in Pilani in 1962, Mā says,

> How is knowledge gained? What a beautiful discussion you have started. Knowledge is *nitya-prāpta* (existing from eternity). It is eternally in you. Had it not been there in you, you would never have asked, "How is it gained?" For example, suppose you have a store, which contains a lot of wealth, groceries, and everything. You do not face any difficulty. But then you ask, "How can we get a grocery store?" Why do you need to know how the knowledge is gained? This is His will only. The Lord has inspired you to ask this question. You are the Self. The thought that you are not He is nothing but ignorance, a veil. But the [veil] is removable. It is like cloud. The clouds cover the sun but once they are removed, the sun is still shining.[154]

In this statement Mā speaks in Advaitic terms about the knowledge which is already there, if covered by a veil. Yet she says that the Lord has inspired him to ask the question to help him remember that he is the Self. Although devotion, and the grace which is inextricably connected with it, is mentioned in Shankara's work, it is considered merely a stage to be moved through, not the modus operandi that it is for the *bhakti* schools.

There is parallel tension between the philosophical schools of *jnāna* yoga and the Vaishnava and Shākta schools of *bhakti* yoga, which is the tension between self-effort and grace and their relative importance. Schools that emphasize *jnāna*, tend to emphasize self-effort; schools that emphasize *bhakti* tend to emphasize grace, or *kripa*, and surrender, or *prapatti*.[155] In chapter 5, we saw that many of Mā's devotees emphasize grace to the point where they feel anything they do will be all right and that Mā will take care of the rest. In fact, Mā does talk repeatedly about grace, saying, "This body says that God's grace is already there everywhere. It is raining all the time in all places."[156] However, Mā also is tireless in emphasizing the importance of self-effort. In Kankhal in 1978, Mā makes an important statement about the relationship between self-effort and grace.

So, it is your duty to prepare your spiritual field to receive the rains of *aurhetu kripa* (undeserved grace) in time. Had it not been your responsibility, what was the use of coming over here and doing all this *sādhana*? What was the necessity of doing this action (*kriyā*)? To think that "He will shower his *kripa* and everything will be all right" is totally wrong. Why do you not rely on his *kripa* for eating and drinking? Why do you do business and have these big factories? Do you not use your hands and minds for these worldly things? Then why do you not use your mind in spiritual realm also? He is very kind, there is no doubt about it. He has given you these hands and this mind only because He is kind. So use them for His work. Then automatically your mind will be ready to receive the rains of His beautiful, ever-raining Grace. How many *āvaranas* (veils) are over your mind. Remove those *āvaranas*. Then your vessel, which is not straight, will become right. But this will be done by a person's own power, not by the Grace of God. No doubt His power will help you because without Him no one will succeed in his efforts.[157]

If we look carefully at the general path that Mā prescribes, whether she describes it as a path of knowledge, a path of yoga, or a path of devotion, it is a fairly rigorous path. It is a path of turning within, or introversion, called *nivritti*. While *pravritti* is looking outside for enjoyment, *nivritti* is looking within for the truth, for God. In Suktal in 1961, Mā describes the critical turn from *pravritti* to *nivritti*:

See, when you do some worldly things, like watching television for example, how many hours in a row can you sit there? Just as movies attract you and you enjoy them for hours and hours, you should develop the habit of sitting in meditation, too. For hours together you have developed this extroverted (*pravritti*) attitude that drags you towards *bhoga*, worldly pleasure. All these days you have been thinking about what to eat, how to sit easily, how to relax, how to talk, etc. All these things have made you extroverted. To achieve the beautiful God, there is a secret. That is called *abhyāsa yoga*, the yoga of practice. But this extrovertedness has made you weak. It pulls you outside and paralyzes your mind. That is why you feel it hard to sit in one posture for long. *Bhoga* and *yoga* are two separate things. You have developed a practice in enjoyment. You have developed the *yoga* of *bhoga*! But the practice of *nivritti*, turning within, makes a person progress towards the Ātma. Once it happens, there is nothing there but calmness and peace.[158]

As we discussed in chapter 5, Mā recommended a personal, unique *sādhana* for each disciple based on his or her aptitude, inclination, and level of attainment. For some, the *sādhana* consisted of only *japa*, for others of *japa* and meditation, for others of elaborate *pūjā*, for others *kīrtan*. For some, they were instructed to do a combination of all four. For most, however, Mā prescribed *trisaṃdhyā*, the practice of performing worship and mantra repetition three times a day, in the early morning, noon, and in the evening.[159] Mā describes the prerequisite to any kind of attainment as getting rid of "I-ness" and "my-ness." When someone asks Mā why his *kundalinī* has not awakened, Mā replies, "How can the *kundalinī* awaken until you have gotten rid of 'my-ness'? 'My' and *kundalinī* do not go together. When you say 'my *kundalinī*' it means you are giving more importance to 'my' than to *kundalinī*. Whether it is *kundalinī* awakening, *samādhi*, or meditation, the first prerequisite is that the feeling of 'I' must go."[160]

Thus, whether Mā was talking in terms of attaining one's personal god or in terms of attaining knowledge, she emphasized practice. She speaks in terms of *tapasya*, or austerity, even in relationship to *bhakti*. During the Samyam Vrata in Suktal in 1961, Mā speaks of the benefits of *tapasya*.

> The very *sādhana* you are doing now sitting for a long time even amidst pain is *tapasya*. One must undergo pain either for God or for the world. If you endure pain for the *ishta*, you will obtain him. All your *anishtas* (undesired things or evils) will disappear and *ishta* will appear. This sitting with pain is very helpful, useful and beneficial. Therefore, always keep in your mind that you are doing *tapasya*. When he keeps doing *tapasya*, the time comes when he feels pleasure in those very pains. The greater the suffering, the greater the pleasure. He starts thinking, "See how much *tapasya* I am doing for God, how He is enabling me to do this *tapasya*." This very feeling turns pain into pleasure. No doubt you will feel pain until you develop this feeling.[161]

Ānandamayī Mā's goals for her devotees were very high, in fact, the highest. She constantly implores them to strive for the ultimate knowledge of the Self and/or union with their Lord. She once said, "You should try to attain the state where death is also dead. You are the children of the Immortal. You are immortal. Try so that that immortality is manifest in you. That is why you are told to realize your Self."[162]

How Mā's Devotees Responded to Her Expectations of Them

What do Mā's devotees understand her expectations for them to be, and how do they respond to them? Almost all of Mā's devotees whom I interviewed took her teaching on the *nivritti mārga*, or the path of turning within, seriously. Half of them took vows of renunciation, some formally and some informally, that precluded marriage, career, and an independent life. They were completely surrendered to Mā's instructions as to where they should live, how they should serve her, and what *sādhana* they should perform. Certainly ashram life for the *sannyāsins* and *brahmahcārinīs* required and still requires self-discipline and self-denial. However, as we discuss more fully in chapter 7, for Mā's women renunciants, in particular, *sādhana* during Mā's lifetime was largely focused on attending Mā.

In terms of householder devotees, there seem to be varying degrees of commitment to the path of turning within as manifested in a *sadhana* of spiritual practice. Only a few devotees, such as Rupa Vishvanathan, emphasize the importance of practices and of self-effort.

> The guru just shows you the path. You must tell yourself, you must manifest your own divinity. . . . I read Mā's words every day! She says effort must be there. It cannot be given like a gift. I can quote! Very few people understand the true divinity of the guru. Only those who have worked for it. They have the maturity. Physical closeness does not give you understanding. The real test of spiritual progress is not how close you were to Mā, but how much you *manifest* divinity.[163]

We have already seen that there are some householder devotees who are dedicated to long hours of *sadhana*, especially women devotees who are freed up from household duties by having servants and can spend time in their *pūjā* rooms during the day while their husbands are at work. Still, the focus of most householder *sadhana* is worship or remembrance of Mā as *ishta devatā*, not meditation on the Self. For most devotees the definition of turning within is dedicating one's daily activities to Mā and having faith that Mā will do the rest. Most devotees believe, as Lalita-Di does, that grace, not self-effort, will carry them through.

> The goal of *sadhana* is liberation from karma, if possible. Though, I strongly believe that since we have the luck to have Mother's hand upon our heads, and her *kripa* always with us, I feel that the liberation will come. If we don't commit sins. A lot of our sins have been washed away by Mā's *kripa*, by having her *darshan*.[164]

Subodh Chattaraj told me that even Mā insisted that certain things cannot be earned.

> I used to do certain practices and have certain experiences. But then I would do the same practices and nothing would happen. I asked Mā why I wasn't getting although I was trying hard. She said, "Those things cannot be earned by practice. It comes with the higher grace. It comes sometimes."[165]

Some devotees seem to feel that Mā's grace is so pervasive that they do not need to do anything to deserve it. Several devotees spoke about Mā's *aurhetu kripa*, or undeserved grace and gave examples of people who came to Mā and received a sudden transformation without any apparent effort. Narendranath Bose, for example, a young businessman with a Western education, spoke to me of his conviction that Mā loves him no matter what he does. He had just finished telling me that Mā had warned him when he was a mischievous little boy, "This body is in every photograph in your house!" I asked him if that had cramped his style. He replied,

> No, it never cramped my style. Never, never. It is very weird. Sometimes I think about it even today. Even today when I am doing something which is regarded as wrong, I just do it. I just do it, because everything in my life, I relate it to Mā. Everything—good, bad, indifferent. Big, small. Sometimes I

know it is wrong. But I know that Mā is not going to throw me away because I'm doing it. So, it's just me.

I asked Naren, "You have experienced her acceptance?" He answered, "Yes, absolutely. I have not the slightest doubt in my mind. I try not to, but I'm also human and am subject to pressure like all humans, and, therefore I succumb to it, but I very rarely get unnerved. Because I'm always sure that Mā will accept me."[166]

Thus, there seem to be three kinds of devotees of Mā. The rare devotee envisions that his or her *sādhana* is leading him or her toward becoming divine like Mā. The majority of devotees lead a life of some degree of renunciation, performing a *bhakti yoga sādhana* with the hope that they will remain with Mā always, whether in this world or the next. A few devotees feel they need only give their lives to Mā, remembering her always, and Mā will do the rest. Mā, however, in her ability to assess the capacities of each disciple, singled out a few disciples for a rigorous *sādhana* of spiritual practices—*japa*, meditation, recitation of sacred texts, and *pūjā*. However, for most devotees she allowed them to focus their entire *sādhana* on her as their *ishta devatā*, surrendering to her will for them. Swami Premananda related that when he first met Mā he challenged Mā as to the necessity of his exerting self-effort when she could give him anything, Mā articulated the proper *bhakti* attitude for him very clearly. He said,

> I was about twenty-three. Mā was so loving, so motherly. I talked to her like my Mother, not my guru. I used to quarrel with her. I would say, "You are God. So, if you wanted to, you could give me *samādhi*. Why don't you? You don't really love me. If you did you would not ask me to do *japa* and *tapasya*." She used to say, "I am not having the *kheyāla* to give it." It was difficult to trick her. . . . One day I went to Mā and said to her, "Mā, what do you want? You are Mā. You are Devī. You are Bhagavān. You should understand what difficulty we have. We can't work in the world, we can't do anything, so we come to you. What do you want from me?" She said, "If you have an ego, if you have your own desire, you will be unhappy. So surrender unconditionally to this body. It is just like in a puppet show. There is a person pulling the strings and the puppet dances. It goes this way and that way, it laughs, it dances. You try to become like that, a puppet in my hands, and whatever I tell you, you do. Don't think on your own. If I say something, do it immediately. Don't use your imagination, your intelligence, or your own conscience to tell what is good or bad. Surrender unconditionally. Just like dough, with no will of its own, ready to be shaped flat or round. Just do it like that. If you can."[167]

Swami Premananda went on to express his own understanding of Mā's instructions.

> God is always doing the best thing for us. He has created us and he wants to take us to him, just like a small child. When a child runs to his mother his mother may beat him or wash him, for his own good. But the child does not understand. He starts crying. Soon he is in his mother's lap. So you have to

be like this. Even if Mā or God is giving you all sorts of suffering, you will not leave, because it is all for your own good. Mā wants to cleanse everything and take you into her lap. So whatever she does, is for our best and we should surrender unconditionally to her and not think of anything else. We need to practice, practice, practice with full faith. . . . I love God as my Mā. I want to have realization of God as my Mā. I want always to be loved by her. I always used to tell her, "Mā, I am full of shortcomings, I am nothing. But whatever I am, with all my sins, I am your child. So whatever you want to do, keep me here or throw me away, you do. That is best for me."[168]

Interestingly, this expression of *bhakti yoga* is echoed almost perfectly in a statement made by Mā that appears in *Sad Vāni*, a collection of Mā's statements recorded by Bhaiji and, therefore, made before 1938:

Where complete self-effacement is the *sādhana*, no other *mantra* or *tantra* is required. Try to become as a little child and without any other effort on your part, the Great Mother of the World will take you in Her arms. But, if on the contrary, you wish to be guided by your own intelligence, you will have yourself to shoulder the entire responsibility for your uplift. Are you not weary of the play of your reason, have you not tasted enough of victory and defeat? Now is the moment to throw yourself into the Mercy of the Almighty as one without shelter and support. Leap into His embrace and you will be released from cares. Remember that it is the pure fool who shall find God.[169]

According to Swami Premananda's version of Mā's teaching on *bhakti* and surrender, *sādhana* does not appear to entail only receiving shelter and support. It includes the possibility of *tapasya*. He emphasizes that one must surrender of the "I" to the point where one has no personal desires and one unquestionably follows the will of God, even if it entails suffering and austerity. In fact, we have heard statements of Mā's in which she rails impatiently at devotees who think they can get something for nothing. Mā is talking here about the Great Mother of the Universe and the Almighty in the abstract. But, for her disciples, God, their Great Mother, is not an abstraction. She is sitting in front of them. The challenge of this kind of *bhakti* is even greater, then, because there is no question of what God intends for you. She tells you and, for your own good, you must obey. Yet, it seems that the path of Mā's devotees, whether it be the path of *bhakti*, *jnāna*, *kundalinī*, or *karma yoga*, was softened tremendously by her motherly love and affection. Devotees clearly felt held in her arms like children, scolded now and then, and sent on their way until they ran back again.

Summary

The *Devī Māhātmya*, echoing the promise of Lord Krishna, says, "Thus does the Devī Bhagavatī, although eternal, manifest herself again and again for the protection of the world, O King."[170] According to her devotees, Ānandamayī Mā is the divine Absolute come to earth to tend to her children, a fulfillment of their desire to know and be known by God. Mā did not deny her divinity; in fact, she confirmed it. She made herself available as the focus of her close devotees' *sādhana* and of their lives. While she may have recommended different paths for different people, she positioned herself at the the beginning and the end of the path as the all-knowing Mother. Mā articulated a *sādhana* in which one becomes "as a little child," a child who understands that no matter what Mother may tell them, it is for their own good. Depending upon the person, the path of surrender to Mā involved varying degrees of egolessness and self-discipline, and varying degrees of self-effort were required to fulfill her expectations. Yet, throughout each devotee's *sādhana*, Mā was there to guide and comfort and, ultimately, to decide what was the best next step. The challenge was surrender of the "I," but the reward was unconditional love and freedom from personal responsibility.

The *sādhana* of surrender to the divine that Mā favors has been more challenging for devotees since Mā's *mahāsamādhi*. While before they could sit before her and receive her comfort, correction, and direction, now they must remember her words and try to hear her voice within. For some devotees this has been a very painful transition. For others, Mā is eternally there. Swami Samatananda speaks of the way devotees approach Mā since her *mahāsamādhi*.

> The individual practices are different, but the goal is Mā. Mā is the goal means that we think that by meditating on Mā we can reach whatever we can think of. If we catch hold of Mā's hand, then Mā will lead us to whatever is needed for us. So we do not form a beautiful idea in our head about the light of consciousness or I'll become this or that. We think, "We will meditate on Mā and we will love Mā and she will show us. Whatever is good for us she will give us. In this life she will give us, and if not, then in the next life we will get it. When Mātājī thinks it is fittest for us, she will give us." So we do not hanker after *vidyā* or *mukti* or anything, because we do not know what is good for us. We pray to you, we love you, and we do not have any type of worldly attachment. This is the way we approach Mā.[171]

In conclusion, in spite of Ānandamayī Mā's insistence that she was just "a little child," she allowed herself to be worshiped as the Divine Mother, as the Mā of all. On the basis of Mā's behavior and her statements about her identity, her devotees related to her as God, whether Bhagavān, Brahman, or Devī, who, having descended age after age to destroy the wicked and protect the righteous, descended once again in Kheora, Bengal, for the sake of His or Her devotees. In the concluding chapter, we ask whether Mā's devotees' belief that God incarnated in this case in the form of a woman empowered Mā's women devotees, in particular, to live a more spiritualized, less conventional life.

SEVEN

Ānandamayī Mā and Gender

ORMAN CUTLER NOTES THAT, in spite of the twentieth century's
romance with the concept of God as "symbol" and its aversion to
the concept of concrete divinity, India still fully embraces God as
possessing an embodied reality and valorizes a personal relationship with an
embodied God. "In India," says Cutler, "a 'personal' relationship between
deity and devotees is possible as a consequence of the embodiment of both.
Deprived of a body, neither human nor deity is capable of particularized,
'personal' interactions."[1] Having determined that the community of
Ānandamayī Mā fully embraces Mā as the embodiment of God and nothing
less, we ask, How have Mā's devotees, particularly the women, been affected
by having had what they consider to be a personal relationship with God in
a woman's body? Can we assume that a relationship of this kind necessarily
empowers women?

The answers to these questions are complex and fraught with ambiguity.
As Caroline Walker Bynum would say, Ānandamayī Mā, in her full
complexity as a gender-related symbol, is certainly polysemous and in some
ways might be " 'about' values other than gender."[2] There are ways in which
Mā's birth in a woman's body particularly inspired and benefited women
and ways in which it was irrelevant. For example, how can Mā's renunciant
women devotees maintain that Mā can never be a model and that they could
never identify with her? How could Mā have lived such an unconventional
life relative to most Hindu women and have advised certain women devotees
to stay at home and devote themselves to their husbands and children? In
the course of reflecting on these questions, we will consider briefly the
cultural construction of gender as it relates to the spiritual path within the
Hindu tradition and as it is reflected in the community of Ānandamayī Mā.
We examine Mā's words on the relevance of gender to spiritual life, as well
as the words of other contemporary Hindu religious figures.

Why Did Mā Take Form as a Woman?

To initiate our exploration of gender and Ānandamayī Mā, we consult the voices of Ānandamayī Mā's women devotees themselves. In twelve of the interviews with my female contributors, after I had asked who they thought Mā was and received the nearly unanimous answer that Mā was not a woman, not a saint, not a guru, but was God incarnate, I asked, "Why do you think Mā took form as a woman?" Sita Gupta, with Rupa Vishvanathan as the translator, was representative of the various dimensions of the issue. At first Sita had some difficulty even relating to the question. Her first response was "For Mā, female or male, it made no difference. For Mā, woman's body, man's body, it made no difference." When I asked, "If she could have chosen any form, why did she choose this one?" Sita-Di replied, "That is for Mā to say." At that point, Rupa interrupted to say, "I feel like this—every now and then, God takes sometimes the form of a father, sometimes a mother, because some feel more comfortable with a father than a mother. I feel some of us are more comfortable with Mother. I'm more comfortable with Mother than Father." Then Sita said, "Didi [Gurupriya Devi] explained, 'This time Mā has come for the ladies.' Didi said this!" Rupa added, "Because we can do personal service for Mā." Sita elaborated,

> We can touch, go ahead, massage her legs. You can't do that with a man. In Vindyachal, Mā used to lie down and one person would be massaging her arm and one person her leg, massaging and talking to Mā and Mā would be laughing. She took off all her clothes and her petticoat used to be there. And she would be laughing and talking. You see, that intimacy you cannot get except with the Mother. So soft, just like a new-born baby, so soft to massage, so smooth. That's a personal feeling. . . . The ladies understood her better and felt closer to her than the men.[3]

These themes—Mā's blindness to gender, the special intimacy possible between female devotees and Mā and, thus, between women and God, the preference for Mother over Father, and the relative inaccessibility of Mā to male devotees—were mirrored in most of the responses. A number of women agreed with Sita Gupta that Mā, as an incarnation of Ultimate Truth, was neither male nor female and that as such she did not have an eye for gender distinctions. However, at the same time, they emphasized that because they were women, they could enjoy a special intimacy with Mā. Because of the cultural prohibitions governing the relationships between unrelated men and women in India, only women could spend time in close proximity to Mā. For example, Vasudha-Di, now age fifty-four, described a special moment with Mā when she was eight:

> When we came from Assam in 1944, Mā was staying on a boat on the Ganges. And my father would bathe in the Gangā three times a day. We used to go with him. We used to see Mā's boat and we would go to it to get *prasād*. We would wash our hands in the Ganges. And Mā would talk. Mā used to swim very nicely and sometimes Mā would jump into the Ganges. I

was only eight years old, but I learned to swim. And sometimes I would hold Mā's feet. And we played. The gentlemen kept their distance from Mā. And Didi couldn't swim, so she stayed on the deck. And afterwards, in the full moonlight, Mā would sing on the boat and we would have ice cream.[4]

This incident is reminiscent of an incident described by Nirmala-Di in chapter 4, in which Mā orchestrated a *līlā*, or divine play, for a few young women, costuming them them as pairs of gods and goddesses and dancing with them. At the end of that story, Nirmala-Di emphasized, "And it was only women!"[5]

Interestingly, two male devotees mentioned the disadvantage of being a man around Mā, one of them expressing the longing to have been more intimate with Mā. Swami Premananda, who had met Mā nearly a half-century ago as a twenty-five-year-old university graduate, made this poignant statement about the fate of being male around Mā:

> When I came to stay with Mā, I could not accept that it was not possible to be near the body of Mother. Her being a lady and I being a man, there were certain limitations. I couldn't be involved with her. There are certain things one shouldn't do. . . . Then I was a foolish boy, because I didn't know all these things one should and shouldn't do. Mā had to teach me. For example, there is this Kanyapeeth, this girl's school. Mā went there one day, but she didn't take me. So some time later, I went there. I went inside. Now, in India, the boys and girls are separated. I went inside the Kanyapeeth and Mā scolded me, right there. She said, "Have you gone insane!" I said, "Mā, I went along with you." She said, "It is all right that you went along, but you should not come in here." I was crying. I said, "I have not done anything wrong!" Then one day, Mā was sleeping there and I said I also wanted to sleep there. And Mā did not take food herself, she had to be fed. So, she was being fed by someone and I said, "I also want to feed you." And her hair, she had very long black hair and I just wanted to comb that. . . . It took me a long time to accept.[6]

What Premananda was longing for, then, was the intimacy that Mā's close women devotees enjoyed while they cared for Mā's physical body as they apparently engaged in the mundane activities of life. However, when engaging in these activities with Mā, her women devotees tell us that these activities were hardly mundane. If we imagine, as Mā's community imagines, an opportunity to swim with God, to sleep next to God, to feed God, or to comb God's hair, we can understand why the men around Mā felt envious.[7]

Several women emphasized, in particular, that the cultural context into which Mā came was one in which women were extremely cloistered, to the extent that they were unable to participate fully in spiritual life. Because Mā took a female form, she offered protection to women wanting to pursue *sādhana*. Malini-Di explained,

> In U. P. [Uttara Pradesh], people are very strict about this. They don't let you go to any *sādhu*. They don't let you go to any person like that. It was

only because Mā had come in the form of a lady that we were allowed to go near Mā. Otherwise, we were not. In U. P., they were very strict about this. . . . And you see, women were always suppressed. But Mā brought out the personalities of the women. . . . And the life of *brahmacharya*, it would never have been allowed, because it is considered very, very wrong not to get the girl married. . . . At the time, things had become so immoral that you couldn't leave girls unmarried.[8]

This point of view is echoed in other responses. Lalita Kumar said, "Mā came in this form especially for the women of this land, because there have been so many rascals masquerading in the form of *mahātmas*, in the *sannyāsin* garb, and taking advantage of women, that it was so utterly safe to be with Mother, for women of all ages."[9] Gita-Di Bose believes that Mā "became Mā' because women prayed to the Divine Feminine. "In India, the women are very much suppressed by the men. That is why she became Mā. Most of the women at the time must have prayed to Shakti. So she came in like a woman. But she is not a woman, she is not a man."[10]

Other women spoke more specifically about Mā's taking form as a woman to enable women to have greater spiritual equality and freedom. Lakshmi Shrivastav, a university professor, spoke of Mā's helping women gain access to formerly male spiritual practices.

> I have read history and also a little bit of anthropology, and I think that in India especially, if the woman changes, then it is easier to change the whole society. I feel that. At the time Mā came, it was 1896. In East Bengal there weren't even trains, just boats. So it was only her coming that introduced women to *kīrtan*, the all night chanting. She introduced women to that. She said, "Why can't the women do that?" There were many things like that. She gave them courage.

Lakshmi was one of many to mention Mā's arranging for women to be allowed to perform *kīrtan*, which, according to Mā's life story, was not accessible to Mā as a young wife. Lakshmi went on to give an example of Mā's inspiring women to be more courageous:

> Once Mātājī was in Banaras staying at the house of a lady. One night Mā went out and she hadn't returned. That lady said to herself, "As a woman, I can't go out at night in a sari." It was quite late. So she just put on a man's *dhoti*, put on a *dushālā* (a shawl), put her hair up in a turban, took a *lati* (a stick) and she went to that place to get Mā. So this is the sort of courage Mā gives.[11]

In this example, it seems clear that Lakshmi saw the "lady" in question as inspired by Mā's fearlessness and refusal to behave in a conventional manner. Mā herself always wore a white *dhoti* wrapped around her in an unconventional way and surely was not afraid to go out at night.

By contrast, Swami Brahmananda, the head of the Kankhal ashram, voluntarily bringing up the question of why Mā was born as a woman, had a different slant on Mā's mission, not surprisingly one involving the uplift of *men*. In the process of explaining his "idea," he nuanced Mā's gender in a different way.

> Mā was a lady. She was not male or female. But because she was a lady, whenever she went into a household, she was accessible to the females. Now what happened, she came to this world to change, to bring change. Now who can change the world? The mother. The household mother can change the boys, not the father. You know, the boy stays twelve, fifteen years with mother. These ladies are future mothers, so they can teach whatever Mā used to teach.

Having just interviewed four female renunciants whom he had told me would help me understand Mā, I asked for clarification. "Did Mā encourage those women to stay in the household or to become *brahmachārinīs?*" Brahmananda replied,

> No, no, she encouraged them to stay in the house and change their sons and their husbands. That was the idea. And in the future, thirty years after Mā's passing, there will be a new generation. That is my idea. And I have seen the boys who came in touch with Mā. They are more forceful than the people of this generation, the younger ones. And they got their teaching from their own mother who got it from Mā.[12]

Not surprisingly, there were no women devotees who believed that Mā's purpose in coming into the world as a woman was to raise a generation of more "forceful" men.

Mā's Accessibility to Women

There seem to be three main ways in which Mā's being a woman particularly benefited and inspired women. The first way, which has been well documented in the interviews throughout this study, is that, because Mā was in a female body, women had greater access to her and, therefore, greater intimacy with her. In watching the films and videotapes of Mā, it is striking to see the number of women, both householders and *brahmachārinīs*, surrounding Mā at public events. I have been able to see the faces of many of the women devotees whom I interviewed hovering around Mā. I can only imagine that, in Mā's private moments, men were absent, and many women had the opportunity to serve God as Mā very closely. It is easy to understand how those women who physically cared for Mā might have been particularly devastated by her death. Chitra, a *brahmachārinī*, movingly expressed the grief of many women close to Mā in a 1984 article in *Ānanda Vārtā*. She says, "My pained heart cries out in anguish to take shelter in the pure haven of love that was our Mother's lap."[13]

While women devotees' privileged access to Mā offered them a rare spiritual opportunity to have a personal relationship with God as Mā, caring for her and being cared for by her, it also offered them an emotional opportunity. Most Hindu marriages, and certainly Bengali ones, require a young woman, who is often a mere teenager, to leave her own mother and spend the rest of her life in the household of her husband, receiving what motherly attention is available, which may be little or none, from her mother-in-law. The heart-wrenching separation of a daughter from her mother at marriage is sung about and ritualized in the time preceding a traditional Hindu wedding, so that nearly every young girl, although prepared for it, also dreads it.[14] After the marriage, depending on the regional and caste customs, a young bride is allowed to visit her own mother only at specific times of the year and, depending on distance, perhaps not even once a year. For married devotees, in the absence of a continuous and nurturing relationship with their own mother, Mā fulfilled that motherly role. Women often mentioned that the kind of intimacy that they enjoyed with Mā mirrored their relationship with their biological Mā. For example, Krishna Bhattacharya, presently in her sixties or seventies, reminisced about a time when Mā invited her to come to Naimisharanya.

> Just like a daughter who after so many days goes to her parent's house, I was looked after by everybody with care. In that way I was. Naimisharanya is a very quiet and peaceful place, and Mā used to ask me every day whether I have seen everything there, and whether I have taken my food, lunch, etc. Mā would let me take her hair down and lie on the cot. We would chat, just as mothers and daughters do. She would say, "What did they feed you? Was the food good?" And I used to ask her about the proper way I should make my rituals and things. And at that time, she used to ask everybody to leave the room, so I could be alone with Mā.[15]

For Mā's *brahmachārinī* devotees, the choice to live with Mā as celibate women meant that they could have a lifelong relationship with *both* mothers, their own biological mothers and their spiritual mothers. For example, when I interviewed the *brahmachārinī* Malini-Di, I also met her mother, who was living in the Kankhal ashram with her. Mother and daughter seemed to be enjoying an intimacy and a proximity not usually possible when a daughter leaves home for her husband's household. In addition, as Malini intimated, whereas an unmarried daughter is considered an embarrassment and a potential disaster, a *brahmachārinī* daughter, safe in the confines of Mā's ashram, can be a source of pride.

Mā as an Advocate for Spiritual Equality for Women

The second way in which Mā's being a woman benefited women was that Mā, because of women's accessibility to her, was in a better position to advocate for their spiritual equality with men. In particular, she was able to inspire some of them, the ones who she determined were suited, to take a vow of lifelong celibacy and become *brahmachārinīs*, pursuing full-time *sādhana*. Eight of the twenty-five women had taken such a vow. This act of renunciation apparently had both associated difficulties and boons. On the one hand, "Mā's girls," as they were called, lived a rather cloistered life in which they had few personal possessions and little or no privacy, were told what to do and where to do it, and engaged in various levels of *tapasya*, or austerities, such as sleeping on a thin mat on the floor. On the other hand, they were just that, "Mā's girls," and as such they enjoyed the enviable position of living and traveling with Mā most of the time. Certainly many of them must have been motivated to become *brahmachārinīs* for this reason. While women householder devotees came and went, based on their husbands' permission and their family responsibilities, "Mā's girls" stayed on, caring for Mā.

Although it would be tempting to think of "Mā's girls" as doing more combing of Mā's hair than meditation, it is apparent that along with physical proximity to Mā came Mā's close scrutiny of their spiritual progress. Swami Gitananda, the only *sannyāsinī* whom I interviewed, described the benefits and the demands of the "girls'" relationship with Mā.

> [The girls] who wanted to be closely related to Mā were treated differently by Mā. She was open with them. She liked to scold them in front of the assembled people. Mā had a free, unrestrained relationship with us and took pleasure in speaking to us. And we girls took pride in our status. Mā would scold us in public for the smallest infractions. . . . It was only for show and then she would say later, "Now, I can scold you with all my heart. I can be very direct with you. I do not have to hide anything." This was our pride that Mā thought we were special. . . . With us Mā felt every little, tiny behavior had to be so fragrant and fruitful as a rose in full bloom. You see, Mā wanted us to blossom into perfection. So she pointed out even the smallest failing so that we will improve and make our life beautiful like a rose.[16]

Chitra's article, "Let Us Be Filled with Sweet Memories," explains the blessings and the challenges inherent in the relationship between Mā and her *brahmachārinīs*.[17] In this article, Chitra reproduces a letter dictated by Mā to her and five of Mā's other "older friends," whom Mā had left in Kishenpur ashram in Dehradun during the "three severe winter months to practice intensive *sādhana*." Although Chitra frames the article by saying that "there is no one now who lavishes grace and compassion on us as did our adored Ma,"[18] practicing *sādhana* in the bitter cold of the Himalayan foothills in December and January without central heating and without Mā must have been pure *tapasya*. Mā, indeed, acknowledges this point in her letter, saying that "we are told that for the sake of concentrated *sādhanā*, *sādhus* and *sannyāsins* [both terms for male practitioners] often stay in cold places since this is congenial to meditation." She says that spending too much time traveling with Mā and "meeting too many people becomes an obstacle." Thus, for their "spiritual welfare," Mā has had the *kheyāla* that they should be away from "this body." Mā chastens,

> Therefore, this splendid opportunity should not be wasted. The aroma of the *sādhanā* of these *tapasvinīs* [female ascetics] must be noticed in their looks,

their way of speaking; each movement should manifest their progress towards Truth. Every effort must be made to speak the truth, to remain steeped in the spiritual, to advance toward immortality.[19]

The letter goes on to address each *brahmachāriṇī* individually with both motherly advice and compassion and guru-like corrections. For example, Mā is happy to hear that Pushpa's and Chitra's inflammation of the throat has subsided. Yet Mā says, "Udas is growing old, wrinkles have started on her face. When will you concentrate on *sādhanā*? Are you going to spend your whole life attending to this body? Complete your *japa* and do your *sādhanā* with enthusiasm and steadiness."[20] She cautions against drinking too much tea in winter and recommends hot water instead. At the same time she says,

> Many a day have you spent watching the sights of the world, joking and laughing in the worldly way; now, friends, be pilgrims on the journey to your real Home! Do not think that just because you have not felt His presence and the touch of Him you are free to while away your time in frivolities, this can never lead to your real welfare.[21]

Mā closes with detailed instructions for daily recitation of sacred texts, *japa,* and meditation.

This letter certainly belies any impression we might have gotten that the *brahmachāriṇīs* close to Mā did not really engage in *sādhana* and only cared for Mā as they would a *mūrti*, or statue of a deity. Yet Mā seems to be acknowledging that tendency. She seems to be calling them to turn their focus away from her and back to themselves and their own spiritual progress, maintaining that "patience and forbearance are necessary for all. How can the foundation be laid without endurance?"[22]

The second evidence of Mā's advocacy for the spiritual equality of women is her establishment of the Kanyapeeth, the Sanskrit school for girls between ages five and twelve, in Banaras. Although it is firmly maintained that Mā never affiliated herself with any institution established in her name, both my interviews and the literature available on Mā point to her active involvement in the school. Swami Samatananda told me, "Our Kanyapeeth girls are famous in Banaras. They speak in Sanskrit. Mā used to watch the girls speaking in Sanskrit, doing dramas from Sanskrit literature. They have received much respect and Mātājī founded this institution. . . for girl's education, for the uplifting of the girls."[23] Uma Chatterjee told me that the Kanyapeeth was technically started by Gurupriya Devi in order "to provide protection for girls who did not desire marriage and education for those who do." Parents, she said, used to send their girls to get a good, spiritual education, but now there are also "economic and domestic reasons." But remarkably, even today, 25 percent of the girls stay on to be lifelong *brahmachāriṇīs,* teaching in the school.[24] Certainly Mā's support of the school and involvement in it reflect her commitment to spiritual education for girls and to the institution of *brahmacharya* and its availability to Hindu girls as an alternative to marriage.

A third demonstration of Mā's advocacy for women's spiritual equality is her arranging for certain women to participate in the Vedic ceremony of *upanayana*, or the investiture with the sacred thread, an initiation available only to boys for nearly two thousand years.[25] The *upanayana* has traditionally marked the passage of a boy of one of the three highest castes into the period of celibate study in which he was to master the Vedas. According to Gurupriya Devi's journal, which is corroborated by my interviews with Mā's devotees, sometime in 1929, in Dacca, "the subject of investing women with the sacred thread had arisen in Mā's *kheyāla* and she herself had taken on a sacred thread."[26] Keshab Bhattacharya, in the midst of telling me about Mā's enthusiasm upon hearing about his *upanayana* in 1971 at the age of eight or nine, said,

> Yes, it was Mā who started the ancient practice of giving the sacred thread to brahman girls. There's a very interesting story of how she was playing with a gold chain of hers and one day, it had three strings, she started putting it around her neck and putting the other end under her arm. She kept it like that for some time, telling Didi, "Look, I'm now a *dvija*, a twice born."[27]

According to Gurupriya Devi, sometime thereafter at the Ramna ashram in Calcutta, Mā gave Bhaiji, who was not a brahman, the sacred thread because she had "the feeling that he was a brahman."[28]

In 1934, according to Didi, right after Mā had given her the name Gurupriya, along with some yellow clothes and the instruction to live as a *brahmachārinī*, Mā "raised one more point":

> "Find out from the scholars in Kāshī [Banaras] whether the ritual of conferring the sacred thread on women is mentioned in our scriptures or not. . . ." At Kāshī we made exhaustive inquiries, from many scholars, about investing with the sacred thread. The unanimous reply was, "This tradition was prevalent in ancient times, but we cannot find an opinion for modern times." Finally we decided we could get the best solution from Pandit Sri Gopinath Kaviraj and so we approached him. Mā also had suggested his name to us. He did some research on the subject and found many examples of instances where women had received the sacred thread. He proposed, "If Mā so desires, she can give the sacred thread to women even now. Mā's will is scriptural. No other opinion is necessary."[29]

And so, in 1935, Mā had Gurupriya Devi invested with the sacred thread, along with Bholanāth's grandniece, Maronī. Swami Samatananda confirmed this sequence of events and offered to show me a copy of a treatise of Kaviraj's "in favor of the sacred thread for women."[30]

Malini-Di told me the rest of the story. After Gurupriya Devi received the sacred thread, Mā had Purnananda, Chandan, Udas, Nirukma, Jaya, and Dika take it. I asked if these people asked to receive the sacred thread. Malini replied, "No, Mā asked everybody. She asked Padmajī—all these people—'Will you take? Will you take?' Some said 'No,' because it meant you had to shave off your hair and take the sacred thread. Then you had to follow a bunch of rules and regulations, and some people felt because of their health they couldn't do." I asked Malini if Mā had asked her and she said, "No, I am not a brahman." She did ask Swami Paramānanda, 'Can we give to non-brahmans also?' and Swamijī said, 'Amongst the men folk, you can, but I don't know about the ladies.' So on that basis, she didn't."[31]

In Dehradun in 1980, Mā talks about a conversation she had with the Mahāmandaleshvara, an important regional head of an order of *sannyāsins*. She says that he came to her respectfully, but concerned, saying, "You have taken this sacred thread. Will you please tell me something about it?" Mā relates the conversation in which Mā argued strongly that the true meaning of the scriptures is that *Kaliyuga*, the present, most degenerate age, is no different from *Kritayuga*, the perfect age; therefore, women deserve to be treated equally. She said that finally the Mahāmandaleshvara relented, saying, "Mā what you have said and done is all correct." In closing the story, Mā says,

> Why did he say so? The reason is that this body put on that sacred thread by herself. She started reciting *Gāyatrī* [mantra] on her own. She did not take any Guru. She did not listen to that *Gāyatrī* from anybody. It automatically came from her heart. That is why this body says, "This mantra does not exist in any educated person alone. It is not the property of any scholar. It exists in everyone and when it comes forth, it seems to be flowing from *Apaurusha* [Not-Man], not from a man but from God."[32]

One other phenomenon demonstrates Mā's advocacy for women's spiritual equality, the planning for the construction of a *yajnashāla*, or building dedicated to the performance of the sacred fire ritual, at the Kankhal ashram, which was done entirely by a committee of women selected by Mā. I found out about this while touring the ashram with the *brahmachārinī*, Malini-Di. She asked me, "Has anyone shown you the *yajnashāla*?" I said that I hadn't even heard of it. She smirked and said, "I'm not surprised. The girls built it." We walked over to the large, formal building, and Malini-Di began to explain:

> *Atinidra Mahāyajna* took place from 6 May, 1981, until 16 May, 1981. And one hundred thirty-five learned *pandits* took part in it. All the *mahātmas* of significance at the time were present for that function. . . . *Atinidra Mahāyajna* is performed for the welfare of the world. There were eleven *kunds* in which the fire was ignited. . . . There was a committee that Mā formed to design this building. The President was Padma Mishra, the Vice President was Parul Banerji, the Treasurer was Nirmala Nahandu, the Secretary was Shanta Patak, known as Pushnananda. And she is the daughter of the Vice President of the country, Mr. G. S. Patak. And myself. We were five. We approached an architect and he designed it for us according to the rules of the *shāstras*. . . . We researched everything. We enjoyed ourselves and we learned a lot about the *yajna*.[33]

Malini-Di was obviously very proud of the building and remembered every detail of the planning and construction, as well as every detail of the fire ritual itself. Lakshmi Shrivastav, another *brahmachārinī*, remembers the process similarly. In telling me about it, she emphasized that "we had control of the accounts, of everything. The treasurer handled that. There were *lakhs* of money. We arranged everything."[34]

It is obvious from these examples that Mā advocated for her women devotees, particularly for her *brahmachārinīs*. She held them very close, gave them a great deal of support and guidance, and offered them many opportunities for spiritual advancement. In addition, particularly in the case of the construction of the *yajnashāla*, Mā empowered the women close to her to learn new skills and take charge of things which were normally within the male domain. In this way, she nurtured a certain kind of independence in her celibate women devotees, which I felt when I interviewed them. The seven *brahmachārinīs* and one *sannyāsinī* whom I met were, as a group, very strong, outspoken, and independent. Although Mā was clearly the center of their lives, they were hardly shrinking *bhaktas*. One can imagine them arguing with Mā, pleading with her, and being fully engaged with her as individual personalities. Perhaps this is what Mā intended, to foster in them as they developed into "pilgrims on the journey to their real Home." Regardless, she gave them every opportunity to develop spiritual parity with men.[35]

Mā as the Perfect Householder, the Perfect *Sādhikā*, and the Perfect *Sannyāsinī*

The third way in which Ānandamayi Mā's birth in a female body might have particularly benefited women was that different women could identify with different stages of her life and be inspired. In chapter 3, we established that Mā was in no way the "perfect wife" according to the *dharmashāstra* paradigm. However, one could imagine that Mā's life with Bholanāth might inspire housewives to make time in their day for *sādhana* and the pursuit of God. Clearly Mā's priority during the years of her "*līlā* of *sādhana*" was not her relationship with her husband but her relationship with God. I did meet many housewives, who, at least since their children were grown, devote large parts of their day to *pūjā*, *japa*, and meditation. I met women in that phase of life who had left husbands to live in Kankhal ashram for part of the year. In fact, Brahmacharini Chandan says,

> The lesson that we have received in this context of the veiled *bahu* [Nirmalā as a young bride] is that, though we complain about our inability to sit for *sadhana* due to our household responsibilities, yet, if there is a real awakening of the desire for attainment even from the worldly point of view, then, despite remaining in the midst of all, an effort can be made to undertake the journey towards that Supreme State."[36]

However, the following section demonstrates that Mā's advice to housewives was largely traditional and that her example was probably lost on most householder women. She certainly did not seem to be saying, "Be the kind of *sādhikā* I was when I was married."

There is no question that Mā's life as a renunciant was one of the factors in inspiring many women to leave the worldly life and become *brahmachārinīs*. However, it may be that Mā's definition of *sādhana* and that of her *brahmachārinīs* were not the same. It may have been difficult for many *brahmachārinīs* to separate their desire to do *sādhana* from their desire to be with Mā. In some ways, being with Mā was their *sādhana* and, try as Mā might have to get the focus off her and onto their own spiritual growth, many women saw the goal of life as being as physically close to Mā as possible. We saw in chapter 5 that few women looked up to Mā as a model, because, as Malini-Di said, you would have to look "way, way up." We turn now to the ways in which Mā's having a woman's body and leading a more unconventional life than most Hindu women did not seem to be major factor in how devotees, particularly women, lived their lives and why this was so.

"Do as I Say, Not as I Do"

While it is apparent that Ānandamayī Mā's life presents a radical challenge to the orthodox concept of marriage, there is a way in which Mā communicated the message, "Do as I say, not as I do." In spite of Mā's advocacy for the spiritual equality of women, Mā seemed to hold many orthodox views on how women, particularly householders, should live their lives. She approved of arranged marriages and, in spite of Bholanāth's extreme concern, instigated the betrothal of Bholanāth's eight-year-old grand niece, Maroni (who lived with them), and her marriage at the age of twelve.[37] Ironically, Mā suggested that it was time for Maroni to marry the man to whom she had been betrothed right after she arranged for Maroni to receive the sacred thread, along with Didi. Mukerji maintains that Mā had Bholanāth marry off Maroni so that he could "discharge his obligations" to her and "resume again his life of *sādhana*."[38] Lipski says that Mā also "counsels: 'There is only one marriage,' and never advises a second marriage even for widows."[39]

Mā's advice to women householders was quite conventional. In 1936 Mā was asked, "What *sādhana* can a housewife do?"

> *Seva* [selfless service] and *japa*. All duties can be performed in a spirit of service and dedication. God himself appears to you in the guise of your various obligations in the world. . . . If you sustain the thought, "this also is one of the many aspects of the Divine," then there need be no conflict between what is worldly and what is religious.[40]

It must be said, however, that although she, like Tryambaka, advised a wife to treat her husband like a god, she also advised a husband to treat his wife like a goddess. For example, when asked if renunciation is a prerequisite to communion with God, Mā says,

> You are not called upon to retire to the forest, nor to become inert, like a stone, unresponsive to what goes on about you. You have to start life from

the position God has placed you in. Be His servant. If you are at home, look upon your son as Balagopal (infant Krishna), your little daughter as Uma (Divine Mother), and your consort as Narayana (God in one form) or Lakshmi (Divine Mother, daughter of Durga). Do not do harm to anybody. Let the little attachment you have developed to people about you continue within its minimum limit. This world is but a *dharmashala* (a lodge for pilgrims where they may stay for a short time). When the call will come for your final exit, all the ties of life will have to be snapped and you won't have a moment's reprise.[41]

In this statement, Mā does seem to be saying that one ultimately needs to progress from householder to *sannyāsin* or *sannyāsinī*, if not in this lifetime, then in a future one.

It seems that Mā asked most housewives, especially those with husbands unsympathetic to spiritual practice, to fulfill their daily duties, to serve their husband and children as God, and to keep their *sādhana* to themselves. Mukerji says that Mā would say,

The efforts you make for your spiritual welfare are to be carefully hidden. Guard them as closely as a miser guards his wealth. You do not have to advertise the fact that you are engaged in *sādhanā*. It is between God and you only. . . . You may do your work with your hands, but nobody can prevent you from keeping your mind on God.[42]

Mā's conservative attitude toward married women was reflected in the fact that, although Mā instituted *kīrtans* for women in Dacca, a radical idea for that time, she also made sure they were in the middle of the night so they would not interfere with the daily duties of *strīdharma*. Mā herself kept neither her *sādhana* nor her *bhāvas* to herself, and she did not fulfill the duties of *strīdharma*. It seems as though the kind of piety that Mā recommends for married women mirrors the kind of piety Caroline Walker Bynum sees in medieval Christian women. Bynum calls it an "inner worldly asceticism" as opposed to a "world-rejecting asceticism," a piety that unites action and contemplation in such a way as to provide continuity in women's lives as they become more spiritualized.[43] This perspective certainly allows for a different reading of Mā's message to married women.

More challenging is Mā's apparent attitude toward the practice of suttee. Mā, along with her mother, Didimā, speaks of the honor of having a *satī* in their family lineage.[44] Lipski quotes Mā as having spoken at some length on the reverence due to one who is able to unflinchingly ascend the funeral pyre.

Once a male devotee asked Ānandamayī Mā whether by committing suicide upon the death of his beloved wife he would be able to join her. In the strongest possible terms She condemned suicide: "To whom belongs the body that you speak of destroying? Is this the way a human being talks? For shame!" And She added that suicide is nothing but a foolish attempt to escape from harvesting one's karma. It only further retards spiritual progress. However, She does not consider that a woman who had become a *satī* (literally chaste women), i.e. a widow who had burnt herself on her husband's funeral pyre, had committed suicide. As far as Ānandamayī Mā was concerned, *sati* was a ritual death, a confirmation of a wife's unconditional loyalty to her husband and an expression of true chastity. "A real *sati* has to be completely steady in mind and body. If entering the fire she suffers, she cannot be called a *sati*." If thus her conduct in life has been totally unblemished, she will be fearless at the time of immolation. In this connection Ānandamayī Mā tells about one of Her ancestors who put one of her fingers into the flame of a candle to test whether she would be able to endure the pain of being burnt. She experienced no pain. Subsequently she ascended her husband's funeral pyre, lay down and remained completely motionless while the flames consumed her body. [45]

Lipski goes on to say that, although Westerners will undoubtedly be shocked by Mā's approval of suttee, it is important to understand that, from her perspective, "motive is all-important. The true *sati* is not escaping from life but is fulfilling her duty according to the *dharma* (right way of living) prevailing within her cultural milieu at the time. She is acting selflessly and shows that she is not attached to this delusive body."[46] Lipski closes the subject by saying, "It must be said that Ānandamayī Mā does not advocate *sati* in the present age."[47]

Although I was unable to find the original source of Mā's remarks on suttee, I have no reason to doubt Lipski's rendering. I believe that Mā's attitude toward suttee derives from a tendency to spiritualize the phenomenon, to idealize asceticism and detachment from the body. It completely disregards the double standard involved in the practice of suttee and the cultural pressures that have brought women throughout history to consider suttee as an option. Mā is seeing suttee purely as the act of an ascetic and, as such, as an act to be honored. Mā's attitude toward suttee reflects her ability to separate the spiritual liberation of women, with its required asceticism and disengagement from attachments, from their social or political liberation.

We can conclude that while Ānandamayī Mā was an advocate of women's *spiritual* equality, in many ways she reinforced the *dharmashāstra* ideal for women that her own life contradicts. Catherine Ojha, having studied thirty-eight female ascetics of Banaras, one of whom was Mā, concludes that although these women are considered to be rebels because of their refusal to live within the bounds of marriage and have adopted a "masculine type of behavior," they "do not profoundly question the established order."

The influence [these rebels] get is not used as a platform in order to criticize such or such fundamental aspect of the social model. . . . When they speak, it is to encourage people to respect their *svadharma*, to urge them to adopt dharmic behavior. When, more particularly, they address themselves to women, it is to ask them to follow with more dignity the rules of this *strīdharma* which their own life belies. The defense of the caste system, and of all the exclusive types of attitudes involved in it is also their preoccupation. They admit themselves that in their private life they may disregard certain rules but that in public it is their duty to keep their distance in order to educate people. In this respect they are not at all different from the majority of *sādhus* who, though they have left the norm behind, are taking the part of *dharma-rakṣaka*, or protectors of the *dharma*. . . . In the case of female ascetics, it may sometimes amount to discouraging other women from doing what they have done themselves. But by strengthening the most orthodox socio-religious values, they are assured to maintain a good reputation.[48]

Although it would be difficult to determine the extent to which Mā was motivated by a need "to maintain a good reputation," it does seem that she often functioned as a "protector of the *dharma*." Rather than expecting all women to follow in her footsteps, she recommended an orthodox life as an "inner-worldly ascetic."

The Cultural Construction of Gender and Ānandamayī Mā

One significant factor seems to inhibit the potential of Ānandamayī Mā, as a gender-related symbol, to serve as a model for women, and that is the ambiguity surrounding her gender. We have seen in the interviews with her devotees that Mā is repeatedly described as neither a man nor a woman or as neither male nor female. Brahmacharini Chandan relates in detail an incident that she considers critical to the life story of Ānandamayī Mā and that communicates the same thing. She says that she heard from Mā's mother, Didimā, that when Mā was nine or ten months old, a "lustrous figure," a *mahātma*, was seen standing very close to little Nirmalā. After meditating next to her and performing *pūjā* to her, the *mahātma* pointed to Nirmalā and said, "This is Mā, neither solely woman nor solely man. You will certainly not be able to keep Her bound in family ties. She will definitely not remain here."[49]

There has been considerable recent scholarly focus on the cultural construction of gender.[50] Shelly Errington defines "gender" as a "cultural system of meaning pertaining to the differences and similarities between men and women as they are lived and interpreted in particular contexts."[51] She explains that while sex refers to human bodies, gender refers to what different cultures make of sex.[52] Using the analogy of a frosted cake, Errington says that, while the body has sometimes been thought of as a cake and the culture as the frosting, on the contrary, the biological givens are the ingredients and the socializing process of a given culture is the cooking process.[53] Human bodies are "asked to bear . . . the culture's gender ideology, its mythologies of the person with specific reference to men and women."[54] Moreover, a person assigned to a gender category may not hold onto that assignment indefinitely. Rather, "a person's gender must continually be affirmed and expressed in social practice," an activity some refer to as "doing gender."[55]

Within the Hindu context, although male and female difference among ordinary people is highly marked, it seems that in the realm of extraordinary people, such as saints, gurus, and renunciants, male-female difference may not be so highly marked. In fact, it may be that the gender of a Hindu saint, guru, or *sannyāsin* or *sannyāsinī* is seen as a kind of third gender; certain male and female holy people are seen as more like each other than like other men and women. This may be in part a by-product of the process of initiation into the life of renunciation. Charles Keyes notes that, although most anthropologists see initiation processes as van Gennep does, as a rite of passage in which a child is transformed from an asexual into a sexual person, in Theravada Buddhist society in Southeast Asia, for example, a man emerges from the renunciant initiation process with an ambiguous gender identity, "a sexual-social identity that is in tension with an ideal [ordinary] male religious identity."[56]

However, within both the tantric and Advaitin frameworks, the ambiguity of the gender of extraordinary Hindu personalities seems to have more to do with the conceptualization of the path to Self-realization. In both traditions, this path is conceived of as a process of transcending the limitations of one's sexual identity, which is itself only a reflection of the limited, dualistic world, into the realm of Ultimate Reality, which is envisioned as having either a perfectly balanced male-female gender (the union of Shiva and Shakti) or a formless, sexless gender (*nirguna* Brahman).[57] Particularly to embark on the Advaitin path to liberation, one must begin by understanding "I am not this body" before one can progress.

This Upanishadic truth has been central to the teachings of Hindu gurus up to the present day. For example, the contemporary Hindu Advaitin, Ramana Maharshi (1879–1950), taught that only by getting rid of *dehātma buddhi*, or the consciousness that "I am this body," can a person realize his true nature. Once he was asked how to root out the sexual impulse. He replied, "By rooting out the false idea of the body being Self. There is no sex in the Self. . . . Only when differentiation ceases will the sexual impulse cease."[58] The Hindu woman saint, Mother Jñānānanda of Madras, by contrast, speaks more in terms of the tantric goal of balancing male and female to transcend sexual gender. According to Charles White, when asked if men and women have exactly equal spiritual characteristics, Jñānānanda says,

> Have you ever seen the statue of Shiva Ardhanari? He is depicted in two sexes but in one body. It is primarily at the gross physical level that we must perceive precise distinctions. When the male and female elements are completely developed and complement each other in the same individual, the soul is fully realized. It is certainly true that men and women have different characteristics. The woman tends to be more emotional, also motherly and loving; whereas the man is more intellectual, perhaps braver. But we cannot rely absolutely on these distinctions. For myself I no longer feel that I inhabit a body of a particular sexual gender. In fact, I sometimes refer to myself with the masculine pronoun.[59]

Within the lives of the *bhakti* saints, as well, according to Ramanujan, "the lines between male and female are crossed and recrossed so many times" as to render them "a kind of third gender."[60] He notes that many male saints wish to become women to have the intimacy with Shiva or Krishna that women saints enjoy. Several famous saints are renowned for their transcendence of gender. The Vaishnava saint Chaitanya, according to O'Flaherty, cultivated a kind of androgyny so that he could experience what it would be like to make love to both Krishna and Rādhā; at times he dressed like a woman and retired each month during menstruation.[61] Ramakrishna Paramahamsa, as well, went through a period of dressing like a woman while he was exploring the *mādhurya bhāva*, or the attitude in which the devotee approaches Krishna as lover.[62] Isherwood says that the reason for this transvestism on the part of Hindu saints is that "if the devotee can make himself seriously believe for a while that he belongs to the opposite sex, he will be well on his way to overcoming the illusion of sex distinction altogether; for he will then know that the distinction is not absolute, as he supposed."[63]

Mahatma Gandhi also minimized the importance of distinctions between men and women. In his letters to the women on the ashram, Gandhi responded to a letter from one ashram sister who requested him to return to protect them.

> In the ashram we all desire to have experience of "the soul." Now the soul is neither male nor female, neither young nor old. The scriptures and our experience tell us that these are the attributes only of the body. The same soul pervades you and me. Then how shall I be able to protect you?[64]

Gandhi himself is renowned for having attained a balance of masculine and feminine characteristics. In another letter, he said, "My ideal is this: a man should remain a man and yet should become woman; similarly a woman should remain woman and yet become man."[65] Erik Erikson remarks,

> I wonder whether there has ever been another political leader who almost prided himself on being half man and half woman, and who so blatantly aspired to be more motherly than women born to the job.... He undoubtedly saw a kind of sublimated maternalism as part of the positive identity of a whole man, and certainly of a *homo religiosus*.[66]

Gandhi's ideal may not be particular to him; it seems to reflect one aspect of the larger Hindu ideal of the *homo religiosus* as well as the *femina religiosa*. The true guru, whether possessing a male or a female body, is propitiated as both mother and father, having supposedly attained the state beyond distinctions.

The ambiguity within the Hindu tradition about the gender of Self-realized beings, then, reflects an ambiguity within the tradition about the gender of God. This ambiguity, however, is less a product of confusion or contradiction than it is a product of the inclusiveness of the tradition. Just as there is great flexibility and interchangeability about the names of God, the faces of God, and the perspectives from which God can be understood, so there is flexibility about God's gender. God is sometimes conceived of as masculine, as Bhagavān, Shiva, and Krishna, and sometimes as feminine, as Bhagavatī, Shakti, Rādhā. Sometimes God is seen as a third androgynous, balanced male-female gender–Shiva-Shakti or Krishna-Rādhā. However, there is a sense in which whatever form of God a Hindu worships, he or she sees that god as encompassing both the form of Ultimate Reality as well as its formlessness. Thus, worshippers of Devī, while they see her as manifesting countless feminine forms, at the same time see her in her most ultimate sense as formless Brahman, a sexless gender.

Ānandamayī Mā on Gender

Not surprisingly, Ānandamayī Mā's position on the gender of ordinary people, of extraordinary people, and of God mirrors the ultimate irrelevance of gender. If we examine Ānandamayī Mā's statements on gender, we find that she, too, maintains that from the perspective of the Self, there is no male and female and that one needs to transcend these distinctions to make any spiritual progress. Once in Dehradun, Mā, reportedly in a trance state, echoed the words of Ramana Maharshi, saying, "All the time, everybody is engaged in bearing a body and feeding it everything that it wants. But there is also a vibration inside and it tells us to be free from this *dehātma buddhi* [this consciousness that "I am this body"]. The main thing is to remove this *dehātma buddhi*."[67] According to Mā, the body is part of and dependent upon this illusory world. In the following statement she creates a pun on the Bengali word *sharīra*, or body, by comparing it to the verb *shara*, which means to move on and slip away. " 'Body' signifies that which slips away, which is constantly changing. If there is no want, no desire, then this kind of body that is ever in the process of perishing does not persist. Thus, after God-realization one can no longer speak of such a body for the Self stands revealed."[68]

We have seen in chapter 6 that while Mā alternates the names of God as well as the masculine and feminine pronouns to refer to God, she maintains that the Absolute, whether called the Self, Bhagavān, Brahman, or even Devī, is neither male nor female. In Brindavan, in November 1967, Mā said, "You are the Self, you are He. He is neither masculine nor feminine. Therefore here, too, there is no question of man or woman. In all men and women, it is He alone. The Self in everybody is genderless. And that Self is He."[69] In other words, the genderlessness of the Absolute is reflected in the genderlessness of human beings.

However, Mā, like Jnānānanda of Madras, also seems to recommend a *sādhana* in which people learn to balance their masculine and feminine qualities as a step toward embracing the genderless Self. In a *satsang* in Poona in 1969, Mā said, "If the manhood in a woman or the womanhood in a man is awakened, the question of sexual difference does not arise. . . . Then He does reveal himself."[70] In Banaras in the same year, Mā made a statement, apparently in reference to a certain woman, that reveals that one of the characteristics of the womanhood of which she speaks is a kind of weakness. Yet, she says that it can be overcome.

Where is there a difference between a man and a woman? There is womanhood in a man and manhood in a woman. They called her *abalā* (weak). Yes, you are *abalā*, without strength, til the time you nurture the desire, need the support. Once manhood is awakened in you there is no question of being *abalā* any more. So there is no question of a man or a woman. Whether you are a man or a woman you must recite the syllable *Om*.[71]

I was unable to find a corresponding example in which Mā spoke about a quality that a man might have to nurture in himself to awaken his womanhood and, therefore, be in a position to have God reveal himself.

It is difficult to determine whether Mā's conviction that both men and women need to become fully male and fully female in order to embrace the Absolute implies that the Absolute is an androgynous third gender, the union of Shiva and Shakti, or a third sexless gender, such as formless Brahman. Since we have seen in previous chapters that Mā often spoke of the Absolute as both ice and water, as both *saguna* and *nirguna*, it is more likely that she conceived of the Absolute as both *saguna*, possessing a perfectly balanced Shiva-Shakti nature, *and nirguna*, without any qualities. If so, she may have thought of herself in the same way.

Regardless of how Mā thought about her own gender, it is not surprising that her devotees would say that she was not a woman and not a man. As Ultimate Reality, she would have to be thought of in one of two ways: as a perfect union of Shiva and Shakti or as formless Brahman. In any case, taking into account the Hindu understanding of the gender of God, as well as the emphasis placed on disidentification with the body, it is not difficult to understand why Mā's women devotees fail to identify with Mā as a woman. If they have listened to Mā well, they have come to believe that they, too, are neither woman nor man but are, instead, the Self of All.

Ānandamayā Mā as Deity: "Looking Way, Way Up"

There is a second important but related factor that seems to inhibit Ānandamayī Mā's potential to serve as a model for women and that is the very fact of her being considered a deity, albeit a deity in female form. In chapter 5, we saw that women devotees had a difficult time even relating to the question of whether or not Mā had been a role model for them because they saw her as the divine other. As we saw in chapter 5, when I asked Malini-Di if Mā was her role model, she replied, "No, you see, to model yourself on Mā was very, very difficult because Mā was the embodiment of perfection." I pushed her a bit further, saying, "But you had somebody to look up to?" Her answer reflects what most of Mā's devotees see as the unbridgeable gulf between the human and the divine: "Really look up! Way, way, up!" While we might have expected that Mā's women devotees would have imitated Mā's life in both minor and major ways, from wearing their hair loose and displaying *bhāvas* to casting aside all worldly goals to pursue Self-realization, we have found that most women felt, as Malini-Di did, that what Mā did was not applicable to them. Those who chose a life of renunciation did not report that they chose it because Mā lived such a life. Instead, they cited other reasons: because Mā had suggested it, because Mā's spiritualizing presence inspired them to renounce the world, or because they wanted to be close to Mā's side.

We have seen that there are ways in which Mā encouraged her women devotees to see her and the things that she did as beyond imitation. She made statements such as this: "The behavior of saints is not to be copied by ordinary people. But one should endeavor to carry out in one's life the teaching or advice received by them."[72] By speaking of her life in terms of "līlā," she participated in the creation of their conviction that she was not a human being. She encouraged devotees to take the path of bhakti and surrender themselves unconditionally to the Almighty, having established that she herself was an incarnation of that Almighty.

Yet, while Mā was establishing herself as beyond emulation, she was also telling her devotees that she went through what seemed like the stages of life, from householder to sādhikā to sannyāsinī, for their sake, by which she seemed to have meant, in order to set an example. It appears, however, that the existence of the conception of Mā as deity inhibited the potential of Mā, the extraordinary woman, to serve as a model for her devotees. It seems that once devotees accepted Mā as embodied deity, no matter how many times she told them that they, too, were God, it was difficult for them to believe her because they naturally assumed that she was more God than they were. Instead of devotees being inspired by the process through which Mā came to know she was God, they marveled at her "līlā of sādhana," which by its mere name communicates that a human being cannot identify with it. Although Mā may have wanted to be available to her devotees as the model of perfect householder, the perfect sādhikā, the perfect renunciant, it seems that they persisted in seeing her as "way, way up" and out of reach.

Ānandamayī Mā is surely not the only female Hindu religious figure whose otherness stood in the way of women identifying with her. Madhu Kishwar and Ruth Vanita note that even in the case of the medieval saint Mīrābaī, who was considered simply an extraordinary woman and not an avatāra, her otherness stands in the way of ordinary women applying her norm to themselves.

> Mirabai had not only to live an extraordinary life, but to prove her extraordinariness by going through ordeals. . . . Having thus proved herself, dared all, broken all barriers, she is exalted and revered, and regains in far greater measure the honor and repute she lost or seemed to have lost by flouting the norms of womanly behavior. She is now perceived as existing beyond such norms. But, by being compelled to be so far beyond the ordinary, she becomes a not easily imitable model. Her way remains literally "anuthi," un-followable. Like Kali who may tread on her husband, like certain south Indian goddesses who behead their husbands, she becomes an object of adoration rather than a model or a guide to action for other women. . . . Being perceived as extraordinary, she is by definition considered to be in a

different category from other women and the freedom allowed her will not be extended to them.[73]

However, we have seen that Mā was not seen by her devotees as an extraordinary woman, as was Mīrābaī; rather, she was seen as a divine being who was beyond extraordinary, beyond compare. As such she was even more likely to be an "object of adoration rather than a model or a guide to action for other women." Yet, a devotee of Mā might respond by saying, "The fact that I cannot identify with Mā is not important. Mā is my Mother, my God incarnate, and, therefore, my association with her, my recognition of her, will carry me to rest with her eternally. I need only sit in the lap of Mother to have it all, both worldly and spiritual fulfillment." For the *bhakta* of Mā, Mā's being "way, way up" is hardly a hardship. He or she undoubtedly feels that sitting in the lap of the Divine Mother is far preferable to walking behind an extraordinary woman, following in her footsteps.

Summary

In this book, through the study of a single figure, Ānandamayī Mā, we have explored the complex terrain of the worlds of the Hindu woman, saint, guru, and *avatāra*. Examining these fundamental aspects of Mā has led us to the realization that none of these worlds is discrete and each is replete with ambiguity and paradox. We have seen that while Mā's devotees maintain that she was not a woman, they also insist that she was the "perfect wife." Her life story, by contrast, reveals a relationship between a husband and wife that is highly unconventional, from the perspective of *dharmashāstra*, and more closely resembles that between a disciple and a guru. Yet, we have also seen that there is precedence within a Shākta culture, such as that in Bengal, for a conventional marriage to evolve into a relationship between a *bhakta* husband and a wife whom he and a larger community has come to worship as an incarnation of the Goddess.

In exploring the world of Hindu sainthood, we have seen that, although Mā's devotees reject the use of the term "saint" to define her, Mā manifested the moral ideals and charismatic qualities sought in identifying a Hindu holy person. Her life was a tribute to the spirit of *sannyāsa*, or renunciation. She rejected the notion of her existence as separate from others, seeing "all persons as organic members of this body." Yet, while Mā is said to have seen the whole world as her garden and been blind to gender and caste, her ashrams hold to strict brahmanical purity regulations and a certain kind of division of labor based on gender. Mā's powerful presence has been well documented by her devotees in descriptions of her ecstatic states and her miraculous powers. She appeared to be at all times the paramount *bhakta*, or devotee of the Lord, totally immersed in a celebration of the One, which she called by different names. The list of her *siddhis*, or miraculous powers, confirms her as an accomplished *yoginī*. Yet, Mā's devotees insist that referring to Mā by any of the terms used to describe a Hindu holy person would relegate her to the level of a perfected being, when, in fact, she is a divine being, perfect from birth.

In the same way, Mā's devotees insist that Mā was not a guru, a person who attains the status of master by following to perfection the path of his or her guru and is thus able to guide others along that same path. The main reason they cite for maintaining that Mā was not a guru is the apparent fact that she did not give *dīkshā*. However, having established that Mā did give *dīkshā*, both directly or indirectly, and instructed each devotee as to their individual *sādhana*, we are left wondering why it seems so critical for devotees to convince others that Mā was not a guru. It seems that there may be two reasons. First, the inner circle of *shishyas*, or disciples, who received initiation from Mā, whether directly or indirectly, may see themselves as an esoteric group who were "special to Mā" and, therefore, especially blessed. They may see the power of their special connection as sealed by the secrecy surrounding it. Second, they may see that although they received their initiation from Mā, her role as their *ishta devatā*, or chosen deity, supersedes her role as guru. They see their living master, then, as the Divine Absolute, and therefore they require no mediation.

When Mā's devotees were asked, "If Mā was not a woman, not a saint, and not a guru, who is Mā?" they responded, "Mā is God." We have seen the multiplicity of concepts reflected in that assertion: Mā is the incarnation of formless Brahman, Mā is the *avatāra* of Devi, Mā is the *avatāra* of Vishnu, or simply Mā is my *ishta devatā*. Regardless of what concept lies behind the term "God," however, devotees seem to hold a common vision that the Divine Absolute came to earth as Mā to be accessible to his or her devotees. The accessibility, or *saulabhya*, of God, both in descending as human *avatāra* and even more intimately as *archā*, or divine image, is articulated and praised by the thirteenth-century philosopher, Pillai Lokāchārya. A commentary on a verse of Pillai's describes God, who is himself full and independent, as allowing himself to be bathed, to be dressed and fed, seeming "to be like one who has no independence."[74] The commentary on the following verse explains that it is God's accessibility "which helps us to be attached to the Lord."[75] So Mā allowed herself not only to walk among her devotees but also, like an *archā*, to be fed, dressed, and massaged by those women devotees who were fortunate enough to be in close proximity to her. Therefore, although all of Mā's close devotees believed that they were relating to the divine in human form, occasionally even receiving God's spiritualizing touch, it was the women who saw themselves as having had the opportunity to "handle" God and, therefore, to become particularly attached to her.

Narendranath Bose has remarked, "For everyone Mā was a different person."[76] Indeed, in each of the extraordinary aspects of Ānandamayī Mā, there is the sense that Mā, as saint, as guru, and as *avatāra*, was willing to be whatever people wanted her to be. She manifested a particular aspect only if she was called upon to do so. One of her favorite aphorisms was "As you play, so you shall hear."[77] Swami Jnanananda, in talking about Mā's miracles, said that miracles "come from the *bhāva* [in this case, attitude or state] of the people. It's the people who drag it from the saint." Mā, herself, in responding to a devotee who asked her to speak to them as a guru, said, "There is no case for the guru-*shishya* relationship if the *shishya* is not there. The guru will only speak if the *shishya* is there." In reference to Mā's identity as a divine incarnation, Swami Samatananda reminds us that Mā always said, "You called for me. You prayed for me. You got this body. As long as you want this body, it will stay. If you don't want this body, it will vanish."[78] In a similar vein, Mā said, "I never say, 'I will do this, I will not do that.' It is you who make me carry out whatever work lies in your power to induce me to perform."[79] We might conclude from these statements that Mā is as we see her; when an ordinary person holds the possibility that these extraordinary aspects of Ānandamayī Mā exist, they are manifested.

Personal Postscript

When I first undertook this study, I welcomed the opportunity to explore the world of a Hindu mystic. However, I was also drawn to exploring the impact that a female saint, guru, or *avatāra* would have on women's lives. Relatedly, I was interested in understanding the worldview of men and women who worship God as the Divine Mother. Therefore, what I have drawn from Mā is just this—her mystical, charismatic presence; her influence on women devotees; and the vision of the world as a manifestation of the Divine Mother. As Gurupriya Devi expressed it, "Mā came for the ladies," and being a woman, what excited me most about this study was the ways in which Mā apparently came for me.

Lina Gupta, in her article "Kali, the Savior" in *After Patriarchy: Feminist Transformations of the World's Religions,* says that women need both alternative models of Ultimate Reality that will emphasize the female experience and positive role models "that reassert the importance of the 'feminine' in all religious experience."[80] Gupta suggests that the goddess Kālī might provide such a model because, in her fierce independence, in her motherly compassion, and in her creative power, she gives "birth to a wider vision of reality than the one embodied in the order of patriarchy."[81] There are definitely ways in which Ānandamayī Mā also provides such a model. There is no question that she was fiercely independent, by any culture's standards. She refused to be restricted by the bonds of family, she traveled wherever and whenever she wanted, and she apparently took action only out of her *kheyāla,* or alignment with the divine will, not out of limited ego. She was the embodiment of motherly love and compassion. Sara Ruddick, the author of *Maternal Thinking: Toward a Politics of Peace,* would undoubtedly find Mā displaying all four elements of "maternal thinking," the practice of which, by mothers and non–mothers alike, she believes can lead to global transformation: holding one's children close while at the same time welcoming change and growth, understanding the particular needs of each child, "attentive love" and acceptance focused on the child as she is, and telling stories intended to strengthen values.[82] Mā's creative power, or *shakti,* is apparent in her single-handed orchestration of a large community, each member of which was committed to following her every direction. When I hear how Mā manifested these qualities, I am reminded of that potential within myself.

As a woman who, though not a devotee, is drawn to Mā, I can select from my understanding of Ānandamayī Mā as a female religious symbol that which inspires me. I can lift up the fact that Mā, in Joseph Campbell's terms, "followed her bliss," that she manifested complete equanimity and fearlessness, and that she flouted the expectations of others. I can contemplate Mā's absorption in the divine and her vision that everything, animate and inanimate, is a manifestation of divinity, and I can strive to respect and care for the world as my garden and to see the divine in each person. I can listen to Mā's words on the importance of *sādhana* and rededicate myself to my spiritual practice. At the same time, I can also choose to live a life in which I celebrate my body and gender as inseparable from my path to God/dess, seeing part of my work as helping other women do the same. Throughout this process, I can imagine any kind of relationship with Mā that serves me on my path, keeping in mind that "as I play, so I will hear."

As a member of the global community, I have a unique opportunity to be moved and changed by the faith of others. Process theology, inspired by the Buddhist idea of dependent origination, maintains that a human being is not same person from moment to moment.[83] From that perspective, the person I was the moment before I heard about Ānandamayī Mā is not the same person I am after having heard of her. There is no question that contemplating that God could come to earth as Ānandamayī Mā has stimulated my imagination to envision and embrace the possibility of God as Mother. As a creative thealogian, having encountered the possibility of God as Mā, I can better embrace the richness of a worldview in which the visible world is alive with the energy of God, our Mother. According to Mā, having at one time been drawn to her, even in my imagination, I am ever changed. As I bring this study to a close, I wonder in what ways I have been and will be changed, remembering Mā's words:

> You may want to banish this body from your mind. But this body won't leave you for a single day—it does not and never will leave your thought. Whoever has once been drawn to love this body will never succeed in wiping out its impression even despite hundreds of attempts. This body rests and shall remain in [her] memory for all times.[84]

Glossary

abhisheka. Annointment; ritual to install the deity into a *murti*, or image of the divine.

āchārya. Master or guru.

ahamkāra. Ego.

ajnā chakra. The energy center in the center of the forehead which is said to be the seat of the guru; the third eye center.

ajnāna. Ignorance.

ajnātva. Lit., "unknown"; used to describe Mā when her whereabouts were unknown.

ālvār. One of the twelve Tamil Vaishnava saint/poets foundational to the *bhakti*, or devotional, movement.

amshāvatāra. A partial *avatāra*, or incarnation of God.

ānanda. Bliss.

aniketanah. No longer having a dwelling place; embodying the spirit of homelessness of a renunciant.

antaryāmin. Inner guru.

anubhava. Direct experience [of the divine].

anuthi. Unable to be followed.

ārati. The circling of oil lamps before a deity as part of a *pūjā*, or worship.

āsana. Seat; yogic posture.

āshram(a). Hermitage; monastery; stage in life.

ātman. According to Advaita Vedanta, the Inner Self of all beings that is identical to Brahman, or Ultimate Reality.

attahāsi. Lit., "laughter like thunder"; Mā is described as having such supreme laughter.

avadhūt(a). One who has attained the highest state of spiritual life according to the Nāth cult.

āvārana. Lit., "obstruction"; veil that obscures right vision and understanding.

223

avatāra. The descent of a deity on earth; an incarnation, especially of Vishnu.

bandhu. Friend.

bangsha. Family line.

bhairavī. A holy woman who is seen as an embodiment of *shakti*, or the divine feminine energy.

bhajan(a). Devotional song.

bhakti. Lit., "devotion," "honor," or "love"; usually referring to the reciprocal relationship of love and friendship between a devotee and a deity.

bhāva. State of spiritual ecstasy; emotion; way of relating to the the divine.

bhukti. The pleasures of the world.

bindī. Auspicious red dot on the forehead.

bodhisattva. In the Mahayana Buddhist tradition, one who has taken a vow to be reborn until all sentient beings have become enlightened.

brahmachārinī. A female celibate.

brahmacharya. The first period of life, that of celibate studenthood.

chakra. Lit., "wheel" or "disc"; in Tantrism one of six "lotuses" or energy centers in the subtle body, the lowest of which is the seat of the *kundalinī shakti.*

chaturvarnāshrama. The interface between the four stages of life (*āshramas*) and the four castes (*varnas*).

darshan(a). The auspicious sight of a deity; a philosophical point of view.

Devī. Goddess; the Divine Mother; a woman embodying a goddess.

dhārana. Lit., "support"; the practice of concentration; an aphorism to be contemplated.

dharma. The righteous way of life; social duty.

dharmashāstra. Religious law; sacred law text.

dhyāna. Meditation.

dīkshā. Spiritual initiation given by the guru to the disciple.

Gāyatrī mantra. The most sacred of Vedic mantras that a brahmin is supposed to recite three times a day as part of the *trisamdhyā* ritual.

ghar. House; shelter.

gopī. Cowherdess; paradigm for a devotee of Lord Krishna.

grihastha or *grihastya.* The second, or householder, stage of life.

gurum eva. Lit., "the guru only"; the doctrine of the *guru-vāda*, or path of the guru, that there is no spiritual attainment independent of the guru.

gurumā. Guru-mother; a female guru.

guru-vāda. The path or way of the guru; a spiritual path whose primary focus is on worshipping the guru.

ishta devatā. One's chosen deity.

jagadguru. The world preceptor.

japa. Mantra repetition.

jati. A social group within which one is born and within which one must marry; a sub-group of the four-fold *varna*, or caste, system.

jīva. Individual soul.

Jīvanmukta. A person who is liberated while still alive; one for whom all sense of duality has ceased.

Karma. Action; ritual action; the result of action; the moral law of cause and effect by which one reaps what one sows.

karmamārga. The path of works.

kheyāl(a). Lit., "thought," "notion," or "spontaneous desire"; used around Mā to indicate the spontaneous impulse of the of the Divine Will.

kīrtan(a). Devotional song or singing session.

kripā. Grace or favor, referring to the grace bestowed upon a devotee by a deity.

kriyā. Activity; spontaneous yogic posture.

kriyamārga. The path of action.

kumārī. Virgin girl.

kundalinī. Esoteric term used to refer to the feminine energy or *shakti,* the latent spiritual power envisioned in the form of a serpent coiled at the base of the spine which, once awakened, rises up the central channel of the subtle body, piercing the *chakras,* or energy centers, eventually uniting with the male principle, Shiva, at the crown of the head.

Mahābhāva. Lit., "the great *bhāva,* or spiritual state"; the highest state of divine absorption and ecstacy.

mahāsamādhi. Lit., "the highest state of divine absorption"; used to refer to the physical death of a great saint.

mahātma. Great soul; honorific title.

Mahāyajna. Greatest Vedic fire sacrifice.

mālā. Garland; garland of flowers offered to a deity or guru; "rosary" of beads for performing *japa,* or mantra repetition.

mārga. Spiritual path.

mātā. Mother; goddess-possessed woman.

mauna. Having taken a vow of silence.

māyā. The illusory power of the divine; that which prevents one from seeing things truly.

moksha. Release from bondage to *karma* and *samsāra;* the goal of the spiritual path.

mudrā. A ritual hand gesture that invokes and seals the relationship between the practitioner and the deity.

mukti. Spiritual liberation.

mūlādhāra. The chakra, or spiritual energy center, at the base of the spine in which the latent *kundalinī shakti* is said to the coiled like a serpent, awaiting its awakening.

mūrti. Lit., "form" or "likeness"; the image of a deity as a focus of worship and *darshan.*

naisthika. Lifelong; used to describe those who have maintained lifelong celibacy.

nāmajapa. Repetition of the name of God.

nāyanmār. One of the sixty-three Tamil Shaiva saint/poets foundational to the *bhakti,* or devotional, movement.

neti neti. Lit., "not this, not that"; referring to a method of analysis common to Advaita Vedanta in which one defines Ultimate Reality, Brahman, by enumerating the things that it is *not.*

nirguna. Lit., "without qualities or characteristics"; referring to Brahman as Ultimate Reality, which is beyond name and form.

nitya. Eternal.

nivritti. Lit., "withdrawal"; the process of turning within for happiness and the truth; spiritual introspection.

nyāsa. A practice in which sounds, usually seed syllables, are indentified with certain corresponding parts of the practitioner's body, the deity's body, and the *yantra*, or spiritual diagram, in order to form a series of microcosmic/macrocosmic relationships.

ojhā. Exorcist.

pakka. Lit., "cooked"; colloquial for "orthodox."

pandit. A learned man; honorific title.

paramparā. Lineage of gurus in a particular sect or teaching tradition.

pativratā. Lit., "she who has taken a vow to her husband"; a devoted wife.

patnī. Wife.

pranām(a). Bowing in obeisance before a deity or superior.

prasād(a). Lit., "favor" or "grace"; food offered to a deity during worship, thus consecrated and served to devotees as the grace of the deity.

pravritti. Lit., "turning outward"; looking outside oneself for happiness and the truth.

pūjā. Lit., "worship"; ritual worship usually involving the presentation of offerings to the deity.

purnāvatāra. A full *avatāra*, or incarnation of God.

rishi. Seer or sage.

rūpa. Form.

sadguru. The true guru.

sādhana. A spiritual practice or discipline; a means to gain liberation.

sādhaka. One who practices a *sādhana*, or spiritual practice.

sādhikā. A female practitioner.

sadhvī. A female ascetic.

saguna. Lit., "with qualities and characteristics"; referring to God as a personalized form of the divine, i.e., Krishna, Shiva, Saraswati.

samādhi. Absorption in the divine; a trance-like state sought in yoga in which the yogi transcends the dualistic world.

samdhyābhāsha. Lit., "twilight language"; referring to the esoteric language used in Tantric texts, to be deciphered only by the initiated.

samkalpa. Spiritual intention.

sampradāya. Lit., "tradition" or "school"; a religious order, teaching tradition, or sect.

samsāra. The world; the wheel of life and death; the cycle of rebirth.

samyam(a). Concentration; a threefold practice of concentration, meditation, and absorption.

sanātana dharma. Lit., "the eternal righteous way of life"; used to refer to the Hindu tradition.

sannyāsa. A male ascetic or renunciant; one who has taken vows to renounce the world.

sannyāsinī. A female ascetic or renunciant.

sant. Saint, usually referring to a holy person in the *nirguna* tradition, in which the divine is conceived of as without qualities.

saptah. An extended devotional chanting session.

satī. The act of a Hindu wife's immolating herself at the death of her husband, called suttee by the British and sometimes referred to in Sanskrit as *sahagamana,* or "going together"; lit., "the good one"; a wife who performs the act of *satī;* a devoted wife.

satsang. Lit., "the company of the truth"; an informal session in which devotees sit with a guru or saint, listen to them speak, engage in dialogue, and/or perform practices together; a congregation.

saulabhya. Benevolence; accessibility.

seva. Selfless service.

shakti. The dynamic, creative power of the universe conceived of as feminine; power.

shaktipāt(a). Lit., "descent of the divine, feminine energy of the universe"; spiritual initiation or *dīkshā* in which the guru transmits his or her fully realized spiritual energy into the disciple by his or her look, thought, touch, or word.

sharīr(a). Body; Mā used to refer to herself as *ei sharīra,* "this body," instead of "I."

shāstra. Codes of conduct.

shishya. Disciple.

shloka. A double verse.

shraddhā. Faith.

siddha. Lit., "accomplished" or "adept," one who has obtained powers (*siddhis*) through yogic and/or tantric practices.

siddhapīth(a). The seat or place of a *siddha.*

siddhi. Yogic insight or power attained through spiritual practice.

smriti. Lit., "what has been committed to memory"; proper name for a certain class of scriptures, as opposed to *shruti,* or revealed scripture.

strī. Woman.

strīdharma. The righteous way of life for a Hindu woman.

svadharma. One's own dharma.

svadīkshā. Self-initiation.

tantra. Lit., "loom"; a system of practices that has as its goal the attainment of the union of the male and female principles, Shiva and Shakti, through ritual practice with their locus in the body.

tāntrika (a). Respectively, a male and female practitioner of *tantra.*

tapas. Heat; the energy generated by the performance of austerities.

tapasya. Austerity.

trisamdhyā. The practice, recommended by Mā, of performing *pūjā* and mantra repetition three times a day: at dawn, noon, and twilight.

upanayana. One of the most important of Hindu rites of passage, or *samskāras,* in which a boy of the upper three castes receives his initiation.

upāya kaushalya. Skill in means, referring originally to the capacity of Gautama Buddha to assess the needs of each of his disciples and teach accordingly.

vanaprastha. The third, or forest-dwelling, stage of life.

vigrahā. Individual form or image.

vishuddha marga. The path of purity.

vrat(a). Vow.

yajna. Vedic fire sacrifice.

yoginī. A female yogi.

yuga. A world era or age consisting of thousands of years, of which there are four of different lengths, the forth and present one being the *Kaliyuga.*

Notes

Chapter One

1. See Marija Gimbutas, *The Civilization of the Goddess* (San Francisco: Harper and Row, 1991).

2. See, for example, Mary Daly, *Beyond God the Father* (Boston: Beacon, 1973); Carol Christ and Judith Plaskow, eds., *Womanspirit Rising: A Feminist Reader in Religion* (San Francisco: Harper and Row, 1979); Charlene Spretnack, ed., *The Politics of Women's Spirituality: Essays on the Rise of Spiritual Power within the Feminist Movement* (New York: Anchor, 1982); and Carol Christ and Judith Plaskow, eds., *Weaving the Visions: Patterns in Feminist Spirituality* (San Francisco: Harper and Row, 1989).

3. Diana Eck, in *Encountering God: A Spiritual Journey from Boseman to Banaras* (Boston: Beacon, 1993), says that "we need to acknowledge our own responsibility for the image of God that we believe in" (p. 48). If our image of God denies or limits others' access to the divine or ignores our interconnectedness, we can participate in an " 'imaginative construction' of the concept of God" (p. 49) which better reflects our ideals.

4. Some feminist scholars have begun to consider appropriating Hindu goddess imagery to stimulate the reimagining of God as female. Rita Gross, in "Hindu Female Deities as a Resource for the Contemporary Rediscovery of the Goddess," in *The Book of the Goddess,* Carl Olsen, ed. (New York: Crossroads, 1983), agrees with feminist theologians that "the male symbolism of deity has been a major contributor to the exclusion of women from positions of respect and authority in Western society and religion" (p. 217). She calls for "a second coming of the Goddess," inspired, in part, by Hindu goddess imagery (p. 218). Lina Gupta, in "Kali the Savior," in *After Patriarchy: Feminist Transformations of the World's Religions,* Paula Cooey, William Eak. in, and Jay McDaniel, eds. (Maryknoll, N.Y.: Orbis, 1991), says that the image of the fearless goddess Kālī could represent for women, both Hindu and non-Hindu, a way of facing and transcending any limitation, even patriarchy (p. 16).

5. Mary Daly promotes a doctrine of the Second Coming, "whether this be conceived as appearing in the form of a woman or a group of women or in terms

of so-called feminine characteristics." See Mary Daly, *Beyond God the Father*, p. 73.

6. See Vidya Dehejia, *Āntāl and Her Path of Love* (Albany: State University of New York Press, 1990); A.K. Ramanujan, "On Women Saints," in *The Divine Consort*, John S. Hawley and Donna Wulff, eds. (Boston: Beacon, 1982); and *Manushi: Women Bhakta Poets* (a reprint of issues 50–52 of *Manushi*, January–June, 1989, dedicated to women *bhakta* poets).

7. There is an article by Charles S. J. White, "Mother Guru: Jñānānanda of Madras, India, in *Unspoken Worlds: Women's Religious Lives in Non-Western Cultures*, Nancy Falk and Rita Gross, eds. (Belmont, Calif.: Wadsworth, 1989), pp. 22–37. A recent popular book by Linda Johnsen, *Daughters of the Goddess: The Women Saints of India* (St. Paul: Yes Publishers, 1994), is far from a scholarly study but is rather a collection of personal essays on the author's encounters with six well-known contemporary women saints, Sri Ma of Kamakhya, Ānandamayī Mā, Anandi Ma, Gurumayi Chidvilasananda, Ma Yoga Shakti, and Ammachi. Most recently, Kirin Narayan has broken new methological ground in her study of the beloved contemporary saint and guru, Swami Prakaśānanda, *Storytellers, Saints, and Scoundrels*, (Philadelphia: University of Pennsylvania Press, 1989), in which she looks at the role of narrative in the teachings of Hindu saints and gurus. An impressive study in French of the living Hindu woman saint and guru Shobha Mā, *La Divinite Conquise* (Nanterre: Societe D'Ethnologie, 1990) by Catherine Ojha, breaks new ground in the study of charismatic women masters.

8. The actual Sanskrit word for the practice of a wife's following her husband on the funeral pyre as described in *dharmashāstra* texts is *sahagamana*, or going with; the Sanskrit name for the women who performs *sahagamana* is *satī*, or virtuous woman. The British coined the term "suttee" for the practice and the woman who performs it. In this study, we will use the term "suttee" to refer to the practice and *satī* to refer to the person performing the practice.

9. Ifi Amadiume, in her introduction to *Male Daughters, Female Husbands* (London: Zed, 1987), undertakes a discussion of what she calls Western female anthropology's "new imperialism," in which women scholars have taken for granted the universal social and cultural inferiority of women and have seen "sexual asymmetry" as a universal fact of life. Amadiume and Trinh Minh-Ha, in *Woman, Native and Other* (Bloomington: Indiana University Press, 1989), represent the new movement among Third World feminist anthropologists. Vandana Shiva, author of *Staying Alive: Women, Ecology and Development* (London: Zed, 1989), and Leila Ahmed, who in *Woman and Gender in Islam* (New Haven: Yale University Press, 1992) refers to many Western women as "patriarchal, colonialist feminists," represent the Hindu and Muslim voices in this movement. They are joined by Western scholars such as Frederique Apffel Marglin and Elizabeth Spellman, who maintain that we cannot talk about gender as separate from other variables such as class and race and who call for scholars engaged in crosscultural studies of women to deconstruct the language of dominance-subordination and superiority-inferiority in light of the particulars they are studying. See Apffel Marglin, "Rationality, the Body and the World: From Production to Regeneration," in *Decolonizing Knowledge: From Development to Dialogue,* Frederique Apffel Marglin and S. A. Marglin, eds. (New York: Oxford University Press, 1996), and "Gender and the Unitary Self: Looking for the Subaltern in Coastal Orissa," in *South Asia Research* (London) 15, no. 1 (1995): 78–140, and Spellman, *Inessential Woman* (Boston: Beacon, 1988).

10. Caroline Walker Bynum in the introduction to Bynum, Stevan Harrell, and Paula Richman, eds. *Gender and Religion: On the Complexity of Religious Symbols* (Boston: Beacon, 1986), p. 2.

11. The list of such scholars is growing longer. See, for example, Frederique Apffel Marglin, *Wives of the God King: The Rituals of the Devadasis of Puri* (Delhi: Oxford University Press, 1985); Ann Gold, *Fruitful Journeys: The Ways of Rajasthani Pilgrims* (Delhi: Oxford University Press, 1989); Kathleen Erndl, *Victory to the Mother: The Hindu Goddess of Northwest India in Myth, Ritual and Symbol* (New York: Oxford University Press, 1993); Mary McGee, *Feasting and Fasting: Vrata Tradition and Its Significance for Hindu Women*, Harvard Divinity School Th.D. dissertation, Cambridge, 1989, and Mary McGee, ed., *Redressing Manu*, forthcoming.

12. See Lynn Teskey Denton, "Varieties of Hindu Female Asceticism," in *Roles and Rituals for Hindu Women*, ed. Julia Leslie (Rutherford, N.J.: Fairleigh Dickinson University Press, 1991), pp. 211–231; and Catherine Ojha, "Feminine Asceticism in Hinduism: Its Tradition and Present Condition," in *Man in India*, 61, no. 3, 1981, pp. 254–285.

13. Kathleen Erndl's work, *Victory to the Mother*, focuses on living women considered receptacles for the goddess. See also her "Worshipping the Goddess: Women's Leadership Roles in the Cult of Śerānvālī," in *Redressing Manu*, edited by Mary McGee, forthcoming. Madhu Khanna has a study of historical Śākta women guru lineages forthcoming. See also, in June McDaniel, *The Madness of the Saints: Ecstatic Religion in Bengal* (Chicago: University of Chicago Press, 1989), the section on women ecstatic saints in Bengal, pp. 191–241.

14. China Galland, in *Longing for Darkness: Tara and the Black Madonna* (New York: Penguin, 1990), p. 158, uses the term "God" in this same way to refer to the Madonna at Einsiedeln, saying that sometimes the word "goddess" connotes a mythological time past rather than actual present time. Chapter 6 shows that, although Mā's devotees sometimes used the word "Devī" to describe the source of Mā's incarnation, they most often used the word "God," I think because we were speaking in English and they understood the power of the word within the Western context.

15. Anil Ganguli, *Anandamayi Ma: The Mother, Bliss-incarnate* (Calcutta: Eureka, 1983), pp. 216–217.

16. *Mahāsamādhi* is the term used by devotees of a Hindu saint or guru to speak of what we would call their "death." It connotes that, although the physical body of the master is gone, he or she has merely passed from the physical world into a permanent state of *samādhi*, or absorption with the divine. Such a person is then considered free from the cycle of birth and death, dwelling permanently in a state of oneness with the Absolute, from which he or she continues to relate to devotees from his or her astral body.

17. For a description of W. C. Smith's "personalist methodology," in which the significance of the data lies in what they mean to the person of faith, see his "Comparative Religion: Whither and Why?" in *The History of Religions: Essays in Methodology*, Mircea Eliade and Joseph Kitagawa, eds. (Chicago: University of Chicago Press, 1959), pp. 34–58. For a discussion of the perils of using methodology as a "device for dominating" and a description of Smith's a-methodological approach, see his "Methodology and the Study of Religion: Some Misgivings," in *Methodological Issues in Religious Studies*, edited by Robert Baird (Chico, Calif.: New Horizons, 1975), pp. 1–30. In a similar vein, Mircea Eliade, in "History of Religions and a New Humanism," in *History of Religions*, 1, no. 1 (1962): 4, says that we must attempt to understand religious phenomena "on their own plane of reference."

18. Three previously mentioned recent studies of contemporary South Asian religious figures or movements come to mind in which the scholar allowed the methodology to arise from the material, seemingly drawing out of the "tool box" of available theoretical approaches without appropriating the material to the single

methodology: Lawrence A. Babb's *Redemptive Encounters: Three Modern Styles in the Hindu Tradition*, (Berkeley: University of California Press, 1986), Narayan's *Storytellers, Saints, and Scoundrels*, and McDaniel's *The Madness of the Saints*.

19. New trends in anthropology, particularly in conducting, presenting, and interpreting fieldwork, such as "self-reflexive anthropology," the valorization of narrative dialogue, and the importance of "polyvocality" are described in *Writing Cultures: The Poetics and Politics of Ethnography*, James Clifford and George E. Marcus, eds. (Berkeley: University of California Press, 1986); *Anthropology as Cultural Critique: An Experimental Moment in the Human Sciences*, George Marcus and Michael Fischer, eds. (Chicago: University of Chicago Press, 1986); *The Anthropology of Experience*, Victor Turner and Edward Bruner, eds. (Chicago: University of Illinois Press, 1986); *Women in the Field: Anthropological Experiences*, Peggy Golde, ed. (Berkeley: University of California Press, 1986); and Richard Shweder's *Thinking through Cultures: Expeditions in Cultural Psychology* (Cambridge: Harvard University Press, 1991).

20. See Richard Shweder's article "Post-Nietzschean Anthropology: The Idea of Multiple Objective Worlds" in his *Thinking through Cultures*, pp. 27–72.

21. Ibid., p. 66.

22. Ibid., p. 68.

23. Eck, *Encountering God*, p. 169.

24. See Eck's discussion of the Hindu concept to *darshana* and its relevance to meeting the challenges of a pluralistic world in ibid., pp. 61–63.

25. To understand the difference between evoking and representing the other's world as a process of creating "an emergent fantasy of a possible world of commonsense reality," see Stephen Tyler's article, "Post-Modern Ethnography: From Document of the Occult to Occult Document" in *Writing Culture*, ed. Clifford and Marcus, pp. 122–140.

26. See n. 9 for the works of Third World anthropologists Amadiume, Trinh Minh-Ha, Shiva, and Ahmed, which criticize Western feminists for universalizing their feminist agendas and generalizing about non-Western women, disregarding class, race, sectarian, and regional variations.

27. Bynum in the introduction to *Gender and Religion*, p. 2.

28. See McKim Marriot, "Constructing an Indian Ethnosociology," *Contributions to Indian Sociology* vol. 23, no. 1, 1989: 1–36; Valentine Daniels's *Fluid Signs: Being a Person the Tamil Way* (Berkeley: University of California Press, 1987); and Gold's *Fruitful Journeys*.

29. Compare this study with Shudha Mazumdar's *Memoirs of an Indian Woman*, Geraldine Fonbes, ed. (Armonk, N.Y.: M. E. Sharpe, 1989), which recounts the first thirty-five years in the life of a Bengali woman only three years younger than Mā. Mazumdar, in contrast to Mā, describes herself as "a middle class woman, aware of and interested in the events happening around her" during this "momentous time for India" (p. xi).

30. See also Narayan's *Storytellers, Saints and Scoundrels*; Karen McCarthy Brown's *Mama Lola: A Voudou Priestess in Brooklyn* (Berkeley: University of California Press, 1991); and Dorinne Kondo's *Crafting Selves* (Chicago: University of Chicago Press, 1990).

31. The site of the tomb where Mā was buried within the Kankhal ashram, now a place of pilgrimage.

32. Interview 14, Kankhal, 11/30/90, p. 2.

33. Interview 17, Kankhal, 12/1/90, p. 3.

34. Gopinath Kaviraj, "Mother," in *Selected Writings of M. M. Gopinath Kaviraj* (Varanasi: M. M. Gopinath Kaviraj Centenary Celebration Committee, 1990), p. 225.

35. Eck, *Encountering God*, p. 65.

36. Ibid., p. 66.

37. Marilyn R. Waldman, "The Power of Productive Paradox: An Exercise in Imagining Religion," Plenary Address, Midwest American Academy of Religion, Western Michigan University, March 1990.

38. Śrī Guru Gītā, Verse 40, in the Nectar of Chanting (South Fallsburg, N.Y.: SYDA Foundation, 1983), p. 18.

39. Interview 36, Calcutta, 1/21/91, p. 20.

40. Interview 21, Kankhal, 12/3/90, p. 2.

41. Interview B, Boston, 11/19/88, p. 11.

42. Interview 30, Calcutta, 1/15/91, p. 12.

43. Interview 18, Kankhal, 12/1/90, p. 6.

44. Iñez Talamantez, "Insiders and Outsiders," a talk given at Harvard University, October 1991.

Chapter Two

1. Gurupriya Devi, Sri Sri Ma Anandamayi, (Calcutta: Shree Shree Anandamayee Charitable Society, 1984), 1:xii–xiii.

2. Bhaiji, *Mother as Revealed to Me* (Calcutta: Shree Shree Anandamayee Charitable Society, 1983).

3. Anil Ganguli, *Anandamayi Ma: The Mother, Bliss-incarnate* (Calcutta: Shree Shree Anandamayee Charitable Society, 1983).

4. Devotees of Mā assume that the most accurate rendering of Mā's life story would be that of her closest devotee, an assumption that contradicts the assumption of Western religious scholarship.

5. Hari Ram Joshi, *Ma Anandamayi Lila* (Varanasi: Shree Shree Anandamyee Charitable Society, 1981).

6. Brahmacarini Chandan, *Svakriya Svarasamrita*, 3 vols. (Kankhal: Shree Shree Ma Anandamayi Ashram, 1981–1983).

7. Bithika Mukerji, *From the Life of Anandamayi Ma*, 2 vols. (Calcutta: Shree Shree Anandamayee Charitable Society, 1980).

8. Bithika Mukerji, "Śrī Ānandamayī Mā: Divine Play of the Spiritual Journey," in *Hindu Spirituality: Vedas through Vedanta*, in *World Spirituality*, Krishna Swaraman, ed., vol. 6 (New York: Crossroad, 1989), pp. 392–412.

9. Alexander Lipski, *The Life and Teaching of Sri Anandamayi Ma* (Delhi: Motilal Banarsidass, 1977).

10. There is a brief section on Ānandamayī Mā in June McDaniel's *The Madness of the Saints: Ecstatic Religion in Bengal* (Chicago: University of Chicago Press, 1989), pp. 193–202. See also "Sacred Biography and the Restructuring of Society: A Study of Anandamayi Ma, Lady Saint of Modern Hinduism," by Katherine Young and Lily Miller, in *Boeings and Bullock-Carts: Studies in Change and Continuity in Indian Civilization, Indian Civilization in Its Local, Regional, and National Aspects*, ed. Direndra Vajpey (Delhi: Chanakya, 1990), pp. 113–147.

11. In Lipski's preface to *The Life and Teaching*, he narrates the development of his relationship with Mā. He first visited Mā's ashram in Banaras and subsequently spent some days with Mā at her ashram in Rajgir. He describes in some detail the "private," or individual meeting, he had with Mā in which he questioned her about the particular obstacles to his spiritual growth and Mā responded with a compassionate but firm list of his "glaring shortcomings" (p. x). His contact with Mā inspired him to study Bengali so that he might read about her further. He has written this book, he says, to expose more people to her inspiring presence.

12. The spiritual biographies of other Hindu religious figures also tend to emphasize the early period in the figure's life. Spiritual biographies seem to fall into two categories: those which emphasize the early, "formative" years in which the ordinary person becomes the saint through a period of testing and spiritual practices, and those which emphasize those same years in an attempt to establish that the "saint" is, in fact, *avatāra*, or God(dess) incarnate, perfect from birth. Ānandamayī Mā's life story is told in such a way as to establish the second identity. See Frank Reynolds and Donald Capps's introduction to *The Biographical Process: Studies in the History and Psychology of Religion* (Paris: Mouton, 1976), pp. 3–5. Ānandamayī Mā's devotees' claim that she is divine in origin is examined in chapter 6.

13. Lipski, *The Life and Teaching*, pp. 28–29.

14. See David Lorenzen, "The Life of Śankarācārya," in Reynolds and Capps, eds., *The Biographical Process*, pp. 87–107, for a brief history of the Hindu genre of hagiography.

15. Edward C. Dimock, "Religious Biography in India: The 'Nectar of the Acts of Caitanya,'" in Reynolds and Capps, eds., *The Biographical Process*, p. 109. Dimock is referring here to Bhagavad Gita, IV, 7–8, in which Lord Krishna says, "Whenever a decrease of righteousness exists, descendants of Bharata, and there is a rising up of unrighteousness, then I give forth myself for the protection of the good and the destruction of evil doers; for the sake of establishing righteousness, I come into being from age to age." Interestingly, the most widely circulated documentary of Ānandamayī Mā begins with this quote from the Bhagavad Gītā, intending to establish Mā's identity as an *avatāra*.

16. See Lorenzen, "The Life of Śankarācārya," p. 92.

17. See Reynolds and Capps, eds., *The Biographical Process*; Michael Williams, ed. *Charisma and Sacred Biography*, JAAR Thematic Studies, 48, 3–4 1982; John Stratton Hawley, ed., *Saints and Virtues* (Berkeley: University of California Press, 1987).

18. Reynolds and Capps, *The Biographical Process*, p. 3.

19. Charles Keyes, introduction to Williams, *Charisma and Sacred Biography*, p. 13–14.

20. Reynolds and Capps, *The Biographical Process*, pp. 3–4.

21. According to Vidya Dehejia in *Āṇṭāḷ and Her Path of Love*, University of New York (Albany: State, Press, 1990), p. 7, Āṇṭāḷ most probably lived around 850 C.E. The two most famous anthologies of the lives of the Tamil saints which include her, the *Kuruparamparāpirapāvam*, or the *6000 Verses on the Glory of the Succession of the Gurus* and the *Divyasūricaritam*, or *The Characters of the Sacred Ones*, were written in the fourteenth and fifteenth centuries respectively.

22. See Swami Saradananda, *Sri Ramakrishna, the Great Master*, translated by Swami Jagadananda (Madras: Ramakrisha Math, 1952) [3d ed., 1963]; *Life of Sri Ramakrishna Compiled from Various Authentic Sources* originally published in 1925, recently (Calcutta, Advaita Ashrama, translated by Swami Budhananda, 1971); and *The Gospel of Sri Ramakrishna* originally published in 1907, authored by a devotee, most recently translated by Swami Nikhilananda (New York: Ramakrishna-Vivekananda Center, 1984).

23. See, for example, Walter Neevel, "The Transformation of Śrī Rāmakrishna" in Bardwell Smith, ed., *Hinduism: New Essays in the History of Religion* (Leiden: Brill, 1976), pp. 53–97; and Arvind Sharma "Ramakrishna Paramahamsa: A Study in a Mystic's Attitudes towards Women' in Rita Gross, ed. *Beyond Androcentrism* (Atlanta: Scholars Press, 1977), pp. 115–124.

24. In the same way, some scholars of the Synoptic Gospels evaluate the relative

importance or historicity of a certain anecdote by determining how many Gospels it appears in.

25. The Shālagrāma Shilā is a piece of black ammonite stone found in the River Gaṇḍakī in Nepal, which has been described in the Skanda Purāna as a sacred representation of Vishnu. It is handed down as a sacred heirloom within Vaishnava brahman families to be used for daily *pūjā*, or worship.

26. Bhaiji, *Mother as Revealed to Me*, p. 8.

27. Mukerji, *From the Life of Anandamayi Ma*, 1:1.

28. Chandan, *Svakriya Svarasamrita*, 1:97.

29. Ibid., p. 55.

30. Mukerji, *From the Life of Anandamayi Ma*, 1:2.

31. Chandan, *Svakriya Svarasamrita*, 1:55.

32. Ibid.

33. Mukerji, *From the Life of Anandamayi Ma*, 1:2.

34. Chandan, *Svakriya Svarasamrita*, 1:56. The *Grihalakshmī* of the household refers to the form of the Goddess of Prosperity, Lakshmī, which rules within the house of a householder. In this case Mokshada Sundarī is both being compared to the Goddess and being lauded as the perfect wife, the *patīvratā*, one who has taken a vow to serve her husband as God. Such qualities as approaching housework as worship and accepting misery as a gift of God, as described by Ganguli in *Anandamayi Ma: The Mother, Bliss-incarnate*, p. 27, complete the picture of Mā's mother as the perfect wife.

35. There is some controversy about the sequence of events surrounding the birth and death of Bipin Bihari and Mokshadā Sundarī's first child. Here we are relating Devi's account in *Sri Sri Ma Anandamayi*, 1:5, which seems to have been the foundation of Mukerji's account. Chandan, however, relates that one and a half years into their marriage, Bipin Bihari took his wife to Kheora. One year later he returned. Soon thereafter the first daughter was born and died around nine months after her birth.

36. Chandan, *Svakriya Svarasamrita*, 1:58.

37. Ibid.

38. Mā usually referred to herself not as "I" but as "this body."

39. Devi, *Sri Sri Ma Anandamayi*, 1:5.

40. Chandan, *Svakriya Svarasamrita*, 1:67–68.

41. Devi, *Sri Sri Ma Anandamayi*, 1:4. This quote is often cited by devotees as evidence of Mā's having been fully conscious since birth.

42. Ganguli, *Anandamayi Ma: The Mother, Bliss-incarnate*, p. 27.

43. Devi, *Sri Sri Ma Anandamayi*, 1:6.

44. Chandan, *Svakriya Svarasamrita*, 2:10–11.

45. Ibid., pp. 16–17.

46. Ibid., p. 13.

47. Joshi, *Ma Anandamayi Lila*, p. 3.

48. Devi, *Sri Sri Ma Anandamayi*, 1:58.

49. Chandan, *Svakriya Svarasamrita*, 2:8.

50. Mukerji, "Śrī Ānandamayī Mā," p. 395.

51. Chandan, *Svakriya Svarasamrita*, 2:32–33.

52. Ibid., p. 27.

53. Mukerji, "Śrī Ānandamayī Mā," p. 395.

54. Chandan, *Svakriya Svarasamrita*, 2:7.

55. Mukerji, *From the Life of Anandamayi Ma*, 1:4.

56. Devi, *Sri Sri Ma Anandamayi*, 1:8.

57. Mukerji, *From the Life of Anandamayi Ma*, 1:4.

58. Ibid.

59. This story was related by Mā to Anil Ganguli, as reported in *Anandamayi Ma: The Mother, Bliss-incarnate*, p. 30. It can be related to the story of the ninth century southern Indian saint, Āṇṭāḷ, who is said to have been helpless to stop the sacrilegious wearing of the garland intended for the deity before it was presented to him out of her identification with the deity.

60. This is a reference to Mā's early demonstration of yogic powers, or *siddhis*, as described in both Buddhist and Hindu texts such as the *Sāmaññaphala-sutta* or the *Yoga-Sūtras* of Patanjali, respectively. These *siddhis* are enumerated by Mircea Eliade in *Yoga and Immortality* and Freedom (Princeton: Princeton University Press, 1969), pp. 88–90 and 178–185. In particular, this incident points to Mā's possession of the classical *siddhi* of *laghiman* (lightness) as described by Patanjali, chapter 3, verse 43: "By making *samyama* [the three-fold practice of concentration, meditation, and absorption] on the relation between the body and the ether, or by acquiring through meditation the lightness of cotton fiber, the yogi can fly through the air." Swami Prabhavananda, *How to Know God: The Yoga Aphorisms of Patanjali*, Christopher Isherwood, trans. (New York: Mentor, 1969), p. 133.

61. Chandan, *Svakriya Svarasamrita*, 2:20–21.

62. Ganguli, *Anandamayi Ma: The Mother, Bliss-incarnate*, p. 29–30.

63. Mukerji, *From the Life of Anandamayi Ma*, 1:7.

64. Ganguli, *Anandamayi Ma: The Mother Bliss-incarnate*, p. 30.

65. Mukerji, *From the Life of Anandamayi Ma*, 1:6.

66. Chandan, *Svakriya Svarasamrita*, 2:17–18.

67. *Mudrās* are the hand poses which often accompany the repetition of mantras. *Nyāsa* is the ritual projection of the mantra into different parts of the body. *Āsanas* are certain body postures taken for meditation.

68. Chandan, *Svakriya Svarasamrita*, 2:56.

69. Mukerji, *From the Life of Anandamayi Ma*, 2:9.

70. Joshi, *Ma Anandamayi Lila*, p. 5. The Kumārī Pūjā is part of the nine-day celebration of Durgā Pūjā. It entails the worship of virgin girl(s) by brahman priests as the pure Goddess.

71. Chandan, *Svakriya Svarasamrita*, 2:41.

72. Joshi, *Ma Anandamayi Lila*, p. 3.

73. Chandan, *Svakriya Svarasamrita*, 1:144.

74. Joshi, *Ma Anandamayi Lila*, p. 4; and Chandan, *Svakriya Svarasamrita*, 2:23.

75. Chandan, *Svakriya Svarasamrita*, 2:62.

76. Ibid., pp. 59–62.

77. Ibid., 1:145.

78. Mukerji, *From the Life of Anandamayi Ma*, 1:6.

79. Ahalyā is the name of the wife of the sage, Gautama, who was seduced by the God, Indra. In revenge, Gautama cursed her and turned her into stone.

80. Devi, *Sri Sri Ma Anandamayi*, p. 8.

81. Mukerji, *From the Life of Anandamayi Ma*, 1:5.

82. Chandan, *Svakriya Svarasamrita*, 2:97.

83. Ibid., pp. 92–93.

84. Mukerji, "Śrī Ānandamayī Mā," p. 395.

85. Chandan, *Svakriya Svarasamrita*, 2:96. Here Didimā is reporting that Nirmalā did not look at Bholanāth at the time of the auspicious first glance, when the bride's face is uncovered so that bride and groom can see each other for the first time. Rather, Nirmalā, her mother reports, was looking at the celestial beings who had gathered at the ceremony.

86. Ibid., pp. 96–97.

87. Mukerji, *From the Life of Anandamayi Ma*, 1:10.

88. Ibid., 1:11.

89. Chandan, *Svakriya Svarasamrita*, 2:98.

90. Ibid., p. 10.

91. Ibid., p. 102.

92. Mukerji, *From the Life of Anandamayi Ma*, 1:12.

93. Chandan, *Svakriya Svarasamrita*, 2:111–112.

94. Ibid., p. 137.

95. Mukerji, *From the Life of Anandamayi Ma*, 1:14.

96. Chandan, *Svakriya Svarasamrita*, 2:109.

97. Ibid., p. 106.

98. Mukerji, *From the Life of Anandamayi Ma*, 1:12.

99. Ganguli, *Anandamayi Ma: The Mother Bliss-incarnate*, p. 32.

100. Mukerji, *From the Life of Anandamayi Ma*, 1:14.

101. Chandan, *Svakriya Svarasamrita*, 2:139.

102. Devi, *Sri Sri Ma Anandamayi*, 1:10.

103. Mukerji, *From the Life of Anandamayi Ma*, 1:15.

104. This is Bithika Mukerji's statement in *From the Life of Anandamayi Ma*, 1:16, which is, by and large, corroborated in all the biographies, with some variation.

105. Ibid., p. 17. Devi, in *Sri Sri Ma Anandamayi*, 1:22, says that it was Bhoodev's wife in Bajitpur who said this.

106. Lipski, *The Life and Teaching*, p. 8.

107. This incident is related in almost all versions. In Chandan's version, however, we have this allusion to *Shashthī* Day, the sixth lunar day, in which the female folk deity, Shashthī, presides over the children's welfare. A cloth is received by a son from his mother on this day, and a *pūjā* of this deity is performed. See Chandan, *Svakriya Svarasamrita*, 3:8.

108. The act of bowing at the feet of an honored person, usually an elder or holy person.

109. As we see in chapter 3, this act of eating the leftover food is considered a sign of devotion on the part of a Hindu wife when she eats her husband's leftover food. The only situation in which a man would eat the leftovers of a woman would be in the case of a woman holy person or guru.

110. Devi, *Sri Sri Ma Anandamayi*, 1:13.

111. *Harināma* means repeating the name of Harī, or God, as one of the forms of Vishnu.

112. Chandan, *Svakriya Svarasamrita*, 3:20–21.

113. Mukerji, *From the Life of Anandamayi Ma*, 1:19.

114. Because of purdah restrictions, women were expected to listen to the *kirtan* from behind a closed door.

115. Chandan, *Svakriya Svarasamrita*, 3:105–107.

116. Ibid., p. 108.

117. See A. K. Datta Gupta's article, "Sri Sri Ma's Self-Initiation," in *Ānanda Vārtā*, vol. 28, no. 2: p. 95.

118. Chandan, *Svakriya Svarasamrita*, 3:120.

119. Ibid, p. 227.

120. Mukerji, *From the Life of Anandamayi Ma*, 1:17.

121. Lipski, *The Life and Teaching*, p. 6. Only Lipski attributes Bholanāth's reluctance to approach his wife sexually to his having received an electric shock.

122. Chandan, *Svakriya Svarasamrita*, 3:86.

123. Ibid., pp. 85–86.

124. Mukerji, *From the Life of Anandamayi Ma*, 1:19.

125. Joshi, *Ma Anandamayi Lila*, 10.

126. Devi, *Sri Sri Ma Anandamayi*, 1:15.

127. Gupta, "Sri Sri Ma's Self Initiation," p. 100.

128. Mukerji, "Śrī Ānandamayī Mā," p. 398.

129. Most of the biographies use words like "awe" or "wonder," with the notable exception of Joshi, who maintains that Ramani Mohan was "greatly upset" and "anxious." See Joshi, *Ma Anandamayi Lila*, p. 10.

130. Devi, *Sri Sri Ma Anandamayi*, 1:16.

131. Ibid., pp. 16–17.

132. Lipski, *The Life and Teaching*, p. 11.

133. Devi, *Sri Sri Ma Anandamayi*, 1:17.

134. Ibid.

135. Mukerji, *From the Life of Anandamayi Ma*, 1:24.

136. Joshi, *Ma Anandamayi Lila*, p. 11.

137. Gupta, "Sri Sri Ma's Self Initiation," p. 101.

138. Ibid., p. 103.

139. Some biographers, such as Gurupriya Devi, refer to this "intensification" as a significant "change in condition" (see Devi, *Sri Sri Ma Anandamayi*, p. 17); others, such as Bithika Mukerji, continue to emphasize that "none observed any change in Sri Anandamayi Ma during or after the period of her spiritual practice. She remained just as she was" ("Śrī Ānandamayī Mā," p. 398).

140. Mukerji, "Śrī Ānandamayī Mā," p. 398.

141. Mukerji, *From the Life of Anandamayi Ma*, 1:25.

142. Gupta, "Sri Sri Ma's Self Initiation," pp. 105–106. This anecdote appears in very few sources.

143. Mukerji, "Śrī Ānandamayī Mā," p. 399.

144. Joshi, *Ma Anandamayi Lila*, p. 12.

145. Gupta, "Sri Sri Ma's Self Initiation" pp. 106–107.

146. Mukerji, "Śrī Ānandamayī Mā," p. 399.

147. Joshi, *Ma Anandamayi Lila*, pp. 14–15.

148. Mukerji, *From the Life of Anandamayi Ma*, 1:23.

149. Ibid., p. 27.

150. Mukerji, "Śrī Ānandamayī Mā," p. 399.

151. Ibid., p. 399.

152. Lipski, *The Life and Teaching*, p. 10.

153. Gupta, "Sri Sri Ma's Self Initiation," p. 104.

154. Joshi, *Ma Anandamayi Lila*, p. 15.

155. Devi, *Sri Sri Ma Anandamayi*, 1:20.

156. Mukerji, *From the Life of Anandamayi Ma*, 1:31.

157. Ibid., p. 34.

158. Ibid., p. 39.

159. Lipski, *The Life and Teaching*, p. 15.

160. Mukerji, *From the Life of Anandamayi Ma*, 1:41–42. Mukerji quotes Mā's own telling of the story, which was too long to be included here but conveys Mā's following her *kheyāla*, or spontaneous divine will, without consciously knowing where it will lead her. The point of this story seems to be that the mysterious red spring, almost divined by Mā, was an indication of the sacredness of the spot.

161. Devi, *Sri Sri Ma Anandamayi*, 1:34.

162. Lipski, *The Life and Teaching*, p. 15.

163. Mukerji, *From the Life of Anandamayi Ma*, 1:44.

164. Devi, *Sri Sri Ma Anandamayi*, 1:214.

165. Mukerji, *From the Life of Anandamayi Ma*, 1:75.

166. Ibid., p. 53.

167. Ibid., p. 56.

168. Ibid., p. 45.

169. Ibid., p. 37.

170. Bhaiji, *Mother as Revealed to Me*, pp. 27–28.

171. Lipski, *The Life and Teaching*, p. 16.

172. Mukerji, *From the Life of Anandamayi Ma*, 1:72.

173. Ibid., pp. 73–74.

174. This incident is related in Mukerji, *From the Life of Anandamayi Ma*, 1:72–74, but I have been unable to determine its original source.

175. Bhaiji, *Mother as Revealed to Me*, pp. 34–35. This account and the following account of Gurupriya Devi are among the first eye-witness accounts of Mā's states of *bhāva* in her biographies. Both Bhaiji and Devi met Mā right before this event.

176. Devi, *Sri Sri Ma Anandamayi*, 1:40–41.

177. Mukerji, *From the Life of Anandamayi Ma*, 1:50.

178. Devi, *Sri Sri Ma Anandamayi*, 1:113.

179. Mukerji, *From the Life of Anandamayi Ma*, 1:89.

180. Devi, *Sri Sri Ma Anandamayi*, 1:131–132.

181. Ibid., p. 38.

182. Ibid., p. 76.

183. Ibid., p. 100.

184. Ibid., p. 162. Devi actually says here, "Then again there was a time when she did not let any water touch her lips for twenty-three days. She did not even wash her mouth." She goes on to say that on the twenty-third day, at 2:30 in the morning, Mā (in Devi's presence) asked for a pot full of water. As Mā drank, Didi reports her saying. "I wanted to see how it feels to live without water. But I found that I was forgetting about drinking water altogether. And if I forgot, you would be faced with a problem. Therefore I drank water though I did not feel the need of it."

185. Ibid., p. 79.

186. Mukerji, *From the Life of Anandamayi Ma*, 1:65.

187. Devi, *Sri Sri Ma Anandamayi*, 1:108–189.

188. Bhaiji, *Mother as Revealed to Me*, pp. 14–15.

189. The Kumbha Melā is a religious festival in which ascetics and yogis from all over India gather every six years in rotation at one of four sacred sites.

190. Devi, *Sri Sri Ma Anandamayi*, 1:174.

191. Mukerji, *From the Life of Anandamayi Ma*, 1:115.

192. Ibid., p. 118.

193. Devi, *Sri Sri Ma Anandamayi*, 1:214.

194. Mukerji, *From the Life of Anandamayi Ma*, 2:2.

195. Ibid., pp. 3–4.

196. Ibid., pp. 5–6.

197. Ibid., p. 15.

198. Ibid., pp. 18–19.

199. Mukerji, *From the Life of Anandamayi Ma*, 1:135.

200. Ibid., p. 136.

201. Ibid., p. 140.

202. Devi, *Sri Sri Ma Anandamayi*, 2:51.

203. Ibid., p. 139.

204. Ibid., p. 27.

205. Mukerji, *From the Life of Anandamayi Ma*, 2:50.

206. Ibid., p. 162.

207. The passing of Bholanāth is reported quite movingly in Mukerji's *From the Life of Anandamayi Ma*, 2:158–165. Since Mā was alone with Bholanāth at the time of his death, Mukerji's version is apparently based on Mā's telling of the story to Devi and other devotees in July 1938. Devi's account is not yet available in English, pending translation from Hindi of her *Sri Sri Ma Anandamayi*, 6.

208. This is the initiation rite that one takes to enter the life of a renunciant. It involves renouncing the rites of Hindu householder *dharma*, undergoing a ritual death, and taking on the symbols of renunciation. See Patrick Olivelle, *Saṃnyāsa Upaniṣads: Hindu Scriptures on Asceticism and Renunciation* (New York: Oxford University Press, 1992), in particular, chapter 4, pp. 82–98.

209. Mā's spiritual biographies maintain that Mā did not give initiation to anyone except Bhaiji and Bholanāth. While Mā was, they say, present at the initiation of many devotees, the actual initiation was given in the early years by Bholanāth, later by her mother, and most recently by selected *sannyāsin* devotees. See chapter 5 for devotees' stories of receiving mantras initiation directly from Mā.

210. Mukerji, "Śri Ānandamayī Mā," p. 404.

211. "Mātri Līlā," in *Ānanda Vārtā*, vol. 29, no. 4, p. 352.

212. Ibid., 344.

213. Mā left no instructions regarding her burial or about the running of the ashrams after her death. Therefore, devotees had to rely on supposition in deciding where Mā intended her burial site to be. For example, some say that a year before her death, Mā instructed that a large, leaning banyan tree at Kankhal ashram be cut down, saying that the site could be used for future ceremonies. Therefore, they knew that *samādhi* shrine was to be built on that spot. Others say that on July 2, 1982, Mā had a conversation with His Holiness Shrī Shankarāchārya of Sringeri in which she told him that she had agreed to be in Kankhal for Durgā Pūjā, which is held in the fall. Therefore, devotees felt impelled to carry her body to Kankhal. Kanti Datta, an older female householder devotee whom I interviewed, told me that a short time before Mā's death, Mā had resisted traveling to Dehradun but had conceded to devotees' wishes to have her attend an event there. After two or three days, she said, Mā said, "Please take me back to Kankhal," but people felt she was not well enough to travel without rest. But after her *samādhi*, they decided to take her body to Kankhal since that had been her last desire, "which had not been carried out" (Interview 17, Kankhal, 11/27/90, p. 7).

214. It is interesting to note that to date no description of Mā's *mahāsāmadhi* in English exists in a spiritual biography. Mukerji, *From the Life of Anandamayi Ma*, vol. 2, takes us only as far as 1939. Lipski published his book five years prior to Mā's passing. Bhaiji and Devi died before Mā. There is no description of the last days of Mā's life or her passing in the commemorative publications distributed at Mā's birthday celebrations after 1982. I have had to rely on the description of Mā's last days in the *Ānanda Vārtā* published in the fall of 1982 ("Mātri Līlā," vol. 29, no. 4) and on short articles in periodicals published the week of her passing (*India Today*, September 4, 1982, pp. 40–41; and *The Times of India*, August 29, 1982, p. 2). Therefore, these last two paragraphs cannot really be considered representative of Mā's spiritual biographies.

Chapter Three

1. *Strīdharmapaddhati*, 1 vv. 2–4, I. Julia Leslie, trans., in *The Perfect Wife: The Orthodox Hindu Woman According to the Stridharmapaddhati of Tryambakayajvan* (Delhi: Oxford University Press, 1989) p. 29.

2. Interview 24, Calcutta, 1/21/91, p. 9.

3. Katherine Young, "Hinduism," in *Women in World Religions*, edited by Arvind Sharma (Albany: State University of New York Press, 1987) p. 60.

4. For example, Mary McGee's *Feasting and Fasting: Vrata Tradition and Its Significance for Hindu Women* (Harvard Divinity School Th.D. dissertation, Cambridge, 1989) juxtaposes an examination of the ideal articulated in *dharmashāstra* texts such as the *Laws of Manu* against the lived experience of Hindu women articulated in her interviews with women in Maharashtra. See also the study of women's *vrats*, or vows, by Anne Mackenzie Pearson, *Because It Gives Me Peace of Mind* (Albany: State University of New York Press, 1996).

5. For an interesting discussion of this tension and its grounding in the prevailing brahman theory of the inherent nature of women, see I. Julia Leslie, *The Perfect Wife*, especially pp. 246–273.

6. *The Laws of Manu*, 3. 55–56, trans. G. Buhler, in *Sacred Books of the East*, ed. Max Muller, vol. 25 (Delhi: Motilal Banarsidass, 1974), p. 85.

7. Ibid., 9.3, p. 328.

8. Ibid., 5.155, p. 196.

9. Ibid., 5.165, p. 197.

10. Leslie, *The Perfect Wife*.

11. Ibid., *Strīdharmapaddhati* v.2–4, p. 29; 48 v.7–8, p. 305.

12. Ibid., 25v. 4–5, p. 276.

13. Ibid., p. 322. Leslie says that Tryambaka classifies both personal daily duties such as bathing and teeth-cleaning and duties to serve her husband as *dharmayuktam*, or religious duties (p. 166).

14. Ibid., *Strīdharmapaddhati* 20r. 6–7, p. 237.

15. Ibid., p. 287.

16. *The Laws of Manu*, 9.96, p. 344. In chapter 9.81, p. 342, it is further said that a wife may be superseded for failure to bear children after the eighth year or to bear sons after the eleventh year.

17. Leslie, *The Perfect Wife, Strīdharmapaddhati* 18r. 4, p. 222.

18. Ibid., p. 210.

19. Ibid., p. 321.

20. Ibid., *Strīdharmapaddhati* 23v. 2, p. 137.

21. Ibid., 22v. 1–3, p. 171. This list reflects Tryambaka's ultraorthodox orientation, as well as the severe discomfort that he and other pandits must have been feeling with the prevailing practices of women in the court.

22. Ibid., p. 318. Although a female renunciant is an anomaly from the perspective of *dharmashāstra*, except within the context of widowhood, there are other paradigms within the Hindu tradition, discussed later in this chapter, in which renunciation is a virtue.

23. Ibid., pp. 320–321.

24. Ibid., *Strīdharmapaddhati* 42r. 3, p. 292.

25. Ibid., p. 293.

26. Ibid.

27. Ibid., p. 300.

28. Ibid., p. 304.

29. Ibid., p. 321.

30. Ibid., p. 328.

31. Manisha Roy, *Bengali Women* (Chicago: University of Chicago Press, 1975); and Lina M. Fruzzetti, *The Gift of a Virgin: Women, Marriage, and Ritual in a Bengali Society* (Bombay: Oxford University Press, 1990).

32. Roy, *Bengali Women*, p. 37. Roy says that the *Shiva-rātrir brata* is a popular ritual in which girls fast all day and in the evening offer food and gifts to Lord Shiva at his temple while praying for him to bless them with a husband like him. She adds, "Almost every Bengali girl who has not been totally uprooted from her culture knows this rite and is thrilled about observing it before she is married."

33. Ibid., p. 160.

34. Ibid. A factor that has allowed men and women to relax their expectations of fulfilling the *dharmashāstra* ideal is the idea that we are currently existing in the *Kaliyuga*, the last and most evil of the four cyclical ages of humankind. It is understood that in *Kaliyuga* the ideal is rarely fulfilled, even by brahmans, and one has to rely more heavily on grace than on self-effort.

35. Ibid., p. 184.

36. Ibid., pp. 32–33.

37. Ibid., pp. 33–34.

38. Ibid., p. 35. For a complete rendering of this famous passage, see "A Wife's Devotion," from "Śakuntalā" by Kālidāsa, in *The Hindu Tradition*, Ainslie T. Embree, ed. (New York: Modern Library, 1966), p. 100.

39. Roy, *Bengali Women*, p. 36.

40. Ibid., pp. 36–37.

41. Fruzzetti, *The Gift of a Virgin*, p. 45.

42. Ibid., p. 128. On pp. 46–57, Fruzzetti describes in some detail the five auspicious rites or *muglas* performed by married women in both households before the wedding ceremony. They each involve the use of a different ritual object which symbolizes fertility, be it a paddle that grinds grain, a drum, or a cooking pot.

43. Ibid., p. 123.

44. Ibid., p. 102.

45. Ibid., p. 131.

46. Ibid., p. 102.

47. Roy, *Bengali Women*, p. 125.

48. Ibid., p. 138.

49. Shudha Mazumdar, *Memoirs of an Indian Woman*, Geraldine Forbes, ed. (Armonk, New York: M.E. sharpe, 1989), the memoirs of a middle-class Bengali woman, born in Calcutta in 1899, is an important resource for understanding the challenges inherent in fulfilling the role of the Hindu wife, even for the elite of Bengali society. See also Margaret Urquhart, *Women of Bengal* (Delhi: Cultural Publishing House, 1983), an account of the life of Bengali women written in 1925 by the wife of a Scottish professor in Calcutta, especially her account of "the religion of all good [Bengali] women—husband worship" (pp. 110–111).

50. Bithika Mukerji's, introduction to Gurupriyā Devī *Sri Sri Ma Anandamayi*, trans. Tara Kini (Calcutta: Shree Anandamayee Charitable Society, 1984–1990), vol. 1, p. xvii.

51. Bithika Mukerji, *From the Life of Anandamayi Ma* (Varanasi: Shree Shree Anandamayee Sangha, 1970, 1981); 1:16.

52. Devi, *Sri Sri Ma Anandamayi*, 1:13.

53. Ibid., p. 35.

54. For a fascinating account of an angry confrontation between Bholanāth and

Mā in 1937 on a pilgrimage to Mount Kailash, see Devi, *Sri Sri Ma Anandamayi*, 5:14–17.

55. Bhaiji, *Mother as Revealed to Me*, trans. G. Das Gupta (Calcutta: Shree Shree Anandamayee Charitable Society, 1983), p. 25.

56. For an analysis of the marriage ritual in Bengal, see Fruzzetti, *Gift of a Virgin*, and for a study of high-caste Nepali women and marriage, see Lynn Bennett, *Dangerous Wives and Sacred Sisters* (New York: Columbia University Press, 1983).

57. Brahmacarini Chandan, *Svakriya Svarasamrita*, (Kankhal: Shree Shree Anandamayi Ashram, 1981–1983), 2:97. Fruzzetti, in *Gift of a Virgin*, p. 32, says that the most important test that a Bengali bride must pass is the examination of her horoscope (*koshthi bicār*).

58. Leslie, *The Perfect Wife*, p. 139. See also pp. 319–320 for a more complete analysis of the prohibition against a life of renunciation for women.

59. In *Bengali Women*, p. 86, Roy notes that during the *Shubha Drishti* the bride is supposed to look at her husband, "while invoking her deity, her husband, with the same kind of material (flowers) worshippers use for deities in temples." Nirmalā's choice to look at deities other than her husband at this crucial juncture suggests a pattern of choosing an independent spiritual life over the responsibilities of marriage and reminds one of Āṇṭāḷ, Akkamahādevī, and Mīrābaī, saint-poets who chose marriage to God over marriage to a human husband.

60. Chandan, *Svakriya Svarasamrita*, 2:95–96. The question of "the normal bond," referring to sexual relations, is discussed later.

61. Ibid., 2:10.

62. This description from Chandan (ibid., 2:133–134) can be compared with Tryambaka's description of daily duties in Leslie's *The Perfect Wife*, pp. 47–48.

63. Mukerji, *From the Life of Anandamayi Ma*, 1:14.

64. Leslie, *The Perfect Wife*, p. 291 (*Strīdharmapaddhati* 42 r.1–3).

65. See Leslie's discussion of the parallels between the *dharma* of the Vedic student and the *dharma* of the *pativratā*, in *The Perfect Wife*, p. 322.

66. Fruzzetti, *The Gift of a Virgin*, p. 14.

67. A. S. Altekar, *The Position of Women in Hindu Civilization from Prehistoric Times to the Present Day* (Delhi: Motilal Banarsidas, 1991), p. 82.

68. Roy, *Bengali Women*, p. 89.

69. Chandan, *Svakriya Svarasamrita*, 2:119.

70. Ibid.

71. Mukerji, *From the Life of Anandamayi Ma*, 1:16.

72. Ibid., p. 17.

73. Ibid., p. 136.

74. Alexander Lipski, *The Life and Teaching of Anandamayi Ma* (Delhi: Motilal Banarsidass, 1977), p.6.

75. Paramahamsa Yogananda, *Autobiography of a Yogi* (Bombay: Yogoda Satsanga Society of India, 1946), pp. 457–458. I am indebted to Alexander Lipski for sharing this reference in a phone conversation, October 1994.

76. See, for example, Paramahamsa Yogananda, *Autobiography of a Yogi* (Bombay: Jaico, 1990), p. 450.

77. Devi, *Sri Sri Ma Anandamayi*, 5:92.

78. An interview with two sisters who were devotees of Mā in 1936 confirms that Bholanāth was, indeed, in the middle of a vow of silence at that time. They said that they were ages six and nine at the time and that "although Bholanāth was *maun*, he was a very jolly fellow. And he used to love children like anything. He was just pulling her [her sister's] hair like this. He was really very loveable." (Interview 8, Varanasi, 11/16/90, pp. 11–12.)

79. If Mā, indeed, did use of the words "violent shock," she may have been referring to the experience of the transmission of *shakti*, or divine energy, known as *shaktipāt* initiation, which is central to the guru-disciple relationship, especially in the tantric path.

80. *The Laws of Manu* 9.81, p. 342.

81. Katherine Young, "Hinduism," p. 75.

82. Roy, *Bengali Women*, p. 91.

83. Mukerji, *From the Life of Anandamayi Ma*, 1:16–17.

84. Chandan, *Svakriya Svarasamrita*, 3:20.

85. Ibid., p. 86.

86. See Anil Ganguli, *Anandamayi Ma: The Mother Bliss-incarnate* (Calcutta: Eureka, 1983), pp. 32–33. The comparison between Mā and Bholanāth's relationship and that of Ramakrishna and Sarada Devi is interesting because the spiritual biographies of Sarada Devi, such as that in *Great Women of India* (Mayavati, Almora: Advaita Ashram, 1953), reveal a similar story but with the genders reversed. Sarada Devi is married to the twenty-three-year-old Ramakrishna at the age of six in 1859, but by the time she is ready to live with her husband at thirteen, he has become an ecstatic *sannyāsin*, or celibate monk. In words similar to Ganguli's, which imply that Bholanāth eventually "caught" Mā's state, it is said that "gradually her spirit caught fire from the contact of her saintly husband. In and through him, she felt a divine presence radiating purity and peace" (p. 479). Ramakrishna, meanwhile, leaves her to pursue the spiritual life in Calcutta. At nineteen, Sarada Devi travels to find her husband, and he asks her, "Did you come here to drag me down to the worldly plane?" She replies, "No, why should I pull you down? I am here to serve you so that you may go ahead on your chosen path" (p. 482). She served him until his death in 1886. Of their marriage, it is said, "Absolutely devoid of anything sensual about it, this union of two immaculate souls in unfathomable love should have some other name. . . . It was a novel kind of wedlock in which both the partners were to observe lifelong celibacy. It was a sacred union of two kindred souls" (p. 476).

87. Christopher Isherwood, *Ramakrishna and His Disciples* (Hollywood, Calif.: Vedanta, 1965), p. 89.

88. In a fascinating passage in Gurupriyā Devī's account of Mā and Bholanāth's trip to Mount Kailash, Didi says, "By the grace of Mā and Bholanāth we were traveling on this pernicious path with such joy" (*Sri Sri Ma Anandamayi*, 5:37.). This is the only place I encountered anyone putting Bholanāth on a par with Mā in dispensing grace.

89. Chandan, *Svakriya Svarasamrita*, 3:120. See chapter 2, pp. 75–76, Note that, according to one of Mā's devotees who met her when she was eighteen in 1936, two years before his death, Bholanāth was uncomfortable with Mā's states of *bhāva*. She reports, "It was in Simla. Mā was lost in singing the name. She had so divine a look, just like a child. All was lost in the *kīrtan*. She was totally absorbed. She was not herself. Bholanāth scolded her, 'Control yourself!' when she went too far. Mā said, 'I am trying. What to do?'" (Interview 17, Kankhal, 11/27/90, p. 1.) Yet, another devotee reports that Bholanāth himself used to exhibit *bhāva* in *kīrtan*: "I used to watch [Bholanāth] in the *kīrtan* and when he was dancing, he used to be like this. His feet were barely touching the ground, only his toes touched the ground." (Interview 32, Calcutta, 1/17/91, p. 7.)

90. Joshi, *Ma Anandamayi Lila*, p. 10.

91. A. K. Datta Gupta, "God as Love," in *Mother as Seen by her Devotees*, ed. by Gopinath Kaviraj (Varanasi: Shree Shree Anandamayee Charitable Society, 1976), p. 24. Also, Bithika Mukerji, "Śrī Ānandamayī Mā: Divine Play of the Spiritual Journey,"

in *World Spirituality*, vol.6, *Hindu Spirituality* (New York: Crossroad, 1989), p. 398, says that Bholanāth "watched amazed" as his wife performed her practices.

92. For example, Joshi, *Ma Anandamayi Lila*, p. 10, says that Bholanāth was "greatly upset at observing frequent changes in the *bhāva* of Mātaji."

93. Alexander Lipski, *The Life and Teaching of Anandamayi Ma* (Delhi: Motilal Banarsidass, 1977), pp. 11–12.

94. Joshi, *Ma Anandamayi Lila*, p. 11.

95. Bhaiji, *Mother as Revealed to Me*, p. 47.

96. Mukerji, *From the Life of Ananadamayi Ma*, 1:27–28.

97. Preparation of food as a religious duty is confirmed in "The Perfect Bride," in *Tales of Ancient India*, translated by J. A. B. van Buitenen (Chicago: University of Chicago Press, 1958), pp. 157–160, in which a prince searches for a bride, challenging all the young women in the kingdom to prepare a complete meal from two pounds of rice.

98. A.K. Datta Gupta, "Sri Sri Mā's Self-Initiation," in *Ānanda Vārtā*, vol. 28, no. 2, pp. 105–106.

99. In *Bengali Women*, pp, 138–139, Roy highlights a phenomenon in urban Bengal in which a barren woman in a household with no small children to look after is encouraged to seek initiation by a guru as "nothing can be better for a woman of her age to be preoccupied with." Obviously Bholanāth might have been looking for a sanctioned institutional framework within which his wife's unusual activities could be understood and controlled.

100. The most vivid telling of the story of Mā's *svadīkshā* is by Mā herself in Gupta's *Ānanda Vārtā* article, pp. 106–107. Joshi met Mā in 1933 and names Bholanāth and Bhaiji as sources.

101. *Svadīkshā* is very rare in the Hindu tradition, even for men. However, Paul Muller-Ortega, in *The Triadic Heart of Śiva* (Albany: State University of New York, 1989), pp. 165–166, says that in Abhinavagupta's tradition of Kashmir Shaivism, self-initiation is considered somewhat commonplace and that a *samsiddhika-guru*, a spontaneously perfected teacher, was preferred because he or she was thought to have been initiated directly by the Goddess. Likewise, Gopinath Kaviraj, in his article "Mother Anandamayi," in *Mother as Seen by Her Devotees*, p. 169, speaks of the *pratibha jnāna*, or self-generated wisdom, mentioned in yogic and tantric literature, in which Divine Grace descends directly upon a soul. However, it is usually considered essential for a spiritual aspirant, however advanced, to have a guru. Even Shrī Krishna Chaitanya, the famous sixteenth-century Bengali saint, who is considered the model of the intoxicated God-man, or *avatāra*, is said to have received mantra initiation from his guru, Īshvāra Puri. Although Ramakrishna Paramahamsa (1836–1886) studied with several gurus and was initiated by them into different paths, *The Gospel of Sri Ramakrishna*, ed. Swami Nikhilananda (New York: Ramakrishna-Vivekananda Centre, 1984), p. 830, he relates a story of a kind of *svadīkshā*. In an account of the initial awakening of his *kundalinī* energy, which is equivalent to *shaktipāt* initiation, or the descent of grace, he says that in meditation when he was twenty-two or twenty-three, he saw a twenty-two or twenty-three-year-old boy, "exactly resembling me," enter his subtle body and travel his central energy channel, touching each of his *chakras*, or energy centers with his tongue, thus awakening them. This is the closest to the description of Mā's *svadīkshā* that I could find in spiritual biographies of other prominent Hindu religious figures. It is significant that this story comes from the Bengali saint and reported *avatāra* who precedes Mā in prominence in Bengal, as the possibilities for hagiography are expanded with each new saint.

The fieldwork of Kathleen Erndl in *Victory to the Mother: The Hindu Goddess of*

Northwest India in Myth, Ritual, and Symbol (New York: Oxford University Press, 1993) demonstrates that it is common for women considered to be possessed by a particular form of the Goddess to claim no human guru. In South India there are two different traditions: the tradition of the lineage of the guru, which is a primarily high-caste phenomenon, and the tradition of goddess possession, which is a primarily-low-caste phenomenon. However, in Bengal and Shākta northern India, these traditions seem to be merged, and a woman possessed by the goddess is said to need no human guru.

102. *The Laws of Manu*, V. v.55, p. 196. Vows are common among women all over India. The *bhakti* movement introduced the idea that men and women could have a private, unmediated relationship with God. For centuries women have undertaken agreements between themselves and God, such as "I will fast on Thursday for the rest of my life if you will provide my son with a son." But Mary McGee's *Feasting and Fasting* demonstrates that most vows are undertaken for the well-being of the woman's husband and children. Most women could not imagine taking a vow for their spiritual advancement. It would be almost unthinkable for a married woman to take a three-year vow of silence.

103. Leslie, in *The Perfect Wife*, p. 253, quotes Tryambaka, 21. v.8–9, as saying that the *gandharvas*, or celestial maidens, gave woman the gift of *shubhām giram*, or a pure or auspicious voice, the implication being that she should use it.

104. Mukerji, *From the Life of Anandamayi Ma*, 1:v.

105. A completely orthodox event.

106. Mukerji, "Śrī Ānandamayī Mā," p. 403.

107. Mukerji, *From the Life of Anandamayi Ma*, 1:85.

108. See Leslie, *The Perfect Wife*, pp. 239–240, for Tryambaka's rulings on raised beds. It is the custom in many parts of rural India today for the husband to sleep on a raised bed, while the wife sleeps on a mat on the floor. Renunciants in India pride themselves on sleeping on the ground with little or no bedding. One of Mā's *brahmachārinīs* described how Mā lovingly and teasingly weaned the "girls" close to her from sleeping with thick mats and pillows and eventually convinced them that this asceticism would help in their search for God.

109. Mukerji, *From the Life of Anandamayi Ma*, p. 133.

110. The significance of cooking for one's husband as part of the *dharma* of the Hindu wife is underlined by Roy in *Bengali Women*, p. 96: "In Bengal, and perhaps all over India, feeding is the principal technique of women, no matter what age they might be, to show affection and love to their men. Food is also used as the means to show the withdrawal of love."

111. Mukerji, *From the Life of Anandamayi Ma*, 1:135.

112. Ibid., 2:9.

113. Ibid., p. 32.

114. Ibid., p. 31.

115. Ibid., pp. 43–45. Akhandananda was the name of one of the Ramakrishna monks who became the third president of the order in 1934.

116. Ibid. pp. 86–135 for an account of this pilgrimage to Tibet, based on Gurupriya Devi's journal.

117. Ibid., pp. 143–145, includes a moving journal entry of confession and apology written by Bhaiji to his wife after he left home to join Mā as a renunciant.

118. Devi, *Sri Sri Ma Anandamayi*, 5:91.

119. Ibid., pp. 91–93.

120. Mukerji, *From the Life of Anandamayi Ma*, 2:146.

121. Ibid., p. 161.

122. Joshi, *Ma Anandamayi Lila*, p. 91.

123. Interview 30, Calcutta, 1/15/91, p. 20.

124. Ibid., pp. 89–90.

125. Mukerji, *From the Life of Anandamayi Ma*, 2:164–165.

126. Ibid. p. 166.

127. Joshi, *Ma Anandamayi Lila*, pp. 91–92.

128. Mukerji, *From the Life of Anandamayi Ma*, 1:136–137.

129. Of the ten devotees I interviewed who knew Mā while Bholanāth was alive, five initiated a conversation about him in which they communicated the great affection in which he was held. They reported that he was much loved by children and devotees alike. Swami Samatananda described his father as a disciple of Bholanāth, which presumes a guru role on Bholanāth's part (Interview 30, Calcutta, 1/15/91, p. 10). Swami Krishnananda speaks of Bholanāth's early role as his guru (Interview 15, Kankhal, 11/30/90, p. 1). Yet, nothing has been written about Bholanāth's life or teachings.

130. Lipski, *Life and Teaching of Anandamayi Ma*, p. 7.

131. Leslie, in *The Perfect Wife*, pp. 324–325, discusses precedents in which women, such as the medieval saint-poet Mīrābāi, flaunt orthodox norms, arguing that their guru's guru—that is, God—told them to do it.

132. Mukerji, *From the Life of Anandamayi Ma*, 1:160.

133. Interview 15, Kankhal, 11/30/90, p. 4.

134. Mukerji, *From the Life of Anandamayi Ma*, 1:16.

135. Traditional Hindu society dictated that women wear their hair braided or held up. Women with loose hair were considered dangerous influences. But this requirement may be more universal. In *Dreamtime: Concerning the Boundary between Wilderness and Civilization* (Cambridge: Basil Blackwell, 1991), anthropologist Hans Peter Duerr remarks, "It appears that at all times and in a number of different societies, long and especially loose and unkempt hair was taken to be a sign that the respective woman, as a sociologist would put it, has extricated herself from social control, or at least was less subject to the pressures of social convention than others" (p. 59).

136. Devi, *Sri Sri Ma Anandamayi*, 3:90.

137. Ibid. p. 93.

138. Carolyn G. Heilbrun. *Writing a Woman's Life* (New York: W. W. Norton, 1988), p. 48.

139. See, for example, section 3 of "The Social Psychology of the World Religions" in H. H. Gerth and C. Wright Mill, trans. and eds., *From Max Weber: Essays on Sociology* (New York: Oxford University Press, 1946), 297ff.

140. Lynn Teskey Denton, "Female Asceticism in Varanasi: A Sociological Outline," Unpublished paper, p. 44. Sarada Devi's (1853–1920) story would have been well known when Mā's life in progress was being documented, beginning with Gurupriyā Devī's journals, written in 1926 and published in 1942.

141. This tension and the scholarly debate it has provoked is beautifully described by Patrick Olivelle in his introduction to *Samnyāsa Upaniṣads: Hindu Scriptures on Asceticism and Renunciation* (New York: Oxford University Press, 1992), pp. 19–78.

142. David Lorenzen, "The Life of Śaṅkarācārya" in *The Biographical Process: Studies in the History and Psychology of Religion*, Frank Reynolds and Donald Capps, eds. (Paris: Mouton, 1976), p. 104. In a contemporary parallel, the recent successors of the four Shankarācāryas, the heads of the regional schools of Advaita Vedānta, have begun to be chosen as boys, in a way that is similar to the selection of the high lamas of the Tibetan Buddhist tradition. Because of the youth of the gurus-to-be, a

concession to the mother-child connection has been made in which the mother is allowed to live in the entourage of the new Shankarācārya, tempering the break with worldly life characteristic of *sannyāsa* initiation. It is a reversal that Mā's mother, Didimā, though a *sannyāsinī* later in her life, continued to be part of Mā's entourage until her death.

143. Devi, *Sri Sri Ma Anandamayi*, 2:147.

144. Mukerji, *From the Life of Anandamayi Ma*, p. 89.

145. Gupta, *Ānanda Vārtā*, vol. 28, no. 2, pp. 105–106. It is not clear why devotees have chosen to deemphasize Bholanāth's Shākta roots. It may reflect an attempt to domesticate Mā through a "Vaishnavafication" of her story. Walter Neevil, "The Transformation of Sri Ramakrishna," in *Hinduism: New Essays in the History of Religions*, ed. Bardwell Smith (Leiden: Brill, 1976), pp. 53–97, maintains that biographers of Ramakrishna made an effort to domesticate his charisma by deemphasizing his Shākta and tantric background and practice, which included ecstatic, even mad episodes, not dissimilar from Mā's, as well as study with a female tantric guru. This process, begun by his foremost disciple, Vivekananda, was aimed at presenting Ramakrishna as a more conventionally acceptable Advaita Vedantin than a God-intoxicated devotee of the Goddess.

146. The works of these four women scholars illuminate the subject of alternative paradigms for women. Prior to their work, scholars had focused on only male ascetic orders within the Hindu tradition. Sanjukta Gupta's, "Women in the Sakta/ Saiva Ethos" in *Roles and Rituals for Hindu Women*, Julia Leslie, ed. (Rutherford, N.J.: Fairleigh Dickinson University Press, 1991), p. 9, discusses the Shākta paradigm as it provides alternatives for women to orthodox *strīdharma*. Catherine Ojha, "Feminine Asceticism in Hinduism: Its Tradition and Present Condition," *Man in India*, vol. 61, no. 3, 1981 pp. 254–285; and Lynn Teskey Denton, "Varieties of Hindu Female Asceticism" in *Roles and Rituals for Hindu Women*, discuss their fieldwork among female ascetics and gurus in Varanasi, including the ashram of Ānandamayī Mā, and highlight many important aspects of the challenge of alternative paradigms to *strīdharma*. June McDaniel, *The Madness of the Saints: Ecstatic Religion in Bengal* (Chicago: University of Chicago Press, 1989), focuses on ecstatic holy men and women of Bengal. In the course of her fieldwork in Bengal, she had no trouble finding people to refer her to Shākta holy women or gurus, while it was virtually impossible to find a Vaishnava holy woman. When she would inquire, "the general response of Vaishnava practitioners was a look of amazement, followed by, 'A holy woman (*sādhikā*)? Why would you want to speak to one of them? Look at all the holy men here. They are much better to speak with'" (p. 192 ff.).

147. See Miranda Shaw's *Passionate Englightenment: Women in Tantric Buddhism* (Princeton, N.J.: Princeton University Press, 1994) for a discussion of woman gurus within the tantric Buddhist context. Madhu Khanna is presently working on a book on female Shākta guru lineages.

148. Joshi, *Ma Anandamayi Lila*, p. 11.

149. Catherine Ojha, "Feminine Asceticism in Hinduism" p. 262.

150. Ibid, p. 271.

151. Lynn Teskey Denton, personal communication, May 11, 1988.

152. See Kathleen Erndl, *Victory to the Mother* and "Worshiping the Goddess: Women's Leadership Roles in the Cult of Śerānvālī," in *Women's Rites, Women's Desires*, Mary McGee, ed., forthcoming, which highlights the *mātās*.

153. Kathleen Erndl, "Worshiping the Goddess: Women's Bhajan Groups in the Cult of Śerānvālī," paper presented to the Conference on Women's Rites at the Center for the Study of World Religion, Harvard University, April 1988, p. 6.

154. Ibid., p. 8.

155. Kathleen Erndl, *Victory to the Mother*, p. 115.

156. June McDaniel, *Madness of the Saints*, pp. 215–228.

157. John Stratton Hawley, "Mirabai as Wife and Yogi," a paper delivered at the Conference on Ascetics and Asceticism, University of Florida, Gainesville, February 1988.

158. Ibid., p. 8.

159. According to Shākta mythology, Kālī, or Shakti, the divine feminine principle, is often pictured as standing on top of Shiva, the divine male principle and her husband.

160. Mukerji, *From the Life of Anandamayi Ma*, 1:118–123.

161. Joshi, *Ma Anandamayi Lila*, p. 92.

162. Satsang Tape no. 22, Banaras, May 1968, pp. 14–17. One of the Sanskrit words for "husband" is bearer or supporter, *bhartri*, from the root *bhṛ*, "to bear". To the extent that *dharmashāstra* texts emphasize the importance of the husband as protector who takes over from his wife's father the task of her protection, Mā is admitting that Bholanāth was, indeed, her husband.

Chapter Four

1. Paramahamsa Yogananda, *Autobiography of a Yogi* (Bombay: Jaico, 1990), p. 448.

2. For a classic description of a Westerner's journey around India in early 1930 from one holy person to another, see Paul Brunton's *A Search in Secret India* (Bombay: B. I. Publications, 1989).

3. See Richard Kieckhefer and George Bond, eds. *Sainthood: Its Manifestations in World Religions* (Berkeley: University of California Press, 1988); and John S. Hawley, ed., *Saints and Virtues* (Berkeley: University of California Press, 1987). Carol Flinders' *Enduring Grace* (San Francisco: Harper, 1993) offers profiles of women saints, as do S. Ghanananda and J. S. Wallace, eds., *Women Saints East and West* (Hollywood, Calif.: Vedanta, 1979).

4. Kieckhefer, Introduction to Kieckhefer and Bond, eds., *Sainthood*, p. viii.

5. Hawley, ed., *Saints and Virtues*, p. xii.

6. Ibid., p. xvi.

7. Ibid., pp. xii–xxiv.

8. Ibid., p. xvii.

9. Diana Eck, *Darśan: Seeing the Divine Image in India* (Chambersburg, Pa.: Anima, 1981), p. 52.

10. Scholarly work on Hindu saints includes works devoted to the lives and philosophies of particular saints; studies on Hindu asceticism and the category of *sādhu;* and studies on the phenomenon of Hindu sainthood. Of particular interest in the first category is William Jackson, "A Life Becomes a Legend: Srī Tyāgarāja as Exemplar," *Journal of the American Academy of Religion* 40, no. 4, (1992): 717–736; Walter Neevil "The Transformation of Sri Ramakrishna," in *Hinduism: New Essays in the History of Religions,* Bardwell Smith, ed. (Leiden: Brill, 1976); and Edward Dimock, "Religious Biography in India: The 'Nectar of the Acts of Caitanya,'" in *The Biographical Process: Studies in the History and Psychology of Religion,* Frank Reynolds and Donald Capps, eds. (Paris: Mouton, 1976), pp. 109–117. On the institution of Hindu asceticism, see G. S. Ghurye, *Indian Sadhus* (Bombay: Popular Prakashan,1964); B. D. Tripati, *Sadhus of India* (Bombay: Popular Prakashan, 1978); M. G. Bhagat, *Ancient Indian Asceticism* (New Delhi: Munishiram Manoharlal, 1976); Patrick Olivelle, *Saṃnyāsa Upaniṣads: Hindu Scriptures on Asceticism and Renunciation* (New York: Oxford

University Press, 1992) and his translation of an eleventh-century text on asceticism, *Vāsudevāśrama Yatidharmaprakāśa : A Treatise on World Renunciation* (Leiden: Brill, 1976); Lise Vail's doctoral dissertation on her fieldwork in Karnataka, *Renunciation, Love and Power in Hindu Monastic Life* (University of Pennsylvania, 1987); and the works on female asceticism in the Bibliography by Ojha, Denton, and Sanjukta Gupta. Important studies of the phenomenon of Hindu sainthood include Lawrence Babb, *Redemptive Encounters: Three Modern Styles in the Hindu Tradition* (Berkeley: University of California Press, 1986); June McDaniel, *The Madness of the Saints: Ecstatic Religion in Bengal* (Chicago: University of Chicago Press, 1989); Kirin Narayan, *Storytellers, Saints, and Scoundrels* (Philadelphia: University of Pennsylvania Press, 1989); and John S. Hawley and Mark Juergensmeyer, eds. *Song of the Saints of India* (New York: Oxford University Press, 1988).

11. See Swami Abhishiktananda, *The Further Shore* (Delhi: ISPCK, 1975), pp. 3–16, for a list of the qualifications of a *sannyāsin*. See Jackson, "A Life Becomes a Legend," pp. 726–732; and Phyllis Granoff, "Holy Warriors: A Preliminary Study of Some Biographies of Saints and Kings in the Classical Indian Tradition," *Journal of Indian Philosophy* 12 (1984): 291, for two different descriptions of common motifs in a Hindu saint's life.

12. Lawrence Babb, "Sathya Sai Baba's Saintly Play," in *Saints and Virtues*, John S. Hawley, ed. (Berkeley: University of California Press, 1988), p. 169. Babb, like Jackson and Granoff, does not question the use of the term "saint."

13. We will use the term *bhāva* to define an ecstatic state of divine absorption, as is most common in Bengal. In a Marathi context, an ecstatic state of divine absorption might be called *samādhi* with accompanying *kriyās* or yogic movements. In Vaishnava theology, *bhāva* usually refers to the four (and sometimes five) classical devotional attitudes toward God: the attitude of a servant toward master (*dāsya*), the attitude of friendship (*sakhya*), the attitude of a mother toward her child (*vātsalya*), and the attitude of a lover toward his or her beloved (*madhurya*).

14. McDaniel, *The Madness of the Saints*, p. 6.

15. Charles Keyes in his introduction to *Charisma and Sacred Biography*, ed. Michael Williams (Journal of the American Academy of Religion, 48, nos. 3 and 4 [1982]: 1–2), says that individuals can be said to be charismatic if they "are deemed by their fellow men to have an especially close relationship with the sacred because they have assimilated some of their actions—either on particular occasions or on a regular basis—to models that are recognized as sacred signs." In the Hindu context, people who exhibit the sacred sign of *bhāva*, or spiritual ecstasy, are considered charismatic.

16. Lalleswarī's poems and life story can be found in B. N. Paramoo's *Ascent of Self: A Reinterpretation of the Mystical Poetry of Lalla-Ded* (Delhi: Motilal Banarsidass, 1978).

17. Shrī Ramakrishna's God-intoxicated state is well-documented. See, for example, *Swami Nikhilananda, trans., The Gospel of Sri Ramakrishna* (New York: Ramakrishna-Vivekanand Center, 1984); and Christopher Isherwood, *Ramakrishna and His Disciples* (Hollywood, Calif: Vedanta, 1965).

18. In the Ramakrishna material, *bhāva* is used to describe his states of ecstasy. See *The Gospel of Ramakrishna*, Swami Nikhilananda, trans., p. 78.

19. In *The Madness of the Saints*, McDaniel notes that many saints of Bengal were known for their contagious states of *bhāva*. For example, disciples of the nineteenth-century Bengali Vaishnava saint, Vijayakrishna Gosvamin, describe themselves as dancing "in the waves of his *bhāva*, which became like a 'sky-high typhoon' " (p. 66) and report that conservative visitors would find themselves dancing in ecstasy with Vijayakrishna. Arcanāpurī Mā, a present-day guru of an ashram in

Calcutta, talks about the contagious state of her guru, Satyānanda: "Thākur [Satyānanda] would spend all day in *bhāva*, and... I became completely lost in Thākur. I, too, began to fall into *bhāva*" (McDaniel, *The Madness of the Saints*, p. 210).

20. Shashibhusan Das Gupta, *Obscure Religious Cults* (Calcutta: Firma KLM, 1976), p. 211.

21. According to Charles Keyes, in his introduction to *Charisma and Sacred Biography* (Michael Williams, ed.), pp. 1–18, there are three signs of charisma: conquest of death, performance of miracles, and gnosis. Keyes maintains that gnosis, the "knowledge that passeth all understanding" is "of much greater significance than miracles" in determining the status of a charismatic religious figure (p. 4). Although gnosis is seen as an inevitable factor in the development of self-realization and a sign of its presence according to the Hindu tradition, it is not highlighted in the various lists of identifying characteristics, perhaps because it is considered so foundational as to be obvious. Ānandamayī Mā's untutored knowledge of the scriptures and spontaneous teachings confirmed her gnosis, but devotees seem to focus more on her egolessness, *kheyāla, bhāvas*, and miracles as an indication of her extraordinariness.

22. Aurobindo Ghose, *The Synthesis of Yoga* (Pondicherry: Arya, 1918), pp. 404–405.

23. *How to Know God: The Yoga Aphorisms of Patanjali*, Swami Prabhavananda, Christopher Isherwood, trans. (New York: Mentor, 1969), pp. 121–140.

24. Mircea Eliade, *Yoga: Immortality and Freedom*, (Princeton, N.J.: Princeton University Press, 1969), pp. 69–70; for a discussion of Patañjali's list of *siddhis*, see pp. 85–90, and for his enumeration of a Buddhist list of *siddhis*, pp. 177–185.

25. Prabhavananda, *How to Know God*, p. 126.

26. *Yoga Sūtra* 3.18, in ibid., pp. 127–128.

27. *Yoga Sūtra* 3.21–22, in ibid., p. 128.

28. *Yoga Sūtra* 3.24, in ibid., p. 129.

29. *Yoga Sūtra* 3.39, in ibid., p. 131.

30. *Yoga Sūtra* 3.40, in ibid., p. 133. This rather unlikely pair of *siddhis* is linked because they are the result of *samyama* on controlling the nerve currents that govern the lungs and the upper part of the body.

31. *Yoga Sūtra* 3.43, in ibid., p. 133.

32. Charles White lists these above powers as reputed to be present in the nineteenth-century saint of Maharashtra, Shirdi Sai Baba, in "The Sai Baba Movement: Approaches to the Study of Indian Saints," *Journal of Asian Studies*, (1972): 31: p. 869. Lawrence Babb in *Redemptive Encounters* describes similar claims by the devotees of the twentieth century saint, Sathya Sai Baba, who says he is the reincarnation of the former saint and is particularly known for his materialization of sacred ash and for curing illnesses. Shashibhusan Das Gupta (*Obscure Religious Cults*, pp. 211–212) offers an alternative list of *siddhis* from the Nāth yogic cult, which he enumerates as *anima*, the power of becoming as small as an atom; *mahimā*, the power of becoming big; *laghimā*, the power of assuming excessive lightness at will; *garimā*, the power of becoming as heavy as one likes; *prāpti*, the power of obtaining everything at will; *prakāmya*, the power of obtaining all objects of pleasure at will; *ishitva*, the power of obtaining supremacy over everything; and *vashitva*, the power of subduing, fascinating, or bewitching.

33. Christopher Isherwood and Swami Prabhavananda, *How to Know God, Yoga Sūtra* 3.51, Ibid., p. 135.

34. See Patrick Olivelle, *Samnyāsa Upaniṣads*, pp. 82–100.

35. Swami Abhishiktananda, *The Further Shore*, p. 7.

36. Patrick Olivelle, *Samnyāsa Upaniṣads*, pp. 100–112.

37. Ibid., p. 102. Olivelle says that "the 'rain residence' was a practice common to all renouncers both within and outside the brahmanical tradition."

38. Bithika Mukerji, "Śrī Ānandamayī Mā: Divine Play of the Spiritual Journey," in *World Spirituality*, Krishna Swaraman, ed.,vol. 6, *Hindu Spirituality* (New York: Crossroad, 1989), p. 405.

39. Interview 34, Calcutta, 1/20/91, pp. 2–3.

40. An elder male swami told me,"She never stayed in someone's house because if she started to, a thousand other people would want her. So she decided not to go to a family, but to stay in a temple. If you build a new house and you want to have a ceremony, she may go there." (Interview 15, Kankhal, 11/30/90)

41. Ghurye, *Indian Sādhus*, p. 17.

42. Jan Gonda, in *Change and Continuity in Indian Religion* (New Delhi: Munishiram Manoharlal, 1985), devotes an entire chapter, pp. 284–315, to the institution of *brahmacharya* and its significance in the Hindu tradition.

43. Patrick Olivelle, *Samnyāsa Upaniṣads*, pp. 32–33.

44. Gonda notes that "the ancient and widespread belief in the 'polluting' effects of sexual intercourse which exposes man to the influence of dangerous powers, the fear of loss of vital power and energy in consequence of *emissio seminis*, the belief in the 'holiness' of procreative power, the conviction that any contact with the holy or divine requires purity and the complete concentration of energy, the belief that the holiness of rites and spiritual life is incompatible with sexual power have all over the world led to various forms of ritual chastity and celibacy" (*Change and Continuity*, p. 293). Yet in the Hindu yoga tradition we see celibacy as part and parcel of an elaborate technology of Self-realization that links abstinence with a carefully mapped out science of energy. See Mircea Eliade's *Yoga and Immortality*, pp. 49–50, for a discussion of the importance, for the yogi's self-realization, of control of the senses and the practice of *brahmacharya*.

45. *Shaktipāt*, literally, the descent of spiritual power, is said to be conferred by a *siddha*, or perfected, guru on a disciple, initiating an awakening of the spiritual energy dormant in the subtle body. It is discussed fully in chapter 5.

46. Interview 16, Kankhal, 11/30/90, pp. 5–6. Readers familiar with Hindi will note that "*Jabardasti mat karo*" actually translates to something closer to "Don't force it." I have been unable to determine whether I heard Swamiji's words inaccurately or whether his interpretation of Mā's words was idiosyncratic.

47. Interview 15, Kankhal, 11/30/90, p. 7.

48. Gurupriya Devi, *Sri Sri Ma Anandamayi*, Tara Kini, trans. (Calcutta: Shree Shree Anandamayee Charitable Society, 1984–1990),1:104.

49. Brahmacarini Chandan, *Svakriya Svarasamrita* (Kankhal: Shree Shree Ma Anandamayi Ashram, 1981–1983), 2:x. We will see in chapter 5 that the language of the guru, particularly in the tantric context, is often called *samdhyābhāsha*, or "twilight language". It is renowned for being cryptic and containing esoteric meaning. The famous Sanskrit pandit and devotee of Mā, Gopinath Kaviraj, said of the disjointed language in which she spoke out of her deep *samādhi* state in Banaras in 1928,"This is truly the language of God. We people with the *samskāras* of this imperfect world cannot understand it."

50. Ibid., pp. 100–103, 162–163.

51. Carolyn Walker Bynum, *Holy Feast, Holy Fast* (Berkeley: University of California Press, 1987). For references to Christian saints whose fasting was associated with not menstruating or sweating and coupled with excreting sweet and healing substances such as oil, see pp. 122–123, 214.

52. Devi, *Sri Sri Ma Anandamayi*, 1:24, writes in the same paragraph about Mā's dietary restrictions in the years 1923 and 1924, her "yogic activities," and a seven-month period of no menstruation. She goes on to say that "the periods became normal for some time and stopped altogether when Mā was twenty-seven or twenty-eight years old." This is curious, because Mā *was* twenty-seven or twenty-eight in 1923 and 1924. Didi herself met Mā in late 1925 or early 1926 when Mā was twenty-nine or thirty years old. Despite the confusion, it seems we can conclude that Mā was not menstruating when Didi began caring for Mā. Bynum reminds us that fasting does suppress menstruation (p. 214).

53. In an interview with Narendranth Bose, he said, "What I know for certain was what Mā's body odor was. I used to love to sort of nuzzle up to her because she had a very, very sweet body odor and I just loved it" (Interview 24, Calcutta, 1/21/91, p. 10). Other female devotees who cared for Mā's body told me that she rarely bathed. Swami Samatananda (Interview 30, Calcutta, 1/15/91, p. 28) said that Mā had a bath only every five or six months.

54. Bynum, *Holy Feast, Holy Fast*, p. 233. The irony of food being considered a precious gift from someone who denies it to herself bears further inquiry in both Christian and Hindu contexts.

55. See Kapil Tiwar, *Dimensions of Renunciation in Advaita Vedanta* (Delhi: Motilal Banarsidass, 1977), pp. 33–34.

56. Mohandas K. Gandhi, *Gandhi: An Autobiography* (Boston: Beacon, 1956), p. 209.

57. One of Mā's oldest swamis recounted to me the story of his pilgrimage on foot from the origin of the Ganges to its end in the Bay of Bengal and back again, having taken the extreme vow of *akash vritti*, or coming from the sky, in which one vows not to ask anyone for anything but only to take what is given or, as he described it, "leaving everything to God" (Interview 15, Kankhal, 11/30/90, pp. 10–15).

58. Ghurye, *Indian Sadhus*, p. 78.

59. This phenomenon of worshiping Mā as a deity is discussed in chapter 6.

60. Rupa Bose (Interview 33, Calcutta, 1/18/91) told of two incidents she had witnessed, one in which Mā was injured in a car accident but refused treatment and the other in which Mā broke her toe but appeared unfazed. These stories are representative of the hundreds of such stories in the testimonial literature of devotees.

61. Interview 41, Varanasi, 11/22/90, p. 2.

62. Devi, *Sri Sri Ma Anandamayi*, 1:15.

63. Prabhavananda Isherwook, *How to Know God, Yoga Sūtra* 2.3, p. 72.

64. Alexander Lipski, *The Life and Teaching of Anandamayi Ma* (Delhi: Motilal Banarsidass, 1977), p. 33.

65. Interview 16, Kankhal, 11/30/90, p. 12.

66. Lipski, *The Life and Teaching*, p. 33.

67. Devi, *Sri Sri Ma Anandamayi*, 1:232.

68. Anil Ganguli, *Anandamayi Ma: The Mother Bliss-incarnate* (Calcutta: Eureka, 1983), pp. 17–18.

69. Mukerji, "Śrī Ānandamayī Mā' pp. 397–398.

70. Interview 19, Kankhal, 12/2/90, p. 12.

71. Interview 16, Kankhal, 11/30/90, p. 6.

72. Interview 37, Calcutta, 1/21/91, p. 1.

73. Interview 24, Calcutta, 1/21/91, p. 2.

74. See John Coleman's conclusion to *Saints and Virtues*, John Hawley, ed., pp. 205–225, for a discussion of this subject with particular reference to the work of William James.

75. See, for example, Trevor Ling, "Indian Sociological Perspectives on Suffering," in *Suffering: Indian Perspectives*, Kapil Tiwari, ed. (Delhi: Motilal Banarsidass, 1986), pp. 270–287, which discusses contemporary Indian social protest movements such as the one led by Swami Narayana, a nineteenth-century Hindu guru and social reformer in Kerala.

76. For example, see J. N. Farquhar, *Modern Religious Movements in India* (New Delhi: Munshiram Manoharlal, 1977), first published in 1917, pp. 387–429, for an analysis of social reform and service from 1828 to 1913.

77. Carl T. Jackson, *Vedanta for the West: The Ramakrishna Movement in the United States* (Bloomington: Indiana University Press, 1994), pp. 76–77.

78. Lipski, *The Life and Teaching*, p. 52.

79. Ganguli, *Anandamayi Ma*, p. 126.

80. Ibid., pp. 171–182.

81. Lipski, *The Life and Teaching*, p. 52.

82. Appar, 6.309.10 (Poem 211) Indira Peterson, trans., *Poems to Śiva: The Hymns of the Tamil Saints* (Princeton, N.J.: Princeton University Press, 1989), p. 45.

83. See, for example, Lawrence Babb, *Redemptive Encounters*, pp. 15–93 for a study of the Radhasoami Movement, founded by Shiv Dayal Singh (1818–1878), which is renowned for its rejection of caste distinctions. See also Leela Mullatti, *The Bhakti Movement and the Status of Women* (New Delhi: Abhinav, 1989), for an analysis of the socioeconomic status of women in contemporary *bhakti* Virashaiva communities of Karnataka.

84. Hawley and Juergensmeyer, *Songs of the Saints*, p. 16.

85. Interview B, Boston, 11/19/89, pp. 13–18.

86. Interview 23, 1/6/91, Ganeshpuri, pp. 2–10.

87. Interview 37, Calcutta, 1/21/91, p. 2.

88. Interview 16, Kankhal, 11/30/90, pp. 15–16. According to Hindu tradition, there are four recurring cosmic ages or *yugas*; the present age, the *Kaliyuga*, is the fourth and furthest from the ideal, righteous age.

89. Interview 33, Calcutta, 1/18/91, p. 10.

90. Interview 21, Kankhal, 12/3/90, p. 5.

91. Interview 32, Calcutta, 1/17/91, p. 3.

92. Interview 14, Kankhal, 11/30/90, p. 2.

93. Satsang Tape no. 36, Dehradun, November 1974, pp. 33–34.

94. Satsang Tape no. 39, Brindavan, January 1975, p. 8.

95. Ibid., pp. 11–13.

96. Satsang Tape no. 8, Suktal, 1960, pp. 44–45.

97. Satsang Tape no. 9, Suktal, November 1961, pp. 13–14.

98. Interview 34, Calcutta, 1/16/91, p. 11.

99. Interview 31, Calcutta, 1/16/91, pp. 2–3.

100. McDaniel, *The Madness of the Saints* p. 231. McDaniel is a resource for studying the phenomenon of religious ecstasy and divine madness in Bengal. For a study of divine madness in Maharashtra, see Anne Feldhaus, ed. and trans. *The Deeds of God in Rddhipur* (New York: Oxford University Press, 1984); for a more comprehensive study, see David Kinsley, "Through the Looking Glass: Divine Madness in India," *History of Religions Journal* 13, no. 4 (1974): 270–305.

101. *Nārada Bhakti Sūtras*, Swami Tyāgīśānanda, trans. (Madras: Sri Ramakrishna Math, 1983), verse 6, p. 2.

102. Ibid., verse 68, p. 19.

103. Olivelle, *Samnyāsa Upaniṣads*, pp. 107–112, points out that even traditional Hindu scriptures on asceticism and renunciation say that the perfect renunciant

assumes the behavior of a *bāla*, a madman, an *unmatta*, a lunatic, or a *pishācha*, a demonic being, and that madness and irrationality are associated with divinity or holiness within the Hindu tradition.

104. See McDaniel, *The Madness of the Saints*, Appendix B, pp. 288–293, for a full listing of these categories.

105. Ibid., pp. 118–127. For a discussion of the *kriyās* associated with the practice of *kundalinī* yoga, see Swami Visnu Tīrtha *Devātma Shakti* (Rishikesh: Yoga Shri Peeth Trust, 1980), pp. 102–105. For classic studies of *kundalinī* yoga, see Arthur Avalon, *The Serpent Power* (New York: Dover, 1974) and Lilian Silburn, *Kundalini: Energy of the Depths* (Albany: State University of New York Press, 1988). For an illuminating study of a nineteenth-century text on tantric Shāktism and *kundalinī* yoga, see Douglas Brooks, *The Secret of the Three Cities: An Introduction to Hindu Śākta Tantrism* (Chicago: University of Chicago Press, 1990).

106. Chandan, *Svakriya Svarasamrita*, Vol. 1:144.

107. Interview 17, Kankhal, 11/27/90, p. 1; Interview 32, Calcutta, 1/17/91, p. 7.

108. Interview 8, Varanasi, 11/16/90, pp. 14–15.

109. Interview 29, Calcutta, 1/14/92, p. 4. Swāmī Tyāgīśānanda, in his commentary on the *Nārada Bhakti Sūtras*, p. 81, says, the true *bhakta* "is not conscious of doing anything of his own accord or for his own sake. He feels like a dry leaf at the mercy of the wind."

110. Interview 21, Kankhal, 12/3/90, p. 1.

111. Interview 29, Calcutta, 1/14/90, p. 4. Chapter 5 addresses the element of contagion and transformation in the presence of a saint or guru.

112. McDaniel, *The Madness of the Saints*, p. 231.

113. Ibid., p. 259.

114. This is acknowledged in Catherine Ojha, "Feminine Asceticism in Hinduism: Its Tradition and Present Condition," *Man in India* 61, no. 3, 1981, p. 280; and in Bynum, *Holy Feast, Holy Fast*, p. 221.

115. Interview 8, Varanasi, 11/16/90, p. 2.

116. Brahmacharini Chandan, *Svakriya Svarasamrita*, 3:186–191.

117. Bhaiji, ed., *Sad Vāni*: Atmananda, trans. (Calcutta: Shree Shree Anandamayee Charitable Society, 1981), no. 68, pp. 103–104.

118. Ānandamayī Mā, *Mātri Vāni*, vol. 2, Atmananda, trans. (Calcutta: Shree Shree Anandamayee Charitable Society 1982), no. 212, p. 152.

119. Hawley and Juergensmeyer, *Songs of the Saints*, p. 48.

120. For a discussion of this ambivalence in the Christian tradition, see Richard Kieckhefer, "Imitators of Christ: Sainthood in the Christian Tradition," in Kieckhefer and Bond, *Sainthood*, p. 23.

121. Phyllis Granoff, "The Miracle of a Hagiography without Miracles: Some Comments on the Jain Lives of the Pratyekabuddha Karakaṇḍa," *Journal of Indian Philosophy* 14 (1986): 389.

122. Ganguli, *Anandamayi Ma*, p. 93.

123. John Carman, in a personal communication, Dec. 5, 1991. "Miracle" has been defined by Charles Keyes in his introduction to *Charisma and Sacred Biography*, p. 3, as "any act that is believed to be impossible given what for any people is known about the normal processes of life and nature."

124. Patañjali's *Yoga Sūtras*, 3: 43, in Prabhavananda, *How to Know God*, p. 133.

125. Interview 15, Kankhal, 11/30/90, p. 17.

126. Yogananda, *Autobiography of a Yogi*, p. 271.

127. Frank Conlon, "A Nineteenth-Century Indian Guru," in *Charisma and*

Sacred Biography, Michael Williams, *Journal of the American Academy of Religion* ed., 48, nos. 3 and 4, (1982):146.

128. Interview 1, Varanasi, 9/5/90, pp. 1–2.

129. Babb, *Redemptive Encounters*, pp. 65–66.

130. Ram Dass, *Miracle of Love* (New Delhi: Munshiram Manoharlal, 1985), p. 44.

131. For an excellent discussion of Sai Baba of Shirdi, see White's "The Sai Baba Movement", 863–78.

132. Interview 36, Calcutta, 1/21/91, pp. 3–4.

133. Interview 33, Calcutta, 1/18/91, pp. 9–10.

134. Interview 8, Varanasi, 11/16/90, pp. 8–9.

135. Interview 29, Calcutta, 1/14/91, pp. 1–2.

136. Interview 19, Kankhal, 12/2/90, p. 11. In a similar story of "mind reading," Rupa Bose relates a time when she gave Mā a *dhoti*, a piece of white cloth which Mā wore as a sari, and Mā gave it away. Rupa said to herself that she wished that Mā had kept her present. Then Mā took the *dhoti* back and gave a different *dhoti* away (Interview 33, Calcutta, 1/18/91, p. 6).

137. Interview 39, Calcutta, 1/24/91, p. 2.

138. In the *Guru Gītā*, the Song of the Guru, verse 72, says,
jñāna shakti samārūḍhas tattva mālā vibhūshitaḥ
bhukti mukti pradātā yas tasmai shrī gurave namaḥ
"Salutations to that Shree Guru who is firmly established in the power of knowledge and is adorned with the garland of the principles (of creation) and who gives worldly fulfillment as well as salvation." *Shree Guru Gita* in *The Nectar of Chanting* (South Fallsburg, N.Y.: SYDA Foundation, 1983), p. 45.

139. Interview 6, Varanasi, 9/22/90, p. 2.

140. Interview 22, Varanasi, 12/11/90, Interview 23, Ganeshpuri, 1/6/91; and Interview 44, South Fallsburg, N.Y., 8/20/93.

141. Interview 20, 12/2/90, pp. 14, 17–18.

142. Interview 34, Kankhal, 12/4/90, p. 1.

143. Interview 6, Varanasi, 9/22/90, p. 2; and the other in Interview 14, Kankhal, 11/30/90, p. 2.

144. Wendy Doniger O'Flaherty, *Dreams, Illusions and Other Realities* (Chicago: University of Chicago Press, 1984), pp. 14–18; for a discussion of the significance of dreams, see chapter 1.

145. Interview 33, Calcutta, 1/18/91, p. 4.

146. Interview 40, Kankhal, 11/27/90, pp. 1–2.

147. Chapter 6 discusses the subject of devotees' experiences of Mā after her death more fully, but for now we touch on stories of her miraculous presence since her death.

148. Interview 24, Calcutta, 1/21/91, pp. 3–4.

149. Interview 30, Calcutta, 1/15/91, p. 12.

150. Interview 28, Calcutta, 1/14/91, pp. 6–8.

151. Yogananda, *Autobiography of Yogi*, chapter 43, pp. 407–427.

152. Interview 18, Kankhal, 12/1/90, p. 5. The belief of Mā's devotees that she knew what they were doing at all times was prevalent in all the interviews.

153. Interview 27, Calcutta, 1/14/91, pp. 1–3. Pushpa related this same story in Ganguli, *Anandamayi Mā*, pp. 100–101.

154. Interview 33, Calcutta, 1/18/91, p. 7.

155. Ganguli, *Anandamayi Ma*, p. 92.

156. Interview 16, Kankhal, 11/30/90, p. 14.

157. Interview 11, Kankhal, 11/27/90, p. 1.

158. Interview 16, Kankhal, 11/30/90, p. 14.

159. See Ganguli, *Anandamayi Ma*, pp. 101–102

Chapter Five

1. Ānandamayī Mā, *Mātri Vāni*, trans. by Atmananda (Calcutta: Shree Shree Anandamayee Charitable Society, 1982), vol. 2 no. 294, pp. 224–225.

2. Ibid., no. 265, p. 199.

3. Ibid. no. 269, pp. 202–203.

4. Ibid., no. 280, p. 213.

5. *Shree Guru Gita* (South Fallsburg, N.Y.: SYDA Foundation, 1981), verse 34, p. 22.

6. Charles White, "The Sai Baba Movement: Approaches to the Study of Indian Saints," *Journal of Asian Studies,* 31, no. 4 (1972): 874.

7. David Miller, "The Guru as the Center of Sacredness," *Sciences Religieuses/ Studies in Religion,* 6/5 (1976–1977): 527.

8. In 1963, Louis Renou, in his introduction to *Hinduism* (New York: Washington Square Press, 1963), discussed the paradigm of the guru and its great influence on the tradition. Jan Gonda devotes an entire chapter to the guru in *Change and Continuity in Indian Religion* (New Delhi: Munisharam Manoharlal, 1985), in which he outlines the history of the guru-disciple relationship from Vedic times to the present. Likewise, David Lannoy's book, *The Speaking Tree* (London: Oxford University Press, 1974), discusses the importance of the guru from a primarily psychoanalytic perspective. In "The Guru as the Center of Sacredness," David Miller maintains that one must understand the guru to understand the Hindu tradition. Shashibhusan Das Gupta, in *Obscure Religious Cults,* (Calcutta: Firma KLM, 1976), enumerates the sects in which the path of the guru, or *guru-vāda,* has been central and further maintains the influence of this path on all of Indian religion. William Cenkner's book on Shankarāchārya, *A Tradition of Teachers: Śankara and the Jagadguru's of Today* (Columbus, Mo.: South Asia Books, 1983), discusses the guru-disciple relationship within the tradition of Advaita Vedanta. Daniel Gold looks at the guru as a focal point of change in his two books, *The Lord as Guru: Hindi Saints in the North Indian Tradition* (New York: Oxford University Press, 1987) and *Comprehending the Guru: Toward a Grammar of Religious Perception* (Atlanta: Scholars Press, 1988). Bettina Baumer's article, "The Guru in the Hindu Tradition," *Studies in Formative Spirituality* 11, no. 3, (1990): 341–353), gives an excellent historical overview of the category of guru. Finally, Douglas Brooks, in *The Secret of the Three Cities: An Introduction to Hindu Śākta Tantrism* (Chicago: University of Chicago Press, 1990), offers an enlightening discussion of the centrality of the guru in tantric Hinduism.

9. See, for example, Raymond B. Williams, *A New Face of Hinduism: The Swaminarayan Religion* (Cambridge: Cambridge University Press, 1984). Lise Vail's article, "Founders, Swamis, and Devotees: Becoming Divine in North Karnataka," in *Gods of Flesh/Gods of Stone: The Embodiment of Divinity in India,* Joanne Waghorne and Norman Cutler, eds. (Chambersburg, Pa.: Anima, 1985), pp. 123–140, is based upon her dissertation, *Renunciation, Love and Power in Hindu Monastic Life* (University of Pennsylvania, 1987), in which she discusses the concept of the interpenetration of guru and disciple based on her fieldwork on a Virashaiva sect in Karnataka. In *Redemptive Encounters: Three Modern Styles in the Hindu Tradition* (Berkeley: University of California Press, 1986), Lawrence Babb discusses the guru in the context of three modern Hindu movements.

10. Gupta, *Obscure Religious Cults*, p. 356.

11. As quoted in Baumer, "The Guru in the Hindu Tradition," p. 352.

12. Gonda, *Change and Continuity*, p. 235.

13. See Baumer, "The Guru in the Hindu Tradition," pp. 341–342, referring to the Muṇḍaka Upanishad, 1.2.12–13, in *The Thirteen Principal Upaniṣads*, ed. and trans. Robert Hume (Delhi: Oxford University Press, 1985), p. 369.

14. Taittirīya Upanishad, 1.3.3., ibid., p. 276.

15. Chāndogya Upanishad, 8.7.2., ibid., p. 268.

16. Shvetāshvatara Upanishad, 6.23, ibid., p. 411.

17. See Baumer, "The Guru in the Hindu Tradition, pp. 343–344.

18. *Mahābhārata*, 7, a.66 C., as cited in Gonda, *Change and Continuity*, p. 252.

19. *Mahābhārata*, 1.123.10–15, trans. and ed., J. A. B. van Buitenen, vol. 1 (Chicago: University of Chicago Press, 1973), pp. 270–271. Jan Gonda, in *Change and Continuity*, p. 230, maintains, however, that the "divine character of the religious teacher, which cannot be disassociated from the divinity of the learned brahman, has always been an Indian tenet."

20. Cenkner, *A Tradition of Teachers*, p. 32.

21. Ibid., p. 34.

22. Chāndogyopaniṣadbhāṣya, 6.14, in Karl Potter, ed., *Encyclopedia of Indian Philosophies: Advaita Vedānta up to Śaṁkara and His Pupils* (Princeton, N.J.: Princeton University Press, 1981), p. 268.

23. William Cenkner, in *The Tradition of Teachers*, pp. 43–44, says that this doctrine is articulated in the revered hymn attributed to Shankara, *Śri Dakṣināmūrtistotra*. Although Karl Potter, in *Encyclopedia of Indian Philosophies*, p. 317, says that this hymn was probably written by a successor of Shankara's, the poem certainly reflects his devotees' assumption that the guru, having realized his divinity, is to be worshiped.

24. Brihadāranyaka Upanishad, III.7, in Robert Hume, ed. and trans. *The Thirteen Principal Upaniṣads* (Delhi: Oxford University Press, 1985), pp. 114–116.

25. Ibid., p. 37. Cenkner refers here to Shankara's commentary on the Brihadāranyaka Upanishad, VI.v1–4 and II.vI.3, in which he traces his lineage through the mothers of the teachers, and to his commentary on the *Māṇḍukyakārikā*, IV.100, in which he praises the triad of Brahman, the lineage of teachers, and his own teacher.

26. Potter, *Encyclopedia of Indian Philosophies*, Shankara's *Brahmasūtrabhāṣya*, I.2.18–20, p. 134, and *Aitareyopaniṣadbhāṣya*, V. 13, p. 277.

27. See Baumer, "The Guru in the Hindu Tradition," p. 345.

28. See *Śiva Sūtra* II.6, plus Kshemarāja's commentary, in *Śiva Sūtras: The Yoga of Supreme Identity*, Jaideva Singh, trans. (Delhi: Motilal Banarsidass, 1979), pp. 102–103.

29. Paul Muller-Ortega, *The Triadic Heart of Śiva* (Albany: State University of New York Press, 1989), pp. 165–167.

30. Gonda, *Change and Continuity*, p. 252.

31. See John S. Hawley and Mark Juergensmeyer, eds., *Songs of the Saints of India* (New York: Oxford University Press, 1988), pp. 43–44.

32. Gonda, *Change and Continuity*, p. 280.

33. As is discussed in chapter 6, while Chaitanya was not the first guru to be considered an *avatāra*—for example, Shankara was portrayed as an *avatāra* of Shiva—Chaitanya's described avatārahood seemed to establish a paradigm for the claim to avatārahood of more contemporary gurus.

34. For example, *Shree Guru Gita*, verse 96, p. 33.

35. Gonda, *Change and Continuity*, pp. 280–281.

36. Klaus Klostermaier, *A Survey of Hinduism* (Albany: State University of New York Press, 1989), p. 173.

37. Although this verse can be found in the hatha yoga text, *Śiva Samhita*, 3.13, Srisa Chandra Vasu, trans. (New York: AMS Press, 1974), p. 47, it was probably an Upanishadic mantra. It is chanted today in Ānandamayī Mā's ashram and in the ashrams of many other gurus.

38. Regarding the contemporary Hindu context, see, for example, Joel Kramer and Diana Alstead, *The Guru Papers: Masks of Authoritarian Power* (Berkeley, Calif.: North Atlantic Books, 1993); Georg Feuerstein, *Holy Madness* (New York: Arkana, 1990); John Wren-Lewis, "Death Knell of the Guru System: Perfectionism versus Enlightenment," *Journal of Humanistic Psychology* 34, no. 2, (1994): 46–61; and Gregory Bogart, "Separating from a Spiritual Teacher," *Journal of Transpersonal Psychology* 24, no. 1 (1992): 1–23. For a discussion of the same issue within the Buddhist community, see Jack Kornfield's "The Emperor's New Clothes: Problems with Teachers," in *A Path with Heart* (New York: Bantam, 1993), pp. 254–271; Kate Wheeler, "Towards a New Spiritual Ethic," *Yoga Journal*, March-April (1994): 32–37; and Stephen Butterfield, "Finnegan at His Wake," *Tricycle*, Vol. III., no. 2 Winter (1994): 64–67.

39. In *The Secret of the Three Cities*, p. 83, Douglas Brooks relates that Bhāskararāya, the eighteenth-century tantric Shākta guru, referred to *dīkshā* as "the first step of the palace of liberation."

40. These forms of *dīkshā*, along with several more found in the *Kularnava Tantra*, are enumerated by June McDaniel in *The Madness of the Saints: Ecstatic Religion in Bengal* (Chicago: University of Chicago Press, 1989), pp. 106–107.

41. Muller-Ortega, *The Triadic Heart of Śiva*, p. 170.

42. Baumer, "The Guru in the Hindu Tradition," p. 343.

43. Brooks, *The Secret of the Three Cities*, pp. 64–65.

44. See Raymond B. Williams, "The Holy Man as the Abode of God in the Swaminarayan Religion," in *Gods of Flesh, Gods of Stone: The Embodiment of Divinity in India*, Joanne Punzo Waghorne and Norman Cutler, eds. (Chambersburg, Pa.: Anima, 1985), pp. 143–145.

45. Vail, "Founders, Swamis, and Devotees," pp. 131–132.

46. McKim Marriott and Ronald Inden, "Toward an Ethnosociology of South Asian Caste Systems," in *The New Wind: Changing Identities in South Asia*, Kenneth David, ed. (The Hague: Mouton, 1977), p. 232. For other works of McKim Marriott, see "Alternative Social Sciences," in *General Education in the Social Sciences: Centennial Reflections* (Chicago: University of Chicago Press, 1992), pp. 262–278; "Interpreting Indian Society: A Monistic Alternative to Dumont's Dualism," *Journal of Asian Studies* 36, no. 1, (1970): 189–195; and "Constructing an Indian Ethnosociology," *Contributions to Indian Sociology*, 23, no. 1 (1989), 1–36.

47. Valentine Daniels, *Fluid Signs: Being a Person the Tamil Way* (Berkeley: University of California Press, 1987), p. 103.

48. Marriott, "Constructing an Indian Ethnosociology," pp. 14–15. In a personal communication on 8/8/92, Marriott conceded that this definition does not take into account the Bengali proclivity to see God as both *nirguna* and *saguna*, as being beyond attributes and possessing attributes.

49. See Vail, "Founders, Swamis, and Devotees," pp. 131–133, for a description of a process of "mutual subtle gift-giving" within the *sampradāya* of Siddhalingēshvara, in which each swami "not only receives qualities such as [his] *śakti*" but also eventually "this results in his *becoming* Siddhalingēśvara."

50. For a discussion of a similar substantial transmission phenomenon, see Mary Douglas, in *Purity and Danger* (London: Ark, 1966), p. 112, in which she speaks of

the Islamic concept of *baraka*, or "success power" in Somalia: "Another characteristic of success power is that it is often contagious. It is transmitted materially. Anything which has been in contact with *baraka* may get *baraka*."

51. I am indebted to Charles Hallissey, a former student of Marriott, for a personal communication on 10/2/92 in which he helped me apply transactional theory to the guru-disciple relationship. There are two parallel phenomena that help to explain the belief in the guru's ability to take on the karma of the devotee. Gloria Raheja, in *The Poison in the Gift* (Chicago: University of Chicago Press, 1988), talks at length about the belief in the brahman's ability to take on impurity. In the Mahāyāna Buddhist tradition, there is the doctrine of the transfer of merit in which a *bodhisattva*, or future Buddha, dedicates his karmic merit to all beings for their eventual liberation (*parināmanā*). See Hans Wolfgang Schumann, *Buddhism: An Outline of Its Teachings and Schools* (Wheaton, Ill.: Quest, 1984), pp. 111–112.

52. Interview 22, Varanasi, 12/11/90, p. 3

53. Interview 35, Calcutta, 1/21/91, p. 12.

54. Interview 30, Calcutta, 1/15/91, p. 12.

55. Interview 11, Kankhal, 11/27/90, pp. 1, 6.

56. Interview 16, Kankhal, 6/18/91.

57. Because I agreed to keep the source of this material particularly confidential, I do not include the specific interview number or the place of the interview.

58. Interview 31, Calcutta, 1/16/91, p. 4.

59. Interview 9, Varanasi, 11/18/90, p. 9.

60. Interview 35, Calcutta, 1/21/91, pp. 6–7. In a similar vein, a Calcutta businessman, Rajkumar Roy, was moved to tears telling me how Mā ordered him to take *dīkshā* and provided everything he needed for the ceremony (Interview 28, Calcutta, 1/14/91, pp. 6–7).

61. Interview 22, Varanasi, 12/11/90, p. 6.

62. Interview 17, Kankhal, 12/1/90, p. 14.

63. Interview 6, Varanasi, 9/2/90, p. 3–4. In chapter 6, we consider what Mā means when she tells devotees, "Nārāyana gave it," or "Parameshvara gave it." Whether she initiates directly or not, she may simply be referring to herself as a channel of the divine, or she may be hinting that she, too, considers herself not the means but the end.

64. Interview 31, Calcutta, 1/16/91, p. 4.

65. Interview 24, Calcutta, 1/21/91, p. 6.

66. Interview 29, Calcutta, 1/14/91, pp. 7–8.

67. Diana L. Eck, in *Darśan: Seeing the Divine Image in India* (Chambersburg, Pa.: Anima, 1981), p. 3, has pointed out the importance of not only seeing but *being seen* by the divine in India.

68. Interview 30, Calcutta, 1/15/91, pp. 8–9.

69. Interview 16, Kankhal, 11/30/90, pp. 3–4.

70. Interview 18, Kankhal, 12/1/90, p. 7.

71. Interview 11, Kankhal, 11/27/90, pp. 1–2. In this description of Swami Turiyananda's *dīkshā*, when he says that Mā's compassionate glance broke down the *samskāras*, he seems to be using a metaphor of purification, almost blowtorching, rather than the metaphor of planting a seed, which is a metaphor of substantial transmission. Yet, since Swamiji in another place in the interview speaks of Mā's planting a seed in the devotee's causal body, which eventually must grow (Interview 11, Kankhal, 11/27/90, pp. 4–5), both metaphors seem to coexist in the minds of Mā's devotees.

72. Interview 7, Ganeshpuri, 10/13/90, pp. 2–3.

73. Interview 2a, Varanasi, 9/7/90, p. 1.

74. Interview 41, Varanasi, 11/22/90, pp. 1–2.

75. Interview 31, Calcutta, 1/17/91, pp. 1–2; interview 37, Calcutta, 1/21/91, p. 7.

76. Interview 27, Calcutta, 1/14/91, p. 3.

77. Interview 30, Calcutta, 1/15/91, p. 11.

78. Interview 23, Ganeshpuri, 1/6/91, pp. 3–4.

79. Interview 44, South Fallsburg, N.Y., 8/20/93, p. 1.

80. Interview 16, Kankhal, 11/30/90, p. 8.

81. Interview 11, Kankhal, 11/27/90, pp. 4–5.

82. Interview 30, Calcutta, 1/15/91, p. 15.

83. Interview 28, Calcutta, 1/14/91, p. 10.

84. Interview 12, Dehradun, 11/19/90, p. 15.

85. Interview 33, Calcutta, 1/18/91, p. 5.

86. Swami Samatnananda, Interview 30, Calcutta, 1/15/91, p. 5.

87. Interview 17, Kankhal, 12/1/90, p. 13.

88. Interview 4, Varanasi, 9/20/90, p. 6.

89. Interview 17, Kankhal, 12/1/90, p. 9.

90. Interview 18, Kankhal, 12/1/90, pp. 1–2.

91. Interview 30, Calcutta, 1/15/91, p. 5.

92. Interview 8, Varanasi, 11/16/90, p. 29.

93. Interview 35, Calcutta, 1/21/91, pp. 4–5.

94. Interview 12, Dehradun, 11/29/90, p. 14.

95. Interview 16, Kankhal, 11/30/90, p. 14.

96. Interview 19, Kankhal, 12/2/90, p. 18.

97. Interview 11, 11/27/90, pp. 4–5.

98. Interview 9, Varanasi, 11/18/90, pp. 1–3.

99. Interview 22, Varanasi, 12/11/90.

100. Interview 30, 1/15/91, p. 14.

101. Interview 20, Kankhal, 12/2/90, p. 20.

102. Interview 4, Varanasi, 9/20/90, p. 1.

103. Interview 30, Calcutta 1/15/91, p. 5.

104. Interview 17, Kankhal, 12/1/90, p. 2.

105. Interview 20, Kankahl, 12/2/90, p. 20.

106. Interview 20, Kankhal, 12/2/90, p. 11.

107. Interview 8, Varanasi, 11/16/90, pp. 32–33.

108. Interview 36, Calcutta, 1/21/91, pp. 9–10.

109. Interview 35, Calcutta, 1/21/91, p. 7.

110. Interview 29, Calcutta, 1/14/91, p. 8.

111. Interview 11, Kankhal, 11/27/90, pp. 3–4.

112. Interview 18, Kankhal, 12/1/90, p. 4.

113. Interview 41, Varanasi, 11/22/90, p. 2.

114. Interview 19, Kankhal, 12/2/90, p. 18.

115. Interview 12, Dehradun, 11/29/90, p. 7.

116. Interview 8, Varanasi, 11/16/90, pp. 19–26.

117. Interview 9, Varanasi, 11/18/90, p. 6.

118. Interview 33, Calcutta, 1/18/91, p. 5.

119. Interview 16, Kankhal, 1/30/90, pp. 11–12.

120. Interview 15, Kankhal, 11/30/90, p. 5.

121. Interview 31, Calcutta, 1/16/91, p. 1.

122. Bithika Mukerji, *From the Life of Ānandamayī Mā*, (Varanasi: Shree Shree Anandamayee Sangha, 1981), 2:143–146.

123. Interview 37, Calcutta, 12/21/91, pp. 3–4.

124. Interview 19, Kankhal, 12/2/90, pp. 6–9.

125. For a discussion of succession in religious movements founded by a charismatic figure, see Timothy Miller, ed., *When Prophets Die: The Postcharismatic Fate of New Religious Movements* (Albany: State University of New York Press, 1991), especially Gene Thursby, "Siddha Yoga: Swami Muktananda and the Seat of Power." pp. 165–182.

126. Interview 16, Kankhal, 11/30/90, p. 9.

127. See, for example, Miller, *When Prophets Die.*

128. Interview 13, Dehradun, 11/19/90, pp. 7–8.

129. Interview 12, Dehradun, 11/29/90, p. 15.

130. Interview 16, Kankhal, 11/30/91, p. 9.

131. Interview 17, Kankhal, 12/1/90, pp. 11–12.

132. Interview 18, Kankhal, 12/1/90, pp. 12–13.

133. Mukerji, *From the Life of Ānandamayī Mā,* 2:147–148. See also Hari Ram Joshi, *Ma Anandamayi Lila* (Varanasi: Shree Shree Anandamayee Charitable Society, 1974), pp. 71–72.

134. A. K. Ramanujan, "On Women Saints," in *The Divine Consort: Rādhā and the Goddesses of India* (Boston: Beacon, 1982), pp. 323–324.

135. See the work of Erndl, Denton, Ojha, and McDaniel in the Bibliography.

136. McDaniel, *The Madness of the Saints,* p. 231.

137. Catherine Ojha, "Feminine Asceticism in Hinduism: Its Tradition and Present Conditions," *Man in India,* vol. 61, no. 3, 1981 pp. 280–281.

138. Kathleen Erndl, *Victory to the Mother: The Hindu Goddess of Northwest India in Myth, Ritual, and Symbol* (New York: Oxford University Press, 1993), pp. 105–134. An parallel conversation occurs in Miranda Shaw, *Passionate Enlightenment: Women in Tantric Buddhism* (Princeton, N.J.: Princeton University Press, 1994), pp. 136–138. Shaw, having established the prevalence of women gurus within the Tibetan tradition, questions the absence of their names from lists of gurus within lineages. In a personal communication, 2/26/92, Shaw also wondered if women within tantric Buddhism and perhaps women, in general, might be less concerned with lineage than men.

139. Satsang Tape no. 8, Suktal, November 1960, p. 36.

140. Satsang Tape no. 20, Brindavan, May 1965, p. 36.

141. Satsang Tape no. 36, Dehradun, November 1974, pp. 24–25.

142. Satsang Tape no. 102, Dehradun, date unknown, pp. 9–12.

143. Ānandamayī Mā, *Mātri Vāni,* Atmananda, trans. (Calcutta: Shree Shree Anandamayee Charitable Society, 1982), vol. 2, no. 332, pp. 267–268.

144. Satsang Tape no. 20, Brindavan, November 1967, p. 14.

145. Satsang Tape no. 98, Kankhal, November 1981, p. 32.

146. Satsang Tape no. 38, Naimisharanya, January 1975, pp. 5–6.

147. See *Mātri Vāni,* 2:229–264, for a section in which Mā offers two of sets instructions for the path of detachment, one for householders and one for renunciants. We see the ordinary norm defined by Mā as the pursuit of liberation in the context of *dharma,* while the extraordinary norm is defined more rigorously as the one-pointed pursuit of liberation.

148. It should be noted that while the *sannyāsins* and *sannyāsinīs* went through a formal *sannyāsa* initiation in which they "cast off" the worldly life, the *brahmachāris* and *brahmachārinīs* either asked Mā if they could stay with her as her "lifelong friend" or were told by Mā to be so.

149. Interview 19, Kankhal, 12/2/90, p. 17.

150. Interview 36, Calcutta, 1/21/91, p. 9.

151. Interview 19, Kankhal, 12/2/90, p. 14.

152. Interview 41, Varanasi, 11/22/90, p. 9.

153. Interview 37, Calcutta, 1/21/91, p. 2.

154. Interview 24, Calcutta, 1/21/91, p. 9.

155. Interview 12, Dehradun, 11/29/90, p. 18.

156. Interview 14, Kankhal, 11/30/90, p. 6.

157. Interview 2, Varanasi, 9/6/90, p. 1.

158. Bhaiji, ed. *Sad Vāni: A Collection of the Teachings of Sri Anandamayi Ma* (Varanasi: Shree Shree Anandamayee Charitable Society, 1975), no. 79, pp. 121–122.

159. Satsang Tape no. 34, Dehradun, November 1974, pp. 6–7.

160. Interview 37, Calcutta, 1/21/91, p. 1.

161. Interview 32, Calcutta, 1/21/91, p. 4.

162. Interview 12, Dehradun, 11/29/90, p. 17.

163. Interview 13, Dehradun, 11/29/90 pp. 14–15.

164. Interview 14, Kankhal, 11/30/90, p. 5.

165. Interview 8, Varanasi, 11/16/90, pp. 32–33.

166. Interview 20, Kankhal, 12/1/90, p. 22.

167. Interview 17, Kankhal, 12/1/90, p. 8.

168. Ibid, p. 12.

169. Interview 19, Kankhal, 12/2/90, p. 18.

170. Interview 41, Varanasi, 11/22/90, p. 2.

171. Interview 30, Calcutta, 1/15/91, pp. 3–8.

172. Interview 37, Calcutta, 1/21/91, pp. 13–14.

173. Satsang Tape no. 83, Bangalore, May 1979, pp. 39–40.

Chapter Six

1. *The Bhagavad-Gītā*, Winthrop Sargeant, trans. (Albany: State University of New York Press, 1984), pp. 206–208.

2. Shang, Sumitra, *Shri Shri Ma Anandamayi: Satsang with the Blissful Mother*, prod. and dir. by PADMA-Film Production, 1980–95. Videocassette.

3. Vijaya Laksmi Pandit, preface to *Woman Saints East and West*, Swami Ghanananda and Sir John Stewart-Wallace, eds. (Hollywood, Calif.: Vedanta, 1955), p. viii.

4. In terms of the Hindu conception of incarnation, see Marvin Harper, *Gurus, Swamis, and Avataras* (Philadelphia: Westminster, 1972); Edward Dimock, "Religious Biography in India: 'The Nectar of the Acts of Chaitanya'" and David Lorenzen, "The Life of Śankarācārya," in *The Biographical Process: Studies in the History and Psychology of Religion*, Frank Reynolds and Donald Capps, eds. (Paris: Mouton, pp. 109–117 and pp. 87–177, respectively; Joanne Punzo Waghorne and Norman Cutler, eds., *Gods of Flesh, Gods of Stone: The Embodiment of Divinity in India* (Chambersburg, Pa.: Anima, 1985), especially Lisa Vail, "Founders, Swamis, and Devotees: Becoming Divine in North Karnataka, pp. 123–142; and Raymond Williams, "The Holy Man as Abode of God in the Swaminarayan Religion," pp. 143–159. For comparative studies of Hindu and Christian conceptions of incarnation, see Geoffrey Parrinder, *Avatara and Incarnation* (London: Faber, 1970), Daniel Bassuk, *Incarnation in Hinduism and Christianity: The Myth of the God-Man* (Atlantic Highlands, N.J.: Humanities Press, 1987); Prashant Miranda, *Avatar and Incarnation: A Comparative Analysis* (New Delhi: Harwan, 1990); and John Carman, *Majesty and Meekness: A Comparative Study of Contrast and Harmony in the Concept of God* (Grand Rapids, Mich.: William B. Eerdmans, 1994), chapter 10, pp. 188–212.

5. Daniel Bassuk, *Incarnation in Hinduism and Christianity*, p. 1.

6. Ibid., p. 6. Bassuk himself uses the terms "man-God" and "God-man" to capture the two ends of these progressions. I reject the gender exclusivity of these terms.

7. Jan Gonda, *Die Reliogionen Indiens* (Stuttgart: Kohlhammer, 1960), vol. 1., p. 269; and *The Bhagavadgītā*, W. D. P. Hill, trans. (London: Oxford University Press, 1928), p. 25.

8. Carman, *Majesty and Meekness*, pp. 191–192.

9. Ibid., p. 198.

10. Ibid., p. 191.

11. Bassuk, *Incarnation in Hinduism and Christianity*, p. 58.

12. Dimock, "Religious Biography in India," p. 113.

13. Swami Saradananda conditions this by saying that the *avatāra* may not have an unbroken memory from childhood, only from the time when "his body and mind mature" *(Sri Ramakrishna, the Great Master* [Madras: Ramakrishna Math, 1952], p. 95).

14. Ibid., pp. 25–26.

15. Christopher Isherwood, *Ramakrishna and His Disciples* (Hollywood, Calif.: Vedanta, 1965), p. 60. It is important to note here that Swami Saradananda first published *Sri Ramakrishna, The Great Master* in 1920, just thirty-six years after the passing of Ramakrishna. Thus, Saradananda's definition and theories of avatarahood would have been available to both Mā and her devotees at that time, including his suggestion that the *sādhana* of an *avatāra* is merely *līlā* undertaken for the benefit of devotees.

16. Ibid., p. 60.

17. Neal Delmonico, "How to Partake in the Love of Krishna," in *Religions of India in Practice*, Donald Lopez, ed. (Princeton, N.J.: Princeton University Press, 1995), p. 244.

18. See Peter Heehs, *Sri Aurobindo* (Delhi: Oxford University Press, 1989), pp. 102–103.

19. Ibid., p. 122.

20. Prema Nandakumar, *The Mother of Sri Aurobindo Ashram* (New Delhi: National Book Trust, 1977), p. 114.

21. Vijay, *Sri Aurobindo and the Mother of Avatarhood* (Pondicherry: Sri Aurobindo Society, 1972), p. 24.

22. Bassuk, *Incarnation in Hinduism and Christianity*, p. 76.

23. Ivy Oneita Duce, *How a Master Works* (Walnut Creek, Calif.: Sufism Reoriented, 1975), p. 4.

24. Charles B. Purdom, *The God Man* (Crescent Beach, S.C.: Sheriar, 1964), p. 24. For more on Meher Baba's theory of avatarhood, see Warren Healy, *Who Is Meher Baba?* (Ahmadnagar, India: Meher, 1979).

25. See Bassuk, *Incarnation in Hinduism and Christianity*, pp. 86–94. For a scholarly study of Satya Sai Baba, see also Lawrence Babb, *Redemptive Encounters: Three Modern Styles in the Hindu Tradition* (Berkeley: University of California Press, 1986).

26. Bassuk, *Incarnation in Hinduism and Christianity*, p. 92.

27. Samuel Sandweiss, *Sai Baba* (San Diego: Birth Day Publishing, 1975), pp. 100–101.

28. Ibid., p. 93.

29. See Charles S. J. White, "The Sai Baba Movement: Approaches to the Study of Indian Saints," *Journal of Asian Studies* 31, no. 1 (1972): 865.

30. William Jackson, "A Life Becomes a Legend: Sri Tyāgarāja as Exemplar," 60, no. 4(1992): *Journal of the American Academy of Religion* p. 734.

31. Sister Nivedita, *Kali the Mother* (Calcutta: Advaita Ashrama, 1989), p. 19.

32. For an illuminating discussion of the Hindu conception of God as many and as One, see Diana Eck, *Encountering God: A Spiritual Journey from Bozeman to Banaras,* (Boston: Beacon, 1993), especially chapter 3, "The Names of God: The Meaning of God's Manyness," pp. 44–80.

33. See J. N. Tiwari, *Goddess Cults in Ancient India* (Delhi: Sundeep, 1985); N. N. Bhattacarya, *The Indian Mother Goddess* (New Delhi: Manohar, 1977); and P. K. Agrawala *Goddesses in Ancient India* (New Delhi: Abhinav, 1984) on the Goddess in the pre-Aryan and early Vedic civilizations. Three excellent sources for study of the Hindu Goddess are James J. Preston, ed., *Mother Worship: Theme and Variations* (Chapel Hill: University of North Carolina Press, 1982); John Stratton Hawley and Donna Marie Wulff, eds., *Devī: Goddesses of India* (Berkeley: University of California Press, 1996); and David Kinsley, *Hindu Goddesses: Visions of the Divine Feminine in the Hindu Religious Tradition* (Berkeley: University of California Press, 1986). Sources on the Shākta and tantric traditions, in particular, include Agehananda Bharati, *The Tantric Tradition* (London: Hillary House, 1965); and N. N. Bhattacharyya, *History of the Śākta Religion* (New Delhi: Munshiram Manoharlal, 1973) and *History of the Tantric Religion* (New Delhi: Manohar, 1987). Works based on Shākta texts include two books by Thomas Coburn, *The Devī Māhātmya: The Crystallization of the Goddess Tradition* (Columbia, Mo.: South Asia Books, 1965) and *Encountering the Goddess* (Albany: State University of New York Press, 1991); and two books by Cheever Mackenzie Brown, *God as Mother: A Feminine Theology in India; An Historical and Theological Study of the Brahmavaivarta Purāṇa* (Hartford, Vt.: Claude Stark, 1974) and *The Triumph of the Goddess: The Canonical Models and Theological Visions of the Devī-Bhāgavata Purāṇa* (Albany: State University of New York Press, 1990). For two studies of goddess cults in northern India based on fieldwork, see Sigrid Westphal-Hellbusch, "Living Goddesses, Past and Present, in North-west India," in *German Scholars on India*, vol. 1 (Varanasi: Chowkhamba Sanskrit Series Office, 1973), pp. 387–405; and a recent work on the cult of Sherānvālī which includes an excellent overview of the myth and theology of Goddess worship, Kathleen Erndl, *Victory to the Mother: The Hindu Goddess of Northwest India in Myth, Ritual, and Symbol* (New York: Oxford University Press, 1993). Much of June McDaniel, *The Madness of the Saints: Ecstatic Religion in Bengal* (Chicago: University of Chicago Press, 1989), includes a discussion of Shātka practice in Bengal.

34. See Coburn, *The Devī Māhātmya*. Coburn maintains that this text made the Sanskritic tradition more contemporary and made the worship of the Goddess more traditional.

35. Erndl, *Victory to the Mother*, pp. 19–20. I am indebted to Erndl's excellent overview of the history of the worship of the Hindu Goddess for this paragraph.

36. Ibid., p. 22.

37. Douglas Brooks, *The Secret of the Three Cities: An Introduction to Hindu Sākta Tantrism* (Chicago: University of Chicago Press, 1990), p. 3.

38. Ibid. See pp. 4–7.

39. N. N. Bhattacharyya, *History of the Tantric Religion*, p. 342.

40. Ibid., p. 343.

41. For an excellent summary of "principal generic features of Hindu Tantrism," see Brooks, *The Secret of the Three Cities*, pp. 55–72.

42. There is considerable overlap between right-handed and left-handed Tantrism and Shāktism. These are not discreet categories but interweaving streams. Brooks, *The Secret of the Three Cities*, is an invaluable resource for understanding the complexity of the Tantric/Shākta world. Brooks demonstrates that even the tantric Shrīvidyā

theologian, Bhāskararaya, who Brooks says "fits squarely within the so-called left current of Tantrism" (p. 211), quotes often from the *Devī Bhāgavata Purāṇa* and claims Vedic status for his work, calling it the *Tripurā Upaniṣad*.

43. *Devī Māhātmya*, 11.43, as quoted in Brown, *The Triumph of the Goddess*, p. 182.

44. Ibid., p. 214.

45. Ibid., pp. 214–215.

46. Rachel Fell McDermott, in her doctoral thesis, "Evidence for the Transformation of the Goddess Kālī: Kamalākānta Bhaṭṭācārya and the Bengali Śākta Padāvalī Tradition" (Harvard University, 1993), speaks of the softening of Bengali Shāktism between the eighteenth and twentieth centuries, in which the goddesses Kālī and Umā "undergo a change in perceived personality through the balm of *bhakti*" (p. 9).

47. *Devī Bhāgavata Purāṇa*, 24.2–4 as quoted in Brown, *The Triumph of the Goddess*, p. 176.

48. Ibid., pp. 132–133.

49. Ibid., p. 184.

50. Ibid., p. 186.

51. N. N. Bhattacharyya, in *History of the Tantric Religion*, says that the *Guhyātiguhya-tantra*, written around the ninth century, making it somewhat contemporary with the *Devī Bhāgavata*, brings the ten *avatāras* of Vishnu in relationship with the ten *Mahāvidyās*, or ten *avatāras* of Devī. There are several variants on the list of the ten *Mahāvidyās*, but the best known are those found in the *Shaktisaṇgama-tantra*: Kālī, Tārā, Chinnamastā, Sundarī, Vagalā, Mātaṇgī, Lakshmī, Shyāmalā, Siddhavidyā-Bhairavī, and Dhūmavatī.

52. Ibid., p. 31–32.

53. Kathleen Erndl, *Victory to the Mother*, p. 31.

54. Brown, *The Triumph of the Goddess*, p. 75.

55. Ibid., p. 176.

56. Ibid., p. 286.

57. Ibid., pp. 142–143.

58. Ibid., p. 209 in *Devī Bhāgavata*, 3. 6.2–4, 7.

59. Ibid., p. 217.

60. Interview 24, Calcutta, 1/12/91, p. 2, 7.

61. Interview 19, Kankhal, 12/2/90, pp. 1–2.

62. Interview 17, Kankhal, 12/1/90, p. 7.

63. Interview 24, Calcutta, 1/12/91, pp. 6–7.

64. Interview 15, Kankhal, 11/30/90, p. 3.

65. Interview 21, Kankhal, 12/3/90, p. 2.

66. Interview 41, Varanasi, 11/22/90, p. 3.

67. Interview 4, Varanasi, 9/20/90, p. 5.

68. Interview 30, Calcutta 1/15/91, p. 16.

69. Interview 9, Varanasi, 11/18/90, pp. 22–23.

70. Interview 36, Calcutta, 1/21/91, p. 2. Chinnamastā is described by Bhattacharyya in *History of the Tantric Religion*, pp. 352–353, in spite of her horrific form, as the form of Devī, who "bestows on her worshipper anything he wants."

71. Interview 14, Kankhal, 11/30/90, p. 5.

72. Interview 17, Kankhal, 12/1/90, p. 10.

73. Interview 41, Varanasi, 11/22/90, p. 2. A fascinating verification of Mā's devotees' seeing Mā as Devī is the booklet, *One Hundred and Eight Names of Shree Shree Ma Anandamayee*, compiled by Saroj Paliwal, Shree Shree Ma Anandamayee

Ashram, Brindavan: 1990. It is modeled after the three traditional texts, the Vishnu, Shiva, and Lalitā Sahasranamas, respectively the One Thousand One Hundred and Eight Names of Vishnu, Shiva, and Lalitā. The authors says that the "rosary of one hundred and eight names of "*Mā-Bhagavān*" [Mā, the Lord] should be repeated to reveal "her *svarūpa*," or her own form (p. viii). The list of names is a list of qualities and forms of Devī, such as Shree Mahalakṣmi, Shree Mantra Shakti, and Shree Mūladharanivasinī, Mother residing in the *mūlādhāra chakra*, or *Kundalinī Shakti*.

74. From the point of view of Advaita Vedānta, the higher Brahman is *nirguna*, one without a second. But lower Brahman, *saguna* Brahman, is *Īshvara*, or God, the cause of diversity, who creates the world out of no motive but out of play or *līlā*. It is this lower Brahman who can be an object of devotion and who, according to Swami Jnanananda, can incarnate. See Karl Potter, ed., *Encyclopedia of Indian Philosophers: Advaita Vedānta up to Śamkara and His Pupils* (Princeton, N.J.: Princeton University Press, 1981), pp. 77-78. It seems that there is apparently some controversy about the position of Advaita Vedānta vis-à-vis the doctrine of incarnation. There is some consensus that Shankara, the famous systematizer of the philosophy of Advaita Vedānta, accepted the doctrine of *avatāra* to the extent that he believed Krishna to be an incarnation of *Īshvara*. However, since the authorship of the *Bhagavadgītābhāṣya* attributed to Shankara has been questioned by certain scholars, it is difficult to reach a definitive conclusion about Shankara's position. See Parrinder, *Avatar and Incarnation*, pp. 50–57.

75. Interview 16, Kankhal, 11/30/90, p. 13.

76. Interview 24, Calcutta, 1/12/91, p. 11.

77. Interview 18, Kankhal, 12/1/909, pp. 9–10.

78. Kaviraj, Introduction to *Mother as Seen by Her Devotees*, p. xi.

79. Ibid., p. 171.

80. Interview 30, Calcutta, 1/15/91, pp. 7–8.

81. Interview 6, Varanasi, 9/22/90, p. 3.

82. Interview 18, Kankhal, 12/1/90, p. 9.

83. Interview 28, Calcutta, 1/14/91, p. 2.

84. Kaviraj, "Mother Anandamayi," in *Mother as Seen by Her Devotees*, p. 165. This article is undoubtedly considered one of the seminal treatises on Mā, along with Kaviraj's introduction to the same volume, which has been reprinted as the ultimate essay in a memorial collection of Kaviraj's essays, *Selected Writings of M. M. Gopinath Kaviraj* (Varanasi: M. M. Gopinath Kaviraj Centenary Celebration Committee, 1990). Many devotees suggested that I read both essays.

85. Kaviraj, "Mother Anandamayi," in *Mother as Seen by Her Devotees*, pp. 167–168.

86. Ibid., p. 169.

87. See Kaviraj, introduction to *Mother as Seen by Her Devotees*, p. xii.

88. Gopinath Kaviraj, "Mother Anandamayi," in *Mother as Seen by Her Devotees*, p. 177.

89. Kavirāj, Introduction to *Mother as Seen by Her Devotees*, p. xiii.

90. Ibid., p. xiii.

91. Kaviraj, "Mother Anandamayi," in *Mother as Seen by Her Devotees*, p. 178.

92. Interview 1, Varanasi, 9/9/90, pp. 2–3.

93. Interview 7, Ganespuri, 10/11/90, p. 5.

94. *Thea* being Greek for Goddess, "thealogy" is a term used in the feminist critique of male-centered religion. See, for example, Naomi Goldenberg, *Changing of the Gods: Feminism and the End of Traditional Religions* (Boston: Beacon, 1979), pp. 96–100. The term is plural here to indicate the lack of consensus about Mā's identity.

95. Interview 30, Calcutta, 1/15/91, pp. 1–2.

96. Erndl, *Victory to the Mother*, p. 31.

97. Ibid., pp. 158–159.

98. Bhaiji, *Dwadash Pradeep*, S. N. Sopory, ed. (Calcutta: Shree Shree Anandamayi Charitable Society, 1976), p. 14.

99. Ibid., p. 15.

100. Bithika Mukerji, "Śrī Ānandamayī Mā: Divine Play of the Spiritual Journey," in *World Spirituality*, vol. 6, *Hindu Spirituality*, Krishna Swaraman, ed. (New York: Crossroad, 1989), p. 394.

101. Gurupriya Devi, *Sri Sri Ma Anandamayi*, Tara Kini, trans. (Calcutta: Shree Shree Anandamayee Charitable Society, 1984), 1:18.

102. Bhaiji, *Mother as Revealed to Me*, G. Das Gupta, trans. (Calcutta: Shree Shree Anandamayee Charitable Society, 1983), p. 143.

103. Bithika Mukerji, *From the Life of Sri Anandamayi Ma*, (Varanasi: Shree Shree Anandamayee Sangha, 1970), 1:21.

104. Ibid. p. 25.

105. Paramahamsa Yogananda, *Autobiography of a Yogi*, (Bombay: Jaico, 1990), p. 450.

106. Alexander Lipski, *The Life and Teaching of Anandamayi Ma*, (Delhi: Motilal Banarsidass, 1977), p. 10. It turns out that this quote is taken from "A Page from My Diary," by A. K. Datta Gupta, in *Mother as Seen by Her Devotees*, pp. 117–126. The article is a verbatim account of a conversation among Mā, A. K. Datta Gupta, Professor Shyama Charan Babu, a Jiten Babu, and various other devotees, which took place on May 22, 1941, in Dehradun. Gupta recorded the conversation, and it was reprinted in this very popular volume. In this particular part of the conversation, found on p. 125, devotee Jiten Babu has asked Mā to say more about the *līlā* of *sādhana*.

107. Eliot Deutsch, *Advaita Vedanta: A Philosophical Reconstruction* (Honolulu: University of Hawaii Press, 1985), p. 34. Shankara himself defines *adhyāsa* in his major work, *Brahmasūtrabhāsya*, as that which "provides the necessary condition on which all distinctions . . . are based" (see Karl Potter, ed., *Encyclopedia of Indian Philosophies: Advaita Vedānta up to Śamkara and His Pupils* [Princeton, N. J.: Princeton University Press, 1981], p. 120–121). Shankara's pupil, Suresvara, in *Naiṣkarmyasiddhi*, defines "superimposition" (*adhyāropa*) in drawing a distinction between the Self and not Self in verse 100: "The Self is self-established and the not-Self is established by another: what we now say is that these two are mutually superimposed (*adhyāropa*) on the basis (*āśreya*) of nescience, just as the rope and the snake are superimposed in the example taken from the empirical world," (*Realization of the Absolute*, A. J. Alston, trans. [London: Shanti Sadan, 1971] p. 126).

108. Deutsch, *Advaita Vedanta*, p. 33.

109. Lipski, *Life and Teaching of Sri Anandamayi Ma*, p. 11. Also, in A. K. Datta Gupta, "A Page from My Diary," in *Mother as Seen by Her Devotees*, p. 123.

110. Anil Ganguli, *Anandamayi Ma: The Mother Bliss-incarnate* (Calcutta: Eureka, 1983), p. 87.

111. Ibid., p. 88.

112. See Ānandamayī Mā, *Mātri Vāni*, Atmananda, trans. (Calcutta: Shree Shree Anandamayee Charitable Society, 1982), 2: 282–283.

113. A.K. Datta Gupta, "Sri Sri Mā's Self-Initiation," in *Ānanda Vārtā*, 28, no. 2 (1981): 93.

114. Ibid.

115. Ibid., pp. 95–96.

116. Ibid., p. 108.

117. Ibid., pp. 109–110.

118. Brahmacharini Chandan, *Svakriya Svarasamrita* (Kankhal: Shree Shree Ma Anandamayi Ashram, 1982), 2:123.

119. Gupta, "Sri Sri Mā's Self-Initiation," p. 104. Mā says that "there were times that nobody was allowed to touch this body." It is not clear what she means by "nobody," since Mā was dependent on others to be fed and cared for. It is difficult to imagine that there was a time when the young women around Mā were not allowed to touch her. Perhaps Mā is referring to her feet, which people were instructed not to touch. Here Mā is implying that the reason for this prohibition was that her feet were too full of *shakti* for an ordinary person to bear without losing consciousness.

In yogic circles, there is a belief that the guru's feet are a powerful repository of *shakti* and that is why one *would* want to touch them. *Shree Guru Gita*, verse 78, for example, says: "The merit gained by bathing in all holy water, up to the seven seas, is not difficult to obtain by (sipping even) one-thousandth part of a drop of the water from the guru's feet." See *The Nectar of Chanting* (South Fallsburg, N. Y.: SYDA Foundation, 1983), p. 28. The well-known guru, Swami Muktānanda, in *Satsang with Baba*, vol. 2. (Ganeshpuri, India: SYDA Foundation, 1974), pp. 212–213, explains, "There is great meaning behind our custom of touching the feet of a holy man, or guru, or bowing down at his feet. . . . The guru's feet are touched because energy is flowing out from his toes. . . . It is again for this reason that great saints, such as Bhagawan Nityananda would not allow devotees to wash their feet, because if their feet were washed the energy particles are washed away."

120. Gupta, "Sri sri Mā's Self-Initiation." p. 104.

121. Interview 19, Kankhal, 12/2/90, p. 12.

122. Mā, *Mātri Vāni*, no. 330, pp. 2:269.

123. Ibid., no. 324, p. 2:274.

124. Ibid., no. 357, pp. 2:287–288.

125. Ibid., no. 356, p. 2:287.

126. Ibid., no. 343, p. 2:275.

127. Ibid., no. 360, p. 2:289.

128. Satsang Tape no. 98, Kankhal, November 1981, pp. 9–22.

129. Satsang Tape no. 11, Pilani, November 1962, pp. 13–14.

130. Satsang Tape no. 21, Brindavan, November 1967, p. 2.

131. Satsang Tape no. 40, Brindavan, January 1975, pp. 21–29.

132. Satsang Tape no. 9, Suktal, November 1961, pp. 29–30.

133. Satsang Tape no. 21, Kurukṣetra, 1977, p. 10.

134. Satsang Tape no. 11, New Delhi, September 1961, p. 16.

135. Satsang Tape no. 91, Rishikesh, November 1980, p. 17.

136. Satsang Tape no. 83, Bangalore, May 1979, pp. 24–26.

137. Satsang Tape no. 11, Pilani, November 1962, pp. 11–12.

138. Satsang Tape no. 10, Pilani, November 1962, p. 34.

139. Satsang Tape no. 9, Suktal, November 1961, p. 32.

140. Satsang Tape no. 26, Haridwar, November 1972, p. 31.

141. Satsang Tape no. 23, Varanasi, May 1968, pp. 26–27.

142. Bhaiji, ed., *Sad Vāni: A Collection of the Teachings of Sri Anandamayi Ma* (Varanasi: Shree Shree Anandamayee Charitable Society, 1975), no. 87, p. 133.

143. Satsang Tape no. 40, Brindavan, January 1975, pp. 4–5.

144. Interview 13, Dehradun, 11/29/90, p. 9.

145. Rachel Fell McDermott, in a personal communication, March 1995, says

that this liberalization of the process of *dīkṣā* on the part of Ramakrishna and later by Ānandamayī Mā may reflect an early-nineteenth-century Bengali reformist response to the challenge of the influence of Christian and Western intellectual ideas. The Hindu Renaissance is characterized by, among other things, a presentation of Hinduism as less parochial and more universal. The Bengali reformer Rammohan Roy (1774–1833), for example, under the influence of Unitarianism and Western ideologies, proposed a synthesis of Hindu monotheism and Christian morality. The Bengali reformer Keshab Chandra Sen (1838–1884), who considered himself a devotee of Jesus Christ and the Goddess Kālī, also experimented with synthesizing elements from Hinduism, Christianity, and Islam.

146. Since Brindavan is the holy pilgrimage site for devotees of Lord Krishna and Kāshi, or Varanasi, is the city of Lord Shiva, this question is really probing Mā's preference between the Vaishnava *bhakti* path and the Shaivite path of Advaita Vedānta. Certainly, that is the way Mā takes it.

147. Satsang Tape no. 98, Kankhal, November 1981, pp. 29–31.

148. Satsang Tape no. 11, Pilani, November, 1962, p. 6. One might question the centrality of *shraddhā*, or faith, within the Advaitin context. This may be another example of Mā's mixing of philosophical categories, which is discussed more fully later.

149. Ibid., p. 35.

150. Satsang Tape no. 102, Dehradun, unknown date, pp. 24–25.

151. I regret not having asked my collaborators more about their sectarian backgrounds. In some cases, as in the case of Keshab Bhattacharya, Interview 9, 11/18/90, for example, it is clear that he himself worshiped Gopāl from childhood and when Mā gave him a Gopāl *mūrti*, he worshiped it side by side with her picture. In other cases, I do not know if the particular devotees used Vaishnava language because they grew up in a Vaishnava family but they now worship Mā as *ishta* or whether they still identify themselves as Vaishnava.

152. Satsang Tape no. 25, Brindavan, November 1969, p. 24. Here the *jīva* is defined, as it is by Shankara, as the Self attached to a gross body and limited by *avidyā*, or ignorance, here described as "dirt." This statement is a description of Shankara's doctrine of *avaccheda-vāda*, or theory of limitation, in which the *jīva* is seen as "a limitation of consciousness, a limitation, owing to mental imposition, of infinity by finitude, of unity by multiplicity." See Deutsch, *Advaita Vedānta*, pp. 52–53.

153. Satsang Tape no. 26, Haridwar, November 1972, p. 27.

154. Satsang Tape no. 10, Pilani, November 1962, p. 44.

155. Among Shrī Vaishnavas, *prapatti* describes the act of taking refuge in Vishnu and is considered fundamental. Among Shākta *bhaktas*, one is more likely to speak of the *kripa*, or grace, of the Goddess.

156. Satsang Tape no. 10, Pilani, November 1962, p. 19.

157. Satsang Tape no. 80, Kankhal, May 1978, p. 18.

158. Satsang Tape no. 8, Suktal, November 1961, pp. 43–44.

159. The traditional brahman *samdhyā* ritual involved repetition of mantras, primarily the *Gāyatrī*, usually accompanied by ritual sipping, breathing, sprinkling of water, offering of water to the sun, and worship with Vedic mantras of Sūrya, the sun, in the morning and Varuna, the guardian of *ritu*, the principle of order, in the evening. See I. Julia Leslie, *The Perfect Wife: The Status and Role of the Orthodox Hindu Woman in the Striharmapaddhati of Tryambakayajvan* (Delhi: Oxford University Press, 1988), p. 105. I assume that for non-Brahmans or non-Hindus, the mantra to be repeated three times a day is not the traditional Brahman *Gāyatrī* mantra, but a mantra appropriate to their background.

160. Satsang Tape no. 43, Ranaghat, March 1975, p. 12.

161. Satsang Tape no. 9, Suktal, November 1961, p. 8.

162. Satsang Tape no. 10, Pilani, November 1962, p. 35.

163. Interview 14, Kankhal, 11/30/90, p. 5.

164. Interview 20, Kankhal, 12/2/90, p. 22.

165. Interview 34, Calcutta, 1/20/91, p. 10. It is not clear what Mā actually said here that Subodh Chattaraj translated as "Higher Grace." I suspect she may have been speaking of *aurhetu kripa*, of which her devotees speak so much and which is discussed later.

166. Interview 24, Calcutta, 1/12/91, p. 12.

167. Interview 12, Dehradun, 11/29/90, pp. 7–8.

168. Ibid., pp. 8–10, p. 16.

169. Bhaiji, *Sad Vāni*, no. 60, p. 91.

170. *Devī Māhātmya*, 12.36, as quoted in Brown, *The Triumph of the Goddess*, p. 133.

171. Interview 30, Calcutta 1/15/91, p. 7.

Chapter Seven

1. Norman Cutler, "Conclusion," in *Gods of Flesh, Gods of Stone: The Embodiment of Divinity in India*, Joanne Punzo Waghorne and Norman Cutler, eds. (Chambersburg, Pa.: Anima, 1985), pp. 169–170.

2. Caroline Walker Bynum, et al., eds., *Gender and Religion: On the Complexity of Symbols* (Boston: Beacon, 1986), p. 2.

3. Interview 17, Kankhal, 12/1/90, pp. 10–11.

4. Interview 37, Calcutta, 1/21/91, p. 9.

5. Interview 31, Kankhal, 1/16/91, pp. 1–2.

6. Interview 12, Dedradun, 11/19/90, pp. 14–15.

7. Caring for Mā as if she were a child—combing her hair, feeding her, and helping her dress—must have evoked in the women who performed these services what the Vaishnava tradition would call *vātsalya*, or the maternal attitude of devotion. Most commonly, *vātsalya* refers to worship of Lord Krishna as Gopāl, the baby and young boy.

8. Interview 19, Kankhal, 12/2/90, pp. 4–5.

9. Interview 20, Kankhal, 12/2/90, p. 21.

10. Interview 24, Calcutta, 1/12/91, p. 16.

11. Interview 13, Dehradun, 11/29/90, pp. 10–11.

12. Interview 18, Kankhal, 12/1/90, pp. 8–9.

13. Chitra, "Let Us Be Filled with Sweet Memories," *Ānanda Vārtā*, vol. 31, no. 1, (1984): 59–63.

14. For traditional songs about the impending separation of mother and daughter, see W. G. Archer, *Songs for the Bride: Wedding Rites of Rural India* (New York: Oxford University Press, 1991). See also William Sax, *The Mountain Goddess: Gender and Politics in a Himalayan Pilgrimage* (New York: Oxford University Press, 1991), for a study of a pilgrimage in Garhwal that traces the trek of the goddess Pārvatī from her parent's home to the home of her husband, Shiva, and back again for periodic visits. See especially the section "A Female Perspective on Residence," pp. 115–126, in which Sax speaks of the anguish of young brides as they leave their natal home and the eagerness with which they await their periodic visits back home. Sax documents this perspective with interviews and translations of traditional songs.

15. Interview 6, Varanasi, 9/22/90, p. 4.

16. Interview 21, Kankhal, 12/3/90, p. 4.

17. Chitra, "Let Us Be Filled with Sweet Memories," pp. 59–63

18. Ibid., p. 59.

19. Ibid., p. 60.

20. Ibid., pp. 60–61.

21. Ibid., p. 62.

22. Ibid., p. 61.

23. Interview 30, Calcutta, 1/15/91, p. 3.

24. Interview 4, Varanasi, 9/20/90, p. 1.

25. According to A. S. Altekar, *The Position of Women in Hindu Civilization from Pre-historic Times to the Present* (Delhi: Motilalal Banarsidass, 1991), p. 9, brahman girls did have an *upanayana* initiation until the turn of the common era.

26. Gurupriya Devi, *Sri Sri Ma Anandamayī*, Tara Kini, trans. (Calcutta: Shree Shree Anandamayee Charitable Society, 1984–1990), 2:160.

27. Interview 9, Varanasi, 11/18/90, pp. 5–6. This incident is reported by ibid., 2: 8–9.

28. Ibid., p. 154.

29. Ibid., p. 160–161.

30. Interview 30, Calcutta, 1/15/91, p. 22.

31. Interview 19, Kankhal, 12/2/90, pp. 15–16.

32. Satsang Tape no. 89, Dehradun, June 1980, pp. 3–9.

33. Interview 19, Kankhal, 12/2/90, pp. 29–31.

34. Interview 13, Dehradun, 11/29/90, p. 13.

35. In this way, Mā could be seen, in the words of Paula Arai, as an "innovator for the sake of tradition." Arai's dissertation, "Zen Nuns: Living Treasures of Japanese Buddhism" (presented for a Ph.D. at Harvard University, 1993), speaks of contemporary Zen nuns in this way, highlighting their striving to attain spiritual equality in order to preserve Zen tradition, which is eroding at the hands of modernity. Ānandamayī Mā, as well, was committed to women's spiritual parity with men to ensure the continuity of ancient spiritual traditions. Her innovations were intended, I believe, to bring men and women back to a more inspired, ideal time, when spiritual education was part of everyone's early life and all phases of life led toward one's eventual turning within.

36. Brahmacharini Chandan, *Svakriya Svarasamrita* (Kankhal: Shree Shree Ma Anandamayee Ashram, 1983), 3:223.

37. Bithika Mukerji, *From the Life of Anandamayi Ma* (Varanasi: Shree Shree Anandamayee Sangha, 1970–1981), 1:159, 2:50.

38. Ibid., 2:51.

39. Alexander Lipski, *The Life and Teaching of Anandamayi Ma* (Delhi: Motilal Banarsidass, 1977), p. 56.

40. Mukerji, *From the Life of Anandamayi Ma*, 2:57.

41. Anil Ganguli, *Anandamayi Ma, The Mother Bliss-incarnate* (Calcutta: Eureka, 1983), pp. 145–146.

42. Mukerji, *From the Life of Anandamayi Ma*, 1:198.

43. Caroline Walker Bynum, *Fragmentation and Redemption: Essays on Gender and the Human Body in Medieval Religion* (New York: Zone, 1991), pp. 50–73.

44. Bhaiji, *Mother as Revealed to Me*, G. Das Gupta, trans. (Calcutta: Shree Shree Amandamayee Charitable Society, 1983), p. 8.

45. Alexander Lipski, *The Life and Teachings of Anandamayi Ma*, pp. 45–46. I have been unable to find the original source of this story, although I have no reason to doubt Lipski, as I have been able to locate many of his other references.

46. Ibid., p. 46.

47. Ibid.

48. Catherine Ojha, "Feminine Asceticism in Hinduism: Its Tradition and Present Condition," *Man In India*, 61, no. 3, 1981, 280–281.

49. Chandan, *Svakriya Svarasamrita*, 2:9–12, 3:32.

50. See, in particular, Shelly Errington, "Recasting Sex, Gender, and Power," in *Power and Difference: Gender in Island Southeast Asia*, Jane Monnig Atkinson and Shelly Errington, eds. (Stanford, Calif.: Stanford University Press, 1990), pp. 1–58, and Jane Monnig Atkinson, "Review Essay: Anthropology," *Signs: Journal of Women in Culture and Society*, 8, no. 2, (1982); 236–258.

51. Errington, "Recasting Sex, Gender, and Power," p. 8.

52. Ibid., pp. 26–27.

53. Ibid., pp. 13–14.

54. Ibid., p. 15.

55. Ibid., p. 22. Errington notes here that when women in America "do gender," they reveal themselves to be nonpowerful.

56. Charles Keyes, "Ambiguous Gender: Male Initiation in a North Thai Buddhist Society," in *Gender and Religion: On the Complexity of Symbols*, Caroline Walker Bynum, Stevan Harrell, and Paula Richman, eds. (Boston: Beacon, 1986), p. 68.

57. The word "Brahman" itself is neither masculine nor feminine, but neuter.

58. Ramana Maharshi, *Talks with Sri Ramana Maharshi*, T. N. Venkataraman, ed. (Tiruvannamalai, India: Sri Ramanashram, 1989), pp. 143–144.

59. Charles White, "Mother Guru: Jñanānanda of Madras, India," in *Unspoken Worlds: Women's Religious Lives in Non-Western Cultures*, Nancy Falk and Rita Gross, eds. San Francisco: Harper, 1980, pp. 29–30.

60. A. K. Ramanujan, "Talking to God in the Mother Tongue," *Manushi: Women Bhakta Poets*, nos. 50–52, January–June, 1989, pp. 9–14.

61. Wendy Doniger O'Flaherty, *Women, Androgynes, and Other Mythical Beasts* (Chicago: University of Chicago Press, 1980), pp. 298–299.

62. Christopher Isherwood, *Ramakrishna and His Disciples* (Hollywood, Calif: Vedanta, 1965), pp. 111–113.

63. Ibid., p. 112.

64. Mahatma Gandhi, *Bapu's Letters to the Ashram Sisters*, Kaka Kalelkar, ed. (Ahmedabad: Navajivan, 1952), p. 26.

65. Ibid., p. 95.

66. Erik H. Erikson, *Gandhi's Truth* (New York: Norton, 1969), pp. 402–403.

67. Satsang Tape no. 34, Dehradun, November 1974, p. 3.

68. Ānandamayī Mā, *Mātri Vāni*, Atmananda, trans. (Shree Shree Anandamayee Charitable Society, 1982), no. 16, p. 9.

69. Satsang Tape no. 20, Vrindaban, November 1967, pp. 9–10.

70. Satsang Tape no. 25, Poona, June 1969, p. 27.

71. Satsang Tape no. 8, Banaras, 1969, p. 38.

72. Bhaiji, ed., *Sad Vāni: A Collection of the Teachings of Sri Anandamayi Ma* (Varanasi: Shree Shree Anandamayee Charitable Society, 1975), no. 79, pp. 121–122.

73. Madhu Kishwar and Ruth Vanita, "Poison to Nectar: The Life and Work of Mirabai," in *Manushi Women Bhakta Poets* (Reprint of *Manushi* nos. 50–52, January–June 1989), p. 92.

74. *Śrīvacanapūṣaṇa viyākkiyānam*, sūtra 38, in *Śrīmat Varavaramuṇitra krantamalai*. (Kāñci: Śrī Kāñci Pirativātipayaṅikaram Aññāṅkarācāriyar, 1966). I am indebted to Vasudha Narayanam for translating this beautiful sutra by Pillai Lokācārya and its commentary. The sutra says, "Diminishing his fullness and independence, [the Lord

in his *archā* form] seems to care for those who do not care for him." In his commentary on this verse, Manavāla Māmunikal says of the Lord: "The Brilliant One who is full of motherly love for his devotee (*āshrita vatsala*) stands to be worshipped because of [the devotee's wish (*icca*). The Lord of the Universe (*jagatpati*) has a bath (*snāna*), drinks [for his thirst], and goes on journeys (*yatra*). Even though independent, this Lord of the universe (*jagannātha*), seems to be like one who has no independence."

75. *Śrīvacana Bhūṣaṇam*, sūtra 39, in Vasudha Narayanan, "Arcāvatāra: On Earth as It Is in Heaven," in *Gods of Flesh, Gods of Stone: The Embodiment of Divinity in India*, Joanne Punzo Waghorne and Norman Cutler, eds. (Chambersburg, Pa.: Anima, 1985), p. 63.

76. Interview 24, Calcutta, 1/12/91, p. 1.

77. Anil Ganguli, *Anandamayi Ma: The Mother Bliss-incarnate*, p. 181.

78. Interview 30, Calcutta, 1/15/91, p. 8.

79. Doris Shang, ed., *Matri Darshan, Ein Photo-Album uber Shri Anandamayi Ma* (Stuhlingen, Germany: Mangalam Verlag S. Schang, 1983), p. 24.

80. Lina Gupta, "Kali, the Savior," in *After Patriarchy: Feminist Transformations of the World's Religions* (Maryknoll, N.Y.: Orbis, 1991), p. 16.

81. Ibid., p. 38.

82. Sara Ruddick, *Maternal Thinking: Toward a Politics of Peace* (New York: Ballantine, 1989), p. 95.

83. For an introduction to process theology, see John Cobb and David Griffin, *Process Theology: An Introductory Exposition* (Philadelphia: Westminster, 1975).

84. Ganguli, *Anandamayi Ma, The Mother Bliss-incarnate*, p. 170.

Bibliography

Archival Material

As the Flower Sheds Its Fragrance: Diary Leaves of a Devotee. Calcutta: Shree Shree Anandamayee Charitable Society, 1983.

Bhaiji. *Dwadash Pradeep.* Edited by S. N. Sopory. Calcutta: Shree Shree Anandamayi Charitable Society, 1976.

———. *Mother as Revealed to Me.* Translated by G. Das Gupta. Calcutta: Shree Shree Anandamayee Charitable Society, 1983.

———, ed. *Sad Vāni: A Collection of the Teaching of Sri Anandamayi Ma.* Translated by Atmananda. Calcutta: Shree Shree Anandamayee Charitable Society, 1981.

Chandan, Brahmacharini. *Svakriya Svarasamrita.* 3 vols. Kankhal: Shree Shree Ma Anandamayi Ashram, 1981–1983.

Chaudhuri, Narayan. *Anandamayi Ma as I Have Known Her.* Varanasi: Shree Shree Anandamayee Charitable Society, 1978.

———. *That Compassionate Touch of Ma Anandamayi.* Delhi: Motilal Banarsidass, 1980.

Ganguli, Anil. *Anandamayi Ma's Inscrutable Kheyal.* Calcutta: Shree Shree Anandamayee Charitable Society, 1980.

Joshi, Hari Ram. *Ma Anandamayi Lila.* Varanasi: Shree Shree Anandamayee Charitable Society, 1981.

Lipski, Alexander. *The Life and Teaching of Sri Anandamayi Ma.* Delhi: Motilal Banarsidass, 1977.

Mā, Ānandamayī. *For Daily Reflection: Contemplation of the Eternal Is the Path.* New Delhi: Navchetan Press, 1970.

———. *Mātri Vāni.* 2 vols. Translated by Atmananda. Calcutta: Shree Shree Anandamayee Charitable Society, 1982.

———. *Words of Sri Anandamayi Ma.* Translated by Atmananda. Calcutta: Shree Shree Anandamayee Society, 1982.

Mother as Seen by Her Devotees, Edited by Gopinath Kaviraj. Varanasi: Shree Shree Anandamayee Charitable Society, 1976.

Mukerji, Bithika. *From the Life of Anandamayi Ma.* 2 vols. Calcutta: Shree Shree Anandamayee Sangha, 1980, 1981.

Schang, Sumitra, ed. *Matri Darshan: Ein Photo-Album uber Shri Anandamayi Ma.* Stuhlingen, Germany: Mangalam Verlag S. Schang, 1983.

Schang, Sumitra. *Shri Shri Ma Anandamayi: Satsang with the Blissful Mother.* Produced and directed by PADMA Film Production. 70 min., 1980–95. Videocassette.

Other Material on Ānandamayī Mā

Ānanda Vārtā. "Sri Sri Ma's Self-Initiation" by A. K. Datta Gupta, vol. 28, no. 2 (April 1981): 93–110.

———. "Mātri Līlā," vol. 29, no. 4 (October 1982): 343–366.

———. "Reflections on Sri Ma's Lila" by Acharya Gita Banerji, vol. 30, no. 3 (July 1983): 212–219.

———. "Let Us Be Filled with Sweet Memories" by Chitra, vol. 31, no. 1 (January 1984): 54–63.

Banerjee, Shyamananda. *Ma Anandamayi, a Mystic Sage.* Calcutta: Shree Shree Anandamayee Charitable Society, 1973.

Devi, Gurupriya. *Sri Sri Ma Anandamayi.* 4 vols. Translated by Tara Kini. Calcutta: Shree Shree Anandamayee Charitable Society, 1984–1990.

Ganguli, Anil. *Anandamayi Ma: The Mother Bliss-incarnate.* Calcutta: Eureka, 1983.

Gupta, A. K. Datta. *In Association with Sri Sri Ma Anandamayi,* vols. 1 and 3. Calcutta: Shree Shree Anandamayee Charitable Society, 1987.

India Today. September 4, 1982, pp. 40–41.

Kaviraj, Gopinath. *Selected Writings of M. M. Gopinath Kaviraj.* Varanasi: M. M. Gopinath Kaviraj Centenary Celebration Committee, 1990.

Madou. *Entretiens avec Atmananda: A La Rencontre de Ma Anandamayi.* Paris: Medirep, 1990.

Mandala, Patrick. *Guru-Kripa ou "La Grace du Guru."* Paris: Dervy Livres, 1984.

Mukerji, Bithika. "Śrī Ānandamayī Mā: Divine Play of the Spiritual Journey." In *World Spirituality,* edited by Krishna Swaraman. Vol. 6, *Hindu Spirituality.* New York: Crossroad, 1989.

Mukhopadhyay, Debaprasad. *Matri-lila Darshan.* Calcutta: Eureka, 1989.

Ojha, Catherine. *La Divinite Conquise.* Nanterre: Societe D'Ethnologie, 1990.

One Hundred and Eight Names of Shree Shree Ma Anandamayee. Compiled by Saroj Paliwal. Brindaban: Shree Shree Ma Anandamayee Ashram, 1990.

Shree Shree Anandamayee Charitable Society, Annual Report, 1988–89. Varanasi: Shree Shree Anandamayee Ma Charitable Society, 1989.

Shree Shree Anandamayee Sangha, Annual Report, 1988–89. Kankhal: Shree Shree Anandamayee Sangha, 1989.

Smaranika: Ninety-First Birth Anniversary Remembrances. Kankhal: Shree Shree Anandamayi Ashram, 1987.

Times of India. August 29, 1982, p. 2.

Young, Katherine, and Lily Miller. "Sacred Biography and the Restructuring of Society: A Study of Anandmayi Ma, Lady Saint of Modern Hinduism." In *Boeings and Bullock Carts.* Vol. 2, *Indian Civilization in Its Local, Regional, and National Aspects,* edited by Direndra Vajpey. Delhi: Chanakya Publications, 1990.

Background Material on Religion, Gender, and Methodology

Ahmed, Leila. *Introduction to Woman and Gender in Islam.* New Haven: Yale University Press, 1992.

Amadiume, Ifi. Introduction to *Male Daughters, Female Husbands.* London: Zed, 1987.

Arai, Paula. "Zen Nuns: Living Treasures of Japanese Buddhism." Ph.D. diss. Harvard University, 1993.

Atkinson, Clarissa, Constance Buchanan, and Margaret Miles, eds. *Immaculate and Powerful: The Female in Sacred Image and Social Reality.* Boston: Beacon, 1985.

Atkinson, Clarissa, and Margaret Miles, eds. *Shaping New Vision: Gender and Values in American Culture.* Ann Arbor: UMI Research Press, 1982.

Atkinson, Jane Monnig. "Review Essay: Anthropology." *Signs: Journal of Women in Culture and Society,* 8, no. 2 (1982): 236-258.

Berger, Peter. *A Rumor of Angels: Modern Society and the Rediscovery of the Supernatural.* New York: Doubleday, 1990.

Brown, Karen McCarthy. *Mama Lola: A Voudou Priestess in Brooklyn.* Berkeley: University of California Press, 1991.

Bynum, Caroline Walker. *Holy Feast, Holy Fast.* Berkeley: University of California Press, 1987.

———. *Fragmentation and Redemption: Essays on Gender and the Human Body in Medieval Religion.* New York: Zone, 1991.

Bynum, Caroline Walker, Stevan Harrell, and Paula Richman, eds. *Gender and Religion: On the Complexity of Symbols.* Boston: Beacon, 1986.

Christ, Carol P., and Judith Plaskow, eds. *Womanspirit Rising: A Feminist Reader in Religion.* San Francisco: Harper and Row, 1979.

———. *Weaving the Visions: Patterns of Feminist Spirituality.* San Francisco: Harper and Row, 1989.

Clifford, James, and George E. Marcus, eds. *Writing Cultures: The Poetics and Politics of Ethnography.* Berkeley: University of California Press, 1986.

Cobb, John, and David Griffin. *Process Theology: An Introductory Exposition.* Philadelphia: Westminster, 1975.

Daly, Mary. *Beyond God the Father.* Boston: Beacon, 1973.

Douglas, Mary, *Purity and Danger.* London: A.K, 1966.

Duerr, Hans Peter. *Dreamtime: Concerning the Boundary between Wilderness and Civilization.* Cambridge: Basil Blackwell, 1991.

Eliade, Mircea. "History of Religions and a New Humanism." *History of Religions* 1, no. 1(1962): 8–11.

———. *Immortality and Freedom.* Princeton, N. J.: Princeton University Press, 1973.

Errington, Shelly. "Recasting Sex, Gender, and Power." In *Power and Difference: Gender in Island Southeast Asia,* edited by Jane Monnig Atkinson and S. Errington. Stanford, Calif.: Stanford University Press, 1990.

Fiorenza, Elisabeth Schussler. "The 'Quilting' of Women's History: Phoebe of Cenchreae." In *Embodied Love: Sexuality and Relationship as Feminist Values.* Paula Cooey, Sharon A. Farmer, and Mary Ellen Ross. San Francisco: Harper and Row, 1987.

Finders, Carol. *Enduring Grace.* San Francisco: Harper, 1993.

Fox, Matthew. *Original Blessing.* Santa Fe: Bear, 1983.

Galland, China. *Longing for Darkness: Tara and the Black Madonna.* New York: Penguin, 1990.

Gerth, H.H. and C. Wright Mill, trans. and eds. *From Max Weber: Essays on Sociology.* New York: Oxford University, 1946.

Geertz, Clifford. *The Interpretation of Cultures.* New York: Basic Books, 1973.

———. *Local Knowledge.* New York: Basic Books, 1983.

Gimbutas, Marija. *The Civilization of the Goddess.* San Francisco: Harper and Row, 1991.

Golde, Peggy. *Women in the Field: Anthropological Experiences.* Berkeley: University of California Press, 1986.

Goldenberg, Naomi. *Changing of the Gods: Feminism and the End of Traditional Religions.* Boston: Beacon, 1979.

Hawley, John Stratton, ed. *Saints and Virtues.* Berkeley: University of California Press, 1987.

Heilbrun, Carolyn G. *Writing a Woman's Life.* New York: W. W. Norton, 1988.

Keyes, Charles. "Ambiguous Gender: Male Initiation in a North Thai Buddhist Society." In *Gender and Religion: On the Complexity of Symbols,* edited by Caroline Walker Bynum, Stevan Harrell, and Paula Richman. Boston: Beacon, 1986.

Kieckhefer, Richard, and George D. Bond, eds. *Sainthood: Its Manifestations in World Religions.* Berkeley: University of California Press, 1988.

Kondo, Dorinne. *Crafting Selves.* Chicago: University of Chicago Press, 1990.

Marcus, George, and Michael Fischer, eds. *Anthropology as Cultural Critique: An Experimental Moment in the Human Sciences.* Chicago: University of Chicago Press, 1986.

Miles, Margaret. *Image as Insight.* Boston: Beacon, 1985.

Minh-Ha, Trinh. *Woman, Native, Other.* Bloomington: Indiana University Press, 1989.

O'Flaherty, Wendy Doniger. *Women, Androgynes, and Other Mythical Beasts.* Chicago: University of Chicago Press, 1980.

Ortner, Sherry B. "Is Female to Male as Nature Is to Culture?" In *Woman, Culture and Society,* edited by Michelle Rosaldo and Louise Lamphere. Palo Alto, Calif.: Stanford University Press, 1974.

Pandit, Vijaya Lakshmi. Preface to *Woman Saints East and West,* edited by Swami Ghanananda and Sir John Stewart-Wallace. Hollywood, Calif.: Vedanta, 1955. vii–viii.

Reynolds, Frank, and Donald Capps, eds. *The Biographical Process: Studies in the History and Psychology of Religion.* Paris: Mouton, 1976.

Ruddick, Sara. *Maternal Thinking: Toward a Politics of Peace.* New York: Ballantine, 1989.

Scott, Joan Wallach. *Gender and the Politics of History.* New York: Columbia University Press, 1986.

Shaw, Miranda. *Passionate Enlightenment: Women in Tantric Buddhism.* New Jersey: Princeton University Press, 1994.

Shweder, Richard. *Thinking through Cultures: Expeditions in Cultural Psychology.* Cambridge: Harvard University Press, 1991.

Smith, W. C. "Comparative Religion: Whither and Why?" In *The History of Religions: Essays in Methodology,* edited by Mircea Eliade and Joseph Kitagawa. Chicago: University of Chicago Press, 1959.

————. "Methodology and the Study of Religion: Some Misgivings." In *Methodological Issues in Religious Studies,* edited by Robert Baird. Chico, Calif.: New Horizons, 1975.

Spellman, Elizabeth. *Inessential Woman.* Boston: Beacon, 1988.

Spretnack, Charlene, ed. *The Politics of Women's Spirituality: Essays on the Rise of Spiritual Power within the Feminist Movement.* New York: Doubleday, 1982.

Talamantez, Inez. "Insiders and Outsiders." Talk given at Harvard University, October 1991.

Turner, Victor, and Edward Bruner. eds. *The Anthropology of Experience.* Chicago: University of Illinois Press, 1986.

Tyler, Stephen. "Post-Modern Ethnography: From Document of the Occult to Occult Document." In *Writing Culture: The Poetics and Politics of Ethnography,* edited by

James Clifford and George E. Marcus. Berkeley: University of California Press, 1986.

Waldman, Marilyn R. "The Power of Productive Paradox: An Exercise in Imagining Religion." Plenary Address, Midwest American Academy of Religion, Western Michigan University March, 1990.

Williams, Michael, ed. *Charisma and Sacred Biography.* Journal of the American Academy of Religion Thematic Studies 48, nos. 3 and 4, 1982.

Woodward, Kenneth. *Making Saints.* New York: Simon and Schuster, 1990.

Secondary Source Material on the Hindu Tradition

Abhayananda, Swami, ed. *The Nectar of Self Awareness.* South Fallsburg, N.Y.: SYDA Foundation, 1979.

Abhishiktananda, Swami. *The Further Shore.* Delhi: ISPCK, 1975.

Agrawala, P. K. *Goddesses in Ancient India.* New Delhi: Abhinav, 1984.

Allston, A. J. *The Devotional Poems of Mirabai.* Delhi: Motilal Banarsidas, 1980.

Altekar, A. S. *The Position of Women in Hindu Civilization: from Prehistoric Times to the Present Day* Delhi: Motilal Banarsidass, 1991.

Archer, W. G. *Songs for the Bride: Wedding Rites of Rural India.* New York: Oxford University Press, 1991.

Avalon, Arthur. *The Serpent Power.* New York: Dover, 1974.

Babb, Lawrence. *Redemptive Encounters: Three Modern Styles in the Hindu Tradition.* Berkeley: University of California Press, 1986.

————. "Sathya Sai Baba's Saintly Play." In *Saints and Virtues,* edited by John Stratton Hawley. Berkeley: University of California Press, 1988.

Bassuk, Daniel E. *Incarnation in Hinduism and Christianity: The Myth of the God-Man.* Atlantic Highlands, N. J.: Humanities Press, 1987.

Baumer, Bettina. "The Guru in the Hindu Tradition." *Studies in Formative Spirituality.* 2, no. 3 (1990): 341–353.

Bennett, Lynn. *Dangerous Wives and Sacred Sisters.* New York: Columbia University Press, 1983.

Bhagat, M. G. *Ancient Indian Asceticism.* New Delhi: Munishiram Manoharlal, 1976.

The Bhagavad Gītā. Translated by W. D. P. Hill. London: Oxford University Press, 1928.

————. *The Bhagavad Gītā.* Translated by Winthrop Sargeant. Albany: State University of New York Press, 1984.

Bharati, Agehananda. *The Tantric Tradition.* London: Hillary House, 1965.

Bhattacharyya, N. N. *History of the Śākta Religion.* New Delhi: Munshiram Manoharlal, 1973.

————. *The Indian Mother Goddess.* New Delhi: Manohar, 1977.

————. *History of the Tantric Religion.* New Delhi: Manohar, 1987.

Bogart, Gregory. "Separating from a Spiritual Teacher." *Journal of Transpersonal Psychology* 24, no. 1 (1992): 1–23.

Brooks, Douglas. *The Secret of the Three Cities: An Introduction to Hindu Śākta Tantrism.* Chicago: University of Chicago Press, 1990.

Brown, Cheever Mackenzie. *God as Mother: A Feminine Theology in India: An Historical and Theological Study of the Bramavaivarta Purāna.* Hartford, Vt.: Claude Stark. 1974.

————. *The Triumph of the Goddess: The Canonical Models and Theological Visions of the Devī-Bhāgavata Purāna.* Albany: State University of New York Press, 1990.

Brunton, Paul. *A Search in Secret India.* Bombay: B. I. Publications, 1989.

Budhananda, Swami, trans. *Life of Sri Ramakrishna Compiled From Various Authentic Sources.* Calcutta: Advaita Ashiram, 1971.

Butterfield, Stephen. "Finnegan at His Wake." *Tricycle* vol. III, no. 2 (Winter 1994): 64–67.

Carman, John. "The Ethics of the Auspicious: Western Encounter with Hindu Values." In *Foundations of Ethics,* edited by Leroy S. Rouner. Boston University Studies in Philosophy and Religion, 4. Notre Dame, Ind.: Notre Dame Press, 1983.

———. "Hagiography and Hindu Historical Consciousness." Paper presented at the Conference on Understanding, Faith and Narrative, Washington, D.C., June 1992.

———. *Majesty and Meekness: A Comparative Study of Contrast and Harmony in the Concept of God.* Grand Rapids, Mich.: William B. Eerdmans, 1994.

Carman, John, and Frederique Apffel Marglin, *Purity and Auspiciousness in Indian Society.* Leiden: E. J. Brill, 1985.

Cenkner, William. *A Tradition of Teachers: Śankara and the Jagadgurus of Today.* Columbia, Mo.: South Asia Books, 1983.

Coburn, Thomas. *The Devī Māhātmya: The Crystallization of the Goddess Tradition.* Columbia, Mo.: South Asia Books, 1965.

———. *Encountering the Goddess.* Albany: State University of New York Press, 1991.

Conlon, Frank. "A Nineteenth-Century Indian Guru." In *Charisma and Sacred Biography,* edited by Michael Williams. *Journal of the American Academy of Religion* 48, Nos. 3 and 4 (1982): 146.

Daniel, Valentine. *Fluid Signs: Being a Person the Tamil Way.* Berkeley: University of California Press, 1987.

Das, Veena. *Structure and Cognition: Aspects of Hindu Caste and Ritual.* Delhi: Oxford University Press, 1980.

Dass, Ram. *Miracle of Love.* New Delhi: Munshiram Manoharlal, 1985.

Dehejia, Vidya. *Āntāl and Her Path of Love.* Albany: State University of New York Press, 1990.

Delmonico, Neal. "How to Partake in the Love of Krishna." In *Religions of India in Practice.* Edited by Donald Lopez. Princeton, N.J.: Princeton University Press, 1955, pp. 244–268.

Denton, Lynn Teskey. Unpublished Paper. "Female Asceticism in Varanasi: A Sociological Outline."

———. "Varieties of Hindu Female Asceticism." In *Roles and Rituals for Hindu Women,* edited by I. Julia Leslie. Rutherford, N.J.: Fairleigh Dickinson University Press, 1991.

Deutsch, Eliot. *Advaita Vedanta: A Philosophical Reconstruction.* Honolulu: University of Hawaii Press, 1985.

Devī Māhātmya or Śrī Durgā-Saptaśati. Translated by Swami Jagadīsarananda. Madras: Ramakrishna Math, 1955.

Dharma, P. C. "The Status of Women in the Vedic Age." *Journal of Indian History* 26, No. 3 (1948): 249–268.

———. "The Status of Women during the Epic Period." *Journal of Indian History* 27, no. 1 (1949): 69-90.

Dimock, Edward. "Religious Biography in India: 'The Nectar of the Acts of Caitanya.'" In *The Biographical Process: Studies in the History and Psychology of Religion,* edited by Frank Reynolds and Donald Capps. Paris: Mouton, 1976.

Duce, Ivy Oneita. *How a Master Works.* Walnut Creek, Calif.: Sufism Reoriented, 1975.

Eck, Diana. *Darśan: Seeing the Divine Image in India.* Chambersburg, Pa.: Anima, 1981.

———. *Encountering God: A Spiritual Journey from Boseman to Banaras.* Boston: Beacon, 1993.

Eliade, Mircea. *Yoga, Immortality and Freedom*. Princeton, N.J.: Princeton University Press, 1973.

Erikson, Erik H. *Gandhi's Truth*. New York: Norton, 1969.

Erndl, Kathleen. "Worshipping the Goddess: Women's Bhajan Groups in the Cult of Śerānvāli." In *Redressing Manu*. Edited by Mary McGee, forthcoming.

———. *Victory to the Mother: The Hindu Goddess of Northwest India in Myth, Ritual, and Symbol*. New York: Oxford University Press, 1993.

———. "Worshiping the Goddess: Women's Leadership Roles in the Cult of Śerānvāli," in *Women's Rites, Women's Desires*, edited by Mary McGee, forthcoming.

Farquhar, J. N. *Modern Religious Movements in India*. New Delhi: Munshiram Manoharlal, 1977.

Feldhaus, Anne, ed. and trans. *The Deeds of God in Rddhipur*. New York: Oxford University Press, 1984.

Feuerstein, Georg. *Holy Madness*. New York: Arkana, 1990.

Forbes, Geraldine. *The New Cambridge History of India*, Vol. 4, *Women in Modern India*, New York: Cambridge University Press, 1996.

Fruzzetti, Lina. *The Gift of a Virgin: Women, Marriage, and Ritual in a Bengali Society*. Delhi: Oxford University Press, 1990.

Gandhi, Mohandas K. *Bapu's Letter to the Ashram Sisters*, edited by Kaka Kalelkar. Ahmedabad: Navajivan, 1952.

———. *Gandhi: An Autobiography*. Boston: Beacon, 1956.

Ghanananda, S., and J. S. Wallace, eds. *Women Saints East and West*. Hollywood, Calif.: Vedanta, 1955.

Ghose, Aurobindo. *The Synthesis of Yoga*. Pondicherry: Arya, 1918.

Ghosh, S. K. *Indian Women through the Ages*. New Delhi: Ashish, 1989.

Ghurye, G. S. *Indian Sadhus*. Bombay: Popular Prakashan, 1964.

Gold, Ann. *Fruitful Journeys: The Ways of Rajasthani Pilgrims*. Delhi: Oxford University Press, 1989.

Gold, Daniel. *The Lord as Guru: Hindi Sants in the North Indian Tradition*. New York: Oxford University Press, 1987.

———. *Comprehending the Guru: Toward a Grammar of Religious Perception*. Atlanta: Scholars Press, 1988.

Gonda, Jan. *Die Religionen Indiens*. Vol. 1. Stuttgart: Kohlhammer, 1960.

———. *Change and Continuity in Indian Religion*. New Delhi: Munishiram Manoharlal, 1985.

Granoff, Phyllis. "Holy Warriors: A Preliminary Study of Some Biographies of Saints and Kings in the Classical Indian Tradition." *Journal of Indian Philosophy* 12 (1984): 290–306.

———. "The Miracle of a Hagiography without Miracles: Some Comments on the Jain Lives of the Pratyekabuddha Karakaṇḍa." *Journal of Indian Philosophy* 14 (1986): 389

Great Women of India. Edited by Swami Madhavananda and Ramesh Chandra Majumdar. Mayavati, Almora: Advaita Ashram, 1953.

Gross, Rita. "Hindu Female Deities as a Resource for the Contemporary Rediscovery of the Goddess." In *The Book of the Goddess*, edited by Carl Olsen, New York: Crossroads, 1983.

Gupta, Lina. "Kali the Savior." In *After Patriarchy: Feminist Transformations of the World's Religions*, edited by Paula Cooey, William Eakin, and Jay McDaniel. Maryknoll, N.Y.: Orbis, 1991.

Gupta, Sanjukta. "Women in the Sakta/Saiva Ethos." In *Roles and Rituals for Hindu Women*, edited by Julia Leslie. Rutherford, N. J.: Fairleigh Dickinson University Press, 1991.

Gupta, Shashibhusan Das. *Obscure Religious Cults.* Calcutta: Firma KLM, 1976.

Hallstrom, Lisa Lassell. "Embodied Truth: The Life and Presence of a Hindu Saint." *Harvard Divinity School Bulletin* 17, no. 2 (1987): 5–6.

Harper, Marvin H. *Gurus, Swamis and Avataras.* Philadelphia: Westminster, 1972.

Hawley, John Stratton. "Mirabai as Wife and Yogi." Presented at the Conference on Ascetics and Asceticism, University of Florida, Gainesville, February 1988.

Hawley, John Stratton and Mark Juergensmeyer, eds. *Songs of the Saints of India.* New York: Oxford University Press, 1988.

Hawley, John Stratton and Donna Marie Wulff, eds. *Devi: Goddesses of India, Berkeley: University of California Press,* 1996.

————, and Donna Marie Wulff, eds. *The Divine Consort.* Boston: Beacon, 1982.

Healy, Warren. *Who Is Meher Baba?* Ahmadnagar, India: Meher, 1979.

Heehs, Peter. *Sri Aurobindo.* Delhi: Oxford University Press, 1989.

Hiltebeitel, Alf. *The Cult of Draupadi.* Chicago: University of Chicago Press, 1988.

————. "Draupadi's Hair." *Puruṣārtha* 5 (1981): 179–214.

How to Know God: The Yoga Aphorisms of Patanjali. Translated by Prabhavananda, Swami. Christopher Isherwood. New York: Mentor, 1969.

Hume, Robert, ed. and trans. *The Thirteen Principal Upaniṣads.* Delhi: Oxford University Press, 1985.

Isherwood, Christopher. *Ramakrishna and His Disciples.* Hollywood, Calif.: Vedanta, 1965.

Jacobson, Doranne, and Susan Wadley. *Women in India: Two Perspectives.* Delhi: Manohar, 1986.

Jackson, Carl T. *Vedanta for the West: The Ramakrishna Movement in the United States.* Bloomington: Indiana University Press, 1994.

Jackson, William. "A Life Becomes a Legend: Srī Tyāgarāja as Exemplar." *Journal of the American Academy of Religion* 60, no. 4 (1992): 717–736.

Johnson, Linda. *Daughters of the Goddess: The Women Saints of India.* St. Paul: Yes Publishers, 1994.

Kālidāsa. "Śakuntalā." In *the Hindu Tradition,* edited by Ainslie T. Embree. New York: Modern Library, 1966.

Keyes, Charles. Introduction to *Charisma and Sacred Biography,* edited by Michael Williams. *Journal of the American Academy of Religion,* vol. 48, nos. 3 and 4 (1982): 1–22.

Kinsley, David. "Through the Looking Glass: Divine Madness in India." *History of Religions Journal* 13 (1974): 270–305.

————. *Hindu Goddesses: Visions of the Divine Feminine in the Hindu Religious Tradition.* Berkeley: University of California Press, 1986.

Klostermaier, Klaus. *A Survey of Hinduism.* Albany: State University of New York Press, 1989.

Kornfield, Jack. "The Emperor's New Clothes: Problems with Teachers." In *A Path with Heart.* New York: Bantam, 1993.

Kramer, Joel, and Diana Alstead. *The Guru Papers: Masks of Authoritarian Power.* Berkeley, Calif.: North Atlantic Books, 1993.

Lannoy, David. *The Speaking Tree.* London: Oxford University Press, 1974.

The Laws of Manu. Translated by G. Buhler. In *Sacred Books of the East,* edited by Max Muller. Delhi: Motilal Banarsidass, 1974.

Leslie, I. Julia. *The Perfect Wife: The Orthodox Hindu Woman According to the Striharmapaddhati of Tryambakayajvan.* Delhi: Oxford University Press, 1989.

Ling, Trevor. "Indian Sociological Perspectives on Suffering." In *Suffering: Indian Perspectives,* edited by Kapil Tiwari. Delhi: Motilal Banarsidass, 1986.

Lorenzen, David. "The Life of Śankarācārya." In *The Biographical Process: Studies in the History and Psychology of Religion*, edited by Frank Reynolds and Donald Capps. Paris: Mouton, 1976.

McDaniel, June. *The Madness of the Saints: Ecstatic Religion in Bengal*. Chicago: University of Chicago Press, 1989.

McDermott, Rachel Fell. "Evidence for the Transformation of the Goddess Kālī: Kamalākānta Bhaṭṭācārya and the Bengali Śākta Padāvalī Tradition." Ph.D. diss., Harvard University, 1993.

McGee, Mary. "Feasting and Fasting: Vrata Tradition and Its Significance for Hindu Women." Harvard Divinity School. Th.D. diss., 1989.

————, ed. *Redressing Manu*, forthcoming.

Madan, T. N. *Non-Renunciation*. New York: Oxford University Press, 1987.

Maharshi, Ramana. *Talks with Sri Ramana Maharshi*. Edited by T. N. Venkataraman. Tiruvannamalai: Sri Ramanashram, 1989.

Manushi Women Bhakta Poets. Reprint of *Manushi*, nos. 50–52, (1989).

Marglin, Frederigue Apffel. *Wives of the God King: The Rituals of the Devadasis of Puri*. Delhi: Oxford University Press, 1985.

————. "Gender and the Unitary Self: Looking for the Subaltern in Coastal Orissa." *South Asia Research* (London) 15, no. 1, (1995): 78–130

————. "Rationality, the Body and the World: From Production to Regneration." In *Decolonizing Knowledge: From Development to Dialogue*, edited with S. A. Marglin. Oxford: Clarendon Press, 1996.

Marriott, McKim. "Interpreting Indian Society: A Monistic Alternative to Dumont's Dualism." *Journal of Asian Studies* 36, no.1 (1970): 189–195.

————. "Constructing an Indian Ethnosociology." *Contributions to Indian Sociology* 23, no. 1 (1989): 1–36.

————. "Alternative Social Sciences." In *General Education in the Social Sciences: Centennial Reflections*, Chicago: University of Chicago Press, 1992.

Marriott, McKim, and Ronald Inden. "Toward an Ethnosociology of South Asian Caste Systems." In *The New Wind: Changing Identities in South Asia*, edited by Kenneth David. The Hague: Mouton, 1977.

Mazumdar, Shudha, *Memoirs of an Indian Woman*. Edited by Geraldine Forbes. Armonk, N. Y.: M. E. Sharpe, 1989.

Michael, R. Blake. "Women of the Śunyampādane: Housewives and Saints in Viraśaivism." *Journal of the American Oriental Society* 103 (1983): 361–368.

Miller, David. "The Guru as the Center of Sacredness." *Sciences Religieuses/Studies in Religion*, 6/5 (1976–77): 527–533.

Miller, Timothy, ed. *When Prophets Die: The Postcharismatic Fate of New Religious Movements*. Albany: State University of New York Press, 1991.

Miranda, Prashant. *Avatar and Incarnation: A Comparative Analysis*. New Delhi: Harwan, 1990.

Mullatti, Leela. *The Bhakti Movement and the Status of Women*. New Delhi: Abhinav, 1989.

Muller-Ortega, Paul. *The Triadic Heart of Śiva*. Albany: State University of New York Press, 1989.

Nandakumar, Prema. *The Mother of Sri Aurobindo Ashram*. New Delhi: National Book Trust, 1977.

Nārada Bhakti Sūtras. Translated by Swāmī Tyāgīśānanda, Madras: Sri Ramakrishna Math, 1978.

Muktananda, Swami. *Satsang with Baba*. Vol. 2. Ganeshpuri, India: SYDA Foundation, 1974.

Narayan, Kirin. "'According to Their Feelings': Teaching and Healing with Stories." In *Stories Lives Tell: Narrative and Dialogue in Education*, edited by Carol Witherell and Nel Noddings. New York: Teachers College Press, 1991.

———. *Storytellers, Saints, and Scoundrels*. Philadelphia: University of Pennsylvania Press, 1989.

Neevel, Walter. "The Transformation of Sri Ramakrishna." In *Hinduism: New Essays in the History of Religions*," edited by Bardwell Smith. Leiden: Brill, 1976.

Nikhilananda, Swami, ed. *The Gospel of Sri Ramakrishna*. New York: Ramakrishna-Vivekananda Center, 1984.

Nivedita, Sister. *Kali the Mother*. Calcutta: Advaita Ashrama, 1989.

O'Flaherty, Wendy Doniger. *Medusa's Hair*. Chicago: University of Chicago Press, 1981.

———. *Dreams, Illusions and Other Realities*. Chicago: University of Chicago Press, 1984.

Ojha, Catherine. "Feminine Asceticism in Hinduism: Its Tradition and Present Condition." *Man in India* 61, no. 3, 254–285.

———. *La Divinite Conguise*. Nanterre: Societe D'Ethnologie, 1990.

Olivelle, Patrick. *Samnyāsa Upaniṣads: Hindu Scriptures on Asceticism and Renunciation*. New York: Oxford University Press, 1992.

———. *Vāsudevāśrama Yatidharmaprakāśa: A Treatise on World Denunciation*, Leiden: Brill, 1976.

Paramoo, B. N. *Ascent of Self: A Reinterpretation of the Mystical Poetry of Lalla-Ded*. Delhi: Motilal Banarsidass, 1978.

Parrinder, Geoffrey. *Avatara and Incarnation*. London: Faber, 1970.

Pearson, Anne Mackenzie. *Because It Gives Me Peace of Mind*. Albany: State University of New York Press, 1996.

Peterson, Indira. *Poems to Śiva: The Hymns of the Tamil Saints*. Princeton, N.J.: Princeton University Press, 1989.

Potter, Karl, ed. *Encyclopedia of Indian Philosophies: Advaita Vedānta up to Śaṃkara and His Pupils*. Princeton, N.J.: Princeton University Press, 1981.

———. *The Spiritual Heritage of India*. Hollywood, Calif.: Vedanta Press, 1979.

Preston, James J., ed. *Mother Worship: Theme and Variations*. Chapel Hill: University of North Carolina Press, 1982.

Purdom, Charles B. *The God Man*. Crescent Beach, S.C.: Sheviar Press, 1964.

Radhakrishnan, S., ed. *The Principal Upaniṣads*. New York: Harper, 1953.

———. and Charles Moore, eds. *Sourcebook in Indian Philosophy*. Princeton, N.J.: Princeton University Press, 1970.

Raheja, Gloria. *The Poison in the Gift*. Chicago: University of Chicago Press, 1988.

Ramanujan, A. K. "On Women Saints." In *The Divine Consort: Rādhā and the Goddesses of India*. Edited by John Stratton Hawley and Donna Wulff. Boston: Beacon, 1982.

———. "Is There an Indian Way of Thinking?" University of Chicago, 1986.

———. "Talking to God in the Mother Tongue." *Manushi: Women Bhakta Poets*, nos. 50–52 (1989): 9–14.

Ranade, R. D. *Mysticism in India: The Poet Saints of Maharashtra*. Albany: State University of New York Press, 1983.

Ray, Satyajit, director. *Devī*. With Sharmila Tagore and Soumitra Chatterjee. Satyajit Ray Productions, 1961.

Renou, Louis. *Hinduism*. New York: Washington Square Press, 1963.

Roy, Manisha. *Bengali Women*. Chicago: University of Chicago Press, 1975.

Sandweiss, Samuel. *Sai Baba*. San Diego: Birth Day Publishing, 1975.

Saradananda, Swami. *Sri Ramakrishna, the Great Master.* Madras: Ramakrishna Math, 1952.

Saraswati, Bedyanath, and Surajit Sinha. *Ascetics of Kashi.* Banaras: N. K. Bose Memorial Foundation, 1978.

Sax, William. *The Mountain Goddess: Gender and Politics in a Himalayan Pilgrimage.* New York: Oxford University Press, 1991.

Schumann, Hans Wolfgang. *Buddhism: An Outline of Its Teachings and Schools.* Wheaton, Ill.: Quest, 1984.

Sharma, Arvind. "Ramakrishna Paramahamsa: A Study in a Mystic's Attitude towards Women," In *Beyond Androcentrism,* edited by Rita Gross. Atlanta: Scholars Press, 1977.

————, ed. *Women in World Religions.* Albany: State University of New York Press, 1987.

Shiva, Vandana. *Staying Alive: Women, Ecology and Development.* London: Zed, 1989.

Shree Guru Gita. in *The Nectar of Chanting.* South Fallsburg, N.Y.: SYDA Foundation, 1983.

Silburn, Lilian. *Kundalini: Energy of the Depths.* Albany: State University of New York Press, 1988.

Śiva Saṃhita. Translated by Srisa Chandra Vasu. New York: AMS Press, 1974.

Śiva Sūtras: The Yoga of Supreme Identity. Translated by Jaideva Singh. Delhi: Motilal Banarsidass, 1979.

Śrīvacanapūṣana viyākkiyām. In *Śrīmat Varavaramunītra Krantamalai.* Kañci: Śrī Kāñci Pirativātipayanikaram Aññānkarācariyar, 1966.

Sureśvara. *Realization of the Absolute.* Translated by A. J. Alston. London: Shanti Sadan, 1971.

Tambiah, Stanley. "At the Confluence of Anthropology, History, and Indology." *Contributions to Indian Sociology* 21, no. 1 (1987): 187–216.

Thompson, Stith. *Motif Index of Folk Literature,* 6 vols. Bloomington: Indiana University Press. 1955–1958.

Thursby, Gene. "Siddha Yoga: Swami Muktananda and the Seat of Power." In *When Prophets Die: The Postcharismatic Fate of Religious Movements,* edited by Timothy Miller. Albany: State University of New York Press, 1991.

Tiwar, Kapil. *Dimensions of Renunciation in Advaita Vedanta.* Delhi: Motilal Banarsidass, 1977.

Tiwari, J. N. *Goddess Cults in Ancient India.* Delhi: Sundeep, 1985.

Tripati, B. D. *Sadhus of India.* Bombay: Popular Prakashan, 1978.

Urquhart, Margaret M. *Women of Bengal.* Delhi: Cultural Publishing House, 1983.

Vail, Lise. "Founders, Swamis, and Devotees: Becoming Divine in North Karnataka." In *Gods of Flesh, Gods of Stone: The Embodiment of Divinity in India,* edited by Joanne Punzo Waghorne and Norman Cutler. Chambersburg, Pa.: Anima, 1985.

————. "Renunciation, Love and Power in Hindu Monastic Life", (Ph.D. diss., University of Pennsylvania, 1987).

Vajpeyi, Dhirendra, ed. *Boeings and Bullock-Carts: Studies in Change and Continuity in Indian Civilization,* vol. 2. Delhi: Chanakya, 1990.

Van Buitenen, J. A. B. trans. *Tales of Ancient India.* Chicago: University of Chicago Press, 1959.

————, trans. and ed. *The Mahābhārata: I. The Book of the Beginning.* Chicago: University of Chicago Press, 1973.

Venkataram, T. N., ed. *Talks with Sri Ramama Maharshi.* Tiruvannamalai: Sri Ramanasraman, 1989.

Vijay. *Sri Aurobindo and the Mother of Avatarhood.* Pondicherry: Sri Aurobindo Society, 1972.

Viṣṇu Tīrtha, Swami. *Devātma Shakti*. Rishikesh: Yoga Shri Peeth Trust, 1980.

Vivekacūḍāmani of Srī Śankarācārya. Translated by Swami Mathavananda. Calcutta: Advaita Ashram, 1982.

Waghorne, Joanne Punzo, and Norman, Cutler, eds. *Gods of Flesh, Gods of Stone: The Embodiment of Divinity in India*. Chambersburg, Pa.: Anima, 1985.

Westphal-Hellbusch, Sigrid. "Living Goddess, Past and Present, in North-West India." In *German Scholars on India*, vol. 1. Varanasi: Chowkhamba Sanskrit Series Office, 1973.

Wheeler, Kate. "Towards a New Spiritual Ethic." *Yoga Journal* (March–April 1994): 32–37.

White, Charles S. J. "The Sai Baba Movement: Approaches to the Study of Indian Saints." *Journal of Asian Studies* 31, no. 4 (1972): 863–878.

———. "Mother Guru: Jñanānanda of Madras, India." In *Unspoken Worlds: Women's Religious Lives in Non-Western Cultures*, edited by Nancy Falk and Rita Gross. San Franciso: Harper, 1980.

Williams, Raymond. "The Holy Man as Abode of God in the Swaminarayan Religion." In *Gods of Flesh, Gods of Stone: The Embodiment of Divinity in India*, edited by Joanne Punzo Waghorne and Norman Cutler. Chambersburg, Pa.: Anima, 1985.

———. *A New Face of Hinduism: The Swami Narayan Religion*. Cambridge: Cambridge University Press, 1984.

Wren-Lewis, John. "Death Knell of the Guru System: Perfectionism versus Enlightenment." *Journal of Humanistic Psychology* 34, no. 2 (1994): 46–61.

Yogananda, Paramahamsa. *Autobiography of a Yogi*. Bombay: Yogoda Satsanga Society of India, 1946.

———. *Autobiography of a Yogi*. Bombay: Jaico, 1990.

Young, Katherine. "Hinduism." In *Women in World Religions*. Edited by Arvind Sharma. Albany: State University of New York Press, 1987.

Index

Ānandamayī Mā (continued)
  lack of successor, 6, 151
  laugh, sound of, 111
  life after husband's death, 51–53
  līlā of sādhana of, 165, 176, 178, 178–82, 184, 209
  literal obedience of, 27, 30
  love of nature of, 28–29, 109
  as "Mā," 33, 43, 48
  mantra of, 36–37, 67, 71, 111
  marriage to Bholanāth. See Ānandamayī Mā–Bholanāth relationship
  miraculous powers of, 115–27, 136, 219–20
  motherliness of, 175–76, 177–78, 195–96, 197, 203, 204, 221
  orthodox concept of marriage, 210–13
  out-of-body experience, 47
  as perfection, 217
  as "perfect wife," 7, 35, 55–56, 61, 62, 79–80, 209, 219
  philosophical flexibility of teachings, 188–91
  powerful gaze of, 142–43
  powerful presence of, 114, 175–87, 183
  powers of photographs of, 123–24, 143, 144–45
  power to spiritually transform, 127–28
  presence after death, 123–24, 144–45
  prohibition against touching, 120–21, 182–83
  and purdah restrictions, 32, 39, 42, 70, 74, 80
  refusal to feed self, 6, 96, 97
  in saguna and nirguna forms, 136
  sainthood and, 7, 87–88, 92–97, 128, 140, 219–20
  self-initiation, 21, 38–41, 71–72, 181, 208
  on selfless service, 101–2
  as Self-realized from birth, 182
  self-referential statements, 182–87
  seven famous aphorisms, 101
  silence vows, 41, 42, 72, 95–96
  spiritual aura of, 66
  spiritual experiences, 38–40, 70–71, 111

  as spiritually exalted, 33, 70, 72, 108–13
  spiritual powers, 37, 40–41, 182–83
  spiritual precocity, 26, 28, 63
  stages in life of, 155, 209–10
  sunny nature of, 26, 27
  trancelike states, 28, 42, 71, 72, 109
  travels of, 47–51, 64, 73–75, 93–94
  unconventionality of, 202
  will of, 172–73
  as woman, 55–85, 200
  and women's spiritual equality, 204–9
Ānandamayī Mā–Bholanāth relationship, 61–85, 219
  alternative paradigms, 81–85
  as arranged marriage, 6, 29–30
  assessment of, 78–85
  and Bholanāth's death, 51, 76–78
  Bholanāth's protectiveness, 6, 68–69, 71, 72, 73, 85
  as challenge to "perfect wife" myth, 63
  compared with dharmashāstra ideal, 7
  horoscope prediction, 29, 30
  Mā as "perfect" Hindu wife, 7, 55–56, 61–62, 70, 79–80, 209
  Mā on purpose of, 84–85
  Mā's devotion to Bholanāth, 35, 55
  and Mā's exalted states, 36–38, 39, 70, 71
  Mā's growing independence in, 80
  Mā's leadership in, 6, 7, 24, 39, 41, 48, 49, 62, 69, 72–75, 140, 151, 219
  Mā's literal obedience in, 33, 42–43, 62, 71, 79–80
  and Mā's travels, 50, 51, 74
  phases of, 32–36, 64–75
  as spiritualized, 69–70
  supremacy of Mā's kheyāla in, 79–87
  unconsumation of marriage, 6, 35, 56, 65–68, 69, 80, 94
  unconventionality of marriage, 6, 56, 71
  wedding ceremony, 30, 62–63, 68
  See also Bholanāth
Ānandamayī Mā: Divine Play of the Spiritual Journey (Mukerji), 99
Ānandamayī Mā: The Mother, Bliss-incarnate (Ganguli), 20, 180

Gautama Buddha, 21, 132, 134
gender, 5, 10, 199–222
  cultural construction of, 213–16
  God as both male and female, 188–
    89, 215–16, 217
  Great Goddess transcending, 170
  Mā on, 216–17
  See also women
Ghurye, G. S., 94, 97
girls' school (Kanyapeeth), 52, 97, 156,
    172, 173, 201, 206
Gitananda, Swami, 15–16, 105, 111, 171,
    205
God
  accessibility of, 220
  descent into perfect being, 162–63
  embodiment concept, 199 (*see also*
    incarnation)
  gender flexibility of, 188–89, 215–
    16, 217
  as guru, 154, 160
  guru's knowledge of, 131, 134, 136
  Hindu saints' madness for, 91, 128
  human ascent to perfection of, 162–
    63
  humans made in image of, 157
  Mā as incarnation of, 5, 7, 15, 80,
    82, 83, 99–100, 140, 152, 156,
    160, 162, 164, 171–75, 178,
    196–97, 199, 200, 217–19, 220–
    21
  Mā on herself as, 182–87, 197
  Mā's absolute devotion to, 107–8
  Mā's description of, 187–89, 216–17
  multicultural complexity of term, 171
  names for, 163, 174, 187
  as sacred feminine. *See* Divine Mother
  unknowability of, 15
  See also avatāra; Divine Mother;
    incarnation
goddess cultures, 3, 4, 70, 82–83, 153
Gonda, Jan, 94–95, 134, 163
Govindās, 61
grace, 137, 160, 163, 191–92, 194–95
Great Goddess (Mahādevī), 3–4, 82, 169,
    187
  nirguna vs. *saguna* forms, 174
Guide to the Dharma of Women, 55
Gumtivale Mātā, 83
Gupta, A. K. Datta, 82, 180, 181
Gupta, Lina, 221

Gupta, Sanjukta, 82
Gupta, Shashibhusan Das, 91–92, 129,
    131
Gupta, Sita, 110, 140, 145, 146, 147,
    152, 159, 171, 200
guru, viii, 7, 12, 129–60
  assumption of negative karma by, 136
  bodilessness and, 214
  for contemporary families, 130
  essential qualities, 132
  Hindu gender construct, 214, 215
  as Hindu saint, 92
  indispensability doctrine, 133–34
  lineage of, 133, 135, 151–55
  Mā as, 64, 137–60, 220, 221
  metaphors for, 153–54, 155, 160
  overview, 130–35
  qualities of, 134–35, 164–65
  as transmitter of *shakti,* 134, 142,
    143–44
  women as, 5, 82, 153
Guru Charita, 134
Guru Gītā, 15, 134
Guru-Māhātmya, 133
guru-vāda, 155, 160

hagiography, 21, 22, 91
Hari, 38
Harinām, 33–34, 35, 70
Harvard Divinity School, 8, 16
Harvard Divinity School Bulletin, 12
Hawley, John S., 84, 88–89, 103, 113
Heilbrun, Carolyn, 80
Hindi language, 10, 20, 51, 75
Hindu Spirituality (journal), 20
Hindu tradition
  author's familiarity with, 11–12
  avatāra concept, 4, 8, 162–67
  bhakti's importance to, viii
  and caste, 102–7
  divine incarnation concept, 8, 162–
    67
  Divine Mother worship, 167–78
  divisibility of persons concept, 136
  and egolessness, 100
  gender constructs, 213–16, 217
  Goddess worship, 3–5, 167–68
  God's embodiment in, 199
  guru as central to, viii, 130–35
  hagiography, 21, 22
  and miracles, 114, 115

Hindu tradition (*continued*)
  on permeable substance, 136
  and piety of indeterminacy, 15, 105,
    115
  and sainthood, 4, 88–92, 100–101,
    108, 128, 215
  terms for religious practitioners, 90
  three major divisions, 4
  womanhood ideals, 55–61
  *See also specific practices, sects, and
    traditions*
householder
  Devī Bhāgavata's positive view of, 170
  inward path for, 193–94
  Mā's instructions for, 146–51, 203,
    205, 210–11
  Mā's life as, 155, 157, 209
  sādhana goals of, 159, 209

incarnation
  Christian vs. Hindu views of, 4, 162
  Hindu concept of, 8, 162–67
  Shākta theory of, 82, 169–70
  See also avatāra; God
India Today (publication), vii
indirect *dīkshā*, 140–44
initiation. *See dīkshā*
Isherwood, Christopher, 69, 165, 215
ishta devatā, 220
Īshvara, 170, 187

Jackson, Carl, 101
Jackson, William, 167
jagadguru, rarity of, 153
japa, 147, 159, 168, 192, 195, 206, 209
Jaya, 207
Jesus Christ, 4, 166, 174
jīvanmukta, 172
Jnanananda, Swami, 95, 98–99, 104–5,
    127, 141, 143–44, 145, 149, 151,
    152, 158, 220
  on Mā as divine, 173–74
Jnanananda of Madras, Mother, 214, 216
jnāna yoga, 190, 191
Joshi, Hari Ram, 20, 76, 77–78, 84,
    152–53
Juergensmeyer, Mark, 113

Kabir, 89, 102–3, 113, 133
Kālī, 3, 24, 34, 42, 46, 47, 48, 82, 83,
    84, 147, 164

as Great Goddess, 169, 174
Mā as incarnation of, 43–44, 73, 176
as model for women, 221
Kālidāsa, 60
Kālī Pūjā, 43–44, 45–46, 73
Kali the Mother (Nivedita), 167
"Kali, the Savior" (Gupta), 221
Kaliyuga, 208
Kalki, 163
Kankhal ashram, 12, 52, 96, 106, 122,
    148, 204, 209
karma, 101, 159, 164, 165, 194
  taking on another's, 117–18, 136, 177
Kaviraj, Gopinath, 15, 48, 51, 140, 175,
    176–77, 180–81, 182, 207
Keyes, Charles, 22, 214
kheyāla, 47, 48, 51, 52, 62, 72, 73, 79,
    99
  definitions of, 99
  and Mā's divine nature, 99–100, 182–
    83
  and Mā's giving *dīkshā*, 138
  and Mā's *līlā*, 179
  and Mā's taking on sacred thread, 207
Kieckhefer, Richard, 88, 89
kirtan, 47, 49, 192
  Chaitanya's powerful, 164
  Mā's ecstatic responses to, 34–35, 36,
    44–45, 70, 109, 110, 181
  Mā's girlhood love of, 28
  Mā's role in women's performance of,
    202, 211
Kishwar, Madhu, 218
Klostermaier, Klaus, 134
kripā. *See* grace
Krishna, Lord, 61, 82, 84, 91, 113, 133,
    161, 196
  incarnations of, 163, 164, 166, 170,
    172, 174, 176, 187, 215
  union with Rādhā, 165, 216
Krishnananda, Swami, 79, 95, 114–15,
    149, 164, 171
Kritayuga, 208
Kumar, Lalita, 120–21, 159, 202
Kumari Puja, 28
Kumbha Melā, 6, 47, 51, 74, 76
kundalinī, 11, 135, 142–44, 168, 193

Lakindar, 61
Lakshmī (Divine Mother), 3, 83, 167
Laksmicharan, Sri, 30

Reynolds, Frank, 22
Richard, Mīrā (the Mother), 165–66
righteous behavior. *See dharma*; dharmashāstra
Roman Catholic Churh, 88
"routinization of charisma," 80–81, 113
Roy, Manisha, 59–60, 61, 65–66, 68
Roy, Rajkumar, 124, 144, 176
Ruddick, Sara, 221

sacred thread, 51, 151, 207, 210
sadguru, 131, 162
    avatāra vs., 164–65
sādhaka, 48, 179–82
sādhana
    of *avatāra*, 165
    of Bholanāth, 50, 74, 75
    of *brahmachāriṇīs*, 193, 204–6
    devotees' pursuit of, 158, 159, 160, 194
    fervor of Mā's, 40 (*see also līlā of sādhana*)
    and genderless Self, 216
    gender restrictions, 201–2
    guru as personal guide in, 145–48
    Mā as goal of, 159–60, 177–78, 195
    Mā's hand in shaping, 51, 94, 148–51, 180, 182, 192–93, 195, 197, 220
    of renunciants, 94
    Self-realization as goal, 157, 159
    of true guru, 165
    of woman householder, 209, 210, 211
sādhikā, 38, 90
Sadhu, Gagan, 34
Sad Vāni, 196
saguna, 136, 170, 174, 217
sahagamana. *See* suttee
Sahajānand Swami, 135
Sai Baba of Shirdi, 117
sainthood, 87–128, 162
    Bengali women, 111
    Christian concepts of, 88, 90
    egolessness of, 100–101
    hagiographies, 21–22, 91
    highest form of human character, 162
    Hindu conception of, 4, 89–92, 100–101, 108, 124, 128
    Hindu gender construct and, 214–15
    Mā and, 7, 87–88, 92–97, 128, 140, 219–20

miracles and, 114–28
rejection of caste by, 102
Sāktism, 5, 168
samādhi, 12, 145, 157
Samatananda, Swami, 17, 123–24, 141, 143, 144, 146, 148, 151, 159, 165, 172, 175, 177, 206, 207, 221
samdhyā. *See* mantra
samkalpa, 172–73
sampradāya, 133, 151–55
Samyam Vrata, 52, 96, 124, 184, 193
sannyāsa, 93–97, 140, 219
sannyāsa dīkshā, 151
Sannyāsa Upanishads, 93
sannyāsin. *See* renunciant
Sanskrit, 4, 12, 40, 52, 56, 57, 89, 206
Saradanada, Swami, 69
Sarasvatī, 168, 176
Sathya Sai Baba, 166–67
Satī, 170
sātī. *See* suttee
satsangs, 8, 184–85, 186, 187
sāttvikā, 170
saulabhya, 220
Sāvitrī, 50
secrecy. *See rahasya*
Self-consciousness, 165, 174–75
self-effort, 172, 194, 195
    tension of grace with, 160, 191, 192
selfless service, 101–2
self-motification, 97
Self-realization, 157–58, 159
    of *avatāra* from birth, 165
    gender ambiguity of, 214, 215–17
    of Mā from birth, 182
Sen, Harkumār, 33, 34, 70, 110
Sen, Ramprasad, 24, 169
Sen, Sarada Shankar, 33
"serpent power," 135
sexual relations, 6, 35, 58, 65–67, 68 (*see also* celibacy)
Shahbagh Gardens, 41–49, 64, 72, 74, 173
Shakti, 84, 215
    avatāra of, 165–66
    Mā on guidance from, 180
    Mā's allusion to self as, 185
    as object of women's prayers, 202
    ten forms of, 173
    union with Shiva, 82, 214, 216, 217
    See also Divine Mother

Printed in the United States
135353LV00005B/75/P

Made in the USA
San Bernardino, CA
17 February 2019